Drunk Jerk: A Chrestomathy of Carousal and Critique
Selected Writings, Interviews, and Images from the Early Twenty-First Century

By Brian M. Clark

ISBN: 979-8-9992116-0-6

Published 2025 by Discriminate Media

Cover illustration licensed from CSA Images (© CSA Images, Inc.). Cover design and book layout by Brian Clark. Apart from grammar and spellcheck, no artificial intelligence was employed in the creation of this book.

Thank You: Aaron Elliot Olson, Adam Gross, Ali Berlinski, Alyssa Mann, Amber Maykut, Amy Szychowski, Andrew Novick, Ben Brunton, Ben Schiff, Christopher "Coop" Cooper, Christopher May, Claudine Rousseau, Dan Andriano, Dustin Newman, Edward Cronenweth, Elizabeth Gonzales, Eric Draper, Eric Mueller, Frank A Fey, Frank Kelly Rich, Gage Skidmore, Gregory Daurer, Grux, Heather Hannoura, Howard Karp, Jamie Sue Taylor, Jaycee Scragz, Jerzy Durczak, Jessica Devine, Jodi Davenport, Joe Bunik, John Moore, John K., John Strege, Jonathan Bitz, Josh Taylor, Justin Simoni, Kaleidoscope Partridge, Karl Christian Krumpholz, Kashfi Halford, Kibae Park, Kristin Brooks, Laura Sheridan, Lindsey Karnopp, Luis Sánchez de Ybargüen, Luke Schmaltz, Magdalena Herrera, Matt Skiba, Max Ribaric, Nick Plumber, Pelle Sten, Ralph Gean, Ranae Griego, Robert Ferbrache, Robert Levine, Scott Lindgren, Shannon Dickey, Shanti Williams, Thomas W. Brown, Tito (ITTOworkshopUS), Tom Lundin, Toshimi Ichiki, Zarateman, and Zhawna Seigwarth.

Drunk Jerk

A Chrestomathy of Carousal and Critique

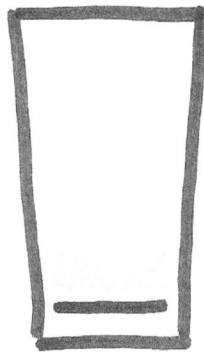

Selected Writings, Interviews, and Images
from the Early Twenty-First Century

Brian M. Clark

DISCRIMINATE MEDIA

— CONTENTS —

— CONTENTS —

Preface

Trashy Texts and Images from 'round About My Turbulent Twenties

First off, if you paid good money for this book, you should feel fuckin' ripped off. I'm serious. This isn't a proper book as such, with a cohesive conceptual throughline, a plot, or an overarching narrative or thesis. Rather, it's an amalgamation of unrelated texts and images cobbled together from disparate sources and presented as a single work for the sake of convenience. Instead of amounting to a "real" book, this trim tome is but a patchwork of papers. ... A menagerie of musings. ... A jumble of jottings. ... A composite concatenation of cogitations. ... You get the fuckin' idea. It's a hash. Even worse, this collection was not prepared with the curatorial assistance of an editor on behalf of a reputable third-party publisher – it was merely thrown together and published by the author, without outside oversight. Like a lowly fuckin' 'zine.

Anyway, since you're already here, I'll explain that this collection came about because I had some "down time" between jobs for a bit at the beginning of 2025 and decided that it might be less than a complete waste of my time to compile a retrospective anthology of the various expressive things that I did roughly two decades prior. As I write this, I'm now entering my late forties, working a fairly "respectable" job in an ostensibly "respectable" field, and doing okay for myself. But a couple of decades ago, I traversed my itinerant twenties and early thirties in something of a state of intellectually and emotionally disheveled *reactive disorder*—bouncing around from city to unfamiliar city, job to menial job, relationship to fleeting relationship—and all the while often doing what would nowadays be described online as "producing content." This book is a backward-looking, cleaned-up compilation of some of that content.

The temporal starting point of the works in this collection is somewhere 'round the turn of the millennium. In my early twenties, I had graduated from college holding a fairly useless Bachelor's Degree in Art, with a Spanish minor, and was living in California's San Francisco Bay Area, not far from where I'd grown up. I was directionless, underemployed, and flummoxed about what the fuck to do with myself as a young adult. On turning eighteen a few years prior, I'd come into some money as a result of an out-of-court legal settlement for a serious childhood accident that could have killed or crippled me – and said money was burning a hole in my proverbial pocket. So, on the heels of finishing college, I bought a one-way ticket to Europe, under the pretext of finding a job somewhere teaching English. Just prior to this, I'd been voraciously reading and idealizing the travelogues of various globetrotting writers (P.J. O'Rourke, George Orwell, Richard Huelsenbeck, Ernest Hemingway, *et al.*), and I figured that working overseas for a bit post-graduation was somethin' to do, anyway.

While living abroad, on a friend's then-still-novel suggestion, I began blogging online about my life as an American expatriate; people back home in The States responded positively to my prose, and I was therefore later prompted by the encouraging feedback to start sporadically writing about other things. After returning to The States in 2002, I then wound up relocating to Denver, Colorado, in 2003 – where I stayed for a few years, first working as an Administrative Assistant peon in a corporate office, and then as an Apartment Complex Manager and part-time Bartender. In 2008 I left Denver for Long Beach, California, where I drearily drew a paycheck working as a Technical Writer at a factory in the adjoining city of Compton; I then departed Long Beach for nearby Hollywood in 2010, a locale where I managed to eke out an abject living as a Bartender (and later, a Rideshare Driver).

Across all these transitions and the span of approximately the first dozen or so years of adulthood, I maintained a couple of blogs, wrote essays and polemics from time to time, and periodically conducted interviews for small press magazines and websites. In 2012, having by then entered my waning early thirties, I grew tired of treading water in the underpaid Sisyphean day-job and side-gig hustle, and so grudgingly went back to school to get a practical postgraduate degree. The return to schooling necessitated that I pull myself together and stop fucking around with non-academic writing; which is around when the most recent closing texts in this collection were penned. So, this book is a retrospective compilation of the essays, missives, rants, vignettes, interviews, and images that I produced in and around my twenties, during roughly the first dozen or so years of the twenty-first century; a somewhat chaotic interregnum bookended by my enrollment in undergrad and grad school.

Some of the texts that appear in this collection were previously published by magazines and websites; others were self-published as blog posts, standalone essays on my personal website, or as social media posts. There are also a few formerly unpublished writings that appear in print for the first time herein. These latter texts generally came about as a result of the unhelpful habit that I had in my twenties and early thirties of going out drinking and jotting down a bunch of ideas on a small pocket notepad, then staggering home bleary-eyed at the end of the night and typing up a cockeyed series of half-formulated paragraphs on my laptop (that I intended to flesh-out into an essay when I woke up the next day), following which I'd save the MsWord DOC file to a desktop folder labeled "Essay Ideas" ... and then never look at the damn thing again until putting together this compendium more than a decade later.

Many of the writings contained herein aren't really the kind of thing that I'd be likely to still author today – some are too caustically critical; some too self-indulgent and self-serving; some too snarky and snide; some too diffidently equivocal and awkwardly personal; some stink of the petulant misanthropy that can only be produced by the disillusionment of young adulthood; and some are just too damn long and sorely in need of a third-party editor. Several of the targets of my erstwhile pedantic criticism that once seemed important to me now come off as somewhat niggling and trivial (*e.g.,* discussion of niche music genres and the subcultures surrounding them, as well as the easily lampooned excesses of the so-called "Art World"). There are also sundry internal contradictions between certain of the texts comprising this book; such as my immature admonitions of others for being "pretentious," comingled with my own authorial flourishes that can only be described at points as ... *glaringly fucking pretentious.* I suppose that with the benefit of hindsight, I should be embarrassed by these kinds of inconsistencies; but given the passage of time and unavoidably clumsy process of growing up, I am not. Nor for that matter am I troubled by (what I imagine will be) plausible critical allegations that the author of these texts was an unattached instantiation of Carl Jung's *Puer Aeternus* archetype, as I have no problem freely acceding to such and don't regard the designation as much of a substantive criticism *per se.*

A few of the more "antagonistic" polemical essays in this book caused me minor headaches at the time that they first were published; this was particularly true of the 2009 anti-pet-ownership screed "Fuck You and Your Stupid, *Stupid* Cat," which resulted in several feline "fur mommies" summarily unfriending me on online social networks and declaring me an irredeemable asshole. I'd intended that essay (and others like it) to be somewhat tongue-in-cheek, or funny-yet-obnoxious, but some people were apparently unable to parse the humor from the obnoxiousness, and only took away the latter. Oh well. (Needless to say, maybe don't take everything that this book comprises *too* seriously.) Anyway, despite all these various faults and shortcomings—even though I've now moved on to other areas of interest and concern, and middle-age has turned me boring and unbelligerent as compared to my younger adult self—on the whole, the prose that makes up these old writings still holds up, so I decided to assemble this retrospective collection, warts and all.

The texts and image selections herein are presented in no particular order other than that I attempted to break up the procession of longer pieces with shorter ones, and tried to pepper the interviews throughout. Accordingly, I would encourage you to skip around willy-nilly. If a text becomes uninteresting (which is more than likely to occur at some point), there's no good reason not to abandon it partway through and move on to another. A few of the quasi-academic essays that are reprinted here originally included footnote citations to third-party sources (science journals, peer-reviewed studies, *et cetera*), but given that the sources originally cited to are now in some cases a-decade-and-a-half old, all the original footnote cites have been removed and instead all relevant outside works referenced, consulted, or alluded to herein are presented in a single list at the end of the book. Nobody is seriously coming here for authoritative academic citations anyway, so it doesn't fuckin' matter.

Omitted from this collection are various reviews written during the time period in question; such as critiques of films and books, and write-ups of live shows and events. Although some of these were published online at the time, generally it now seems to me that they don't bear republication here. Also not included within are a few interviews I conducted that didn't end up standing the test of time; such as an interview with an underground filmmaker, an interview with an "art prankster," and a few conversations with musicians. Some of these excluded texts are still available online (*see, e.g.,* Drunkard.com and LAist.com), but I didn't think that they were fit for reprinting here, so they're probably not worth your time to look up online, either.

* * *

In putting together this book at the outset of 2025, rereading all this old shit from decades ago, I was (perhaps predictably) struck by how many things have changed in the intervening years since these texts were first written. The bulk of this volume's contents comes from a period which, at the time, was described online as "Web 2.0" — an allegedly exciting new era of interactive Internet use. The Web 2.0 nomenclature was employed by tech journalists of the era to denote a shift away from the early Internet of the 1990s, which had been a static one-way communication interface that users logged-on to from land-wired computers, to passively consume content in the form of fixed webpages. Web 2.0 was an Internet that was innovatively pivoting to user-generated content and online interaction; user-created blogs, and early social media like MakeOutClub.com and Friendster.com, then MySpace.com, and finally Facebook and Twitter.

The writings in this book were authored in the midst of, and immediately after, the shift to Web 2.0. It was, initially at least, a time when the Internet was still sort of a quirky niche phenomenon. Google was yet in its infancy, and the "go-to" online search engine at the time was AltaVista. The online world then felt like "The Wild West" or "a blank canvas," or some other suitable simile for fresh, unexplored expressive territory that anyone could enter without seeking the imprimatur of established third-party "gatekeepers." As a recent-ish twenty-something college graduate in the first few years of the new millennium, I could blog freely and self-indulgently to online strangers about my puerile drunken misadventures, without much concern that prospective employers or my relatives might encounter my blog or website; because they were generally normies who weren't really quite fully "on" the Internet, yet. (In retrospect, this phenomenon was both disinhibiting and emboldening in ways that were probably less-than-healthy.)

It was a time when music consumption was still shifting from physical media to MP3 audio file downloads, preceding online digital streaming; when digital cameras were in the process of rendering film-based cameras obsolete, but phone-embedded cameras didn't yet exist; when the notion of online dating was the punchline to a joke

– something that only desperate "losers" did, and which almost nobody would freely admit to; when cellphones were becoming increasingly common, but were only capable of SMS text messaging and *actual telephone conversations*. Smartphones with apps didn't appear until near the end of the aughts, and were cost-prohibitive for a while before they saw wide adoption by the public. Online video was quite novel, making its debut partway through the decade with the likes of YouTube and Skype; then followed by mobile interfaces like Snapchat and Vine. Podcasts appeared following the introduction of Apple's iPod MP3 player and spent the first half of the aughts on par with the obscurity of ham radio, before eventually being taken semi-seriously towards the end of the decade. TikTok wasn't a "thing" yet. It all inevitably changed though; and relatively quickly and dramatically. By the end of the aughts, advances in technology and the proliferation of low-cost of access had ushered in a cultural sea change—ubiquitous smartphones, widespread adoption of social media, a 24-7 instantaneous global news cycle, online shaming, doxing, "influencers," revenge porn, and the beginnings of online cancel culture were all swirling around in the zeitgeist— because by then most people (including prospective employers and my relatives) were indeed very much "on" the Internet, and were carrying it around in their pockets.

So, if nothing else—even if perusing this book leaves you thinking that I am, or was, a calumnious, self-absorbed bloviator—the texts comprising it serve as a snapshot of some of the things that were going on in culture 'round about the first dozen years of the twenty-first century; before the omnipresence of social media and online culture, before "digital natives" had entered adult society, when the menace of Artificial Intelligence was still just an abstract far-off Sci-Fi film premise. Maybe that's at least worth something. But to be clear, you should still feel fuckin' ripped off if you paid good money for this book, because—like I said at the top—it's not a proper book as such.

– Brian M. Clark
  March 2025
  Denver, Colorado

Why I Drink

A Case Against Prohibitionism

2009

Sixteen years ago, I was sitting with a friend on a suburban sidewalk curb on a sunny afternoon in Northern California, "shooting the shit" over a shared 22 oz. bottle of Mountain Dew. We were both sixteen years old, and clad in well-worn Converse All Star shoes, plain brown pants, threadbare black hoodies, and Punk Rock t-shirts. The two of us were your typically pollyannaish and hopelessly idealistic middle-class, suburban, American teenagers; vaguely passionate and sanguine about far-off, abstract social causes of some sort or other, willfully disaffected and under the deluded impression that by listening to enough indie-label music and reading enough underground 'zines we might somehow be able to suss-out—between the two of us—just what was wrong with "the world." In other words, we were a pair of green, stargazing idiots.

I recall the teenage version of myself saying to my friend, "Hey, man ... have you ever thought about what the world would be like without stimulants? Like, what if there were just, like, *no* mood-altering chemicals out there: no pot, no acid, no 'shrooms, no cocaine, and no *alcohol?* Wouldn't that be *so great?* I mean—think about it—it would probably be a way, *way* better world to live in, because people

Teenage '90s bullshit.

wouldn't be able to escape their problems the way they do now. People wouldn't be able to just get drunk or high and then avoid dealing with all the fucked-up shit that goes on in the world – they'd have to face all the ugliness and actually *solve* problems like poverty, racism, sexism, inequality and war. They'd have no chemical escapism, so they'd, like, have to actually face up to how fucked up everything is, and fix things." My friend paused a moment, contemplatively furrowed his brow, and then nodded in stoic, sober agreement, "Yeah, man ... yeah, that would be a better world for sure."

Sigh.

Yes, I actually said that (or at least something along those lines) sixteen years ago. I recently turned thirty-two—yes, *twice* the age I was when my young friend and I longingly contemplated a stimulant-free and problem-free planet—and nowadays, I couldn't disagree with my sixteen-year-old self more.

Having long since turned a consummate inebriate, these days I regard the notion that intoxicants are just distractions—hindering humanity's ability to create some peaceful, hand-holding utopia—as comically simplistic; laughable.

In fact, I'd now actually argue that stimulants are more likely a key element of the social glue that bonds civilized society together, entrenching people in a shared commonality of experience – helping to keep us, to whatever extent, from tearing each other's throats out, so to speak. Because, irrespective of one's stature in the world or station in life, stimulants are one of the few things that can make life bearable—if not enjoyable—for *everyone*, equally.

My drug of choice is alcohol. Perhaps you prefer another—that's fine—but booze is the intoxicant most agreeable to my own particular set of needs. I *love* alcohol ... love it, *man*. One of the reasons that I'm so fond of booze is simply that, pragmatically speaking, it just makes life easier for me. Because what I couldn't have realized as an unworldly teenager sixteen years ago, is that being an adult is a real tiresome pain in the ass a lot of the time. Sure, those of us in the modernized West have transcended the assorted woes of our forbears' past: we're not fighting off wild animals with our bare hands anymore, nor are we dying by the millions of plague or starvation. But nevertheless, modern, grownup, everyday life can still be a real headache: rent, insurance, phone bills, gas bills, water bills, electrical bills, medical bills ... taxes, debt, collection agencies, inflation, recession, depression ... soul-crushing day jobs, deadlines, unpaid invoices, downsizing ... gridlock, fender benders, parking tickets, roadside repairs, police sirens ... backaches, Doctors' appointments, root canals ... pugnacious panhandlers, door-to-door solicitors, vengeful neighbors, nagging relatives, barking dogs, obnoxious know-it-all teenagers ... the head-game pitfalls of modern dating ... *et cetera*. This is the stuff of contemporary adult life (at least it is for me anyway), and it frequently strays into head-throbbingly stress-inducing *I-want-to-punch-walls-or-fucking-kill-somebody* territory. Unsurprisingly, often enough something is needed to, as they say, "take the edge off." In my own case, this is alcohol. Booze is the soporific balm that lets the misanthropic beast in my head get some rest, and thereby makes all the little nuisances of modern life bearable and worth putting up with.

The author, "taking the edge off" at a bar in Hollywood, California, 2009.

I recently found myself standing in line at my local supermarket, at 9:00 p.m. on a Wednesday, buying groceries for one. Long since having burned-out from working a lame nine-to-five office job; I stood there with a pounding headache and a sore neck; crossing my fingers and hoping that my credit card wouldn't be declined at

3

the register; while waiting for the overfed hog-of-a-woman in front of me (who was paying with wadded-up small denomination bills, coins, and coupons, *and* wasn't even attempting to keep her screaming brood of snot-faced rug rats under control); summoning every last ounce of patience I had left, to just remain calm, collected, and minimally polite. As the vein in my forehead bulged with frustrated impatience and I fantasized about buying an AK-47 and indiscriminately massacring everyone in the place, I was nevertheless comforted by the notion that—thank God—there was a twelve-pack of ice-cold beer waiting for me in the fridge at home.

This thought, this simple consolation, carried me through the tedium of the moment; as similarly booze-related consolations have carried me through similarly wearisome situations many times before. It's just a small slice of solace, I know, but the point is that whatever the bedeviling frustrations and tribulations of my day-to-day life may be, it is comforting to know that I can go home; close the door on the outside world, crack open a cold can of beer, close my eyes, tip my head back, savor its crisp, nonjudgmental, liquid kiss ... and wash my

The author, working a tedious day job in Compton, California, 2009.

humdrum troubles away. Within twenty minutes or so of having consumed the first can and moved on to the rest—as if by some sort of neurochemical magic!—I feel *just fucking fine*, thank you very much. Moreover, I don't even remember whatever it was that I was so annoyed about in the first place. Soon enough, I'm laughing at my own jokes and having conversations with the furniture – totally alone and in a state of ephemeral, alcohol-induced bliss.

And that's just *one* of the many, many reasons that I love alcohol. I also love it because it motivates me. It inspires me to do fun, funny, oftentimes crazily-stupid things. It prompts me to tell cocky boors at the bar exactly what I think of them (and to hell with the consequences!), it assures me that I'm witty (even when I'm very likely not), and imbues me with the distorted self-confidence to chat up strange, foxy girls I've never met before. Alcohol reminds me that—never mind the nine-to-five job that pays the bills—sometimes it's a good idea to "live a little" ... and maybe that might mean drunkenly knocking over a row of Vespa scooters outside a hipster coffee shop and running like hell. You never know what'll happen when you're loaded out of your gourd – and in the disenchanting, spirit-crushing, punch-clock, workaday world that we've somehow managed to fashion for ourselves, that's an invaluable quality to say the least.

Sitting on a curb in the suburban sun at age sixteen, I had ample time to worry about distant phantoms like poverty because I was a starry-eyed kid with no idea what the fuck he was talking about. It's easy—very easy—when you haven't really dealt with much of life or reality yet, to distill "the world" down to facile binary positions: poverty versus affluence, war versus peace, herd-minded "conformity" versus trailblazing "individuality," escapism versus "dealing" with reality, *et cetera*. And of course, what I didn't realize and couldn't fathom as a teenager is that it obviously just isn't that simple. Both life and the world are actually pretty goddamned complicated much of the time; neither fits nicely into a set of stark, polarized extremes operating in black-and-white dualistic opposition. Real-world economics isn't merely a metaphorical "pie," and social class isn't as simple as who arbitrarily gets the biggest proverbial "slice" of that pie. Racism, sexism, and xenophobia are amorphous, ever-changing concepts involving a confluence of culture, history, politics, group psychology, and an array of other mercurial complex factors. War is wrapped up in a miasma of economics and trade, historical grudges, barrier issues, conflicting political philosophies, race relations, religious schisms, and a host of other interweaving insoluble dilemmas. The problems people face—from large to small—often have many facets and multiple seemingly valid perspectives to them. In short (as many have long noted), "life" and "the world" are filled with few black-and-white absolutes and are often just blurry gradations of gray. So, assuming that if people just sobered up they could "fix" the aforementioned problems is, at best, an overly simplistic proposition which fails to take into account just how multifaceted both people and "the world" actually are ... and yet that's *exactly* what some folks— lots'a folks, actually—tend to do.

Although it is popularly conceived of by its denizens as "the land of the free," sadly, The United States of America seems to be eternally besieged by many citizens of the Captain Bringdown variety. Yes, counterintuitive as it may be, there are many absolutist, sanctimonious, buzzkill busybodies among us who can only be described as *prohibitionists* – actively engaged in the advocacy of some form of censure here in what is ostensibly touted by its own citizens as "the land of the free."

Prohibitionist bullshit, 1918.

Prohibitionists come in many flavors, and have set their sights on more than just mood-altering stimulants: there are those self-appointed public health crusaders who'd like to outlaw all smoking; there are those who'd like to ban certain foods; there are those vigilant guardians of morality (paradoxically, at both extremes of the political spectrum) who'd like to put an end to pornography; there are those emotionally oversensitive, concerned Orwellian citizens who'd like to redact certain epithets and insults (and in some cases *all* profanity) from our cultural vocabulary; there are those who think that every dope-dealing hippie ought to be in jail; and naturally, there are those teetotaling do-gooders who'd like to see the country go "dry" again. Presumably, these vacuous people gain some sense of self-worth by attempting

Fucking assholes, 1920.

to dictate, by way of legislation, the social mores and palpable liberties of the rest of us (the power to control what other people do is, ironically, intoxicating in its own way). As far as I'm concerned, they're all myopic, uptight jackasses.

The problem with prohibitionists of all stripes is that their thinking is stunted; they tend to view things in the same sort of oversimplified, dumbed-down, dualistic way that my teenage friend and I did sixteen years ago. When confronted with the overwhelming myriad complexities of life and the world, these reproachful souls say to themselves, *Golly, if only we could rid the world of an evil like booze* (or pornography, or videogames, or blasphemy, or ... whatever), *everything would be so much better for everyone.* And that's just callow, shortsighted, and silly – excusable in a teenager, perhaps, but deplorably misguided when carried into adulthood. Because even if it *were* feasible (which it very rarely is) to extirpate some particular flavor of so-called "vice," I'd still question the premise that doing so would in any way make the world (or our society in particular) a better place. After all, much of the Islamic world is free from the sins of alcohol, porn, and gambling – but at what price? And Communist North Korea keeps an airtight lid on all sorts of social and moral deviance within its borders – but who'd want to live *there?* Perhaps it's a bit of a false dichotomy to draw, but still ... is *any* tightly controlled society objectively somehow a "better" world than the modern, permissive West in which we live? The assumption that the prohibition of some particular variety of behavior or substance would have positive social consequences is just that – an unfounded, speculative assumption. Wishful thinking. Yet prohibitionists rarely falter in their convictions that whatever they're out to ban will be a social panacea, freeing us from the wickedness of ourselves.

And it's not only prohibitionists' basic assumptions that are generally unsupported; their argumentative strategies are usually pretty unsound as well. When railing against booze, for example, prohibitionists tend to present the most extreme position as though it were the norm; all drinkers are alcoholics. Or they'll cite impressive-sounding statistics about how many crimes are committed (indirectly) "because of" alcohol, how many people die every year in fraternity hazings due to alcohol poisoning, or—most often—how many people are killed annually as a result of drunk driving. And they lazily assume that these casuistries are valid arguments in support of the notion that alcohol should be banned outright. But they *aren't* valid arguments – under any real scrutiny, they're belied as absurd, over-simplified absolutism, and an appeal to emotion rather than reason.

Dumbass logo of The American Prohibition Party.

Consider: when impugning hooch, the typical prohibitionist tactic is to present a grim-sounding statistic or factoid that suits their argument, isolated and out of context. They'll pull on heartstrings by pointing out how many people die in the U.S. annually from booze-related mishaps of some sort, but will neglect to present that figure alongside other causes of death, and/or relative to the total number of deaths – which is willfully deceptive. In keeping with this kind of cherry-picking of relevant data, they'll also ignore inconvenient statistics and factoids – like the fact that studies have indicated that moderate alcohol consumption actually may *lower* one's risk of dying of heart disease, which is the *leading* killer in America.

Also misleading (and usually omitted from these sorts of discussions) is the method in which the parameters of some prohibitionist-friendly statistic-generating studies are defined – as, for example, it's sometimes the case that a study will rank a person who has more than two drinks a day as "an excessive drinker" (which is a bit of a stretch, as far as I'm concerned). Or similarly, the fact that—for the purposes of these studies—the U.S. federal government classifies a fatal accident as "alcohol-related" if it involves a driver, a biker, or a pedestrian with a blood alcohol content of 0.01 percent or more, whether or not drinking actually contributed to the accident. Yes, that's right, if *the fucking pedestrian* is drunk, it's still tallied as an "alcohol related" accident, even if alcohol didn't contribute to the accident – so some of the numbers bandied about by prohibitionists when discussing this issue ought to also be taken with more than a grain of salt.

Prohibitionists are also wont to present problems as being of an all-or-nothing variety, wherein the only way to address a given issue is to either unilaterally embrace their proposed solution, or simply accept that there is no other reasonable option for harm mitigation; which is rarely actually the case. For example: yes, a tragically high percentage of American teenagers die in booze-related accidents annually – but how does that percentage compare to populations in Europe, where the drinking age is generally lower, and the enticing taboo of forbidden Demon Rum holds less sway over the young? One way to alleviate the problem might be to ban alcohol outright or stiffen drunk driving penalties—yes, that's one possible option—but another might be to simply increase the driving age and/or lower the drinking age, so as to acclimate teens to responsible drinking earlier in life, *à la* certain European models. Such middle-road options at least bear *considering*, but they tend to be dismissed out-of-hand by axe-grinding all-or-nothing prohibitionists.

Regardless—let's set all that aside—because when it really comes down to it, the fact that there are unfortunately some people out there who're actually stupid and irresponsible enough to drive while hammered ultimately only reflects upon *those individuals* – and that's what's really

at issue here: individual choice. The ability to make decisions for oneself. Every day, lots of people drink alcohol and have the forbearance of mind not to get behind the wheel of a three-ton motor vehicle and go careening down the freeway in a deadly game of vehicular pinball. Because they're responsible adults who're cognizant of the fact that drunk driving is the apex of Moron Mountain—just above playing Russian Roulette, running with scissors, and juggling switchblades—and I for one find it insulting when it's insinuated that I'm somehow responsible by proxy for the minority of nitwitted blockheads who are actually dumb enough to drive under the influence. But that kind of guilt-by-association angle is oftentimes the crux of the prohibitionist mindset.

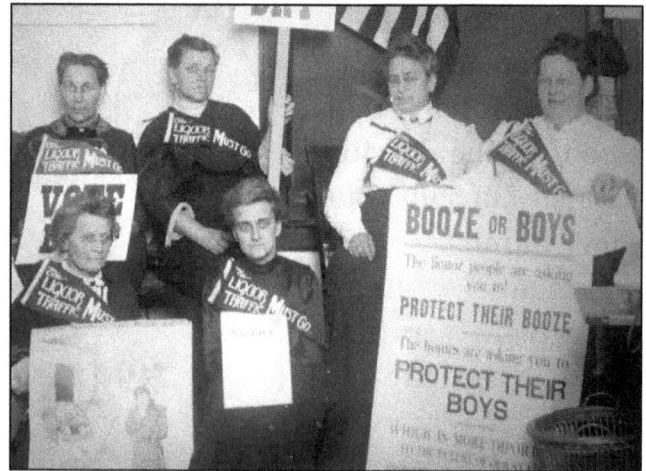

The joyless scolds of The Women's Christian Temperance Union, 1914.

To illustrate how silly this kind of prohibitionist quasi-logic is, allow me to draw a similarly irrational, emotionally-seated parallel, if I may: When I was in college, the Women's Student Union at my university fleetingly sponsored a campaign to put so-called "socially aware" slogans on the plastic urinal-cake-holders in all the men's restroom urinals on campus. Each of these bore the message, *You hold in your hands the power to stop rape.* After a brief uproar, the urinal-cake-holders were removed by edict of the university's administration. Why? Because they clearly implied that *all* men are in some way complicit in rape (and somehow have the power to stop it), simply because the act is committed by *some* men. Which is absurd and patently insulting to roughly half the population. Suggesting that all men are responsible for rape is akin to implying that *all* homosexuals are responsible for the proliferation of AIDS ... or that *all* Muslims are responsible for jihadist terrorism ... or that *all* dog owners should be held accountable for every mauling by a junkyard mutt ... or that *all* drinkers are responsible for drunk driving. With too broad

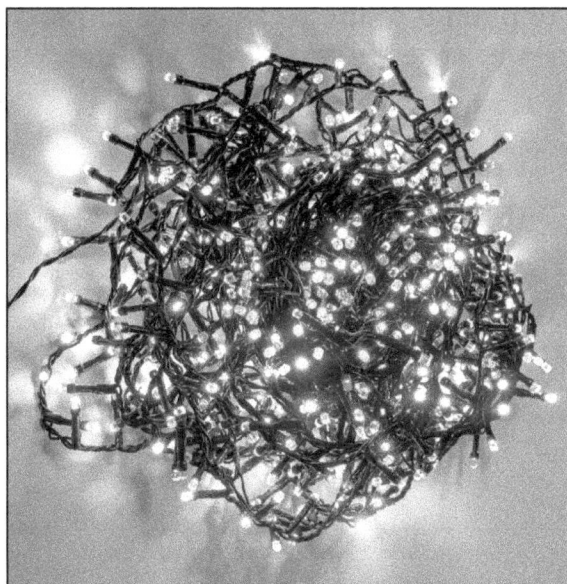
Watch out for these!

a brush, it tars the majority for the misdeeds of a small minority—a few bad apples—and it's a poor argument for imposing restrictions upon a group of otherwise reasonable people. In fact, I'd even assert that in principle, as an argumentative strategy it's really no less bigoted than good ol' fashioned bigotry – *They're all the same you know, they're all of the same type and kind.* Any such broad-sweeping conjectures are invariably inaccurate and impractical to the point of uselessness – yet they're often a

central tenet of prohibitionist rhetoric when calling for the imposition of bans.

Imagine if this sort of specious prohibitionist reasoning were applied to other areas of life? Every yuletide some negligible percentage of dumbfucks across the country plug too many Christmas tree lights into a single electrical socket and don't water their trees enough, causing them to dry out ... some nonzero subset of that percentage of trees catch fire, burn the house down and kill the entire family inside – so should we be banning Christmas lights or indoor trees? Plenty of children drown in swimming pools every year – so should we therefore outlaw swimming pools? Airplanes provide us with global transportation, but some of them crash and kill people – should they be proscribed as well? What about cars? The automotive death toll is far from insignificant – should they be outlawed? I could go on, but you get the point.

No reasonable person would seriously argue that pools, lighted Christmas trees, cars or airplanes be banned – because as ostensibly responsible citizens of a free culture we accept the fact that some of the pleasures and conveniences of life come with risks, and when the benefits of those pleasures and conveniences outweigh the risks then they ought to be permitted, for the common good. Prohibitionists of all kinds can't get their heads around this idea. They look at the most extreme anomalies on the fringes of whatever behavior they're in favor of curtailing, posit those extreme anomalies as the norm, and then insist that they constitute a threat to society as a whole. Which is ridiculous, not to mention intellectually disingenuous. As with so much of the gray area that is life, it's silly to let a few bad apples dictate how everyone else is treated – to do so is to pander to the lowest elements in all of us, by treating everyone like the worst among us.

I realize that this will probably sound preachy and obvious, but the simple fact of the matter is that with liberty comes responsibility. Having the freedom to drive a car carries with it the liability of having an accident. Having the freedom to drink carries with it the responsibility of not doing patently stupid things like driving a car while drunk. The fact that some marginal percentage of the otherwise overwhelmingly reasonable populace is too immature and negligent to handle those responsibilities by no means ought to reflect negatively upon the majority of those who can. Some people are just screwups, and when they demonstrate that enough, society obligingly steps in and revokes their

The author, relaxing on the streets of Long Beach, California, 2009.

driver's license, takes away their kids, or, in some cases, imprisons them. It's a shame, but that's the price that comes with the rest of us—most of us—having the well-deserved liberties to drive cars, raise children, and (most importantly, for me anyway) drink booze.

The right to chemically adjust one's mental state via alcohol and other intoxicants is an indispensable freedom—a tangible liberty that goes hand-in-hand with the pursuit of happiness—and one that deserves more sticking up for, more often. In a byzantine and often topsy-turvy world, stimulants like booze help us "take the edge off," without regard to race, class, or creed. In this sense, they're a great unifier; from the wealthiest investment banker to the most impoverished wino, they ameliorate the tedium of the human condition, and in so doing allow each of us the opportunity to relax and enjoy life – regardless of whether we're sleeping in the penthouse suite, or in the gutter. What could possibly be more intrinsically American than that?

Prohibitionists may *think* that they mean well—they believe that they're trying to help us by saving us from ourselves—but they're not helping anybody. Their brains are choked with hubris inasmuch that they actually believe that *they* somehow know what's best for *everyone else.* Like earnest, deluded, misguidedly well-meaning teenagers, they presume that they've got a quick "fix" for the inherently flawed nature of life and the world. They don't. So, the next time you hear some gaggle of uptight no-fun-nicks pining about how "there ought to be a law" against something-or-other, ask yourself: *Who the fuck do a bunch of bothered busybodies think they are to tell the rest of us what we ought to be drinking, smoking, eating, saying, or watching?* The self-righteous gall of it all is incredulous – and more drinkers (and pot smokers, and gamblers, *et al.*) ought to challenge it more vocally, more often, because it's bullshit.

Reality TV Show Pitch for The British Television Market

2008

Simon Cowell, Gordon Ramsay, and Steven Patrick Morrissey are each driven blindfolded in separate unmarked vans and dropped off in the middle of the Mexican city of Ciudad Juárez at sundown, wearing pinstriped three-piece suits and burnished leather loafers. Each is given 2,000 Mexican pesos, an obviously fake Canadian passport, and an English-to-Spanish traveler's pocket dictionary. Meanwhile, the Juárez and Sinaloa cartels have each been informed that the three Britons are in-country and working at the behest of the *other* cartel—their territorial rivals—in collaboration with the U.S. Drug Enforcement Agency. Through a mix of moxie, gumption, and sheer pluckiness, each man must attempt to make it out of Mexico alive.

(SPOILER: They all die.)

Befuddled by Belief

Why What People Believe Is Less Telling Than Why They Believe It

2004

For a long time now, I have had this running theory about belief: that the vast majority of people tend to believe in precisely those things or qualities that they themselves *aren't,* or don't embody. Take the Catholics, for instance. One needn't invoke the heretic-torturing sadism of the Spanish Inquisition, the revanchism of the Crusades, the bellicose brutality of the Conquistadors' escapades in Central and South America, the papal accession with the Nazis during the Second Word War, or the more recent scandals involving boy-diddling Catholic priests in the United States – just take as a point of analysis a regular, average, everyday Catholic guy. The Catholic "Joe Schmoe" trope, as it were. Imagine any stereotypical East Coast Italian-American "Guido" or West Coast Latino "Cholo," and you'd be remiss to omit the crucifix surely hanging from a pendulous chain 'round their necks as an outward signifier of their ostensibly devout Catholicism. Do these kinds'a regular workaday Catholic dudes tend to instantiate Jesus Christ of Nazareth's teachings *vis-à-vis* compassion, tolerance, forgiveness, humility, and charity? Are they morally unimpeachable and incorruptible, and awash in unqualified beatific "love" for all humankind like Jesus ... or are they more likely to flatten your *fucking faggot nose* if you inadvertently insult them or look askance at their ol' lady too long? I'm guessing the latter.

Carlo Gambino, mafioso crime boss ... and devout Catholic.

Likewise, are most practicing Buddhists interested in Buddhism because they possess the qualities of mind that Buddhism ascribes salience to—serenity, equanimity, tranquility, *et cetera*—or instead, are they practitioners of Buddhism because they're characterologically neurotic and stressed-out ruminating overthinkers who yearn for the placid mental state that Buddhism purports to offer? Again, I'm inclined to think it's the latter. Similarly, the so-called "Religion of Peace" hasn't exactly been living up to that docile appellation as of late. ...

"The Religion of Peace" in action.

It's not just religion, however. It's also politics. Take progressivist liberals—a group which promotes "tolerance" and "diversity"—are in my own anecdotal experience, some of the most intolerant and repressive of individuals out there. Supposedly fixated on both "diversity" and "free speech," they are at once intent on censoring, silencing, or rendering mute any and all viewpoints that differ from their own. Progressivist liberals are often so intolerant of dissent that they can rarely sustain coherence within their own ideological ranks, on account of internecine feuding of the sort aptly parodied in *Monty Python's Life of Brian* – through the factionalism fictionally depicted between The People's Front of Judea and The Judean People's Front ("Splitters!"). What about libertarians? Those loudly pining for anarcho-capitalism in online forums tend not to actualize such beliefs by leaving the comfortable suburbs for lawless failed states in the developing world, where they can freely engage in "voluntary exchange" without interference from "big government." Or how about starry-eyed communalists? Ever met an obnoxiously ardent Communist or Socialist?

"Splitters!"

They tend to be fuckin' rich kids; children of affluence and privilege, living off the largesse of their "capitalist swine" parents; blinkeredly striving towards a utopian arcadia of equality that deviates from their own cushy upbringings. They rarely embody or actualize the ideals of Marx and Engels in their real-world lives (and, it bears mention, nor do the leaders of actual Communist countries). Conversely, the working poor often idolize the gaudily rich, providing a viewership market for covetous programming like *Lifestyles of The Rich and Famous*, *MTV Cribs*, and their ilk – which allow the poor to enviously pine for opulent homes and goods beyond their means. What they *want*, not what they *are*.

It feels like there's something of a pattern here. ...

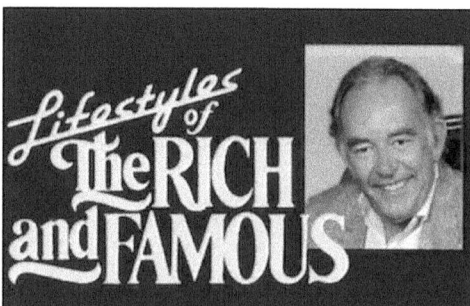
Something to aspire to, at least.

So I guess that it's not particularly surprising that most contemporary Americans claim to believe in equality—"all men are created equal" being a lodestar of the nation—while living in a country that has one of the larger disparities between rich and poor in the world. Or that Americans tout "freedom" as being the cornerstone of their way of life, while concurrently incarcerating a larger percentage of their fellow citizens per capita than any other developed nation in the Western World. (It's the "land of the free," but if you smoke reefer, you go to jail. Wait ... *what?*)

This observation about human nature is hardly new. As philosopher Will Durant put it back in 1926, "It is notorious that the principles which we apply in our actual living are largely opposite to those which we preach in our churches and our books. The professed ethic of Europe and America is pacifistic Christianity; the actual ethic is the militaristic code of the

Ye Olde Schoole Pacifistic Christianity of Europe.

marauding Teutons." But it is perhaps noteworthy and less commented upon, however, that the phenomenon goes in both directions. The outwardly presenting "nice" guys are often the inverse of "nice" – but so are the outwardly presenting "bad boys."

For example, in my experience, those who adhere to Anton LaVey's brand of solipsistic, amoral, materialist, and nominally hedonistic Satanism, do so because it is a philosophy that embodies all the characteristics that they themselves *lack*. Most self-described "Satanists" idealize and aspire to things like "power" and "strength" because

Heh, heh, heh ... like ... uh ... like ... hail Satan ... dude.

those are things they *don't* possess. Self-identified Satanists are, on the whole, meek, feeble, and disenfranchised – socially, sexually, and often economically. Living in their parents' musty basements; metaphorically, if not literally. Satanists esteem the concept of social hierarchy, while typically languishing at the bottom of it; lionizing "individuality" while all dressing similarly, wearing the same hokey jewelry, and generally taking their "individualistic" cues on culture from *each other*. Not exactly paragons of "individuality" or living out an uninhibited "do what thou wilt" philosophy. Ironically then, in tangible terms, Satanists on the whole are probably less likely to be "dangerous" as a group than Christians.

What's curious, to me, is that—given how so many people seem to be so overfond of telling everyone else what they believe in, to the extent that it becomes a foundation of their identity as an individual—they are somehow completely oblivious to the fact that most if not all of their own personal actions often run counter to the things they claim to "believe" in or at least present themselves as believing in. It's almost like there's some kind of cognitive dissonance that's just hardwired into human nature regarding belief. Although there are certainly exceptions— sometimes glaring ones—it seems to me that a lot

Hippies – probably insufferable assholes.

of people tend to idealize those qualities in their belief system, for which they as individuals are somehow deficient. It's as if people on some subconscious level know who they really are, and what they lack, and they therefore gravitate towards ideological ideals that revere the very qualities that they don't possess.

What's ultimately intriguing about people isn't *what* they claim to believe in as an overarching philosophy or worldview, but what one might be able to surmise about *why* they need to believe in it. Something to maybe keep in mind the next time you meet someone who seems to present themselves to the world as being entirely goodly and wholesome, and espouses a worldview predicated on kindness, tolerance, and love. Given the track record of human nature when it comes to "belief," healthy skepticism of such people seems to be warranted. Otherwise stated; it's reasonably safe to assume that most peace-n-love Hippies are undercover assholes aiming towards kindness, and most black-clad Metalheads are closeted overcompensating softies striving towards truculent toughness. It sure seems that way.

Does this topsy-turvy phenomenon apply to me? Probably. But if so, I'm just as blind to it as everyone else. Oh well. *C'est la vie.*

Metalheads – likely harmless.

True Alcohol Action!

An Interview with Adam Parfrey

2006

Adam Parfrey (April 12, 1957 – May 10, 2018) was a prolific American author, journalist, editor, recording and visual artist, art exhibition curator, and all-around *bon vivant*, who is best known for having helmed the notorious publishing company Feral House. The son of Hollywood film and television actor Woodrow Parfrey, Adam grew up amongst celebrities from a young age. During his lifetime, Parfrey was dubbed "America's Most Dangerous Publisher," but objected that he would have preferred to be known as "America's Most Interesting Publisher."

In 1992, Parfrey's Feral House imprint published *Cad: A Handbook for Heels* ("The Forgotten Lore of the Red-Blooded American Male"), a celebration of men's magazines of the late '50s. At a time when hipsters hadn't yet cottoned on to bachelor pad music and exotic cocktails, *Cad* brimmed with essays and illustrations on everything from burlesque, Exotica music, tiki culture, Russ Meyer, adventure tales (both true and fictive); as well as booze-related essays on the nuances of a "perfect" martini, the history of rum, and the definition of good scotch. As to whether the book inspired or presaged the decade's infatuation with all things retro is moot – it was a balls-out throwback to a bygone era, standing in diametric opposition to the constricting buzz-kill mores of '90s Political Correctness at its height. Parfrey's Feral House continued publishing comprehensive studies of postwar men's culture into the 2000s, including 2003's *It's A Man's World: Men's Adventure Magazines* and 2004's *Sin-A-Rama: Sleaze Sex Paperbacks Of The Sixties*. Parfrey was interviewed via email for *Modern Drunkard*.

Brian M. Clark: There's a widely-held perception that people in postwar America were square, straight-laced, and full of hang-ups, yet it seems to me that, if anything, Americans have more hang-ups about drinking now than they did back when Dean Martin and his ilk were the arbiters of style and etiquette.

Adam Parfrey: It seems like there's not enough free time, not enough time to get fucked-up these days. We're stuck in a situation where we have to complete projects, make money, work double shifts to make a go of things. It's easier societally to drink in countries like Japan and Russia, certainly. Also, all those victim group restrictions engineered by people like

MADD are making a victim of me! Let me drink!

BMC: In the books you've published on men's culture, a common thread is the hedonistic intermingling of adventure and sex with booze. In the postwar era, a "man's man" fought hard, drank hard, and reveled in the pleasures of the flesh. Today, the idea of mixing sex with booze (or booze with adventure) is more than a little taboo.

AP: *Cad* was the most proscribed book I ever published. It was banned in Canada, having been seized from some alternative store in Vancouver. Some bookstore owners screamed at my distributor sales reps, "We nailed this door shut long ago. Get this book the fuck out of here." It was as if the bookstore owners considered it a history of the Holocaust, but from the Nazi point of view. Very strange.

BMC: In one of your articles in *Cad*, you touched on the idea that psychedelic drugs of the '60s were often viewed by men such as Gershon Legman as a threat to a preexistent "booze-centric attitude to eroticism" – *i.e.* the idea that alcohol was, "the magic potion that unshackled social inhibitions," while drugs just clouded people's minds. Would you agree with the sentiment that, whereas psychedelics help people get outside themselves, alcohol forces people to get inside themselves?

AP: There's a good reason for psychedelics, to get short-term benefits of schizophrenia without having to live with it after you come down. There are obvious insights that can be gleaned there. They will certainly cloud your mind if you continue taking these psychedelics. But alcohol is getting a thumbs up from medical America now; that a couple few drinks a night, and the reduction of stress is better for you than killing yourself with anxiety. These discoveries are going to be a social and societal boon for drinking in the near future at least.

BMC: Back then, a gentleman drunkard knew how to handle his liquor with decorum and class, while in contrast, a "rummy" got surly and violent. Nowadays, anyone who drinks regularly and to excess is perceived as an "alcoholic." How would you view Americans' attitudes towards booze as having changed in the last several decades, and what do you suppose has led to such a change?

AP: I'm old enough to remember a time (the early- to mid-'60s) when my folks had parties and went to parties where everyone drank, and drank a lot. Sometimes there were fights and screaming matches, but life went on and people dealt with it as a normal occurrence. I remember when this old souse, Jason Robards Jr., was at my parents' place drinking all night, doing a

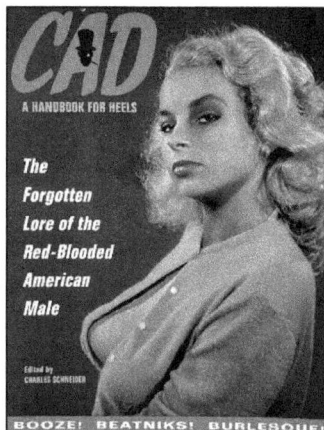

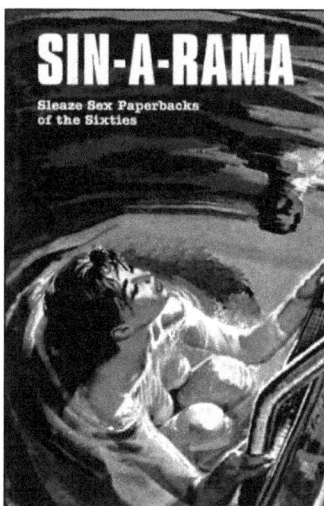

couple runs to liquor stores. When I woke in the morning to go to school the fucker was still drinking and ordered me (the hosts' kid) back to bed. Even though the sun was out, he told me that it was not time for school, and to get

Jason Robards Jr., old souse.

back to my room. I snuck out the back door. School was a bit more inviting to me that morning with a fucked-up actor on a bender back at home.

Another time, when I was older, I was baby-sitting the kids next door – the actor Aldo Ray's kids, Paul and Eric. Aldo Ray was a big bastard who played Green Berets in John Wayne movies. His best friend at the time was Ed Wood. So one night, Aldo Ray gets back home, and he brings with him a couple sauced old geezers. I didn't know who they were, but they smelled like puke and cheap liquor and they scared the shit out of little me. But they insisted I stay and listen to them

Aldo Ray, big bastard.

argue with each other about whether they thought it was okay to let me go home.

My feeling about liquor and drugs is this: the problem isn't the drugs or the liquor, it's the people themselves. Many people don't know how to handle the stuff, but how would anyone get to high or inspired moments without them? Imagine

popular music without liquor or drugs. Impossible to imagine.

BMC: What's your favorite drink and why?

AP: A friend just turned me on to this Haitian rum, Barbancourt. It's really tasty and good. It's supposedly used for voodoo ceremonies. I wouldn't expect anything good to come out of Haiti, but Barbancourt Rum proved me wrong.

BMC: Do you have any favorite bars? If so, what's so special about them?

AP: I remember a couple dives in Hoboken in the mid-'80s that sold 30¢ beers all day and night and 50¢ shots. You couldn't see the faces of a lot of their customers; they were face-down on the bar.

BMC: Would you be kind enough to share a particularly entertaining drinking story?

AP: Well, I was once with Boyd Rice and a couple girls at this place called Henry Ford's in Portland, Oregon, and we were guzzling a up storm. I forget the joke I told, but Boyd was laughing so long and so hard that we all joined in and kept at it for like five or ten minutes. Then I noticed the bar pianist clutching at his chest and spilling forward onto his face, suffering a massive heart attack. I was trying to call Boyd's attention to this, but all my faces and finger-pointing made him laugh even louder and harder. I think that must have been the last thing this pianist heard as he was dying. Our drunk voices laughing and screaming as loud as can be.

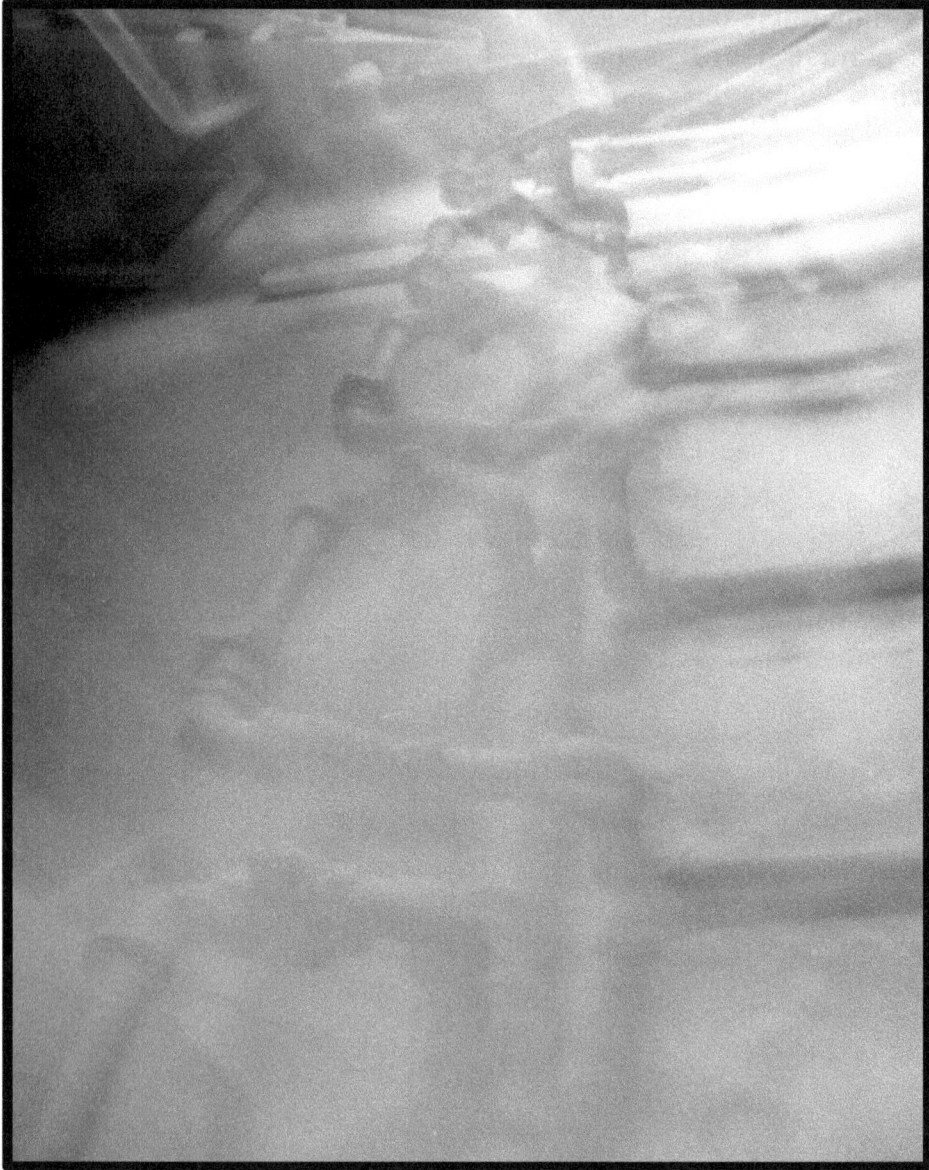

Free Holiday Medical Advice from Your Local Bartender

2013

Today is the last Sunday before Thanksgiving. In less than a week, you'll find yourself inextricably trapped at an overlong table, staring down at a plate of dry turkey and soggy stuffing; murmuring curses under your breath and praying for a swift and merciful death while you feign a smile at your asshole relatives' prying questions about why you haven't been promoted yet, or why you aren't married yet, or why you haven't had a kid yet, or whatever other petty little indicia of "success" they've been trying to foist on you for your entire goddamn motherfucking life like the heartless cocksucking bastards they are. And this flagrant indignity—this cruel affront to your autonomy as a self-sufficient adult—will fall upon you after you've already endured the oppressive horror of battling with insufferable holiday traffic to the airport, followed by the Kafkaesque dehumanization of modern air travel that wearies the body and mind while jaundicing the very soul. You'll be thoroughly burned-out, exhausted, and cowed, long before you take your first bite of gritty, desiccated turkey – but that's not even the worst of it. After you've suffered through the meal and the tedious obligatory conversation that comes with it, the heartless bastards will probably have you relegated to sleeping on a lumpy foldout bed in some godforsaken guest bedroom with a drafty window and over-starched sheets that reek of mildew, next to a dickhead cousin who snores like a burly lumberjack and farts like an obese trucker. It will be horrible. Just goddamn horrible. At the risk of being crass, you'll be lucky if you can steal away for five minutes every couple of days just to jerk off in the bathroom like a thirteen-year-old – and let's be honest here, it can't get much worse than that, friend.

In short, as usual, Thanksgiving is going to be a downright shitty holiday this year – so much so, that by the end of it you'll likely be envying the passengers on The Titanic. So, as your friend and confidant, I am obliged to state that it would behoove you to start relaxing and blowing off steam preemptively – by which I mean today. Having already personally conferred in great detail with your physician, I assure you that it's definitely in your best interest to come down to my bar today for some delightfully soothing, reasonably priced Happy Hour cocktails, between the hours of 3:00 in the afternoon and 7:00 in the evening. We serve this one drink— *perchance you've heard of it?*—it's called the "Old Fashioned." At a mere $8.00, it very well may be the only armament with which you might fortify yourself against the bleak, ignominious terrors that soon await you at Thanksgiving. Your Doctor and I both reckon that two or three Old Fashioneds are probably a very good idea for you today, for health reasons. Stress will fuckin' kill you, and Thanksgiving is guaranteed to be stressful. I, your friend, want you to live. So don't be a goddamn fucking cretin, for Chrissakes – come down to the bar for a drink or two, while you still have time!

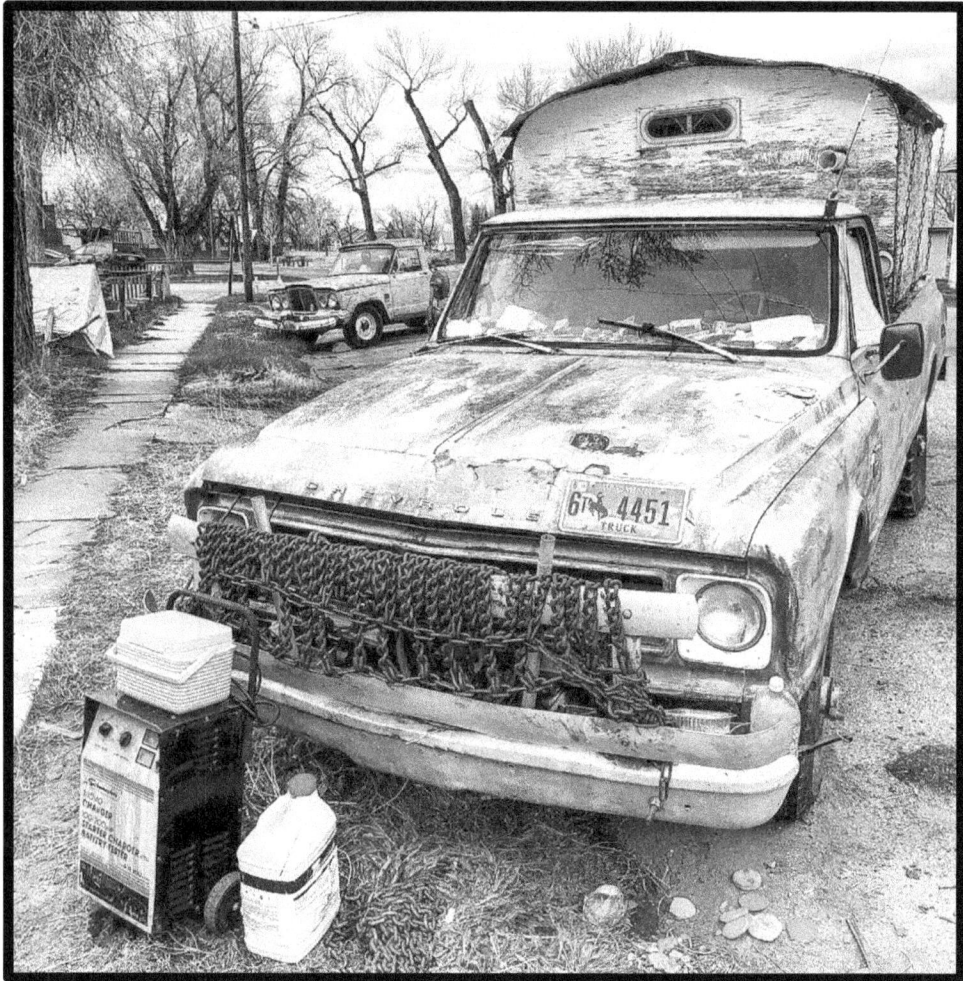

The Amazing Ralph Gean

The Tumultuous Tale of a Tenacious Troubadour

2007

Few individuals alive have had as longstanding or committed a relationship to Rock n' Roll as Ralph F. Gean. Even fewer can claim to have led lives remotely as multi-faceted, colorful, and downright *weird* as the inimitable man otherwise known as "The Star Trekkin' Rock n' Roll Cowboy." Ralph's been writing, performing, and recording his own music pretty much nonstop since the mid-1950s, and began his career opening arena shows alongside the big names of the day; but fifty years later, rather than enjoying the fruits of decades of fame and success, Ralph instead remains in relative obscurity, largely unknown except to devoted fans of "outsider" music. He's endured more than a few years of living

Ralph Gean in the 1960s.

in hovels, sleeping in his old Ford van, and playing on street corners for food money; and yet despite receiving little recognition or reward for his musical labors, Ralph's never abandoned his lifelong dream of Rock n' Roll glory, even as he now enters his late sixties.

I first saw Ralph perform in Denver, Colorado, in 2003 at an all-ages showspace and warehouse that I was living in at the time called Monkey Mania. An unassuming man with sloping shoulders, a missing front tooth, and long, stringy gray hair, Ralph was clad in a pair of sweatpants, a tattered cowboy hat, and what could possibly be the tackiest oversized tie-dyed shirt I've ever seen – none of which suggested "rock energy." Ralph had been booked to play that night alongside several local Punk and Indie bands composed of teenagers young enough to be his grandchildren, and while his inclusion on the bill may have seemed an anomaly at first, as soon as he took the stage it became immediately apparent to all in attendance that not only did he fit right in, but was actually the highlight of the show.

Ralph playing live, early 2000s.

As with many Punk shows I've been to over the years, the other bands that performed that night blend together in my memory; too many guitars, too many amps turned up all the way, too many tattoos, too many piercings, too much hair dye, and way too much shouting – but not nearly enough substantive content, sincerity, or anything resembling genuine passion. Ralph, on the other hand, stuck out like a sore thumb, not only because of his age and attire, but also because musically he was everything the other acts weren't; he ambled up to the stage with just his timeworn acoustic guitar (which was missing a string), humbly stepped up to the microphone, thanked everyone for coming, and then proceeded to captivate the otherwise jaded and cynical audience with a series of genuinely odd, funny, ebullient, and just plain *fun* Rock and Country songs about murder, lust, and the Old West; which he bellowed out in his signature full-throated baritone, and frenetically strummed with more zeal and unpretentious enthusiasm than all the scream-laden angst-rock bands that had preceded him put together. How Ralph ended up playing one-man shows at Punk warehouses in his early sixties, half a century after he began his career in Rock n' Roll, is a bit of a long story, filled with fleeting glory, abject despair, run-ins with the feds, shitty day-jobs and love triangles gone wrong, but then ... that's what Rock n' Roll is all about, after all.

Ralph F. Gean was born in 1942, in Port Arthur, Texas, to a musically inclined mother (he would eventually record several of her compositions) and a father who worked as both a jukebox salesman and Victrola repairman; thus, young Ralph was exposed to music—and lots of it—at a very early age. He displayed such a love for singing that, in 1945 (at the age of three) Ralph's mother took him into a studio to cut his first recordings; a cappella renditions of "Jesus Loves Me" and other religious traditionals (technically making Ralph's studio debut antecedent to that of his hero, Elvis Presley). Enjoying a relatively normal childhood and adolescence, like many American teens of the 1950s era, Ralph was bitten by the Rock' n' Roll bug, and during the summer of 1959 the

Ralph as an adolescent, 1950s.

Ralph as an early teen.

teenaged Ralph worked at a carnival and saved up enough money to buy his first guitar. He immediately set about mastering the instrument and began writing and performing his own songs while still a student at Thomas Jefferson Sr. High (where Janis Joplin happened to be a classmate). Ralph rashly dropped out of school at seventeen to join the U.S. Air Force, but—as he was interested mostly in Rock n' Roll, fancy clothes, fast cars, and girls—he quickly realized that he wasn't cut out for military service. Ralph managed to find a loophole in Air Force rules through which he was able to slip, and set out to become a professional Rock n' Roller instead.

Ralph Gean's career in Rock n' Roll took off in the early 1960s. Having achieved a modicum of local notoriety for his performances of both originals and covers of contemporary Rock standards (a regular practice in the early days of the genre), in 1962 he was invited to make his first proper studio recording, cutting an original track called "Here I Am" for Ray Doggett Productions. "Here I Am" was recorded with B.J. Thomas (later made famous for "Raindrops Keep Fallin' On My Head") and Thomas' band at the time, The Triumphs, as well as a vocal group called The Epics. Curiously, a B-side to the single was never recorded, and "Here I Am" never saw commercial release.

Undeterred, Ralph went back into the studio that same year and recorded "Weeping Willow Tree" b/w "Experimental Love," which was released soon thereafter by Lori Records. For his second studio foray (but first actual single), Ralph was backed by Freddie Koenig & The Jades, and supplemented by a female vocal trio known as The Lively Sisters (with future Country star Mickey Gilley on piano). "Weeping Willow Tree" quickly became a regional hit in the Houston, Texas, area, and Ralph's career as a Rock n' Roller was officially underway.

Ralph and his guitar, 1950s.

Due to circumstances beyond Ralph's control, the momentum created by the success of "Weeping Willow Tree" would be squandered; it took a full two years for Ralph's second single to be released. Gallant Records financed the recording of Ralph's second 45 and in 1964 released "One Night In San Antonio" b/w "Hey Dr. Casey," the latter being Ralph's novelty tribute to the television series *Ben Casey*. This, too, was well received locally, and Ralph's career was—by all accounts—headed nowhere but up. Throughout this period, Ralph was regularly opening big arena shows for national acts like Roy

Orbison, Glenn Campbell, Roy Head, and others; and soon enough his songs were being covered by his contemporaries (Sunny & The Sunliners did a rendition of "One Night In San Antonio" and Vance Charles & The Sonics recorded the Ralph-penned track "Closer To Me").

It seemed that young Ralph was surely poised for national Rock n' Roll success, and he well-nigh had it, but for one thing: the so-called "British Invasion" spearheaded by The Beatles, and its attendant bottoming-out of national interest in Rockabilly-inspired American Rock n' Roll. As Ralph would later recount, "By the time my second single finally came out, we were in the middle of Beatlemania. All I ever heard was 'Beatles, Beatles, Beatles'." Undaunted by the public's sudden, fickle shift in taste, Ralph put up $200 of his own money to go into the studio and record a third single, "Electricity" b/w "I'm

Ralph in the early 1960s.

Counting On You," but he couldn't find any record labels interested in releasing or distributing it, as his American brand of Rock n' Roll had fallen out of fashion while teenagers instead embraced the so-called "Fab Four," The Rolling Stones, and other British imports.

Ralph with his early vinyl singles.

His brush with success having dissipated much more quickly than it had taken to develop, Ralph Gean did what seemed the most reasonable thing to him at the time; he acquired his high school equivalency certificate and got married, tying the knot with a young lady by the name of Sadie Onetta Slaughter in 1967. Both lifelong Mormons, the young couple headed up to Idaho, where Ralph sought employment through The Church of Jesus Christ of Latter-Day Saints, and through which he eventually found a job as a crop processor and boxcar unloader. A year later, Ralph enrolled in junior college at Rick's College in Rexburg (now a part of Brigham Young University), where he undertook the study of geology and paleontology, while working part time as a campus groundskeeper. Barely able to make ends meet, Ralph and Sadie lived in a small trailer where they conceived their first of what would eventually become four children: Evangelynn, Ralph III, Charles, and Melissa (for whom Ralph would later compose an eponymous love song).

Things were tight for the Geans in Idaho. Ralph earned barely enough to pay the rent, let alone feed his wife and new child. Nonetheless, amid his college studies, part-time employment, and duties as a new father, he managed to find his way into the role of a gangster in the college's theater production of *Kiss Me Kate*, the cast of which included a handful of big-name Broadway actors. The production saw eleven performances in both Idaho and Utah, receiving glowing print reviews locally and as far away as New York City, and turned Ralph into something of an on-campus celebrity. Despite this second minor stint in the limelight, however, Ralph just couldn't keep it together as a college student, part-time groundskeeper, and father; and was forced to drop out after just a year of studying at Rick's.

Ralph in Idaho.

As the 1960s came to an end, the Geans moved back to Texas, where Ralph undertook a string of menial jobs to support his family, including: service station attendant, janitor, office clerk, short-order cook, cafeteria manager trainee, laundry attendant, Procter & Gamble soap salesman, hospital orderly, factory worker, lumber mill worker, TV repairman's assistant, layer of seismography wire, patio foundation digger, and a few others.

Having managed to get somewhat back on their feet in Texas, by the early 1970s, Ralph eventually relocated the family yet again, this time to the global capital of the Mormon faith; Salt Lake City, Utah. Not long after their arrival, Ralph and Sadie decided to break from the orthodox Mormon Church and became involved with a Mormon splinter sect led by Rulon Alred, whom the press had derisively dubbed "The Mormon Manson." Unlike conventional Mormonism of the time, Alred's sect encouraged the historically traditional Mormon practice of polygamy, and thus was at odds with both the church and the law. As Ralph would later explain, "It was very controversial, and it confuses a lot of people. ... Bigamy is when a guy is married to several different gals who don't know about each other, but polygamy is where everybody knows about it and accepts it, and I believed in that idea at that time. I'd like to think that if I'd stuck with it, I'd have had a minimum of eight wives." Contrary to his aspirations, however, Ralph only managed to acquire two; his extant bride, Sadie, and a second, Ruth Evans. The three were officially married by Alred's sect in Murray, Utah, and maintained a polygamous relationship—children and all—for two years, from 1974 to 1976; during which time Ralph would eventually construct a roofless wooden shack in the Utah desert to house his growing brood.

The Geans' Utah desert shack.

We started out in the same house, but things got worse and worse. ... So we moved out to the country, but that didn't last, either - one [wife] wanted to stay in the country, and the other one wanted to stay in town. So then we moved back to Salt Lake [City], into the same apartment building. One was in an apartment upstairs, the other one was in an apartment downstairs, and I was spending three days with each of them. And that's really a crazy way to live.

Ralph in the late 1970s.

Despite the commitments of not one, but two wives (and a job), Ralph continued to write songs, which he began to record on the recent invention of the hand-held cassette tape recorder. Unfortunately, notwithstanding the best of intentions, Ralph's polygamous marriage steadily deteriorated over the course of two years, and his first wife, Sadie, eventually left the arrangement, taking with her their four children. Ralph and his second wife, Ruth, remained in Salt Lake City, and the two had their own child, Annette Spring, in 1977. That same year, Rulon Alred was assassinated by a rival Mormon sect headed by Ervil LeBaron, following which the Gean family was officially excommunicated from The Church of Jesus Christ of Latter-day Saints; something Ralph has sorely lamented ever since. Subsequent to their excommunication, Ralph and Ruth's relationship also began to erode and eventually foundered much like the one that had preceded it, with Ruth leaving Ralph and taking their young daughter with her.

And so, as the decade of the 1970s came to an end—having been officially banished from his church, his five children and two ex-wives gone from his life, his college studies left unfinished, and his career as an *almost* famous Rock n' Roll star left more than a decade-and-a-half behind—a single and lonely Ralph Gean entered into a deep and prolonged depression, for which he would eventually be forced to seek treatment. In due course, Ralph found his way back to Texas yet again, essentially homeless and with no prospects of things getting much better any time soon.

By 1980, the down-and-out Ralph had managed to make it back up to Salt Lake City a second time and was living in the unsecured basement of a low-rent hotel that he dubbed "Skid Row Manor." He spent a year and a half living out of the hotel, supporting himself by

Ralph busking on the streets of Salt Lake City, Utah.

playing guitar on the streets of Salt Lake City, despite constant harassment from the local police. As he would later reminisce,

> In a lot of ways, it was great. … It tightened up my playing and really broadened my repertoire. And there were some really nice moments. One time, a guy liked me so much that he cashed his whole paycheck and gave it to me. Another guy gave me the jacket right off his back. … Although some people tried to give me drugs. I'd have to tell them, "I can't do that. Playing on the streets, I'm in enough trouble with the police as it is."

Desperate for cash, Ralph managed to get occasionally caught up in a currency counterfeiting ring led by a friend of his whom he'd met out in the desert during his polygamous shack-living days. Although he was only peripherally involved in the counterfeiting scheme in 1974 and again in 1979, in early 1981 this came to an abrupt halt when U.S. Secret Service agents appeared at Ralph's "Skid Row Manor" door and asked him to take a visit downtown with them. He narrowly evaded arrest by complying with the agents' requests for information about the extent of his involvement in years previous; and aside from having to sign a pledge never to become re-involved in the counterfeiting underworld, Ralph survived the ordeal unscathed and was essentially "scared straight" for the rest of his adult life.

Dona Mae Donohoo and Ralph Gean.

During the year and a half that he survived as a busker, Ralph made the acquaintance of Dona Mae Donohoo, a married woman with a deep-seated love of music and an interest in helping him out. They recorded a number of songs together and eventually developed a lifelong relationship that nebulously shifted from amorous to platonic (and back again), but never led to marriage. Although Ralph had never abandoned music entirely during his years as a polygamist in the 1970s, it had taken a backseat to his duties as a husband and father; but at the onset of the 1980s, he again

Ralph singing with Big Bang & The Boulders.

resolved to become a full-time Rock n' Roller. With the help of Donohoo, Ralph managed to get back on his feet, and by 1983 he was on stage once again.

For the next three years, Ralph fronted a number of Rock, Rockabilly, and Country acts, including: Big Bang & The Boulders, Rockin' Ralph Gean & Dreamsteam, Gean & Country Curfew, Kickin' Country, Heritage Review, Satsuma, Electricity, Banderos, John Doe & The Nobodys, and Dream Steam. Enjoying spirited local interest, Ralph and his assorted bands performed regularly at bars, small venues, and fairs throughout Utah and Wyoming. All told, during this three-year period, Ralph reports that the bands he worked with collectively earned more than $30,000, and while enjoying nowhere near the attention he'd received in the late 1950s and early 1960s, for all intents and purposes, he was nonetheless a professional full-time musician once again.

Following the dissolution of the of last of Ralph's Salt Lake-based groups in 1986, he was asked to write several murder-themed songs for an independent film titled *The Nuthouse*, and although the movie was never made, the assignment yielded what would later become such crowd favorites as "Homicidal Me" and "Hard To Be A Killer." Aside from this one-off assignment, however, things had pretty much dried up for Ralph in Salt Lake City; and with no new prospects for starting up another band, in 1987 he and Donohoo moved to Denver, Colorado, where the two would remain, albeit separately, for the following two decades.

Upon his arrival in Denver, Ralph soon landed an idyllic job (for him anyway) as a live-in caretaker for the millionaire heir to a mining fortune named John Spencer. Spencer, a recovering alcoholic, suffered from what Ralph described as "emotional problems," and consequently his inheritance was overseen as a trust, part of which provided for Ralph's living with Spencer and, in doing so, helping him function in the day-to-day world.

> All I have to do is make sure he doesn't get into trouble or accidentally hurt himself. ... And really, it's the easiest thing I've ever done in my life, since John is able to do just about everything for himself. He works at Bayaud Industries, and he spends every dime he makes on the Lotto. He's won a few hundred dollars that way, and when he wins, it makes him really happy – I don't think he has any idea how much money he really has. And they pay me to take him on vacations, too. We recently toured the sites of famous Western gunfights. ... I'm telling you, this is the kind of job I've always dreamed about.

Over the course of the next decade, the two became close friends, and Spencer even began playing music and recording with Ralph.

At the turn of a new decade, the 1990s, Ralph began a spate of one-man acoustic guitar performances inside his old Ford van (which had served as both home and recording studio for him at certain points). Still relatively new to town and fearful that the local police wouldn't approve of street corner minstrels such as himself, Ralph would park his van outside of Denver's Wax Trax Records, open its sliding door, and play from inside, figuring that if the cops showed up, he could just close the door and drive off. Eventually, he realized that, unlike Salt Lake City, Denver's police force had better things to do than harass

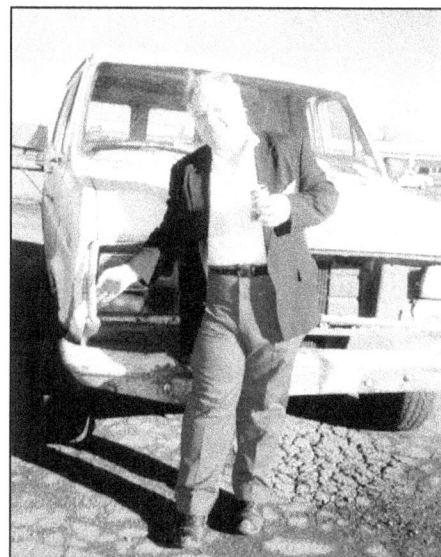

Ralph and his old Ford van.

street musicians, and by 1994 Ralph was strumming his acoustic guitar and singing outside Wax Trax on a weekly basis. After scouring the oldies vinyl section for old Rock n' Roll 45s and chatting with the store's employees, Ralph would play outside until he'd made enough money to buy a steak at a nearby restaurant, after which he'd return home to watch the program *Xena: Warrior Princess* (the Aphrodite character from which would eventually inspire his song "Goddess Of Love").

Ralph playing outside Wax Trax Records.

Ralph playing live at Denver's 7 South, 1990s.

Around this time, Ralph made the acquaintance of Shannon Dickey, a savvy music maven Wax Trax employee who took an active interest in Ralph's music and prompted him to begin performing at local venues. Acting as Ralph's manager, Dickey brought Ralph's music to the attention of a number of Denver's more eccentric music enthusiasts, including "incredibly strange" music aficionado Boyd Rice, The Apples In Stereo bassist Eric Allen, Tom Lundin, and Gregory "Ego" Daurer (whose "Kill For A Cigarette" Ralph

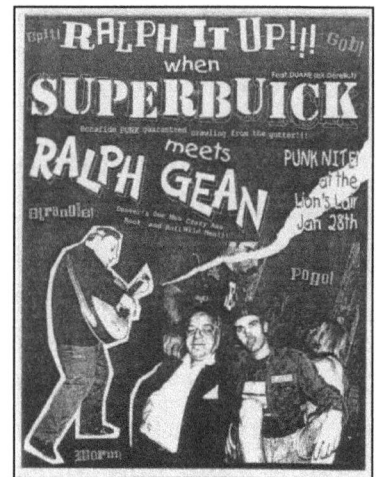

would go on to cover in later years). This began a comeback of sorts for Ralph's theretofore washed-up career, and with Dickey as his manager, the next few years saw Ralph performing regularly throughout Denver, both as a solo act and with Rockabilly backing bands composed of musicians young enough to be his kids. Due to the often off-color subject matter of many of his songs, Ralph eventually evolved such a devoted following amongst Denver's in-the-know hipster crowd that by 1996 he was featured on the cover of the city's free weekly paper, *Westword*.

A year later, in 1997, with the assistance of several enthusiastic fans/friends, the first ever CD collection of Ralph's music was released under the exasperating title *A Star Unborn or What Would Have Been If What Is Hadn't Happened: The Amazing Story Of Ralph Gean*. It contained a selection of cuts from the preceding thirty years of Ralph's career,

Ralph playing a standing-room only show at the Lion's Lair, 1990s.

including some of his early 45s, a few of his 1980s full band recordings, and a number of solo tracks recorded on hand-held cassette decks. The disc sparked an immediate wave of interest in Ralph's music among a diverse fan base comprising Rockabilly and Country enthusiasts, and collectors of "incredibly strange" outsider music in general. San Francisco's Punk Rock 'zine, *MAXIMUM ROCKNROLL* said of the disc, "Musically, it veers from psychotic shit-kicking to bent Rock n' Roll, parodistic plodding heavy rock, scary Casio nuttiness worthy of latter-day 'beat of the Traps.' ... [Gean] doesn't need any 'bonus' respect points for his age." *Exotica/Etcetera* said, "The man has presence, the man has a sound, and both come across with power." And *Rock & Blues News* was bold enough to declare, "[Gean's] problem has always been that he was ahead of his time. It took ten years for The Rev. Horton Heat and the psychobillies to catch up with Ralph Gean."

The Reverend Horton Heat, Ralph Gean, and Shannon Dickey, 1990s.

In the years that followed in the second half of the 1990s, Ralph would go on to perform with the likes of Paul Burlison and Rocky Burnette, and with bands such as The Mutilators, The Volts, and The Humpers; as well as open for bands such as The Reverend Horton Heat, and John Sinclair (of MC5 fame). He was brought into the studio to record a few songs with Jello Biafra of The Dead Kennedys and later with Eric Allen of The Apples In Stereo (neither of these sessions ever saw commercial release), and even flown out to San Francisco to play to more than 1,500 people at an "Incredibly Strange Wrestling" event.

This newfound interest of young people came despite several problems with the release of Ralph's *A Star Unborn* CD, which was issued and distributed by World Serpent Distribution – a niche underground imprint based out of London, England, which specialized nearly exclusively in European Post-Industrial Goth and Neofolk music, not American Rock n' Roll or Rockabilly. While the disc saw excellent distribution in Europe and was well received there, the story in North America was altogether different. *A Star Unborn* was not only difficult to find outside of hip independent record shops that carried

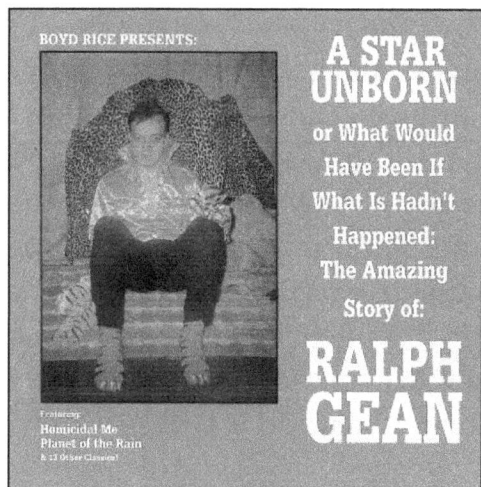

A Star Unborn or What Would Have Been If What Is Hadn't Happened: The Amazing Story of Ralph Gean, CD from World Serpent, 1997.

the often willfully obscure releases on World Serpent, but was usually filed in the Industrial/Experimental section of such shops and marked-up as a British import – making it often twice as expensive as domestic independent CDs. As if that weren't frustrating enough, World Serpent declared bankruptcy and went out of business not too long after the release of *A Star Unborn*, thus making the disc all but impossible to find and effectively out-of-print not long after its release. As a result, Ralph's short-lived debut CD was going up on eBay—and selling—for exorbitant amounts of money (as much as sixfold the price of new retail CDs, in one instance), as a rarity and collector's item, but was all but entirely unavailable to the general public in the United States, and had earned Ralph next to nothing in the way of royalties.

Meanwhile, starting in 1996, Ralph began making a series of trips to Memphis, Tennessee's Sun Studio, where Elvis Presley had kicked off the initial Rock n' Roll phenomenon. During each visit, Ralph paid to record with the studio's in-house band, committing to tape a half-dozen or so songs per session, including his own originals and classic Rock n' Roll era covers. Although he had no specific intention of releasing these recordings, Ralph continued to make journeys to Memphis whenever he'd saved up enough money and vacation time, mostly for the fun and nostalgia of recording at the legendary studio. "I've always wanted to do my own Sun session with my songs. ... I couldn't believe how good it all turned out [and] just to be standing where all those greats stood – it was wonderful."

Unfortunately, by the end of the 1990s, most of Denver's hipster crowd had lost interest in Ralph Gean. The mid-1990s era rejuvenation of "retro" culture and its corresponding revival of interest in the genres of Swing, Surf, and Rockabilly music had petered out by the end of the decade, and Ralph was again generally ignored and forgotten. When I met Ralph in 2003 the only gigs he could manage to get were at sparsely attended Punk Rock warehouses like the aforementioned Monkey Mania, and local Mexican restaurants, where he'd often play up to three sets without any amplification, and only be compensated with a meal and whatever tips he could make from patrons. This wouldn't have

Ralph playing live on college radio, KCVU 1190, Boulder, Colorado, early 2000s.

been so bad, except that Ralph's job as a caretaker for John Spencer ended not long after I made his acquaintance, and he soon found himself effectively homeless and without income of any sort whatsoever. Things suddenly got rough for Ralph Gean, yet again, and there were several weeks during which he had nowhere else to stay aside from on the futon outside my bedroom, in the basement of Monkey Mania. Eventually, however, Ralph managed to find permanent subsidized housing on the outskirts of Denver, and for the most part has been doing quite well these days. He still performs on a regular basis at local bars and restaurants, and has recently started getting decent gigs again, opening for local bands at proper venues from time to time. He still writes new songs and is still as excited and enthusiastic as ever about his career in Rock music.

Ralph in 2006.

What's distinctive about Ralph Gean (aside from the tumultuous turns his life has taken over the years) is that despite decades of repeated setbacks, he's never lost touch with his original lifelong aspirations. Most of the kids in the bands that Ralph opens up for won't "make it" in the music business; and once they realize that, will likely throw in the towel after a few years, moving on to "real" jobs and careers, and reminiscing from time to time about their salad days spent "living on the edge" and playing in a band. Not Ralph. He's implacable. He'll never stop—not until his body forces him to anyway—because he just loves Rock n' Roll too much; writing songs, recording, and most of all, performing for live audiences. The man gets a genuine kick out of entertaining people and puts on a great show, all by himself. If a crowd wants to hear murder songs, he'll play murder songs, if they want Elvis covers, they'll get Elvis covers - he doesn't particularly seem to care, as long as everyone's having a good time. And most often, with nothing but a microphone and an acoustic guitar, he manages to steal the show from whatever Rock band he's opening for. Ralph is unflaggingly charming, sincere, funny, and he's got almost forty years of practice on anyone he might be playing with, so it really shouldn't come as too much of a shocker.

At the risk of overselling "The Star Trekkin' Rock n' Roll Cowboy," I'd argue that Ralph's music captures something that's increasingly rare in this day and age: a sincere love for writing and playing that has little to do with "success" or commercial viability. In an era when every Tom, Dick, and Harry wants to be instantly catapulted to international stardom via *American Idol* without ever paying their dues (let alone writing a single song), Ralph Gean is a man who's paid his dues in spades ... and then some. He's well past ever becoming a Pop star at this point, but nonetheless continues to write and perform for whoever will listen, simply because he loves it. Ralph was around when Rock n' Roll was born, and although he might've just missed the boat on American Rock n' Roll's first wave by a few short years, he hasn't lost sight of its original balls-out spirit of pure *fun*; irrespective of the varied, occasionally misguided directions it's taken in the decades since.

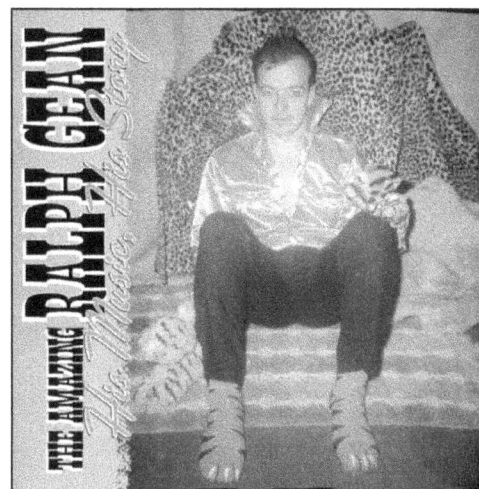
The Amazing Ralph Gean –
His Music, His Story,
2 x CD from Discriminate Audio, 2007.

Your Tax Dollars Paid for This Whisper into the Wind

2005

The next time you hear a hidebound conservative bitching about the profligate use of taxpayer dollars on The National Endowment for The Arts, The Public Broadcasting Service, or Welfare; and the next time you hear a peacenik liberal pissing and moaning about extravagant U.S. military spending, or Homeland Security; and the next time you hear a *laissez-faire* libertarian whine about crony capitalism and unfair tax subsidies for big agribusiness or sports arenas – keep in mind that American taxpayers are still shilling out non-negligible funds to finance government-sanctioned prayer. Yes, we still fuckin' pay people to *pray* in this country. The United States Senate and The United States House of Representatives *both* have paid chaplains who open legislative sessions with fuckin' prayers. They're nondenominational prayers, but still, they're fuckin' *paid prayers*. So goddamn stupid.

At least the NEA gives us spuriously transgressive "feminist" art to make fun of; and at least the military drops bombs on people, both of which—whether you agree with them or not—constitute actually fuckin' *doing* something tangible. Prayer is, by definition, a non-action. It's whispering into the wind and wishing for magic, like a six-year-old pining for the day Santa will finally bring her a pony for Christmas. It's fucking idiotic. If we're going to squander taxpayer dollars on paid prayer, then we might as well start giving out cash for Native American rain dances, or hire voodoo priestesses to lay curses on Al-Qaeda – it's the height of wasteful, useless, magic-minded nitwittery ... and we're *paying* for it.

For more information on this ludicrously fucking pointless waste of U.S. taxpayer money, visit Chaplain.House.gov or Senate.gov.

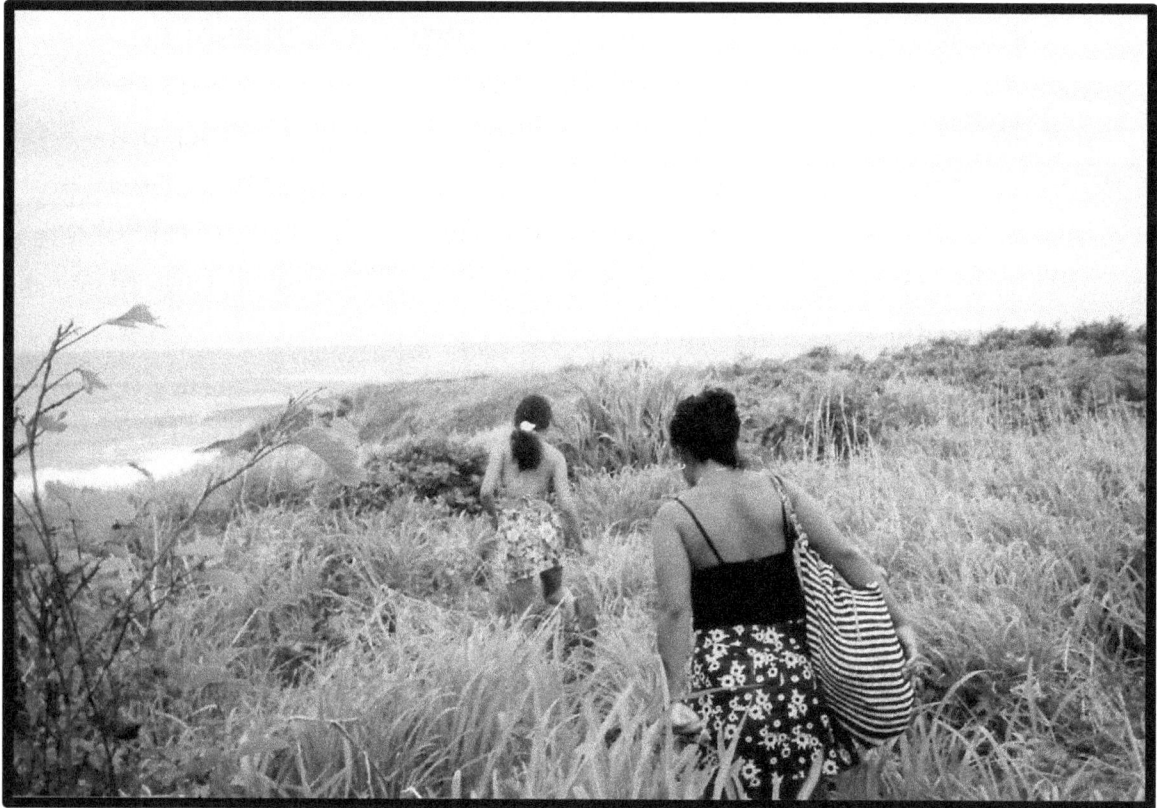

A Tropical Motel 6 By the Sea

Living and Working at Costa Rica's Hotel Iguanazul

2013

Back at the end of the 1990s, I spent a couple of summers working abroad through a program that provided American college students with affordable, short-term work visas for selected countries. One year I worked briefly as a barback at a gigantic pub called The Old Oak in Cork, Ireland. The other year, I worked as a bilingual hotel concierge at The Hotel Iguanazul in the Guanacaste province of Costa Rica. Both of these experiences were simultaneously great and horrible; great in that they got me out of the United States for a few months in my early twenties, and gave me a superficially-legit excuse to drunkenly explore a new part of the world; horrible in that doing so involved performing menial labor for intolerable assholes, at paupers' wages. I haven't thought about either of these jobs in ages, but one of my former American coworkers at The Hotel Iguanazul recently emailed me with links to an episode of a Travel Channel show titled *Hotel Impossible* (think *Kitchen Nightmares* or *Bar Rescue*) which recently did an episode on our erstwhile Costa Rican employer and place of residence, The Hotel Iguanazul.

I used to live and work at this Tropical Motel 6 By the Sea, earning $1.50 an hour as a bilingual liaison between English-speaking American tourists and the jaded Spanish-speaking Costa Ricans who were paid less than $1.00 an hour to cater to them. The bulk of the hotel's clientele were working-class Americans from Florida who took advantage of the cheap direct flights out of Miami and lopsided currency exchange rate; and who, once in-country, shamelessly indulged in the easy excesses of Costa Rica's famously lax drug enforcement and non-criminalization of prostitution. They were, on the whole, rude, cocksure, and entitled; in a king-for-a-day sort of way. In a word, they were bastards.

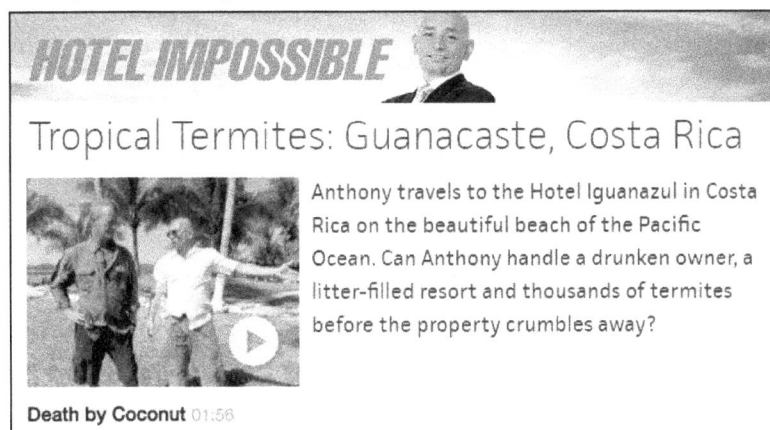

HOTEL IMPOSSIBLE

Tropical Termites: Guanacaste, Costa Rica

Anthony travels to the Hotel Iguanazul in Costa Rica on the beautiful beach of the Pacific Ocean. Can Anthony handle a drunken owner, a litter-filled resort and thousands of termites before the property crumbles away?

Death by Coconut 01:56

Even though I only made a-buck-fifty an hour, it wasn't the worst job I'd ever had. It was, however, the worst place I've ever lived. The hotel rooms rented to guests were nice—"posh," even—but the servants' quarters where the staff lived were borderline squalid. It was like camping on a mattress in a hut, in the jungle. My American college friends were skeptical when I got back home and said that my onetime roommate and I slept under mosquito nets every night at The Hotel Iguanazul because we found a scorpions' nest in our room, but the fact is, we *did*. There was *a goddamn scorpions' nest* in my fucking room in the servants' quarters area of The Hotel Iguanazul. ...

"Rustic."

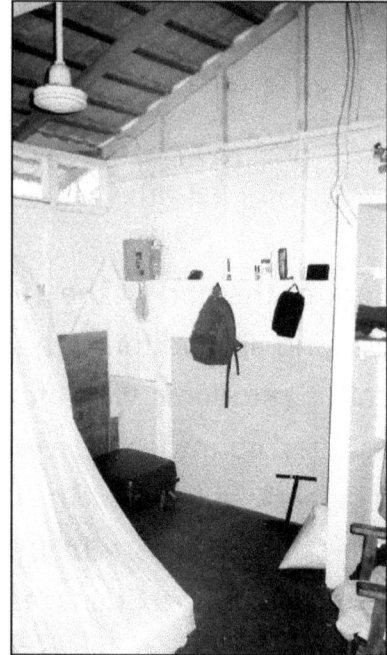

Mosquito netting tucked under my mattress on the floor. Also pictured: less than ideal jungle roofing insulation.

Anyway, it's just petty *schadenfreude* on my part, and nobody will find this nearly as amusing as my former coworker and I do, but there are a couple of clips online of The Hotel Iguanazul's Canadian trainwreck of a proprietor, Dave, being called-out by the host of *Hotel Impossible* for being a lush who's let the place go to hell over the years. It's been fifteen years since I lived and worked there, and from the online clips of *Hotel Impossible*, it looks as though not much has changed. Which is a damned shame, because it's an amazing and picturesque place, but unfortunately its ownership and management appear to still be of dubious competence. Hopefully, proprietorship and management of The Hotel Iguanazul will change hands, and someone will turn it

Our communal sink. At least we had running water – most of the locals didn't.

into The Ritz By The Sea that it deserves to be; and hopefully, when they do so, they'll fumigate for scorpions in the servants' quarters.

...

Beethoven's Blue Balls

2005

I'm of the opinion that German composer Ludwig Van Beethoven was the greatest artist ever to have trod the face of the earth. Granted, he may not have been as much of a mind-bogglingly-confounding autistic-polymath-genius-weirdo as the likes of, say, Sir Isaac Newton, but—setting The Sciences aside—as far as I'm concerned, when it comes to The Arts, Beethoven's creative genius overshadows even the likes of DaVinci, Michelangelo, *et al.* His "Eroica" symphony, "Ode to Joy," "Egmont," his Fifth Symphony, and so on – these are pinnacles of human achievement far and above any static work like a mere painting or sculpture, and far more emotive. As the venerable American critic H.L. Mencken once opined, "The feelings that Beethoven put into his music were the feelings of a god." And it's true, really. It's hard to wrap one's head around now, but Ludwig Van Beethoven reinvented Western music. The man was in a league all his own; a titan of tunes. Paramount.

Of course, during his lifetime, despite his renowned talent as a hit-machine composer, poor Ludwig couldn't really get any decent action from the ladies. He pursued many women (some of his offhand musical sketches to them survive as timeless classics of the Western canon), but—although he was indeed "famous" by the standards of the day—he never married, and ultimately died alone. Partly as a result of his rotten luck in love, Ludwig was a saturnine depressive, a heavy drinker, and often suicidal. You see, the problem for the ever-dejected Ludwig in class-stratified Vienna of the early nineteenth century, was that his surname was preceded by a "Van" instead of the aristocratic "Von" that piqued the amorous interests of *fräuleins* at the time. So not only was he an ornery eccentric genius, but by virtue of his social class, he also wasn't "marriageable," as they say nowadays. It's a dang shame, really, to see that kind of culturally-entrenched myopic philistinism—petty bigotry, if you will—so profoundly affect such a brilliant, for-the-ages talent.

Perhaps you've heard Ludwig's earworm "Für Elise"? It's a catchy ditty that he wrote for some entirely forgettable broad named Elise who probably wouldn't fuck him. Or maybe you're familiar with his "Moonlight Sonata"? It's a classic tune that the sullen, lovelorn bastard composed for a rich girl named Julie or "Giulietta" – who of course was also entirely forgettable, also contributed zilch to the history of Western culture, and also probably wouldn't fuck him. As I say, I personally regard the guy as the preeminent artist in the annals of recorded history; certainly the greatest composer of all time, anyway. Nonetheless, the poor forlorn sonofabitch still couldn't find love because his last name had an "a" instead of an "o" in it.

Further proof that "the fairer sex" are inerrantly pure of heart and have their priorities straight.

¡Borracho, Borracho, Borracho!

A Spanish Travelogue

2002

The following is an online journal kept on an intermittently regular-ish basis from January through April of 2002; while I was working as an English teacher in Madrid, Spain, and living in a shared-flat with about a dozen or so other foreigners from throughout Europe, Scandinavia, Asia, South America, and The United States. Being that this was back in the days before the existence of such things as social media and smartphones, digital cameras were rare and expensive – and I certainly didn't own one. The few photographs accompanying the text were shot on film, on an automatic camera, and were later developed on my return to the United States, then digitally scanned.

You Keep a Diary.
January 4, 2002, 7:07 p.m.

Normally, I would be opposed to this sort of thing. One of the downsides to the Internet is that it gives every half-witted dumbshit his or her own personal "digital soap box" from which to rant and banter at the rest of the world; but a friend back in the San Francisco Bay Area suggested that I start an online WebLog or "blog," and just write about my life here, rather than sporadically send-out unsolicited emails to people back home as I've occasionally done in the past while travelling in Ireland and Costa Rica. Ergo, I am now one of those half-witted dumbshits on the Internet with a personal, digital soap box. The Anal Cunt song "You keep a diary" immediately comes to mind. ... *Amen.*

Mierda Española.
January 5, 2002, 5:09 p.m.

I realized the other day that I've been living and working outside the United States for over a year now; three-plus months in Ireland and the rest in Spain. Kind of odd, considering how little I actually miss The States most of the time.

Sure, I miss all the stupid shit you take for granted. I miss my car. I miss decent record stores where I can find things I might actually like. I miss bookstores that carry titles in English besides Steven King, Ernest Hemingway, and Harry Potter. I miss speaking English with people I relate to. I miss 24-hour diners probably more than anything. But otherwise ... I dunno – not much else to say. I just don't really care either way.

I'll be back stateside someday. Today is not that day.

Karma Will Have Its Way with Me Yet.
January 8, 2002, 5:35 p.m.

So, I live on the sixth floor of a fairly old building in the Alonso Martinez area of Madrid – at the corner of a semi-busy intersection which features a constellation of bars and a 7-Eleven convenience store. It is often very, *very* crowded on Friday and Saturday nights, with all sorts of dumbasses

milling around 7-Eleven, drinking boxed wine, or just wandering around the street drunk, singing "Viva España" or various other ass-backwards Spanish ballads.

A month or so ago, I was having a "party" (using that word liberally) in my room, and I was quite drunk, so to impress the guests, I started throwing little cocktail onions at the passing taxis below. Lots of fun because, amid the noise and commotion, nobody can really tell where the flying onions are coming from. This was so much fun that it then escalated into soaring slices of ham. I somehow, gloriously, managed to hit one taxi square on the front windshield with a nice rectangular slice of ham, which was then promptly pushed off by a windshield-wiper. Good, harmless fun indeed! Later that night, some drunk Rastafarians were drinking below my window and belting out some awful reggae shit at 5:00 a.m., so I threw a tomato at them. I missed, but that's not the point. The point is that, in all cases, I was never seen.

So, all of this had the effect of instilling in me the sentiment, *Wow! I can throw food out my window at people and cars, and nobody will ever know where it's coming from since I'm way up on the sixth floor!* That was about a month ago.

So, this last weekend I was entertaining a couple of American girls in my room, and again I was quite drunk, and again the street corner was filled with people and cars. The same sequence of events pretty much transpired, except that all I had in my fridge this time was ... eggs. We hit a taxi on the trunk. We hit a sports car on the hood, and they drove off in a rush. We almost hit some people with some cocktail weenies, too, but that didn't really count. So all of that was quite fine and dandy. Good clean fun. Until ... I lean out the side window and toss an egg down at a stopped taxi, but I don't really put all the "umph" needed to hit the taxi, and the egg falls short. I duck my head inside the window and hear, "*¡Hijo de puta cabrón!*"

So, some poor bastard was strolling down the sidewalk with his *amigos*, and I hit him on the head with an egg. Oops! That wasn't so nice, but ... these things happen. But then my stupid drunk ass decides to look out the window to see who I'd hit, and the motherfucker and his friends see my head poke out and they start pointing and yelling. So now they know where I live. ...

And that was it. They never did anything. They never tried to get into my building. They never tried to break my windows. Nothing. We all went out drinking after that, 'til 6:00 a.m., and when we came back – nothing. So, I am still waiting for Karma to kick my ass. The retribution will come, I am sure of it. But you can never really be ready for that sort of thing.

Yes'm.
January 9, 2002, 6:17 p.m.

So, they are doing a musical of *Driving Ms. Daisy* here. In Spanish. In a theater in downtown Madrid. *Driving Ms. Daisy* – the Spanish musical. *Amazing.*

Military English.
January 10, 2002, 10:07 p.m.

So, I got my new schedule of classes today. Looks like, starting Monday, I'll be teaching Advanced English to a cadre of twelve officers from the Spanish Army. Yup. Apparently, they need to prepare for the NATO language exam, and it is my job to teach them how to say things like, "Assault formation, Green Squadron go!" Hah. The textbook is pretty amusing. It's called *Military English for Users* and is filled with word games, puzzles, and "Military English" activities. The highlights, though, are the cartoons and diagrams. *Peanuts*-style drawings of army men shooting at each other, tanks blowing things up, and airplanes dropping bombs n' such. Below each cartoon there is text like:

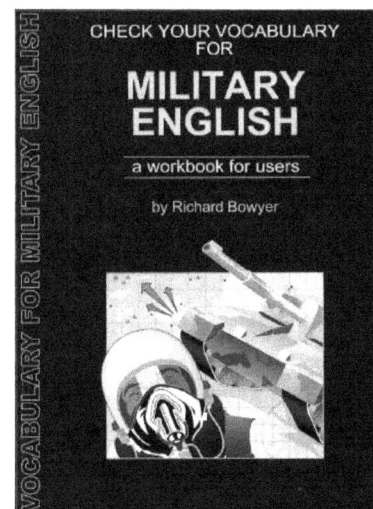

CHECK YOUR VOCABULARY FOR

MILITARY ENGLISH

a workbook for users

by Richard Bowyer

VOCABULARY FOR MILITARY ENGLISH

"They are _____ fire."

Possible answers:

    A. making
    B. leaving
    C. friendly
    D. exchanging

Answer?

    D. exchanging (fire)

It's great. I'm pumped. It's bringing back all sorts of G.I. Joe flashbacks already, and I haven't even started the class yet. With any luck the people will be cool, and I can turn phrases like "Drop your weapons!" into "Drop your weapons *motherfucker*!" That would make me a happy pedagogue indeed.

Megabyte me.
January 11, 2002, 8:30 p.m.

I learned today that the term "*bite*" means "dick" in French colloquial slang. Therefore, the term "megabyte" is immensely hilarious to the French (so they say anyway). When she's drunk, my French housemate Faustine always refers to her boyfriend as "*Zee megabyte!*" Now I get it.

Faustine, wasted.

Bienvenidos al Ejército Español.
January 14, 2002, 9:15 p.m.

Well, I am sorry to report that my experience teaching English to the Spanish Army wasn't half as swell as I was hoping it would be. First of all, I had to take the slow bus way out to the boondocks of north Madrid, then when I finally got to the military base I had to pass through a *weak-ass* security checkpoint (they didn't even frisk me, or look for explosives in my shoes!), then the building

I was supposed to teach in was locked, so I had to find some grunt with keys to open it, and then only a handful of my students actually showed up to class (all in full camo and stormtrooper boots, however). The classroom was freezing cold and poorly lit, and I couldn't hear anyone (nor could they hear me), because throughout the entire class, the fucking drum corps were marching around outside the building making a godawful racket with some snare drums and a poorly-played trumpet.

Add to this some major confusion about what actual class I was supposed to be teaching and to whom; not Advanced English – Basic English, and not to officers preparing for the NATO exam – to grunts who are my age (early twenties), most of whom didn't know where the class was supposed to be, didn't know who I was, and didn't really know who *they* were either. So, as a result of this, I didn't have any of the right books, or even the right attendance sheet, and when I phoned my company's office to figure out what was up, they freaked out at me, as if the mix-up was somehow *my* fault. Of course it wasn't ... but did my boss apologize later? Of course not. Annoying, indeed.

Anyway, all of my students are from the Artillery Division, and so far my favorite is the guy whose job it is to load shells into the anti-aircraft guns. Seriously – that's his fucking job. I made everyone go around the room and say their name and what they do, and he says, "Um ... hell-o, I am named Jose, and I put the bullets in the big guns for shooting down the airplanes." Amen to that, Jose – *¡Viva España!*

The Fine Art of Spanish Pornography.
January 15, 2002, 8:59 p.m.

You wouldn't believe some of the porn they have in this country, you just wouldn't. Allow me to explicate for y'all:

One of the more subtle U.S.-Europe differences is that of government-sanctioned sexual hang-ups. America, having been founded by Protestant fanatics fleeing sectarian repression in England, still clings to the novel concept of "morality" (read as "censorship") in public broadcasting. This has long since died off in

Europe, of course (just look at Scandinavia). Kidding (sort of). Anyway, in short, broadcasting regulations and the concept of "socially acceptable television" vary quite a bit between Europe and The States.

For instance, despite the overload of gore films and garbage like "professional" wrestling spewing out of America, real corpses are never shown on television in the United States – this is not so in Europe. Here in Spain, when there is a ten-car pileup on the freeway, and they show it on the news, you get the pleasure of seeing the gore up close and nasty – in America, you are stuck looking at crumpled cars shot at a distance and close-ups of shattered glass on the asphalt. Consequently (believe it or not), last year a few of my Spanish businessmen students initially speculated that 9/11 was a "hoax" – their logic being: *If thousands of people died, why aren't there any corpses on any of the news footage?* And I found myself explaining, "Because in America they don't put dead bodies on TV, and all of that footage is taken from the American news." But I digress.

So anyway, some things are a little different; like the fact that they show hardcore pornography on regular television here. Oh, yes—that's right—hardcore porno, broadcast for free, to the general public. After about 10:30 p.m. any night of the week, you get upwards of three channels of smut broadcast into your house, free of charge (at least in my flat we do – and I seriously doubt that my stingy, uptight landlord is paying for the porn for the rest of us).

Now, the first channel is pretty much your run-of-the-mill, imported-from-Los-Angeles *Playboy* silliness; naked girls spraying themselves with hoses on a beach somewhere, or some shit like that – *boring*. Then there is the second channel, which is equally-bland Spanish porn; a naked girl or two on a bed somewhere rubbing telephone receivers all over their bodies, saying in Spanish, "I'm here for you, call me big boy!" – *boring*. Dull. Tacky. Pedestrian.

But then there is the third free porn channel, which is something entirely different. It is something *sui generis*. It is something very, *very* special. On more than one occasion members of my hodgepodge international household have gathered 'round the communal television set to stare transfixed—in quiet awe and horror—at what goes on, on free porn channel number three.

Free porn channel number three is—dare I say it?—*the most amazing concept Art project I've ever seen in my entire life*. That's right motherfucker, avant-garde Art. Maybe it's "outsider art," but it is certainly Art ... because it's not really "smut," that's for goddamn sure. So, this is what I'm talking about:

Okay, basically you have this kind of plain-looking South American woman somewhere in her thirties, and um, she is on TV every single day of the week. Every day she is there, on the screen, fucking more than a few corpulent, repulsive men on a mattress on the floor of a half-decorated warehouse. This is a bit depressing, especially considering that she never seems to be even so much as amused by the act of "love making" she's engaged in, let alone enjoying it, but other than that – not particularly out of the ordinary.

Oh, and did I mention that there are people sitting around on couches situated around the mattress, drinking cocktails and chatting with each other – completely indifferent to the fact that this South American woman is fucking some dude (actually, usually two dudes), literally right at their feet?

Muy sexy.

Oh, and did I mention that the men doing the fucking are wearing *fluorescent pink-and-green glam-rock wigs and masquerade masks*? Oh, and sometimes they wear Skeletor (from the *He-Man* cartoon) masks, or *Scream* masks. Oh, and add to this the fact that there is no sound – only dubbed-over goofy Central American mariachi and salsa music played in endless loops. It's *amazing* stuff. It's a fascinating program, really. It's just so completely surreal and mystifying. Like way more fucked up than anything someone like Hans Bellmer could have come up with in his wildest dreams.

The first time I beheld this bawdy program, me and three of my housemates were flipping through the channels and we see this ruddy fat guy in a pink wig and a masquerade

51

mask fucking the South American woman doggie-style, while she is performing fellatio on a skinny guy with a cast on his arm, who is wearing a *Scream* mask, and all the while there are two couches full of homely people inattentively drinking cocktails and ignoring the threesome on the mattress at their feet,

¡Qué sexy!

and there is a song playing that goes, "*¡Te quiero, te quiero, te quieeeeeeeero! ¡Cha-cha-cha!*" Yup, I shit you not.

The best thing about it is that it is nearly the most un-erotic, un-sexual, un-arousing thing you could possibly imagine. I mean, from my perspective, there is nothing sexy or prurient involved whatsoever. It's completely beyond me how anyone could successfully jack off to this stuff. It just wouldn't work. It just ... wouldn't.

For a while, the working theory (first posited by my gay Argentine housemate, Diego) was that this was a "hidden camera" program of some sort, and that all the people involved were just completely fucked-in-the-head and insane. That's sort of plausible, I guess, but improbable, really. However, I think I may have figured it out.

This is my running theory; so, the way I envisage it, this warehouse is located somewhere in the outskirts of Madrid, and basically it is like a one-woman brothel or something, where you can go and pay some money and fuck this chick. But if you wanna' fuck the woman (I'm sure it's cheap) you have to agree to be filmed and broadcast on live porno-TV. So, sleazy, dirtball Spanish men (like porcine hairy men and lanky men with casts on their arms) head down there, throw down their money, and hump this woman. The ones who wear the fucked-up masks and wigs are those that don't want to be recognized on television by their girlfriends / wives / family, and the people on the couches drinking cocktails are just waiting in line to hump the South American woman; or they work for the porno-TV station, or whatever. I surmise that sort of makes sense, in a way. That's the most logical explanation I can think of anyway.

Regardless, it may not be licentious, but I daresay that it's Art. It's definitely Art. Art, I tell you ... *Art*!

El Templo de Debod.
January 20, 2002, 4:14 p.m.

It's been ass-cold here lately. Too cold to wander around town at night listening to my Discman, like I like to do. So lately I've been stuck inside, or in crowded smoky bars, which sucks. When it's warmer, one of my favorite things to do here to kill boredom when I'm restless, is to walk down to the Temple of Debod at about midnight ... because it's *eeeeeeeeviiiiiiil*.

The Temple of Debod is this ancient Egyptian shrine which the government of Egypt bequeathed to Spain for reasons unbeknownst to me. They shipped the whole thing up here piece-by-piece and reassembled it on a spot near Plaza España that overlooks the southern half of the city. The front part of the building is surrounded by a large pool of water, and at sunset they illuminate it with spotlights, and you can stand on this ledge and have a superb vista looking out on the lights of the city below. It's real *purty*.

The Temple of Debod at night.

For some reason the Temple of Debod just strikes me as really bitchin'. I like hanging out there. I wander around it at night in a hoodie listening to Sludge Metal, and I feel some serious *bona fide* badassedness running through my veins. Because I am a big fucking dork, of course.

Moriré ... Me Voy a Morir.
January 21, 2002, 10:59 p.m.

Nothing interesting to report, really. Another dumb Monday. Still pounding my head into a wall, trying to teach English to the Artillery Division of the Spanish Army. I was hanging out in the mess hall before class today, drinking a coffee, surrounded by chain-smoking, beer-sipping camo-clad Spaniards, and Alien Ant Farm's rendition of Michael Jackson's "Smooth Criminal" came on the radio. The bartender sang along poorly in Spanglish. It was a magical and surreal moment – you kind of had to be there.

My job is such a hoot sometimes. I guess in theory it's a "job" because they pay me, but in practice it's often more of a Dadaist performance piece or something along those lines. I was teaching the English future tenses today (will do, going to do, will be doing, will have done, *et cetera*), and to illustrate some point I was attempting to make and clear up somebody's misapprehension about the difference between the "future simple" and the "future continuous," I wrote up on the chalkboard:

> I will die.
>
> I am going to die.

For some reason, this still amuses me, even now. So tell me, hotshot, you're a native English-speaker; do *you* know the difference?

¡Quiero Matar ... Toda La Noche!
January 23, 2002, 11:51 p.m.

So, today was a shitty day. I didn't get enough sleep last night, I missed breakfast, and I had a shitty headache all day long. The novelty of my "job" has long since worn off, and now it's just a big annoyance, which doesn't pay well enough to validate the trouble. The Army fuckers are a big

One of the bazillion Catholic churches, doesn't matter which.

camo-clad pain in my ass at this point, and it's only been a week.

Anyway, I learned how to say "breast" or "boob" in colloquial French today. So all afternoon I kept calling my French housemates "one boob" and "two boobs" in French. I thought it was funny anyway.

I can also say "son of a whore" and "ass-face," and now because I know the word for "boob" I can say "whore boobs," "ass-boobs" and "boob-face." All of which are going to be oh-so useful, of course.

Que le Jodan al Ejército Español.
January 25, 2002, 9:11 p.m.

Today was a pretty good day. I taught two executives at an international security company the term "carpet-muncher," and they taught me that you can euphemistically call a girl a dyke in Spanish by saying she's a "*tortilliera*" which is Spanish for "tortilla-maker" (nobody seems to know why – it's inexplicable). That's what it's all about. Shit like that.

Fuck the Spanish Army though, I hate those fuckers. Yesterday, out of nowhere, the Colonel and his entourage came to "inspect" my class. I presume they were "making their rounds" of the base and decided to pop in. Fuckers. So, I'm standing there trying to teach the camo-clad Army guys, and the door opens and there stands The Colonel and his phalanx of Army yes-men. All my students jump to their feet and salute him. I stand there motionless, unsure of what I'm supposed to do. He mumbles something to me in inaudible and unintelligible sub-sonic Spanish, which I can't make out (my Spanish is pretty good, but it's not *that* good). I stare at him like a deer caught in headlights. Making an effort to enunciate and project his voice at me this time, he says, "Humm ... there aren't many students today, are there?" and I say, "Uh ... I dunno, I just took over this class from another teacher." Uncomfortable

¡Borracho, Borracho, Borracho!

silence. He gives me a funny look, which in the international language of facial expressions translates to; *You fuckin' dumbass foreigner.* I smile stupidly. He and his goons close the door and leave. Fuckers. I don't get paid minimum wage to take that kind of shit. I get paid to teach executives about carpet-munchers.

Anyway, it's Friday night. I'm getting drunk and going to some "German electronic music show" at this club called NASTI, which I think is usually a gay disco. I have no idea who or what is playing, but shit, German electronic music sounds like it's worth my five euro. I've got nothing better to do anyway. Maybe they'll bust out with "Autobahn." I hope so, but I doubt it. Full report tomorrow.

Musik Non-Stop.
January 26, 2002, 4:59 p.m.

The "German electronic music show" last night was terrible. I've been to quite a few shows over the years, and last night's performance by Tak Tak Tak was probably the first time I've ever stormed out of a show after only five minutes – and I paid €9.00 to get in.

The spectacle I witnessed last night was the real-world embodiment of every negative stereotype that Americans hold about Europeans, everything lame about "electronic music" and everything detestable about "fashion" – just completely shitty. Tak Tak Tak was two scrawny German guys in their mid-twenties wearing matching black t-shirts, who were standing on a stage smoking cigarettes, idly sipping cocktails, and every now and then absentmindedly twiddling knobs on a big mixing board. The "music" they were "making" was of the generic *boom-tsk-boom-tsk-boom-tsk* Techno-esque variety that can be found at any number of bars, clubs, and discotheques throughout Europe. There was nothing "live" about it – there weren't even fucking turntables involved. Basically, they had like a dozen tracks or so of pre-recorded music, which they were "mixing" in and out with volume knobs. Lots of 808 bass kicks, octave square-wave basslines, and phasers (the kind of shit any idiot with an '80s sound module and a MIDI-controller can sequence in about ten minutes). So there was

about five minutes of just that—two guys twiddling volume knobs on a mixer—then this short blond German girl with glitter on her cheeks comes out and starts singing in English about pussycats or something. Unbearable.

I was drunk, and it probably would have been fun if the crowd was dancing or something—anything—but they were all too preoccupied with trying to look cosmopolitan and vogueish in their white turtlenecks and thick-rimmed glasses. So, as I said, I stormed out after about five minutes. Nine euro down the drain.

Do You Like American Music?
January 27, 2002, 8:32 p.m.

Well, last night was a doozy. First off, I went to see an indie Noise Rock band from The States at Gruta 77, which is way out in the boonies of southern Madrid. It doesn't matter what they were called. I wouldn't say they were "great," but they were good. But then, any American Rock band is good compared to any Spanish Rock band, so I guess that isn't saying much. After that, I repaired back to my flat and found most of my housemates drinking and watching TV. So, I continued drinking with them. All told, by the end of the night, I had consumed the following: sangria, beer, wine, whiskey, champagne, more beer, and two unidentified shots. Today I am accordingly hungover, but it was a good evening of ruckus (I got in after 5:30 a.m.), so it was worth it.

My housemates and I went out "dancing" with my landlord, a thirty-something, socially maladroit Spanish weirdo who wears bellbottom jeans and tight-fitting button-up shirts, and who shamelessly hits on girls at discos like no other. He's an aspirant philanderer who seems to lack the kind of "game" that it takes to "seal the deal," with the ladies. That's my impression, anyway. He bought us all drinks, and at one point I had him doing drunken Irish jigs with me (kind of) at a place called Più. There was some mayhem of the typical drunken cavorting variety between discos, then a bunch of us came home and watched the infamous "surrealist porn channel" for a while and had a rousing discussion on the importance of penis size. (The verdict? It matters.)

I Am the Ugly American ... I Know What I Am.
February 3, 2002, 4:51 p.m.

It's Sunday afternoon. I've been too busy over the last three days to set aside any time to be a geek at an Internet café and post on this journal. Quick summary of my weekend:

Thursday night I experienced some wicked insomnia. I finally capitulated at about 4:30 a.m. and started drinking coffee, reading, and listening to music. I had to "get up" at 6:15 for work on Friday morning so I could catch the train to Tres Cantos, which takes about an hour. Made it to work at 8:00, totally delirious and seeing spots in my peripheral vision. Did a horrible job – even more so than usual. Tried to teach but just rambled in circles like a senile old man. Came home and slept for an hour before I had to go do it all again. Finally came home at 5:00 p.m. and slept for three hours or so. Woke up, had a coffee, and started drinking sangria-in-a-box. Got properly lubricated pretty quickly – as did everybody else I live with. The defenestration of food began again (though not out of *my* window, for once). It was canned Swedish meatballs this time. Predictably enough, the only person who succeeded in actually hitting anyone on the sidewalk below was my Swedish housemate Hermine (she used to work at IKEA, so she's a professional). Pretty damn amusing. That stuff never gets old.

Met my new housemates. Two more Yankee girls, from Boston. They seem alright, but now there are way too many Americans living in the flat – that is to say, seven, including myself. It's starting to get fractious, and I predict will turn into MTV's *The Real World* pretty damn quick. Anyway, left the flat at around midnight and finally made it to one of those "Gothic / Industrial" bars I've been curious to check out. Good God! The place was so fucking wretched, it was shameful. All it was, was this really dark bar where they were blasting bad late '80s "Industrial Dance Music," and hiding in the shadows were a bunch of pallid, rotund, awkward people with white face paint on. I gave the place a once-around and then left. Didn't want the cooties to rub off on me. Went back to the flat. Kept drinking with the housemates.

Went to a "party" in some Spaniard's apartment at about 2:00 a.m. or so. My housemate John and I pretended to be a gay couple for a little while, which was amusing. Shortly thereafter, we left. After leaving the "party," John, my other American housemate Jay and I drunkenly ran around on the streets screaming "*Go Raiders! Raaaaaaaiders! Cowboys suck!*" while kicking garbage cans and throwing around big cardboard boxes. My compatriots and I managed to piss off a group of Spaniards for being audacious enough to be drunken "ugly Americans" shouting nonsense in English in their country. Verbal insults were exchanged. One of them mooned us at a distance. Lots of macho posturing then took place on both sides, but there was no altercation. We had Jay on our side, and he is this big and burly ex-football player who looks formidable; like he could really hurt you if he wanted to. He claims he's a pacifist – but then it must be easy to make such claims when nobody in their right mind would want to fuck with you in the first place. Following not getting into a fight with the locals, we went to this disco called Speakeasy. It was awful, of course. Most of them are. But that's the main fucking thing that people do here at night for kicks – hit the discotheques. *Ugh.* After that, returned home and whipped up some food, woke up some of my housemates while I was in the kitchen, because I was yelling something at Hermine, but I now don't remember what.

Me, John ... drunk.

Woke up Saturday morning with a mild hangover. Ate some eggs and felt better. Later in the day, I ended up going out drinking with my new Yankee housemates. Got too drunk again and ended up at this disco-bar called Millenio. It was more than awful, of course. I despise discotheques (which is all anyone does here at night for fun), so I usually just goof off to amuse myself while everyone else dances "seriously."

The intolerable virago windbag from Indiana who lives in my flat apparently hates my guts and refers to me as "the snob." Damn fucking straight. I'm inclined to think she's a fucking "idiot," so that's fine. Anyway, that was my weekend. Not looking forward to work tomorrow morning.

Top quote of the weekend is from my housemate John: "Brian, I can't keep going to discos with you, because I always get caught up in your 'let's make fun of everything' stuff, and then I totally ruin my chances with *las damas!*"

Meatpacking, Southpark, and Rape Camps.
February 5, 2002, 10:18 p.m.

It's funny how quickly things can turn around sometimes. Just yesterday I was completely frustrated with work and looking for an escape hatch; plotting my departure from this land of olive trees, sangria, jamón serrano, and crabby old midget ladies.

Yesterday was shitty. It was my last day of teaching to the Artillery Division of the Spanish Army, and they were being whiny shits as usual. "But wait, what's on the NATO exam? What should I study? How many times can I take it over if I don't pass?" Bla, bla, bla ... whine, whine, whine. I had no answers for them. I'm just an English teacher for an outside contractor, nothing to do with NATO, as far as I know.

But regardless, I'm through with all of that camouflage-n'-boots business now. Now things are different. I picked up three new classes today, and all of them are "totally cake," *dude*.

> #1. Hour-and-a-half, two days a week, teaching TOEFL preparation to four executives at Campofrío ("Cold Country" in English), Spain's equivalent to Oscar

Meyer. I get to take the train at 7:00 a.m. to a meat-packing plant way out in the sticks, which smells like honey-glazed ham. *Yum!*

#2. Two hours, one day a week, teaching intermediate English to Spain's economic adviser to NATO. Military fella' – kind of a bore, but a nice guy. He served in Bosnia, and I'm gonna' get all the juicy goods out of him. Like, "Did they *really* have 'rape camps' out there? ... Like *really*, for *reals*? That shit's *craaaaaazy.*"

#3. Private beginner English lessons for a thirteen-year-old boy. I dig this kid. He is great. His room is full of Warhammer figures and *Lord of The Rings* posters and *Southpark* crap. He has a PlayStation and everything. His parents are totally rich, and he's living it up – it's great. He only knows the bare basics of English, like the verb "to be," so today we just talked about all the stuff that he's into, like, "Orcs are green." "Sauron is evil." "Cartman is fat." *et cetera*. It was nothing short of rapturous for me to get fuckin' *paid* to do that. So now, instead of trying to beat Phrasal Verbs into the heads of impatient military motherfuckers, I get to talk about wizards and dragons with a thirteen-year-old kid.

My job has become a cakewalk again, and I can deal with that. *Phew!*

My Country, 'Tis of Thee, Sweet Land of Stupidity, Of Thee I Bitch.
February 7, 2002, 6:20 p.m.

So, I live in a "shared flat" in the center of Madrid, Spain. There are nine bedrooms, three bathrooms, a kitchen, and a TV room. Two of the bedrooms are "doubles," so there are a total of eleven inhabitants (twelve including the landlord). The place has a pretty high turnover rate – in the six months or so that I've lived here I've lived with people from: Spain, France, Italy, Sweden, Finland, England, Switzerland, Germany,

Argentina, Brazil, The Philippines, Nepal, and the good ol' US of A. The dynamics have always been awkwardly disjointed and engaging, if not frustrating and nerve-wracking. Everyone trying to get along, deal with each other, and even understand each other, and has produced quite a few amusing and "educational" situations, to say the least. It's a big fucking melting pot of unfiltered multiculturalism. But now everything is completely different. When I first moved in, I was the only American living in the flat – now we Yanks are the overwhelming majority ... and this troubles me.

The current demographics of my flat are as follows: two Swedish girls, a pair of French sisters, a Filipino, and *seven* Americans (California: two, Massachusetts: one, New Hampshire: one, Missouri: two, Indiana: one). This makes me a very unhappy Yankee indeed. Because most of the Americans are wantonly fucking dumb! Call me crazy, but my philosophy is; if you're living in Europe and you don't know what the Second World War was fought over, at the very least you deserve to be browbeaten with the fact that you are the personification of every negative stereotype about Americans held the world over – and that's going easy. All-too-common statements from my countrymen like "Communism and Fascism ... well, they're basically the same thing anyway, right?" leave me speechless and facepalming. I rest my case.

Blame Canada.
February 9, 2002, 6:06 p.m.

It's a nice, sunny Saturday afternoon here in the fine, fine capital of España. Unfortunately, I am a little hungover. Last night wasn't particularly eventful. Everyone I live with went out dancing at Ducados Café, while I stayed home by my lonesome, got drunk on wine, and blasted old Punk music throughout the flat. Following that nonsense, I went and sat in this bar called Nueva Vision, guzzled beer, and smoked cigarillos for about twenty minutes while waiting for my Spanish friends Vicente and Luis to show up.

Following that nonsense, Vicente insisted that we go to this big Irish pub called O'Neill's, at which I drank some Guinness and got into an argument with a pompous douche about the evils of The United States of America. Total motherfucker, he was. When I was introduced to him (in Spanish) and asked him where he was from, he responded, "*Soy norteamericano*" (I'm North American). So, I replied, in English, "Oh, you're an American? So am I. What part of The States are you from?" Oh, *no*. No, no, *no*. He most certainly is *not* an American, and in fact was aggrieved—nay, *insulted!*—by the audacity of such a presumption on my part. He is a proud Canadian—thank you very much—and how *dare* I suggest that he's a fucking American simply because he said he's from *North America* rather than deigning to specify that he's from Canada. Heaven forfend. My mistake. I had committed a grievous *faux pas*, clearly. I tried to politely backpedal a touch by name-dropping various Canadian things I like or liked: Shadowy Men on a Shadowy Planet; Superconductor; *The Kids in the Hall* ... alas, my conciliatory name-dropping was to no avail. He'd never heard of Shadowy Men or Superconductor, and really preferred discussing the sundry evils of U.S. foreign policy going back half a century. And, so, that was the subject of conversation.

While my interlocutor stopped short of stating outright that the U.S. had "asked" for last year's attack on the Twin Towers, his opprobrium for not just the Bush Administration's military response in Afghanistan, but pretty much *all* U.S. foreign policy going back decades, verged on venomous. And I—as an American—am to whatever extent, at fault. In brief, his argument was, *You are paying taxes and voting for a government that kills innocent people around the world; therefore, you are indirectly responsible for*

murdering those people. It's really that simple. I attempted to disabuse him of this ham-handed idea; I tried to explain that I'm no American triumphalist, I hadn't voted for "W," and furthermore I was born in 1977 (so, in fact have only been voting for a few years), and so I hardly feel responsible for the bombing of Laos by the Nixon Administration ... but he was unpersuadable and unappeasable.

My knowledge of Canadian history is admittedly limited, but apparently, The Great White Canadian North was blamelessly minted out of winter-fresh dandelion petals from the Lilly-white vulva of The Earth Mother Goddess, *sans* a drop of ethically questionable bloodshed in the intervening years. Whereas The United States of America, in his view, is merely an "Evil Empire" engaged in a sort of expansionist neo-colonialism on a global scale, and I, by dint of my having been born there, am a *de facto* Emissary of Evil. A hapless surrogate for George W. Bush in Spain. Yeah, total asshole. If Canada is remotely as humorless, sanctimonious, and preachy as this dickhead, then it's no wonder that all their decent entertainers end up moving to The States to "make it" (where, according to this guy's logic, they are each as individuals perfidiously funding The Yankee War Machine).

Following that nonsense, I accompanied my housemate John to a disco called Black Jack, where I imbibed too much and had an exhilarating time being an Ambassador of Evil by proxy. I finally got home at about 4:45 a.m. and crashed in my bed. And wouldn't you know it, I somehow plumb forgot to brush my teeth! Anyway, today is Saturday, and I feel kind of shitty. It's the official commencing of Carnival (the Spanish and Latin American equivalent to Mardi Gras), so everyone I know is going to a bunch of parades and festivals. I, however, will be avoiding such Amateur Hour nonsense.

Amusing Tidbits Concerning the English and Spanish Languages
February 12, 2002, 10:48 p.m.

So today I taught some executives the difference between the following idiomatic Phrasal Verbs:

#1. "to shoot down" (a plane) versus "to shoot up" (drugs);

#2. "to turn on" (a light) versus "to be turned on" (to be sexually aroused);

#3. "to get off of" (to exit) versus "to get off on" (to be sexually gratified by);

#4. "to jack up" (a car, or prices) versus "to jack off" (to masturbate).

God, I love my job sometimes.

In a semi-related story, here are the three most amusing errors made by foreigners attempting to speak Spanish in Spain:

#1. Confusing the word *"cono"* (ice cream cone) with the word *"coño"* (cunt). This produces splendid statements (in Spanish) like, "Wow, the cunts at McDonald's are so cheap!"

#2. Confusing the word *"pollo"* (chicken) with the word *"polla"* (dick). This produces even more marvelous utterances (in Spanish) like, "I love to eat dick. Dick is my favorite food. I'll eat dick with just about anything."

#3. Confusing the word *"año"* (year) with the word *"ano"* (anus). You get the idea ...

Ha, ha, ha! Never gets old. *Never.*

Rock on ... Man!
February 16, 2002, 8:21 p.m.

Ugh ... Typical Friday night. Drank a little, moseyed around town a bit. Nothing particularly special, really. Hung out with my housemate John, who was in superb form last night: "I just want to fucking kick some dumb little Spaniard's ass!" It was great. He's great. He's always full of surprises.

So anyway, it's Saturday and tonight I'm hanging out with this eccentric thirty-something guy I met in a bar. He's a professor of "Film

Criticism" from The States, who's over here teaching for the year. Totally weird guy. Doesn't fit in Spain at all. Tall, pale dude with long black hair who wears mostly black and carries his Film Criticism syllabus around with him all the time. Anyway, we like a lot of the same movies and some of the same bands, and had some engrossing conversations at the bar. So he's alright by me. Anyway, the guy's Spanish is just completely gawdawful. I mean, he sounds like a suburban soccer mom saying, "*Ho-la, bwee-nos deeee-yaas!*" It's pretty amusing, actually, as (given his appearance), Spaniards just have no idea what to make of him. So I'm gonna' take him to Malasaña and show him around. Maybe go to Louie Louie, or try to find a Punk place or something. We'll see. When he called me earlier, he ended the conversation by saying: "Ok, well I'll see you in a couple of hours, okay? ... Rock on man!" No kidding: "Rock on ... man!" That's how this guy actually talks: "Rock on ... man!"

Somewhere in the Malasaña neighborhood.

Resaca y Vergüenza.
February 17, 2002, 7:27 p.m.

So I hung out with the Film Criticism Professor last night. He is totally great on so many levels. He's thirty-six years old, has a Ph.D., usually wears all black, and looks like he was once a member of Pigface or Ministry or something. The man's vocabulary usage is totally hilarious, too. I called him up last night and said, "Hey, so what's up, what are you doing?" to which he replies: "Oh, you know, I'm just *hanging heavy* here at the pad." I shit you not, ladies and gents, the man

unironically says things like "hanging heavy" and doesn't miss a beat. He's great.

But my evening with this gentleman was kind of a trainwreck. Basically, we spent the night talking about geeky film stuff while bar-hopping all over Malasaña – until alcohol made both of those activities impossible. We spent a good deal of time at Nueva Vision, which was full of skinheads for some reason (actually, there were only probably about eight or nine of 'em, but that's full enough for me). Following the consumption of a couple of "minis" there (a total misnomer, by the way), I somehow managed to get way too drunk and started behaving accordingly. In the end, we managed to hit about ten bars before I was crippled by alcohol and had to shamble home (sometime around 4:00 a.m.). All told, I only had about ten beers and half a box of sangria, but I found myself in quite an unbecoming state, nonetheless. At 4:30 a.m. I woke up my poor Swedish housemate, Hermine, because she could hear me through the wall as I was violently vomiting into my trash can for about fifteen minutes.

Today I awoke at the bright and precocious hour of 5:00 p.m., to find that I had spent all the money in my wallet and smoked all my cigarillos during the course of the evening, like a goddamn fuckin' wastrel. Yup. I am a champion. *Winner.* Presently, I'm drinking coffee and trying to feel okay, with mild success. I never behaved like this when I was a college kid. I was practically straight-edge back then. Somehow, I always get everything backwards.

The Real World.
February 20, 2002, 10:19 p.m.

The last two days have been kind of ridiculous in a lot of ways. I stayed up all night last night, listening to Heavy Metal, reading, and drinking hot cocoa, then I taught class this morning totally delirious, and slept away the afternoon. I'll probably end up doing the same thing tonight. That is the state my life has been reduced to as of late: sleep, work, eat, read, eat, Internet café, drink coffee, read, sleep, drink sangria-in-a-box, work ... rinse and repeat. Yesterday, however, was pretty funny and eventful anyway.

¡Borracho, Borracho, Borracho!

One of the dumber American chicks I live with has this charming habit of a hootin' and a hollerin' while watching *Operación Triunfo* (the Spanish version of the U.K.'s *Popstars*), a pop pablum program that doesn't end until after 1:00 in the morning. Well, my housemate John gets up at 6:30 a.m. like I do, and his room is right next to the TV room, so he is constantly pleading with her to keep the noise down after midnight. Well, I guess that the night before last, she just decided to be a bitch back at him about it and declared, "No, we can watch TV whenever we want to, so sorry, but you just have to deal with it." And that night John was kept up by her hootin' and hollerin' at the TV, and didn't get enough sleep. ...

So yesterday, I woke up at 6:30 a.m., and I drearily shuffled out into the TV room, and John is sitting there blaring the TV loud enough to wake up half the flat, and he shouts at me on my way out the front door, "Hey Brian! Good morning! How the hell are you? Have a good day at work, man! See you later!" Having only gotten about an hour or so of sleep myself, and therefore being fairly delirious, and confronted with a situation like that, I chuckled to myself for a few minutes on my walk to the metro.

Then, when I got home from my morning class at around 10:00 a.m., John is sitting in his room playing bongo drums – so fucking loudly that it was reverberating throughout the whole flat. So the idiot girl from Indiana—*la Indiana Idiota*—comes storming out of her room histrionically hollerin' "What the fuck are you doing? It's fucking 10:00 a.m., haven't you ever heard of quiet?" – to which our hero John replies, "Look, I can do whatever I want whenever I want, so—sorry—but you just have to deal with it." I laughed my ass off some more.

So I went into my room to take a little *siesta* before my afternoon class, from which I was promptly awoken by a clamoring racket of yelling coming from the kitchen – in English. I get out of

John, smugly looking askance.

bed, head down to the kitchen to find out what the hell all the commotion is about, and encounter Hermine, the Swedish girl, dumbfoundedly watching John and the Indiana Idiota go at it – American style. Petty obloquy and coarse language of the most absurd variety were flying back and forth at full volume. "Your Spanish is pathetic! You sound like a dumb fucking hick!" ... "Fuck you John, you're twenty-nine and you act like you're fucking eighteen!" ... "Well, everyone in this *piso* can't stand you, because you're so fucking loud, dumb, and obnoxious!" *et cetera, et cetera, et cetera* ... Finally, the Indiana Idiota started crying semi-hysterically and made a hurried exit from the kitchen, though she did manage to get in the parting recrimination, "Fuck you! I hate you! Fuck you John!" following which she cowered in her room to cry for a few hours. The whole thing was just so completely glorious. It was like a Greek drama unfolded in my very own living room! I went into my room and lay in bed snickering for at least ten minutes (which unfortunately interfered with my *siesta* time, though it was worth it, of course).

Later that night, our landlord called a "house meeting" to discuss the issue of noise. I was hoping for a full-on class-war conflagration amongst the Americans (Midwesterners versus East Coast Ivy Leaguers, or Midwesterners versus West Coasters), but everyone just sat there and listened while he delivered an entirely predictable speech in Spanglish about respecting other people's right to sleep. Oh well.

So, the drama continues to unfold. MTV's *The Real World* has nothing on my flat. *Nothing.* Do they have Swedes, Frogs, and a Mormon Filipino named Chaz who eats bread-and-mayonnaise sandwiches? Nope – they ain't got shit on us. But regardless, my original point holds; there are too many Americans now. If everyone were from a different country, this kind of drama wouldn't be happening, because everyone would be on their best behavior – they'd be acting like *de facto* "cultural diplomats" for their respective nations. But since the majority of the flat is now Yankees (and even the non-Yankees speak near-fluent English), everybody just lets their hair down and acts like an obnoxious ass. And, as Americans, we all seem to excel at that.

Is It "Cool" If It's "Ironic"?
February 23, 2002, 11:56 p.m.

Well, it's Saturday night, and I'm boycotting Madrid's nightlife to be a geek. Last night I stayed up all night, and then slept from 2:00 p.m. to 8:30 p.m., and now I'm just not in the mood to run around like a drunken fool again.

So last night I hung out with the Film Criticism Professor again. It was pretty much a repeat of last weekend, except that I paced my drinking a bit and didn't get totally sick this time. We bar-hopped around Malasaña for a while, spent some time at El Garaje Sonico and Tupperware, and then I came home and ate a bunch of greasy food, before trying unsuccessfully to sleep before the sun came up.

So, last night the man was wearing a fluorescent lime-green t-shirt and a leopard print fur jacket. Nobody but nobody dresses like that here. If it weren't for the fact that he's the spitting image of Nick Cave, one might've mistaken him for a Glam Rocker or something; instead, it screamed "irony." I'm not really sure that "works" here. ...

"Rock on, man!"

This guy is so great on so many levels, the least of which being that he ends every conversation (both on the telephone and in person) with an enthusiastic "Rock on, man!"

My Delightful Sunday Afternoon.
February 24, 2002, 10:06 p.m.

For once in my life, I awoke of my own volition at 8:00 a.m. on a Sunday morning. I then had myself a picturesque morning fit for a Disney film – I showered, dressed, and then fixed myself up a fine-ass breakfast consisting of: two sunny-side-up eggs, two pieces of toast, three slices of fried ham, and a nice steaming cup of coffee. It was lovely.

Then I put some heavy music in my Discman and sauntered down to Madrid's be-all-end-all of flea markets, el Rastro. El Rastro is this weekly open-air market that takes over the entire neighborhood of La Latina and extends for literally dozens of city blocks in every direction. It's completely overwhelming, at the very least, and has no U.S. parallel that I know of (though I wouldn't be surprised if Los Angeles had something similar). Supposedly, you can find just about anything there, from just about any period in Spain's history, though I suspect it's really a question of luck – which I seem to lack.

Curios, knickknacks, sundries, tchotchkes, n' bric-a-brac.

I was on a mission to find military memorabilia from the Second World War era, to hopefully later be resold on eBay at a markup. Alas, I had no luck in my quest, though I did stumble upon a pair of Soviet cufflinks from around the 1960s (I'm guessing), and a chintzy Nazi belt buckle, which was obviously made sometime after the fall of the Third Reich (I passed on both of these items). In matter of fact, given that I know nothing about military memorabilia from any era, I wouldn't have been able to spot what would or would not be of "value" online anyway, so the exercise was pretty pointless – but I guess I had to figure that out by actually standing there and realizing, *I have absolutely no idea what any of this shit is worth.* Oh well. Anyhow, there was a lot of other swell shit though, which I might've bought, were it not so big as to be un-transportable back to The States, or just too expensive for my minimum-wage-earning English Teacher's blood. In the end, I came home empty-handed, but I've convinced myself that it was worth getting up at 8:00 a.m. anyway, just for the "cultural experience" of it.

Extranjeros Sin Papeles.
February 26, 2002, 4:58 p.m.

I have this morning class with some executives from a meat processing company called Campofrío. The class is at this industrial slaughterhouse way out in the boondocks of southern Madrid, in a suburb called Villa Verde. To get to the class, I have to take the train for about half an hour, and then walk through this industrial warehouse district – sometimes before the sun has come up. It's the kind of neighborhood where you find half-destroyed toilets and tied-off used condoms on the side of the road (there's usually at least one dismal analog to it in every major city).

Well, this morning as I was trekking to class at daybreak, I was privileged enough to behold one of nature's rare spectacles: two African prostitutes in pumps and miniskirts, smoking cigarettes and warming themselves around a trashcan fire. As I walked past, they momentarily paused chatting in whichever African language they speak, smiled at me, and then resumed their conversation, which consisted primarily of chirps and whistles (I jest, of course!).

Fucking illegal immigrants working in our country without papers, man ... don'cha just fucking hate 'em? Oh, wait. ... *I'm* (sort of) part of that cohort. ... Well, fuck me then.

Somewhere in downtown Madrid.

But seriously, Madrid is very, very much a "cosmopolitan" European city, and the immigrant population here is a very special thing indeed. The Spanish are such docile, tolerant, pliant, bleeding-hearted pushovers when it comes to stuff like that, that there are people from just about everywhere living in this damn city, all of whom can be seen daily on the city's metro. Anyway, as an immigrant of dubious legal status myself, here is my quick, lazy analysis of the immigrant population of Madrid:

<u>South and Central Americans</u>:

Due to the language factor, South and Central Americans tend to fit pretty seamlessly into Spanish culture and society, though the Spaniards tend to look down on them quite a bit (I presume that it's of a piece with the curious dynamics that sometimes exist between Brits and Americans / Australians / Canadians / Kiwis). In particular, I've noticed that Colombians seem to be a particular target of scorn and derision from Spaniards. In one of my Business English classes for executives once, half the class was occupied one day by a hearty discussion of how Colombians are all just a bunch of good-for-nothing layabouts who've taken over the city's public parks – dealing drugs, drinking too much, and neglecting their kids. Back in The States, one might call that sort of generalization "racist," but the Spanish don't tend to countenance such PC hang-ups – at least not most of the ones I've met anyway.

Asians:

It doesn't matter where an Asian in Spain is actually from; they are referred to under the lazy sobriquet *"Chinos,"* and that's just the way it is. Asians have a total monopoly on the late-night convenience store racket here. So much so in fact, that you don't even say *"Voy a la tienda."* (I'm going to the store), you say, *"Voy al Chino."* (I'm going to the Chinamen's). Because it's just true, that's why. Otherwise, they're essentially invisible in the culture, from what I've observed. They keep to themselves, siloed away in their own little insulated cultural pockets somewhere. Probably just glad to be way the fuck away from the Khmer Rouge, or the Red Guard, or whomever was making their homeland a hellhole

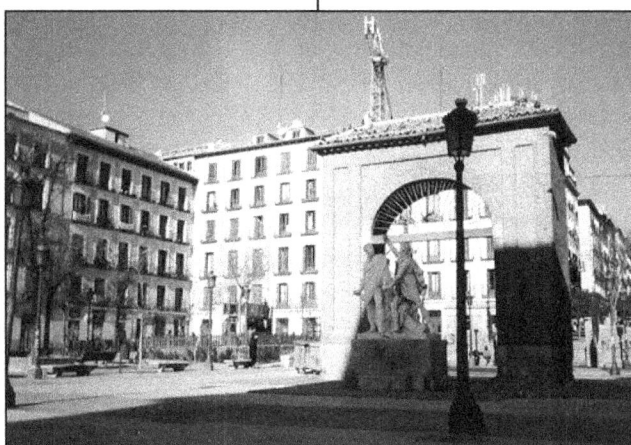
Madrid's Plaza Dos de Mayo in Malasaña, haven of Moroccan hashish pushers.

when they fled to Spain. It does throw me off a bit, I must confess, every time I meet an Asian person in Spain who speaks their native Asian language, and Spanish ... but no English.

Moroccans:

A few of 'em superficially resemble Osama Bin Laden (and I presume that some of them maybe wouldn't mind hanging out with him) but it seems their main purpose in this country is to offer to sell me hashish in Plaza Dos de Mayo every fucking day. (Oh, and they sell scarves on the metro too, but only when they know I'm nowhere near Dos de Mayo).

Turks:

Every Turk outside of Türkiye is working in a Dönner Kebab shop somewhere in Spain. I've never met one anywhere else ... have you?

Africans:

Industrious multi-functional individuals to be sure! They sell bootlegged CDs by the scores in the metro, they hawk hash in the public parks, they assertively participate in "the world's oldest profession" on Calle Montero, and they like to hang out just below my window at 4:00 a.m., drinking boxed wine and singing as loud as they can (and they're such toughies that they're undeterred by flying tomatoes and eggs!).

Bosnians and Serbs:

Okay, so I don't pretend to know the nuanced differences between Bosnia, Serbia, Hurts-to-go-pee-in-ya, or whatever, but I do know that here in Madrid there is no shortage of dispossessed refugees from the Balkan region (or wherever exactly it is that my American tax dollars went to bombing). These women drive me absolutely fuckin' nuts. I say "women" because there are no men from this country in Madrid whatsoever—only women and children—and they spend all their time roaming the metro system begging alms by ceaselessly reciting this obnoxious monotonal mantra about how they have forty mouths to feed and they've seen war (*seen* it), and bla, bla, bla. I don't care if they are fleeing genocide, they need to learn some common fucking decency: Point 1: If you want money from me, don't ever fucking touch me – period. Point 2: When I'm standing on the metro with my Discman on, and I'm wearing my "fuck off" face, that means: *Fuck off, I can't hear you because I have my discman on and no, I won't turn it off to listen to your mantra because I heard it yesterday, and really, I don't care about what Slobodan Milosevic did to your family.* (I jest ... of course! Kidding. Kidding.). But seriously though, the Spanish homeless have it so much worse than these people, and yet they get so much more charity from everybody because they play the "I'm a war victim!" card, and absolutely everybody buys it and gives them something.

Gitanos (a.k.a. "Roma" a.k.a. "Gypsies"):

Technically, these people aren't really "foreigners," but they definitely exist outside of mainstream Spanish culture and society. It's hard to explain how the Roma people work. Most of them seem to be pickpockets of some sort. The scam is that the old Roma ladies approach tourists with their hand-woven lace (or whatever it is) and just get all up in the tourists' faces with some rambling pitch in Spanglish about the lace (often sort of forcing it into the tourists' hands), and meanwhile their brood of pocket-slitting teenage boys are making off with the tourists' wallets and purses, all through cunning subterfuge. That's the general perception anyway. I don't know to what extent any of this is or isn't accurate, but it's part of the reason that I started wearing a wallet chain, even though I'm not a skateboarder. From what I do know, I will say this much: in the handful of places that I've lived in and been to (various parts of the U.S., the U.K., Ireland, and Costa Rica) I've never seen a group of people—a demographic, ethnicity, or "race"—in a so-called First World nation treated anywhere nearly as poorly as the Roma. These people don't just live in "bad" neighborhoods or "ghettos" – they live literally outside of society, in a Dickensian sort of limbo. In

Madrid the Roma live in tent city shanty towns on the outskirts of town, and in Granada they live in caves up on the hillside overlooking the city. Very strange.

Russians:

For some reason, the Russians are the creepiest of all foreigners in Spain. They tend to be these big, shaven-headed tough guys in leather jackets who always roam the metro system in twos or threes, and always seem to be looking over their shoulders. I have no way of verifying this allegation, but I just know they're all affiliated with the Russian mafia, and are only here in Spain to traffic stolen diamonds up from Africa, through Spain, and into northern Europe. I just know it.

Giris:

The term *Giri* here in Spain is roughly analogous to the term *Gringo* in the Americas; it applies to any non-Spaniard who's Caucasian – be they German, French, British, American, or what have you. So, I'm a *giri*, or more specifically, a "Yankee" (pronounced "*Janqui*"), as in, "Yankee go home!" *Giris'* main function in Spanish society is to support pickpockets, petty thieves, prostitutes, the university exchange programs, and the tourism industry. I am proud to say that I have absolutely nothing to do with any of that shit. After all, my ass belongs to NATO now.

Not a Party.
March 2, 2002, 3:20 p.m.

So a couple days ago, a friend-of-a-friend of mine from The States flew into town. He's on a tour of Spain and France for no particular reason. He's basically I guess what you'd call, like, an Indie Rock "hipster" – I don't really mean that in a necessarily derogatory way ... it's just that he's the spitting image of Elliot Smith in both countenance and style of dress. He's the kind of guy I picture when I hear the word "hipster." Alright guy though; seems cool enough to me, having just met him.

Somehow I managed to end up having a mini-party in my room last night, which consisted of four Spaniards I've managed to befriend, and five Americans (John, the new hipster guy, The Film Criticism Professor, one of the American chicks, and myself). Really unusual mix of people. It wasn't even really a real "party" at all, but my humorless live-in-landlord got unreasonably upset with me and blew the whole thing out of proportion, so we were out drinking on the street by around midnight. Eventually we ended up at my friend Luis' apartment, drinking Calimochos and listening to heinous Northern European Death Metal compilations.

Later, as we were wandering around town looking for some Irish bar called Finnegan's, we bumped into my Mormon Filipino housemate, who was all by himself in Chueca, the gay district. Needless to say, he was totally embarrassed, though I'm *sure* he was just passing through. ... He's comically square. He won't even say the word "fuck" – so I make it a point to cuss like a sailor around him as much as possible.

Segovia.
March 4, 2002, 10:57 a.m.

Yesterday consisted entirely of a day trip to Segovia – roughly two hours north of Madrid by train. The Hipster, The Film Professor, one of the American girls, and myself all met up at my apartment at 9:30 a.m., and barely made the 10:15 train.

Me in front of Segovia's "flamboyant" gothic cathedral.

The Hipster had stayed up all night, and as a result, got progressively more delirious throughout the day (at one point he was giggling to himself about pigeons). This appeared to be largely performative.

Segovia itself was bitterly cold and conspicuously devoid of its usual throngs of tourists (it being a Sunday in the off-season). We were there for maybe eight hours, during which we partook of all the famous old shit: the Roman aqueduct, the gothic cathedral, and the Disney-esqe medieval castle. All of which was fine and dandy.

Segovia's medieval castle, The Alcázar.

Amusingly enough, The Hipster and The Film Professor are both to some degree afraid of heights, so at the top of the castle they were both kneeling and warily sticking their heads out over the edge of the wall – meanwhile the American girl was hanging around the side of a parapet saying, "Hey, take a picture of me like this!"

At some point in the afternoon we had a long and leisurely Spanish lunch at a mildly touristy restaurant, at which The Hipster ordered a plate of unidentified seafood which turned out to be: squid, crayfish, and some kind of ambiguous "fish." He had some trouble with it. Also dining at this restaurant were half-a-dozen American frat boy types wearing baseball caps and gaudy multicolor Mexican ponchos. In consideration of the fact that they were in a foreign country full of exotic regional foods, every one of them had decided to order pizza for lunch – every, single, one.

¡Borracho, Borracho, Borracho!

Enseñando Inglés.
March 6, 2002, 6:19 p.m.

Yesterday was a good day to be an English teacher. First off, I had my weekly two-hour class with General Martín of the Spanish Army – Spain's economic advisor to NATO. Most of the class was just the usual grammar bullshit, but I did manage to toss in some goofiness at the end; there is this English-learning magazine here called *Speak Up!*, which comes with cassette tapes for "listening comprehension." So I found an old issue with an article on the movement to legalize marijuana in the U.K., and incorporated it into yesterday's class, which was mildly amusing. I had the Spanish general listening to a stoned-sounding Scottish guy debate a stuffy English guy about the positive and negative effects of smoking dope, then I made him read the article aloud, which had some great moments like, "Marijuana is also referred to as 'pot,' 'reefer,' 'dope,' 'viper weed,' and 'Mary Jane'." (imagine all of this in a thick, stumbling Spanish accent). His homework is to write a short essay about his opinion on the subject. I think I can reliably infer what it'll be. ...

Following that, I had my one-hour class with the twelve-year-old rich kid. He was sick— febrile and kind of delirious—so we didn't really have a real "class" yesterday; instead we just talked about Warhammer shit. I somehow managed to miss that whole phenomenon as a teen, so I really had very little to contribute to the conversation. I tried to explain Dungeons & Dragons to him, but it was obvious that he didn't really give a shit. Not enough all-out war, I suppose.

Anyway, it was great – easiest money I ever made. Good day.

Holy Toledo!
March 9, 2002, 2:06 p.m.

Damn, it's been a busy couple of days entertaining international guests. A friend-of-a-friend from Germany flew down on Tuesday, and since then we've all been cavorting around like fools. I took them out for beer and tapas a few times, and we went to a tiki bar called Hawaii, where they serve drinks out of volcanoes with dry ice in them; and the other day we visited that famous *chocolatería* downtown and had chocolate and churros, which was okay. The night before last, we went to a semi-authentic Flamenco show, slurped some sangria, and generally had a jolly old time of it.

Hermine n' me at Hawaii.

Friday we all took a day trip to Toledo and did all the touristy stuff you do in Toledo.

Toledo is downright eerie. It's this labyrinthine network of narrow streets that wind circuitously in all directions and lead to dead ends. If The Winchester Mystery House were a city, it would be Toledo. Once upon a time (pre-Columbus, that is), it used to be evenly split into enclaves of Jews, Muslims, and Christians, but then the latter decided it would be fun to have an Inquisition and expelled the rest. (Not cool, Christians!) I wanted to go check out the remaining non-Christian buildings, but didn't succeed due to time constraints; the mosque was "under construction" and covered in a big blue tarp, and we didn't really have enough time to try to find one of the old Synagogues because we had to catch the train back to Madrid.

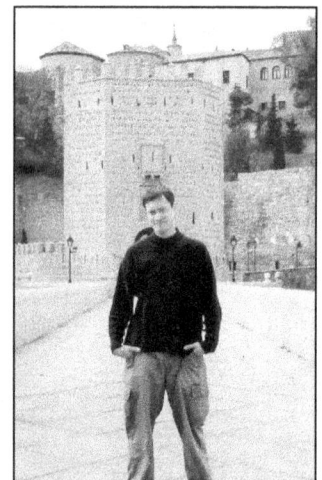
The gates of Toledo.

Oh, Give Me A Home, Where the Buffalo Roam.
March 19, 2002, 3:37 p.m.

Welp, my soused sojourn in Spain is nearing its end. It's strange to imagine I'll be back on American soil in about a month. I've been living consecutively overseas for more than a year now, and I think I've gotten used to it. It's nice being a foreigner in that you can sort of just tune everyone around you out and do your own thing. You can pretend that you don't speak Spanish when being panhandled or solicited by hookers around Calle Montero (a.k.a. "*Calle de las Putas*" ... Whore Street); you can "play dumb" linguistically when you're bored in a conversation, smile-and-nod or "dip out," and nobody takes offense; you can also presume that whenever you feel like you don't "fit it" it's just a cultural thing and it's not *you*. Of course, none of that applies when you're on your home turf.

Last I checked, I despised living in the San Francisco Bay Area, but the precise reasons why have faded and blurred in my memory. But fuck it, I'm excited to go back anyway – I've lived abroad a couple of other times, in other countries, but actually miss The States this time. Not for any of the silly shit like so-called "freedom" or whatnot, but the important stuff; I miss having a car and driving it around in the middle of the night. I miss 24-hour diners and bottomless cups of coffee. I miss owning a VCR and renting movies in English, to be watched in the privacy of my own home, without commercial interruptions. I miss eclectic bookstores with a wide variety of titles in English, and I miss "world-class" capacious record stores like Amoeba and Rasputin Records, where you can get just about anything under the sun.

Of course, I love Spain and I love Madrid—someday I'll be back, for sure—but I'm tired of being a foreigner and being treated as such. I'm tired of being surrounded by hundreds of thousands of chain-smoking wine snobs and *fútbol* fans. I'm tired of only comprehending eighty percent of what's going on around me at any given time. I'm also tired of some of the screwy mannerisms here – like the normalcy of protractedly staring at strangers on the metro and the absence of a personal space "bubble" when walking around in public (I am not making either of these up!). I'm tired of having superficial friendships with native Spaniards based on little more than a shared interest in independent music and, "Hey, will you explain the lyrics to Melvins songs to me, because they don't seem to make any sense?" (They don't make any sense!). I'm tired of getting up at 6:15 in the morning to stand on a jam-packed train for an hour, to "teach" English for an hour, and (after factoring in travel and prep time) not even making the equivalent of minimum wage to show for it. I'm tired of only being able to buy what I can carry in my arms when I go shopping, and I miss American-style shopping (they don't call 'em *super*markets for nothing, you know). I'm also tired of hearing, seeing, smelling, and tasting a litany of bitter criticism for "American cultural imperialism," George W. Bush's ostensible global misdeeds, and the barbarism of the American Second Amendment and the death penalty – during every initial encounter I have with European students, co-workers, bar-goers, *et al*.

The Spanish adore ham like you would not fuckin' believe.

Not that Spain is without its upsides. The buildings and plazas are easy on the eyes, and the weather is usually quite nice. The food is inexpensive, healthy, tantalizingly tasty, and made somehow just ... *better* – and you can *eat* the hot chocolate. The workday is interrupted by a two-hour nap-and-snack time during which most folks leave the office for beers, tapas, and perchance a quick *siesta*, just to break up the afternoon. People stay out way well into the wee hours of the night; even the old ladies. Alcohol is dirt-cheap and consumed at all hours of the day. Hashish and marijuana are both legal to possess, and smoking such in public is usually considered okay, depending on where you are. You can get anywhere in the city on the metro, usually in under an hour, for about 80¢ – and it's reasonably safe and clean. The urban street crime tends to be dominated by pickpockets and purse snatchers, rather than drug-related shootings and six-on-one muggings. And if, say, some unfortunate and "impecunious" Spaniard is beset by a horrific disease, the government won't just let 'em die in the street like we do in The States, which I figure is a nice gesture. Oh, and topless babes on magazine covers and all over television is a plus too.

This is Madrid's main post office, if you can believe it.

Yes, Spain is very, *very* nice, and highly recommended by me ... but regardless, I have run my race here, and am ready for a change of scenery, even if it is going to be the Bay Area again.

Cannabis ... Yes? ... No!
March 20, 2002, 7:35 p.m.

Last week, during my private class with General Germán Martín, Spain's economic advisor to NATO, I assigned him a "reading comprehension" activity titled "Cannabis – Legalize It?" culled from *Speak Up!* magazine. This was accompanied by a "listening comprehension" cassette, which featured a debate on the subject amongst a Scottish man, an English man, and an American woman. The General's homework for the week was to write a short composition about his opinion on the subject.

So, I submit for you (unaltered), the essay "Cannabis" by General Martín of the Spanish Army:

"Cannabis"

Firstly a short summary will be given about the title:

- Who is damaged by "cannabis"

- Who is beneficiary by "cannabis"

- Which are the solutions to this problem.

Regarding the first point, the damaged by cannabis are not only the consumers, also the consumer's family and the public health.

The consumers are damaged because the risks of cannabis are lung cancer, emphysema and heart disease, and the others social problems.

The consumer's family are damaged because in many cases their have pay the drug, and they have take care of consumer.

The public health are damaged by cannabis, because they have pay the differents illness caused by cannabis.

Secondly, the beneficiary are the "mafia" who control the world-market of drugs.

Finally, the solutions to this problem is knowledge consumers about the damages of cannabis and to fight the world-market and the unlawful consumption.

[signed]

– Germán Martín

Now, to be fair, this isn't actually that bad considering his level of English, although he did have a whole week to write it, and obviously used a Spanish-English dictionary extensively. Regardless, I for one, am convinced by his argument, "The solutions to this problem is knowledge consumers about the damages of cannabis." Amen to that. As far as I'm concerned, it passes muster.

Amy.
March 22, 2002, 12:02 p.m.

One of the nice perks about having a totally generic name like Brian Clark is that you often get mistaken for someone else. For instance, yesterday I received the following email:

Brian,

Amy just called me and she is trying to reach you but does not have your number. She thinks you check your mail and will get this message and call her. She is at home until 3PM or you can call her cell, ▮▮▮▮▮▮▮▮. Please call her.

Mike P.

To which I replied:

Hey, Mike,

Look, I'm getting really tired of this kind of stuff. Don't get me wrong, I mean, Amy's cool, but she's just so damn unreliable sometimes. I mean, how the hell could she "lose" my number? What is that about? She has my number memorized (at least she used to). So, frankly, I'm not buying it. And actually, the more I think about it, I'm just tired of her bullshit games in general, so you just tell that bitch she can call ME if she wants, but otherwise she can go fuck herself.

– Brian

We'll see what happens.

We Haven't Had That Spirit Here Since 1969.
March 27, 2002, 7:27 p.m.

Last night I hung out with The Film Professor, John, and some English teacher chick from Tennessee. We went and watched an American movie in English with Spanish subtitles, and then ditched the English teacher and stayed out drinking till 5:00 in the morning. We ended the evening at this bitchin' old bar in Malasaña called Hotel California, where I was accosted by a drunk Spanish mod chick who came over to talk to us because she said that she could tell I was an American, because only an American would have a "silly" haircut like mine, and smoke a big cigar (like her uncle smokes) in a bar like this at 5:00 in the morning. Then she started apologizing profusely because she thought she'd offended me, when in truth, I was flattered – that's exactly the look I'm going for!

So, tonight John and I are taking the metro to the main train station, then a night train to Barcelona, where we are supposed to cross paths with the American Hipster guy who was in Madrid a few weeks ago, but who's been cavorting around France since then. Hopefully, we will find him somehow, and merriment will be had by all.

My Madrid Metro Pass.

They say Barcelona is the only city in Europe where you can still get "real" absinthe (not the fake kind they sell in the U.K. and the rest of the E.U.). So, since the opportunity is right there at my feet, I'm debating whether or not I should partake in this longstanding pretentious custom or not. Picasso, Hemingway, Van Gogh, and lots of other "creatives" were big into the stuff. Of course, the hullabaloo surrounding absinthe is completely disproportionate to its supposed quasi-hallucinogenic effects. Just because some ostensibly "creative" types used to drink it habitually and then a few of them were driven mad (as if that were a rarity), some bureaucrat felt the need to make the stuff illegal. Otherwise, it probably would have fallen into obscurity like however many other niche European liqueurs that don't get exported outside of whatever bucolic hamlet has been making them since Ye Olde Medieval Tymes. But no, absinthe is illegal in most of the Western world, so therefore ... it's just *so fucking cool! "Oh, my God, dude, you live in Spain! Have you had ... A-B-S-I-N-T-H-E-? Oh, man I so want to go to Spain to try that stuff, so bad! Fuuuuuck!"* Supposedly it tastes like black licorice. We shall see. ...

Karma Will Have Its Way with Me Yet.
March 28, 2002, 9:21 p.m.

Oh hell, everything is all fucked up. Last night John and I packed our bags, said our goodbyes, and headed out to the train station, only to wait in a long line which led to, "Sorry, the trains to Barcelona are all full – today *and* tomorrow. Yep, sorry, fuck off." So, no Barcelona – I'm still here in Madrid. Fuck.

So last night John and I met up with The Film Professor at El Pobre Gaspar ("Poor Gaspar") and had some tapas and beer, following which we all took a cab over to Joy Esclava ("Joy Slave"), Madrid's second hippest (and likewise penultimately expensive) discotheque. It's astounding that you can fit that many insufferable Eurotrash douchbags into one discotheque, but yes, it can be done. I'll spare you the details of this escapade, but basically it came down to this: we paid too much to get in, we paid *way* too much for drinks, and the music was godawful.

The real excitement of the evening came at about 5:00 a.m., when I had a full-on, face-to-face, spittle-flecks-flying-out-of-the-mouth battle of words with my uptight live-in landlord. He's about twenty-eight or twenty-nine, but acts like he's at least thirty-five, and has all these silly rules. The crux of his rules system being this:

#1. You can't have overnight guests in your room unless they pay for a night;

#2. You can only have visitors to the flat between the hours of 4:00 p.m. and 9:00 p.m.;

#3. No parties;

#4. No noise (TV, music, *et cetera*) after midnight on weeknights;

#5. Wash your dishes and clean up after yourself;

... and that's about it.

Now, unlike a couple of the coquettish female tenants who are on his "good" side (and get away with fucking murder as a result of it), I haven't really actually broken any of these "rules" over the last year or so. I've hewed to and abided by all of them, technically speaking. I don't have late-night parties, I don't wake people up on the weekdays, I wash my dishes and clean up after myself, and when I have overnight guests – they pay. However, I *do* do things which he simply cannot grok. Things that make no apparent sense.

Anyway, so last night I came in at about 4:30 a.m., and in my state of drunken stupor, I figured it would be "funny" to set up a table in the middle of the entryway. (Don't ask me why, it was just "funny," okay?) So John and I were sitting in his room with the door ajar, and Mr. live-in landlord comes home from a long night of (presumably) unashamedly hitting on much younger girls at bars, and he sees the table in the entryway and pretty much flips his lid. I believe the term is "high dudgeon." He storms into the room tempestuously and—with spit flying everywhere—just lays into me in Spanish. "Why do you do stuff like this? You think you're pretty fucking clever? You think you're pretty funny? Why do you have be such an asshole all the time? Why do you have to fuck with everything all the time?" (*et cetera.*)

This sort of took me by surprise, considering that all I'd done was put a table in the entryway, and really … what's the real harm in *that?* But then he started citing all these examples of other prankish stuff I've done; stuff I had no idea he'd even known about. It seems that somehow, Mr. live-in landlord knows about every "unusual" thing I've ever done in the flat. Every fucking thing. He knows about how I used to throw eggs and sandwich meat at taxis down on the street below my window. He knows that it was me who, in the wee hours of the morning last Saturday night, threw a full bottle of dish soap across the courtyard into a neighbor's open window (I was drunk, and, damn it, it was funny). And he knows about nearly every other minor infraction, transgression, and misdeed that I've committed over the last year or so.

Which means that somebody fucking sold me out. One of the other jerks who lives here, who has axe to grind with me went and fucking told on me. I have my suspicions as to who this might be … there are several Americans from the Midwest who aren't exactly "fond" of me anymore, and one in particular who has no scruples whatsoever—the Indiana Idiota—I certainly wouldn't put it past her … Ah, but fuck it. Really, I don't care. I'm moving out in a matter of days anyway.

In the end, the beautiful thing about all this is that Mr. Live-in landlord is completely right; I am an asshole, and some of the quizzical random things I've done to amuse myself make no sense. But, like I told him – *Who have I harmed? Which rules have I broken?* I mean, really, come on.

Do I wash my dishes? *Yes.* Does everybody else? *No.* Do I make a mess? *No.* Does everybody else? *Yes.* Do I try and sneak people in overnight without paying? *No.* Do other people? *Yes.* Were the French girls kicked out or chewed out (as I was last night) when they had a loud party on a Monday night, and some of us didn't make it to work the next day for insufficient sleep? *No.* So—yes—I may be an asshole, but there's certainly no "rule" against that. The charge of "asshole" certainly wouldn't hold up in court, now would it? So I say, *fuck it.* My shenanigans have been harmless. If the worst thing I ever do in my life is throw an egg out my window at some poor bastard on the street, then I won't even bother

repenting for my sins, because Lord knows that ain't *shit*! Amen.

After our yelling match, John told me he was really impressed with the ease with which I was able to argue in Spanish. Considering how long I've been here, I speak it pretty damn well, and without a noticeable accent. I later realized, however, that during my verbal sparring with the landlord, I'd been tripped up by one of those sneaky "false cognates"—words that sound like they should be English-Spanish cognates (basically the same in both languages—"taxi," "computadora," "hotel," *et cetera*), but actually aren't. Sort of like cross-lingual malapropisms, I guess. In attempting to say, "You have no sense of humor!" I said, "*¡Tu no tienes un sentido de humor!*" … but "*humor*" means "mood" in Spanish. So I think that what I maybe actually said was, "You have no feeling of mood!" Which, of course, makes no sense. But now I'm not sure if that's actually correct, or not. Damnit.

Anyway, these are the things we ESLers have to deal with all the time; uncertainty regarding if you actually fuckin' said what you thought you fuckin' said. Other examples of Spanish-English "false cognates" (many of which lead to humorous linguistic gaffes) include the following:

Embarasada ≠ Embarassed.
Embarasada = Pregnant.

Dinero ≠ Dinner.
Dinero = Money.

Bizarro ≠ Bizarre.
Bizarro = Brave.

Raro ≠ Rare.
Raro = Strange.

Molestar ≠ Molest.
Molestar = Annoy.

Actualmente ≠ Actually.
Actualmente = Currently.

Asistir ≠ Assist.
Asistir = Attend.

Sopa ≠ Soap.
Sopa = Soup.

Sensitivo ≠ Sensitive.
Sensitivo = Sensible.

Sensible ≠ Sensible.
Sensible = Sensitive.

It's difficult to keep track of all this shit. Especially when you're loaded at 4:45 a.m. and shouting back at your furious landlord, attempting to explain things like absurdist pranks and Dadaism in a language that isn't your own.

Shaved Heads, Firearms ... And Alcohol!
March 30, 2002, 6:55 p.m.

Tonight I'm pumped because I've been invited to a private party hosted by The United States Marine Corps. That's right, the USMC is having a shindig and I get to go. I'm supposed to be at the U.S. embassy by 9:30 p.m., to be transported via automobile to the party, which is at an undisclosed location. I'm hoping we get to ride in an armored limo or a Humvee or something, but I have a feeling it'll be an unmarked "civilian" car. We'll see.

The funny thing is that there are only like a total of fifteen or sixteen marines here in Madrid, and they all guard the American embassy. But since 9/11, they have to strive to do everything unobserved, so their parties have to be "secret" *soirées*, and the address to their house/compound can't be given out. It just makes the whole thing so much cooler.

Shaved Heads, Beer ... And Boredom.
March 31, 2002, 7:41 p.m.

Well, I am sorry to inform you that the United States Marine Corps do not know how to party hearty. Nope. No. Nada.

Last night, my American hostess and I showed up at the U.S. embassy at the appointed time and met with some camo-clad folks on duty, who were quite amiable, outgoing, and heavily armed. After about fifteen minutes of hanging around the lobby of the embassy, a U.S. "diplomatic" minivan showed up to take us to the *fiesta*. This was basically a normal white Ford, except that it had bullet-proof windows and "diplomatic" plates. Having "diplomatic" plates conveys "diplomatic immunity," which means that the driver should—nay, *must*—drive as nimbly and fast as fucking possible on both freeways and suburban streets (just to make sure that nobody from Al-Qaeda follows you and finds out the location of the secret battle-station hideout). This was cool.

When we finally got to the U.S. Marines' house/compound (which is way the fuck out in the suburbs) the fun abruptly ground to a halt as quickly as the diplomatic van. The marines live in a lavish suburban mansion which contains (among other amenities and perks): a pool, a tennis court, a weight room, a pool table, a full bar, a gargantuan big-screen TV (with video games, DVD player, VCR, *et cetera*), and lots of odd U.S. military regalia and flags and stuff. Not that any of that necessarily makes for a fun night when you're stuck with a handful of marines and their guests sitting around languidly watching the NCAA "final four" of U.S. college basketball and eating beer nuts. Not easily defeated, I got quite drunk on free Guinness, smoked a cigar in the backyard (not in the house – this is U.S. government property, after all), and didn't make an ass out of myself in the slightest. Somehow I don't reckon that kind of behavior would have been appreciated by all the humorless tight-asses who lived there.

The highlight of the evening (aside from all the mind-blowing excitement of American college basketball!) was watching the AFN for about forty-five minutes. The AFN, or American Forces Network, is the corniest television station I've ever seen. Basically, it's broadcast all over the world to servicemen on duty, who are stuck in boats or on bases or whatever. Since it's a U.S. government channel, it has to be non-profit and can't show real commercials, nor can it afford to produce halfway decent programming. So, what you get on the AFN are all these pitiable documentaries on "The Wealth of American History" or "Coming Challenges of The Twenty-First Century" intermittently interrupted by "commercials" which are really just non-profit public service ads directed specifically at the military. Stuff like, "Loose lips sink ships!" and "Don't let your military identification card fall into enemy hands!" Totally surreal.

Porto, Day One.
April 10, 2002, 1:02 p.m.

I'm writing this here journal entry in the city of Porto, Portugal. Damn.

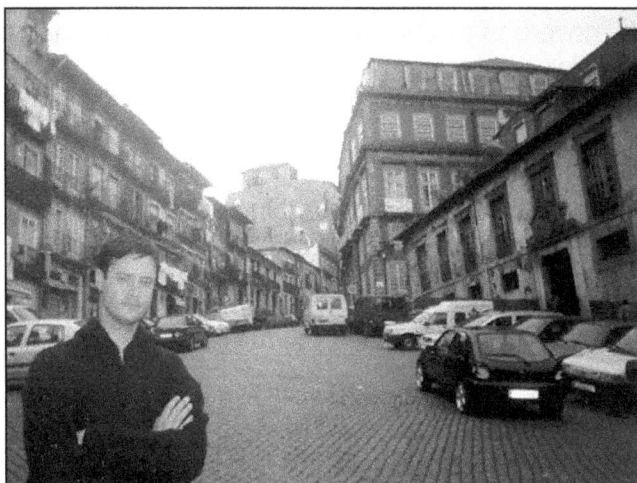

Been traveling with John and The Hipster for like … three … four days now, I don't really know. Sunday evening we took the night train from Madrid to Vigo, Galicia, where we spent two nights and two contentedly lackadaisical days. I can't say much for Vigo, really. It's the largest city in Galicia, but the highlight of my two-day stay there consisted of me and The Hipster peeing into the Atlantic Ocean late Monday night. Not that

there's ever much going on anywhere on a Monday night, but shit, the crowd at the Tropical Disco Pub downtown never surpassed six guys sitting at the bar ogling the female bartender. The only other real highlight of Vigo we experienced was The American Bar, which was surreally themed in a cross between kitschy Americana and more Native American Indian crap than would ever be necessary, anywhere.

Following two days of lounging around Vigo, there was a two-hour bus trip to Porto, in northern Portugal, where we are presently. Porto is nice indeed. Awesome architecture, warrens of winding old serpentine streets and back alleys, a river crisscrossed by multiple bridges and lined with a small fleet of old-school wine boats, and shit … I dunno, more cool old stuff. We've all agreed that it's the most underrated city any of us has seen in Europe.

So far, the people seem very friendly, for the most part, although spoken Portuguese is basically indecipherable to me. Everyone seems to understand you if you speak to them in Spanish, but their responses are inscrutable and completely over my fuckin' head. Portuguese sounds kind of like a French person trying to speak Spanish after having had a dental operation and still benumbed by Novocain (or something to that extent). The food is good, though not nearly as "amazing" as everyone says (I'm particularly fond of the fried cod balls myself).

Incidentally, Porto is the home of Port wine – I tried some, and yes, it's some damn fierce stuff, but I actually quite liked it. I also tried the

Portuguese cherry liquor, Ginjinha. It kind of tastes like alcohol-laced cherry Robitussin, though it's not nearly as bad as I've heard it made it out to be previously.

Porto, Day Two.
April 11, 2002, 6:05 p.m.

Today I ate a Portuguese dish which was truly baffling. I don't remember the name, but basically it went like this: a slice of bread, a slice or two of fried ham, a piece of beefsteak, some sliced sausage, a piece of cheese, a sliced hotdog, some more cheese, another piece of bread, a fried egg, then topped with some bizarre barbecue-esque meat sauce, all served in a bowl surrounded by french fries. I suppose one could call this a "sandwich," though that doesn't really do it justice. I don't know what the fuck it was, really, but I ate it several hours ago, and my stomach still feels like it's full of lead shot.

The Portuguese francesinha "sandwich" – fucking brutal.

Tomorrow: Lisbon.

Lisboa e Sintra.
April 16, 2002, 4:13 p.m.

Well, I'm finally back in Madrid. We were in Lisbon for three days, but I had a helluva time finding an Internet café (that is, one that actually worked and wasn't closed), and I was too busy to deal with this journal thing anyway. But now that I'm back in Madrid, I will whip-out a quick retrospective recap of Lisbon:

Humm ... well, we arrived in Lisbon after spending far too many hours on the train seated near a shrieking Portuguese toddler, who I really, really, *really* wanted to beat to death after about five minutes. Within seconds of being dropped off in Lisbon's main plaza, we were accosted by salesmen of all kinds; first a guy slinging sunglasses, then a guy hawking hashish, then a guy attempting to offload a (presumably stolen) camcorder, then another guy pushing hashish, and so forth. Lisbon is a lot like San Francisco – it's hilly, it's on a bay, it has a bridge that looks very much like The Golden Gate, and there are a shitload of foreigners roaming about. The only real difference would be that visiting Lisbon for three days costs about an eighth of what it would cost to visit San Francisco for the same amount of time.

During our stay in Lisbon, John, The Hipster and I did a bunch of touristy stuff such as visit the Jerónimos Monastery, the São Jorge Castle, the Belém Tower, the Art Museum, and the Coach Museum, where I succeeded in pissing off The Hipster by hollering at him in my best southern "hick" voice, "C'mon now boy! Let's get a move on f'er Chrissake!" (He stayed annoyed at me for most of the rest of the afternoon.) Other than that, we ambled around town, ate well for fairly cheap (the Portuguese make several varieties of damn fine soup), and brushed-off the hash dealers again, and again, and again.

Me on a rampart (or whatever) of the São Jorge Castle.

The Hipster headed back to Madrid a couple of days early to catch a plane to The States, and after he left, John and I took a day trip out to Sintra, which is about forty-five minutes from Lisbon by train. There we toured a seriously bad-ass Moorish castle, an ostentatiously lavish palace of some kind, and some gardens.

Sintra – metal as fuck, dude.

That evening, John and I caught the night train back to Madrid, and *voila!* – here I am. All in all, it was an affordable, relaxing, fun week-long vacation, and nobody really got on anybody's nerves *that* much, which I bet is a rarity among travelers.

Happy Trails To You, Until, We Meet … Again …?
April 17, 2002, 6:59 p.m.

Today is my last day in Spain. I will miss it. I love this fucking country … but someday I'll be back, I know it.

So, I spent my last day here breezily chillin' with my Spanish friends Vicente and Concha, drinking wine and having tapas around La Puerta del Sol. It was a nice final afternoon. Tonight I'm meeting up with a guy I used to work with in Costa Rica for dinner in Malasaña.

"Tostada," Luis, and Vicente – Spanish rockers.

Tomorrow I fly out of Barajas International Airport, change planes in Paris, and arrive in Boston sometime in the evening. I'm meeting up with some Bostonian friends I haven't seen in ages, then it's onward Cal-i-for-ni-a. Ergo, this will be my final journal entry—or, at least a hiatus—because this here journal was about living in Europa, and livin' in America is a different ball of yarn entirely. *Adiós.*

August 19th, 1998

Valued Customer,

We here at Saefway take great pride in each and every item we offer to the community under our SELEQUT label. Behind each Saefway product can be found the excellence and commitment of extensive marketing, research, advertising, and, most importantly, Quality Assurance. Quality Assurance, or QA, is at the crux of our SELEQUT label's success. As a member of the Saefway QA team, my commitment to excellence shines through everything I do, and the document you now hold in your hands is no exception.

Hello, my name is Brian Clark, and I am a "temp" employee for the Quality Assurance lab at Saefway Corporate Headquarters in Walnut Creek, California. I live and work in cubicle #B3615, in building B, and I have security clearance, which gains me access to all restricted QA and product development labs onsite. As impressive as that might sound, in truth, it is ... shit. Total shit. I spend mind-boggling hours performing mind-bogglingly menial, asinine, shit-labor. Drudgery. Meaningless, banal tasks which could be performed with little difficulty by a monkey. I count the minutes. I count the dots on the ceiling tiles. I count the counting. There are no windows in my section of the building. There is no sunlight. Nine hours a day, five days a week – I spend the majority of my time here. And thus ... I get bored.

Fucking bored. ...   F. U. C. K. I. N. G.   B. O. R. E.D.

The document that you now hold in your hands is the fruition of my boredom, a copy of the highly sought-after and critically acclaimed *Saefway Prison Diaries*. There are a mere ten copies in existence. Consider yourself lucky—for the moment—for you (along with nine other lucky souls), have received a ***FREE*** copy of this influential and rare document, compliments of your friends and associates here at Saefway Corporate Headquarters.

Your first question, naturally, is, "What the fuck are the *Saefway Prison Diaries,* asshole?" Well, naturally, HIGH ART, motherfucker. *The Saefway Prison Diaries* is best described as a three-part collection of mind-poems, or perhaps visual-essays, or even a singular collage-novel, or whatever sounds most pretentious to you. Regardless, a singular work in no way influenced by or referenced with ANYTHING Max Ernst EVER put his grubby little fingers on – end of discussion. A totally original concept from start to finish. At any rate, "collages," made using a copy machine, *Webster's II New College Dictionary, The Office Max 1998-1999 Office Products Catalog*, a 'zine, and a photograph.

The first set of pitchers is entitled "Three Walls I Call Home," and deals representationally and non-rationally with the concepts of isolation, detachment, and alienation which occur naturally during any serious amount of time spent in a cubicle. The second set, "Promised Land," is primarily concerned with the longing for freedom, which in turn produces hallucinations. Much like the illusory oasis often seen in the desert, these images are hallucinatory landscapes—images of paradise—fixated upon a point … in a cubicle. The final set of pitchers encompasses a narrative centered on anger, rage, and frustration, and is entitled "Meditations on A Fat Wallet, for Which I've Sold My Soul." These involve issues of anger, rage, and frustration … and death.

So there you have it, *The Saefway Prison Diaries*, a cry for help from one under the thumb of fluorescence and THE MAN. I was paid a mere $13.00 an hour to produce this work, but the amount of SOUL put into its creation is immeasurable. I can only hope that this might amuse you for a few moments while you sit on the can.

Sincerely,

Brian M. Clark
Quality Assurance

SAEFWAY SELEQUT

Presents:

The Saefway Prison Diaries

A high-concept "art" piece by
Brian M. Clark

SAEFWAY

— Chapter One —

Three Walls I Call Home

work·sta·tion (wûrk′stā′shən) *n.* An area, as in an office, with equipment and furnishings for one worker, often including a computer or computer terminal.

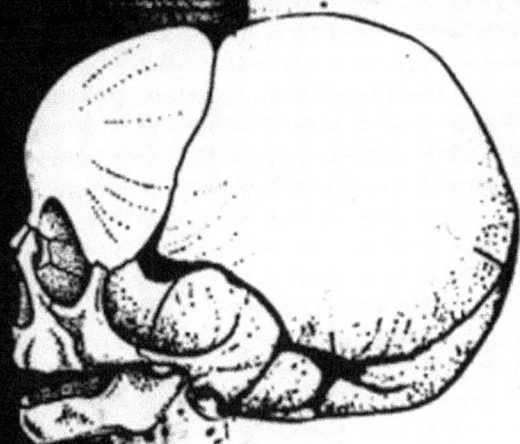

shut•eye (shŭt′ī′) *n. Slang.* SLEEP 1a, b.

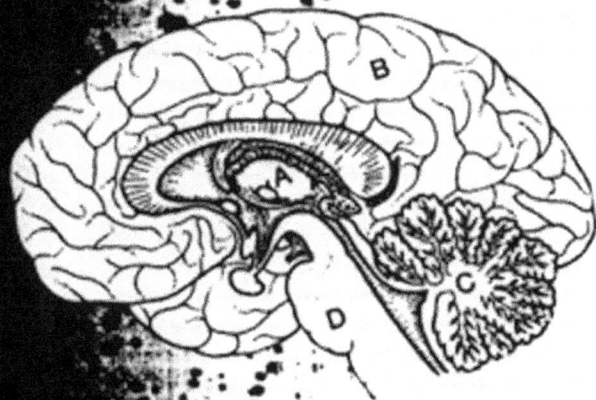

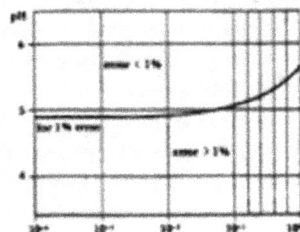

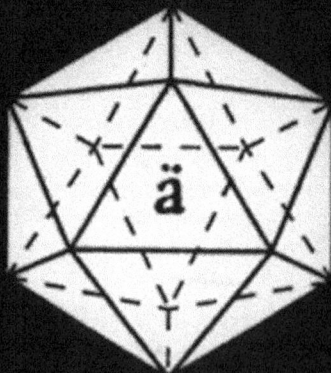

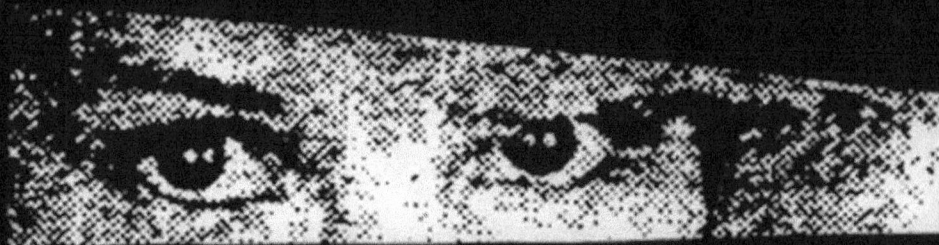

about 300,000 megahertz.

radiation sickness •

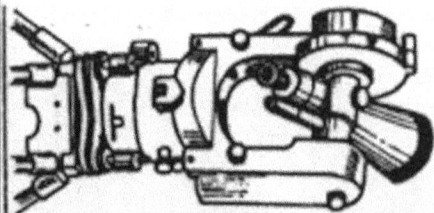

radiation sickne

radiation sickness

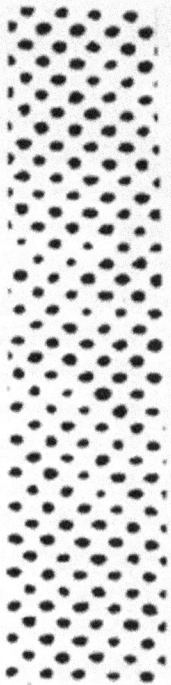

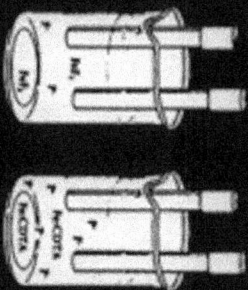

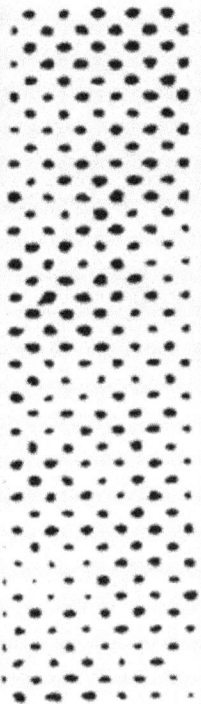

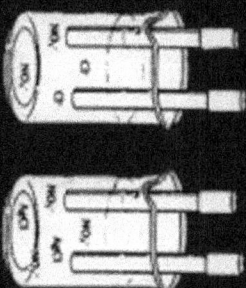

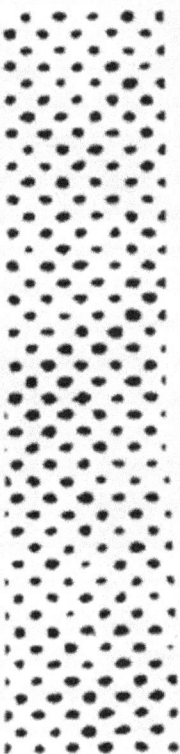

soft membranous bones of fetuses

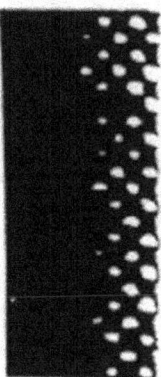

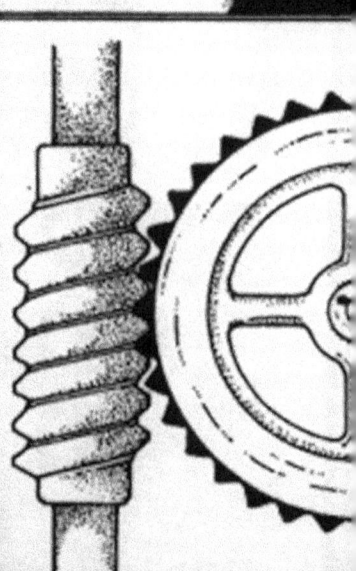
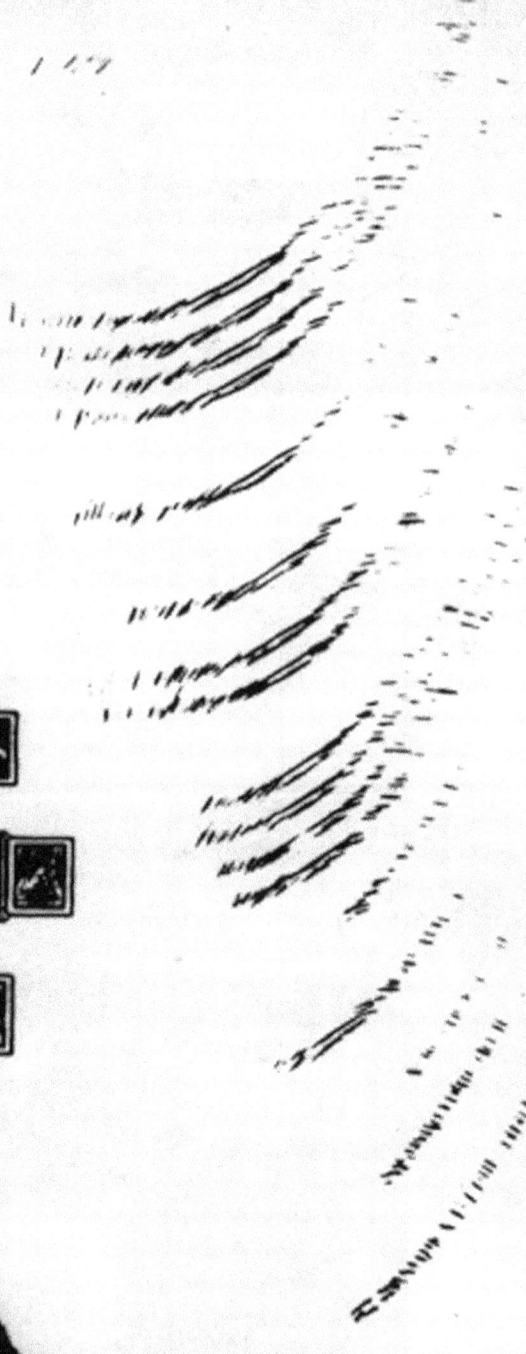
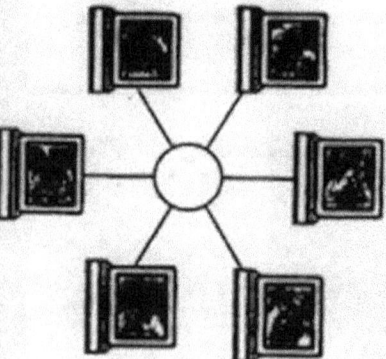

Informal.

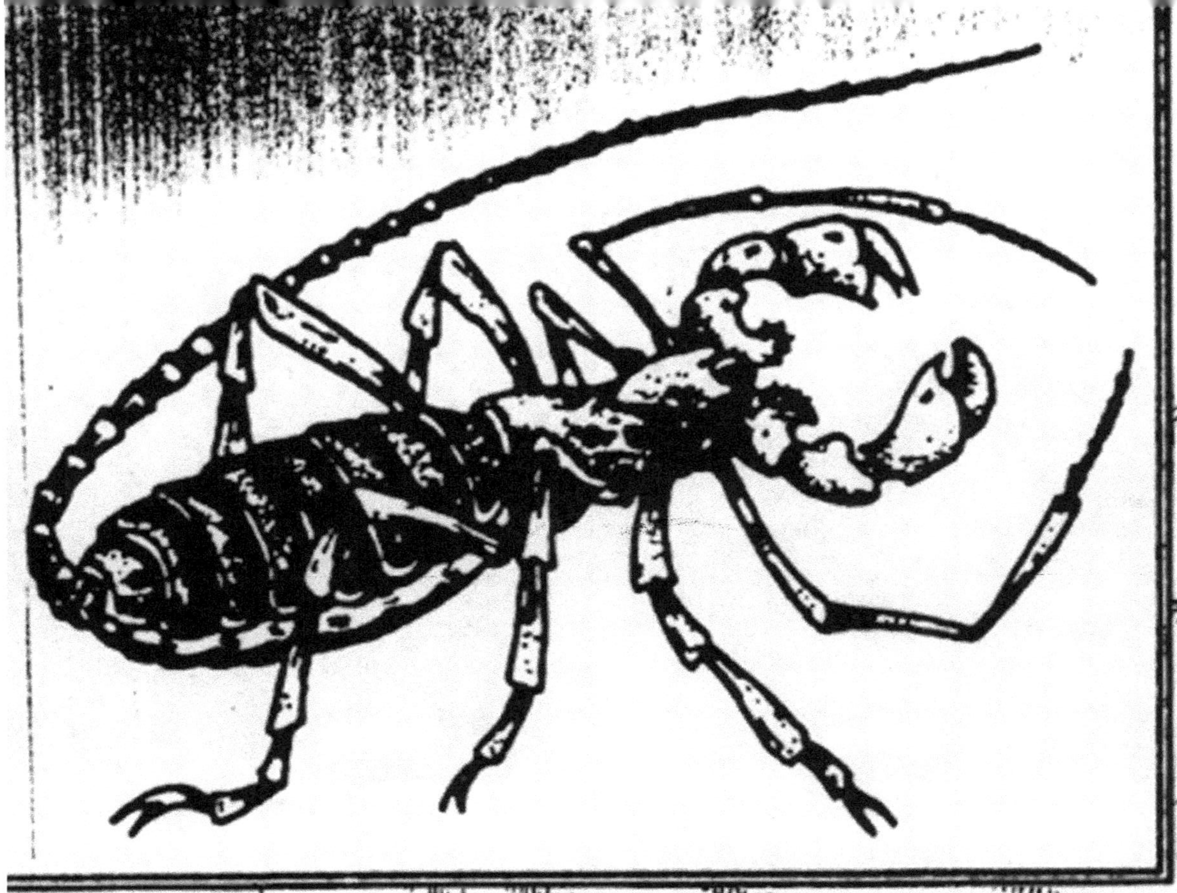

…ly allergenic foods on the ingredient list … include milk, eggs, peanuts, soybeans, tree nuts … and wheat

… other allergenic foods exist and these should also …

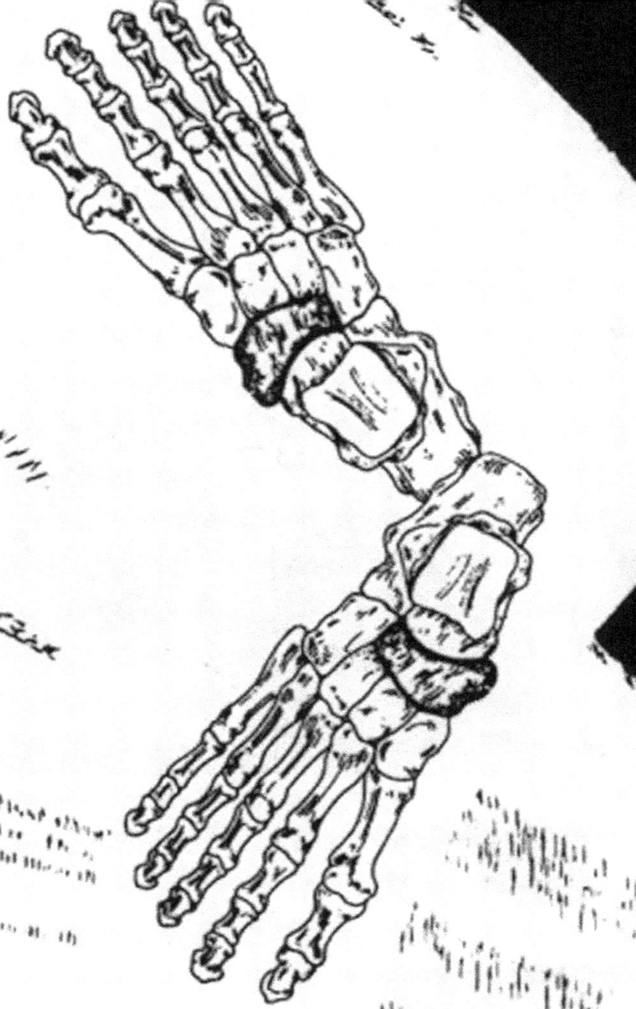

ēt'

e e

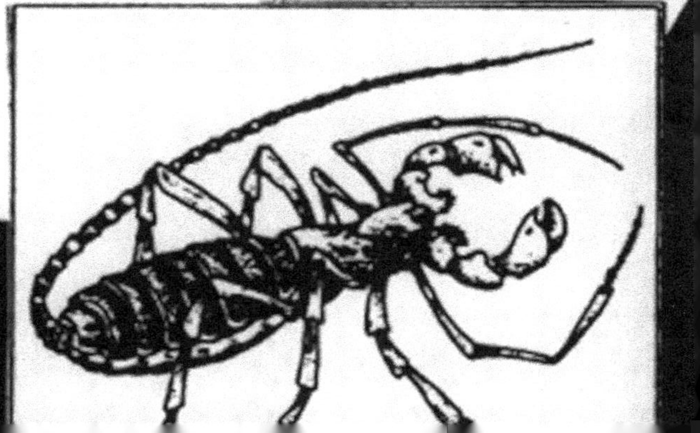

Label the sources of ingredients when the ingredients are derived from common allergenic
unless it can be demonstrated that the ingredient contains no protein from the allergenic so

Consumers may not understand the sources of certain ingredients. For example, whey and casein should be identified as derived from milk.

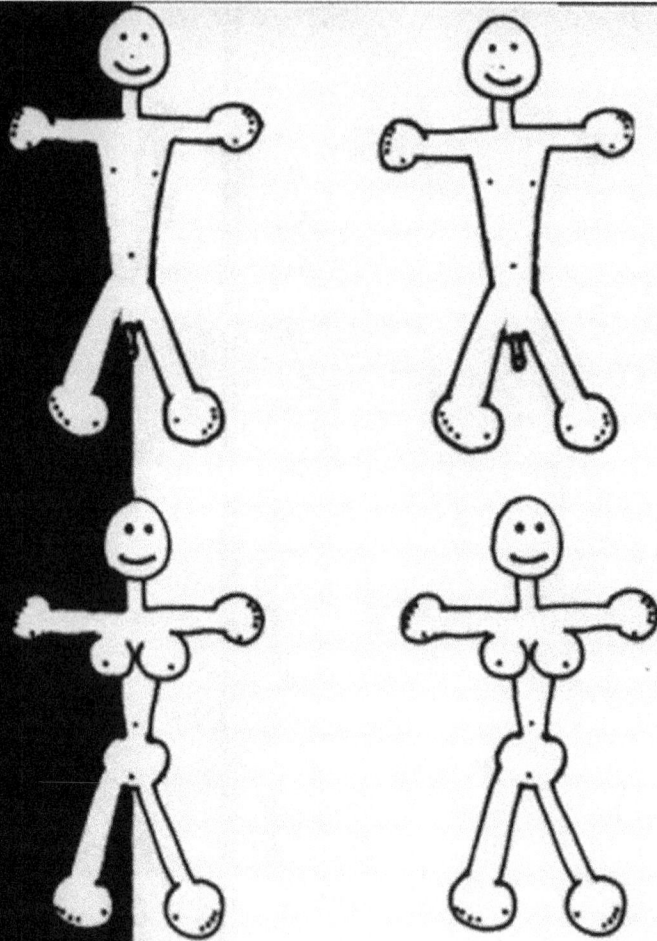

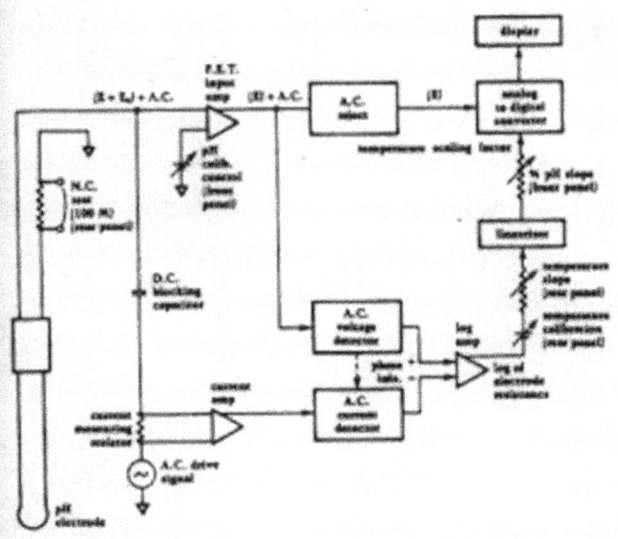

Fig. 18: Ag_2SO_4 is added to remove Cl^- in the determination of NO_3^-.

Pus in the blood.

— Chapter Two —

Promised Land

Plate One –   *"Chance Meeting of My Fist and Your Face, In the Hallway"*

Plate Two –   *"Das Boot!"*

Plate Three –*"Passover ... "*

Plate Four –   *"Self-Portrait with Energon Cubicles"*

work·sta·tion (wûrk′stā′shən) *n.* An area, as in an office, with equipment and furnishings for one worker, often including a computer or computer terminal.

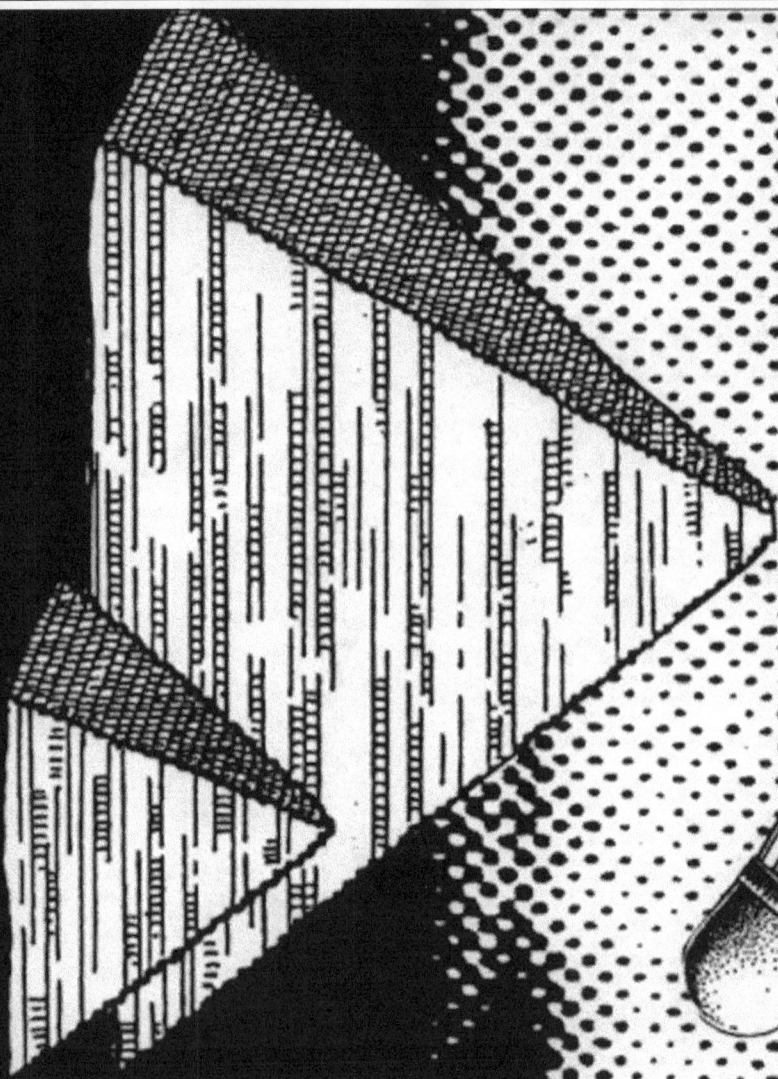

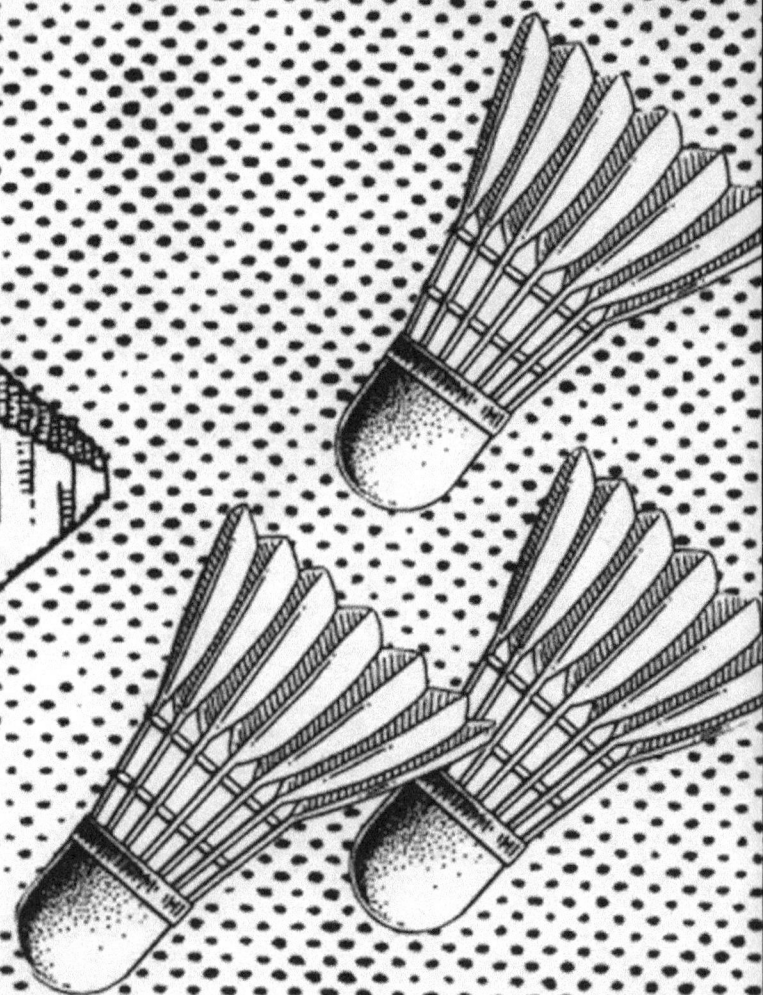

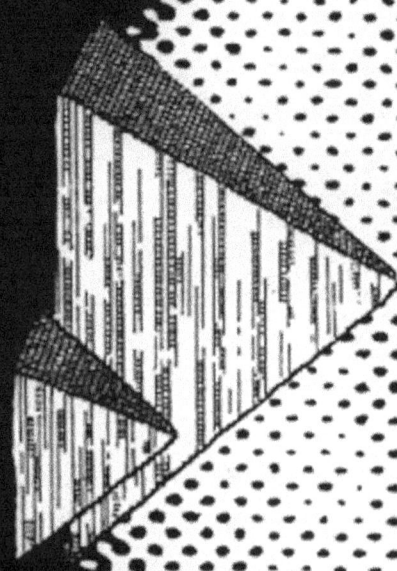

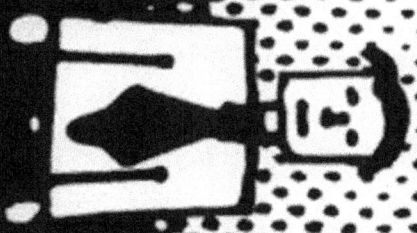
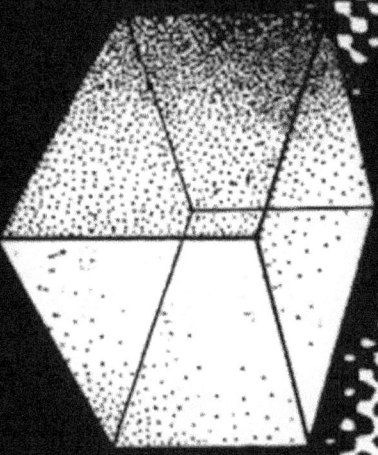
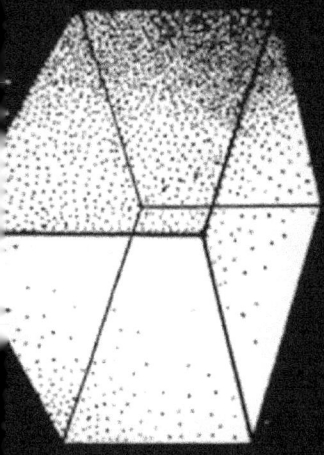

A slender larval

shuttlecock

— **Chapter Three** —

Meditations On a Fat Wallet, For Which I've Sold My Soul

Plate One –   *"Untitled, Part One"*

Plate Two –   *"Untitled, The Sequel"*

Plate Three –*"Untitled, The Return"*

Plate Four –   *"Untitled, Revenge of the Untitled"*

Plate Five –   *"Tilted ... "*

work·sta·tion (wûrk′stā′shən) *n.* An area, as in an office, with equipment and furnishings for one worker, often including a computer or computer terminal.

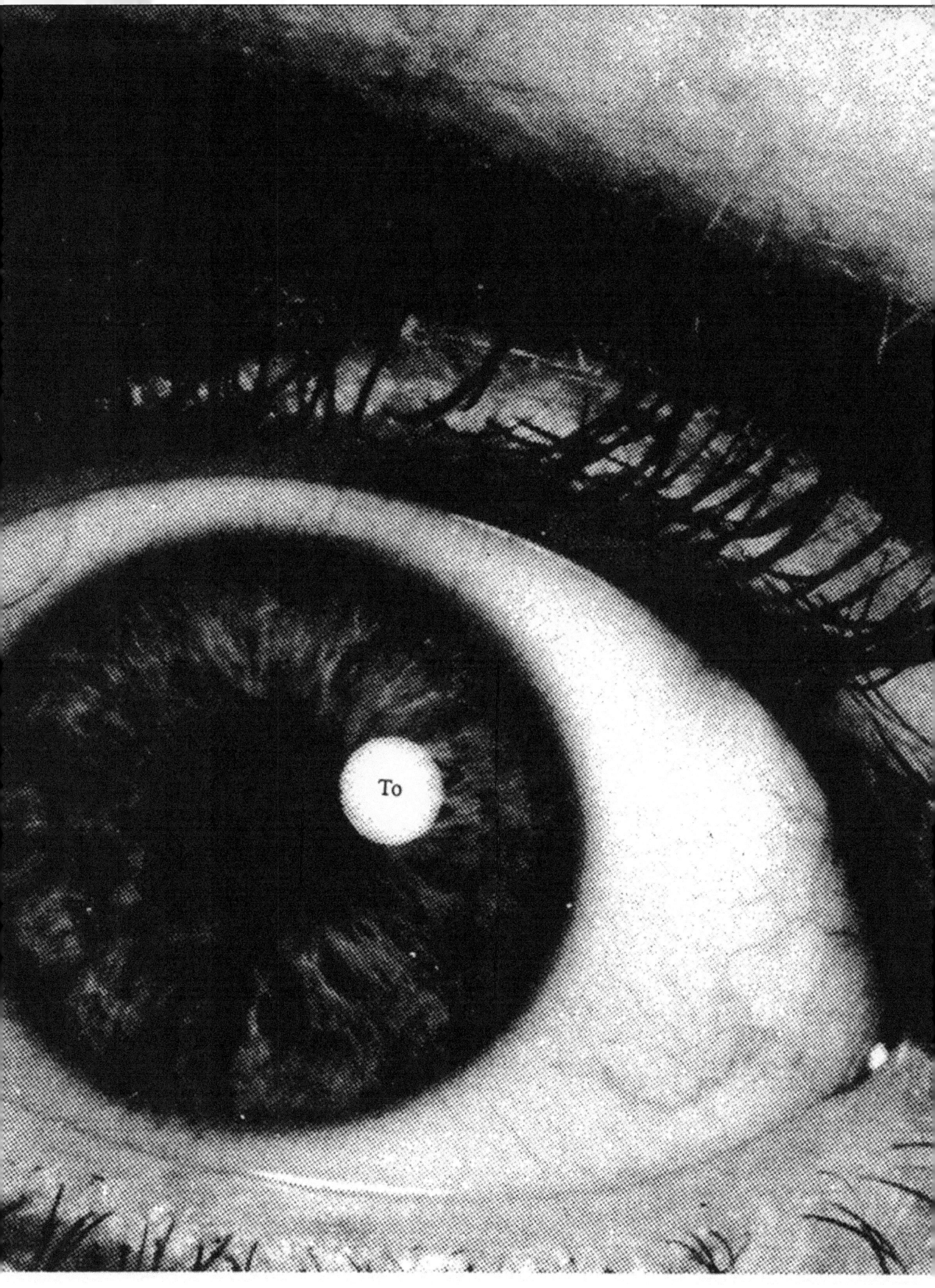

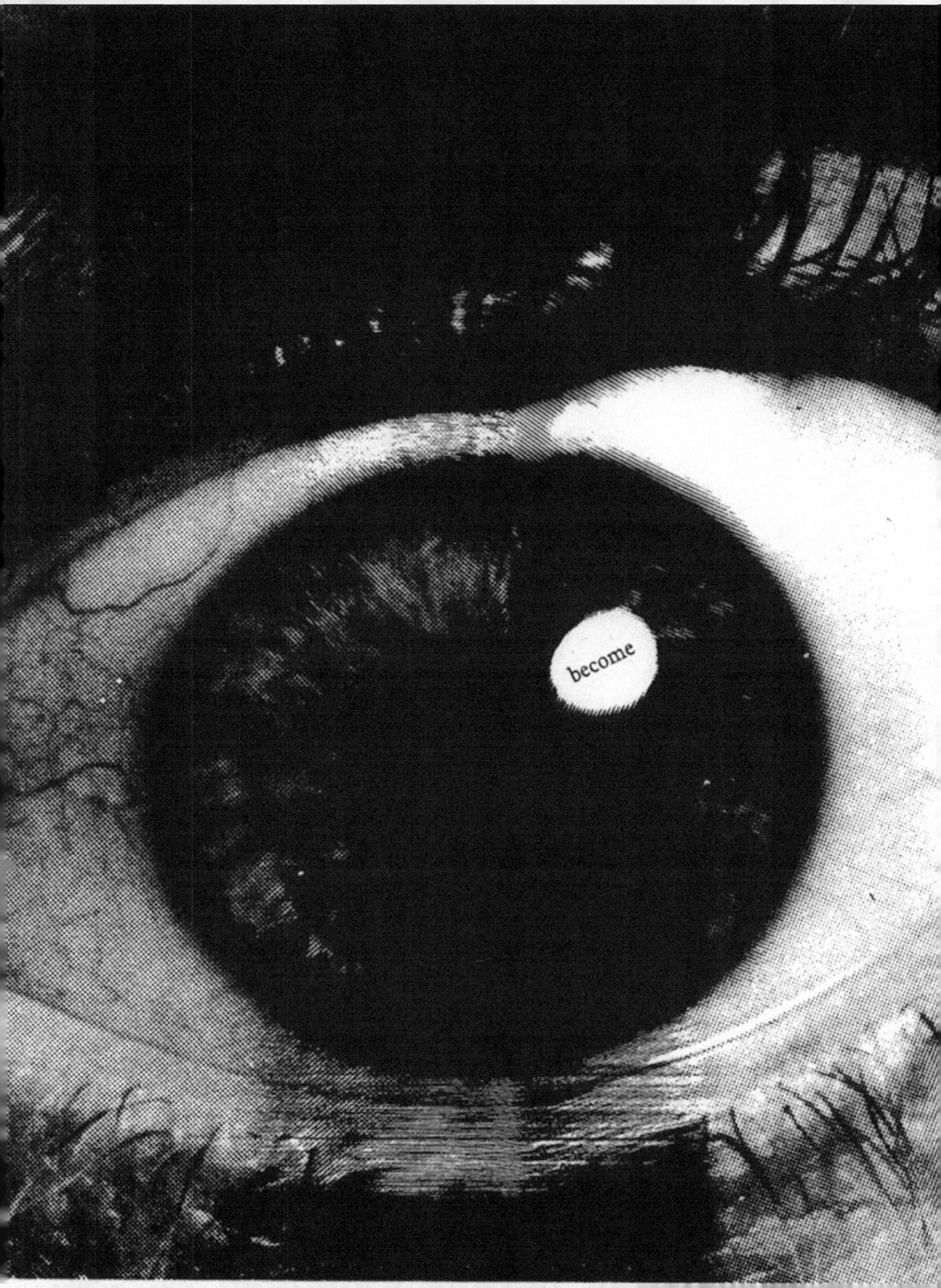
become

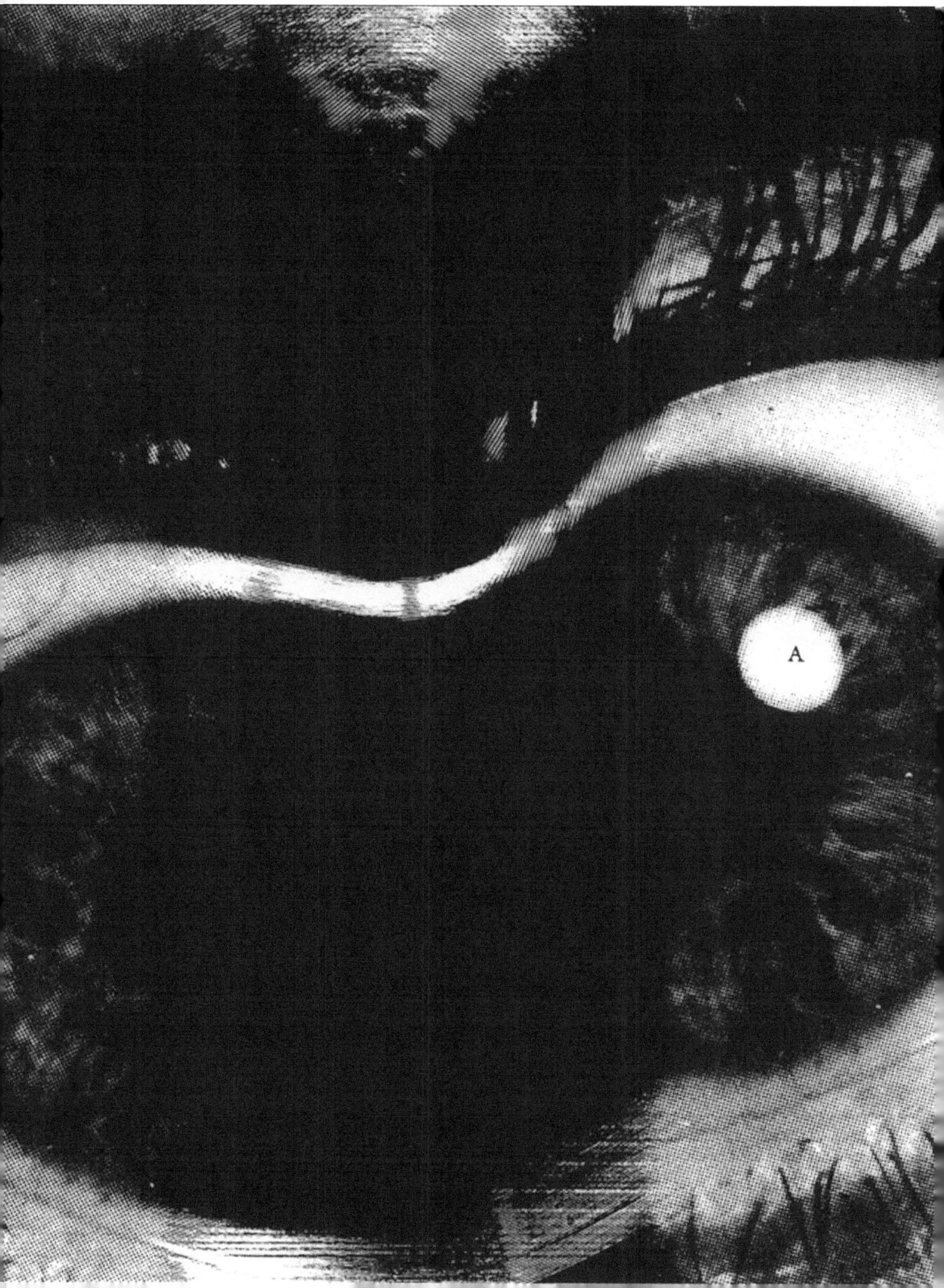

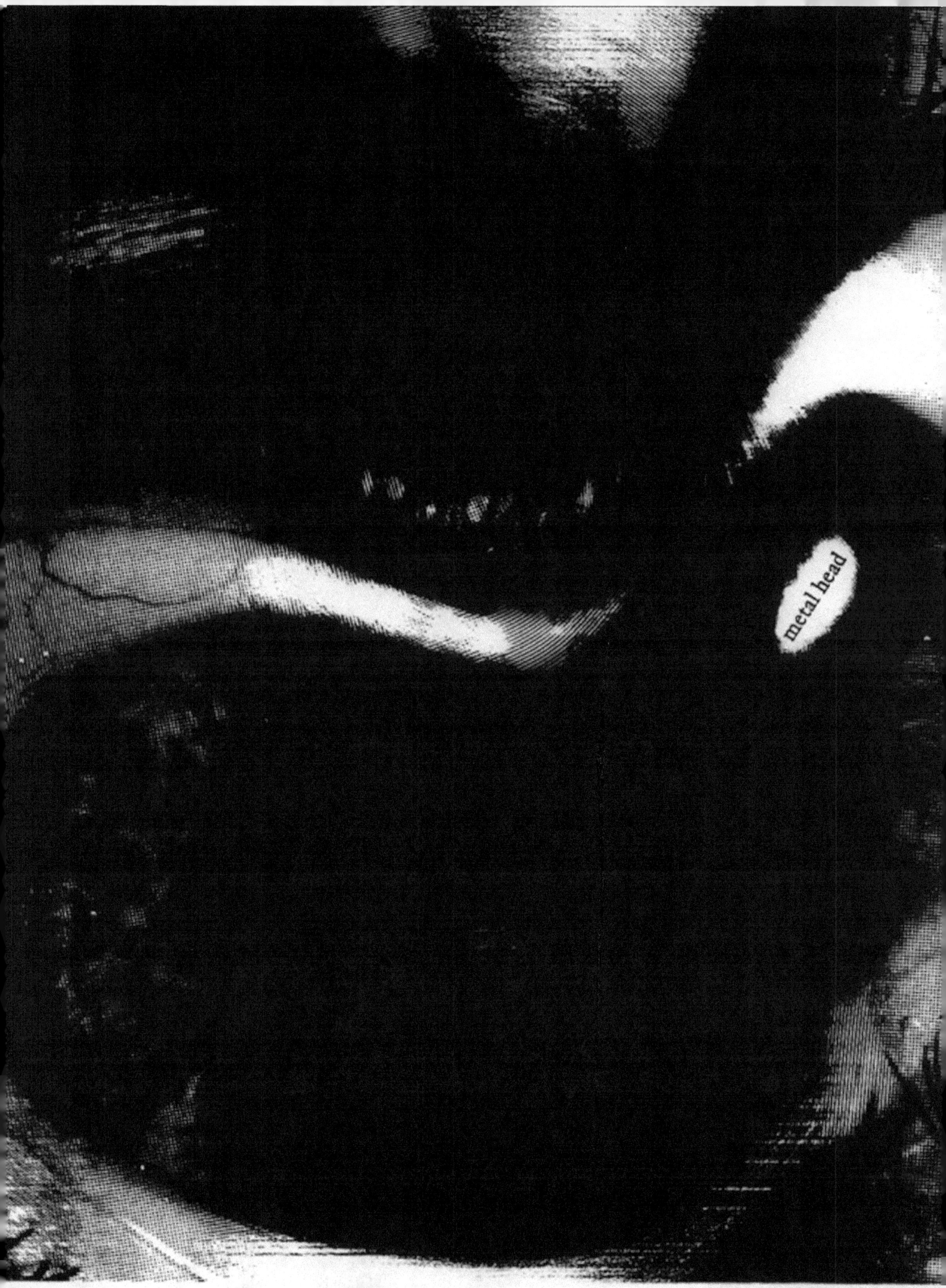
metal head

for crushing

Authenticity Versus Irony

2003

Irony poisoned almost the whole world, and it's only going to keep spreading. That's why a wave of authenticity is going to definitely arise against it. Because you can't really experience life, you can't really live in an ironic way. I mean, what the fuck is this guy Beck doing? I can't even watch him on stage. It's ridiculous. I don't understand. What is this kind of, *"Yeah I'm into it but not really. I'm just kind of checking it out. I'm kind of break dancing, but not really, because I am too cool to really break dance."* What the fuck are all these people breeding? The whole aesthetic premise of irony is just rotten to the core. When I got to New York and I went to concerts, I realized nobody really fucking dances because they are too cool. But really they just don't know how to feel because the people on stage don't fucking know how to feel.
  – Eugene Hutz, lead singer of Gogol Bordello

Nice quote. I agree (in theory), and I like Hutz's band (to an extent) … but I'm not so sure I necessarily "buy it" fully. When I saw Gogol Bordello play live in San Francisco a year or so ago, I could have sworn that the violin player was wearing a Clash t-shirt, the logo of which had been covered up by a Sex Pistols patch (*i.e.* his shirt looked like some misprinted Sex Pistols shirt featuring a picture of The Clash). If that ain't an "ironic" gesture, then I don't know what is. (*Ho, ho, ho – vee are zee zany eastern European gypsies who don' undastand zee famous English Punk Rock bands!*) And Hutz's over-emphasized fumbles with the English language seem pretty iffy to me too. When he says things like "I was thirteen beers drunk!" on their album *Multi Contra Culti vs. Irony*, that can't be *entirely* accidental. But it's part of their whole *we're-a-bunch-of-wacky-post-punk-multi-cultural-immigrants* shtick. Smells like *irony* to me, Eugene.

But irony (like a lot of things in life) is one of those things that's "funny" when *you* do it, but annoying and stupid when *other people* do it – it's completely subjective. Some people think Neil Hamburger is an unfunny idiot with an "ironic" schtick – others regard him as a comic genius in the vein of Andy Kaufman. It depends on how you look at it, but I tend to be of the latter opinion. There are lots of things like that in culture. I'd argue that, while Eugene Hutz may not realize it, "authenticity" is also often in the eye of the beholder.

Maybe the people who go to concerts in New York are shy and insecure? Maybe the women don't want to "invite the male gaze," and maybe the men are afraid of seeming effeminate? Maybe they're hungover? Maybe they're shitty dancers? Maybe they've all been in horrible car accidents and are wearing leg braces? *Or maybe they just don't feel like dancing?* (I know that when I'm at shows, I'm usually disinclined to break into a fuckin' jig.) Or fuck, maybe they all really *are* "too cool" to cut a rug? Who knows? (*Who cares?*) But at least they aren't so vain and full of hubris that they presuppose they've got the inside scoop on so-called "authenticity." All dancing issues aside, *that* would be really fucking annoying, Eugene. …

Spoiled for Choice

On Condiments, Foreskins, and Genocides

2012

Believe it or not, there are heady academic philosophers out there who somehow make a living debating the counterintuitive notion of whether human beings have "free will" in a materialistic universe. I have an inclination on the topic, but I think it's actually sort of a boring question, in that it's ultimately unknowable and whatever debate there is to be had on the subject is comprised of purely hypothetical thought experiments. More interesting to me, irrespective of how one falls on the "free will" versus "determinism" debate, is considering all the external influences on us as humans that direct our decisions in liminal-yet-demonstrable ways; ways which clearly implicate our capacity and inclination to choose in concrete, real-world terms.

Choice, Condiments, and Cut Cocks

Take mayonnaise, for instance. When it comes to ostensibly subjective issues of "taste" (in both the gustatory sense of "taste" and "taste" as in a sense of discriminating acumen), mayonnaise deserves discussion. In the country of my citizenship, The United States of America, mayonnaise is generally relegated to the role of a secondary dressing added to sandwiches and burgers, or used as a binding in "salads" like tuna salad and egg salad. Americans overwhelmingly tend to reserve other condiments and dressings for dipping. French fries, onion rings, chicken tenders, tater tots, and other fried "finger foods" are generally doused by Americans with ketchup, ranch dressing, barbeque sauce, or some species of mustard ... but rarely mayonnaise. However, as put by the Vincent Vega character in the hit 1994 film *Pulp Fiction*, "You know what they put on french fries in Holland instead of ketchup? ... Mayonnaise. ... I seen 'em do it, man, they fuckin' drown 'em in that shit." It's true. In "The Low Countries" of Europe—The Netherlands, Belgium, and Luxembourg—mayonnaise is apparently the go-to dressing of choice for french fries (or, as they call them, *frietjes*, *pommes frites*, or *fritten*, depending on the country). In other words, mayonnaise is The Low Countries' ketchup. Why? I have no fuckin' idea, but I think it's a weird thing to stop and contemplate, at least a little. And the ketchup-versus-mayonnaise disparity is just the "tip of the iceberg," as it were, of cultural incongruities between The United States and Europe's Low Countries – there's also the issue of the tip of the cocks (and no, I don't mean roosters, I mean dicks. Johnsons. Willies. Peters. Penises).

Like most American guys, when I was born in the late 1970s, my parents had my cock's foreskin sliced off, or at least allowed the hospital to slice it off. Did my mom n' pop take any time to mull over whether this was a good idea or not, before ceding to the procedure on my unconsenting babbling behalf? ... Or, rather, did they just accede to my infantile schlong-snipping because that was simply "what one does" in America in the late 1970s? I dunno. I haven't asked them about it, and I don't plan to. But it's weird, because apparently over in Europe's Low Countries, most chaps' cocks' caps are left *au naturel* – un-clipped, unlike mine. And that's odd. One would presume that we'd all be in agreement in the modern Western World with respect to the comparative merits and demerits of foreskin filching, but apparently, we are not. Which is peculiar, and—like the relative regional prevalence of condiments—I think that it says something larger about choice and decision making generally.

Does this transatlantic cultural schism suggest that the majority of Americans have meticulously sampled a wide-ranging suite of prospective condiments and then discriminatingly deliberated about which dipping sauces and dressings are best suited for their particular taste buds as an accompaniment to fries ... and that most of them independently arrived at ketchup? Or that most Belgians have likewise fastidiously parsed all available slatherin' sauces before deciding that mayonnaise is their preference for *pommes frites*? Does it mean that the majority of American and Dutch parents judiciously research male circumcision and—after having compared peer-reviewed scientific studies about its ostensible benefits and alleged downsides—arrive at antipodal conclusions that line up roughly with their nationalities? No. Of course not. These are social conventions that just sort of slowly evolve over time in the aggregate. We all accede to them as part of the normative status quo of the culture in which we're brought up, often half-knowingly at best; and for the most part, the majority of us just "go with the flow" regarding most things that are considered "normal" in our society. We are, in a word, "habituated" to them.

People may be dimly aware of the rote automaticity underlying this phenomenon, but if one asks most people about stuff like this—*Why do you prefer ketchup on your fries instead of mayonnaise?*—they generally act like the question is preposterous, and obviously so. *Because ketchup is what goes on fries, that's why.* And, given the lack of conscious deliberative choice involved on an individual level most of the time by many people, that's a bit odd, given that most of us like to believe that we "own" our decisions, as unique and idiosyncratic individuals. It's even odder on the issue of less seemingly trivial "choices" – like circumcision. One would surmise that parents would actually stop and research that issue, but my inclination is to think that the bulk of them don't – they just "go with the flow" of whatever is the norm in the culture that they happen to live in. Statistical incidence of the practice varying by country would certainly suggest as much, anyway.

Choice and the Narrowmindedness of Nationalism

Having once travelled in Europe, I found it odd how overcompensatingly proud many Europeans were of their nations' long-ago-salient accomplishments, at a time when their modern international import was often nominal at best, and their national economies were on par with that of single U.S. states. For example, the Spanish monuments to Christopher Columbus' discovery of the New World are ostentatious and ubiquitous across Spain, and Spaniards will still trot out this half-a-millennium-old accomplishment-by-proxy as something that Yanquis like me ought to still be appreciative of and grateful for. Likewise, the Irish can't quickly enough interject and remind the overseas Yank traveler of The Emerald Isle's sundry contributions to Western Civilization ("Yer President John F. Kennedy was Irish, don'cha know?") as though that should matter to an American expatriate in his early-twenties at the turn of the Millennium. And of course, wherever one goes (not just in Europe), one will hear about how the locality in which one is situated has the best cuisine the world has to offer, the prettiest women in the world, the best football club, *et cetera*. All dumb shit that the local townies are "proud" of about where they happen to have been born and raised – none of which really makes a lot of sense objectively, at a distance.

The fact that European football hooligans from picayune backwaters with unpronounceable names will congregate and beat the living shit out of hooligans from equally provincial boondocks over a fuckin' soccer game is, well – pretty weird. (And yes, I am aware that Americans have their own dumb, insular Yankees-versus-Red-Sox rivalries that are tantamount to any in the European football world.) This kind of "local pride" thing is wearying and silly, but also entirely predictable and prosaic. Misplaced pride of ownership in the happenstance of one's place of birth is even "universal" and desirable, according to the primeval Greek historian Herodotus, who is alleged to have written:

> If anyone, no matter who, were given the opportunity of choosing from amongst all the nations in the world the set of beliefs which he thought best, he would inevitably—after careful considerations of their relative merits—choose that of his own country. Everyone without exception believes his own native customs, and the religion he was brought up in, to be the best; and that being so, it is unlikely that anyone but a madman would mock at such things. There is abundant evidence that this is the universal feeling about the ancient customs of one's country.

Herodotus' attitude on the topic is far from unusual. As he correctly points out, it's pretty much the norm, everywhere. Most people, in most places, most of the time, seem to be pretty convinced that where they're from and what they're used to is preferable to other possible alternatives. Many people act like all of their sclerotic inherited cultural preferences are *theirs*, and defend them passionately with an air of dogmatism.

Given the desultory nature of a lot of traditions and norms, it would seem that many common cultural practices should come in for critical review and analysis – but they rarely do. Ergo, rather than prompting introspection and cultural self-reflection concerning the norms and mores of one's own culture, these kinds of observations as to cultural difference are more likely to produce amusement, disgust, and prejudice. Encountering photographs in *National Geographic* of African bushpeople with purposefully distended lips, necks, and earlobes, does not generally prompt the typical Westerner to reconsider the reasonableness of their own customs, norms, habits, and fashions – but rather, tends to elicit finger pointing and snorting laughter. And that's fine, to some extent. The Rousseauian "noble savage" myth thing is silly, and there are few persuasive arguments to be made in favor of neck distensions, at least that I'm aware of. But the same goes for comparable aspects of the West; the cosmetics and fashion industries, luxury goods, "conspicuous consumption," lip-fillers and pectoral implants ... and various other wasteful and inefficient "normal" practices that are ubiquitous in Western culture. I imagine that an African bushman would find humorous absurdity in the American penchant for costly and unnecessary seasonal lawn care and maintenance, for example.

Choice and The Fickleness of Faith

It's trite to point out that the majority of people adopt the religion of their parents and their society. It's not exactly likely that around 974 million Indians each individually decided that Hinduism is "The One True Faith"; or that 243 million Americans stumbled on some variant of Christianity as "The One True Faith"; and so on with "The One True Faith" being Islam, Buddhism (and the rest) in various parts of the world in which those religions are dominant. It's trite, sure, but it's still fuckin' *true* – most people tend to just fall into whatever religion they were raised with. There is, perhaps, nothing more consequential in a person's life—at least philosophically, if not practically—than one's religious conception of life's meaning, the world, and one's place in it. And yet, looking at the numbers, it seems as though the majority of the global populace have decided to just "go with the flow" of the culture they happen to live in, and simply adopt the faith that they were steeped and marinated in as kids. That's odd. Odder than condiments and circumcision, even.

The absurdity of cultural and cross-cultural religious adoption seems unsurprising, however, if not intuitive – at least in modern times. Although, historically, plenty of ruinous internecine wars were fought in Europe alone over Christian doctrinal hair-splitting, nowadays people often gloss over intercultural religious differences with mollifying notions like the ecumenical idea that all religions are aiming toward veneration of the same universal God; and that it's just that different cultures have different regional interpretations and understandings of how, when, and why one should exalt God. In other words, the idea goes that Yahweh, Jehovah, Allah, Brahma, Gaya (*et al.*) are just different names for, and interpretations of, the same universal overarching spiritual force that binds the universe. I don't buy it, but I can see how that kind of apologetical rationalization is alluring to believers. Less easy to explain away with feel-good universalism, however, are different cultures' attitudes towards what is and isn't acceptable to eat; whether that's according to God or just social norms.

Choice and The Caprice of Cuisine

Why is it considered acceptable in The United States to eat cows and pigs, but utterly abhorrent to consume cats and dogs? It's not self-evident. Pigs are supposedly just as intelligent as, if not more intelligent than, cats and dogs. Pork isn't kosher in Judaism, and it's *haram* in Islam; yet pork is deemed perfectly acceptable as everyday food throughout the United States. Meanwhile, in parts of Asia, consuming cats and dogs is not unheard of; and conversely, in most of India the eating of beef is proscribed because cattle are deemed sacred in Hinduism, Jainism, and some sects of Buddhism. So, there's not really a lot of rhyme or reason to these culinary customs across the globe – and yet people obviously take them pretty dang seriously. Try eating a dog in the United States sometime and you'd better be ready to be fuckin' lynched; but don't hold your breath waiting for a logical explanation from American canine-lovers as to why they recoil in horror at the idea of dog-eating, but they're still comfortable with eating dogs' ostensible intellectual superiors – pigs.

Food is just one obvious exemplar of cross-cultural differences that pops out as an arresting difference in norms between societies. But there are many others, and the variations among customs and standards—big and small—in different cultures, can have sweeping effects at the societal level.

Choice and The Sway of Society

The Japanese have long notoriously clocked on average more hours per workweek than Americans; who in turn still work more hours on average than the French and other European nations. Countries' comparative metrics of sociocultural health (gross national product, happiness indexes, rates of obesity, average life expectancy, childhood mortality rates, *et cetera*) can vary accordingly – sometimes drastically. But these cold statistical metrics fail to capture the fact that how people even *think* in different cultures, and how they see the world, are often quite different.

For example, concepts of time differ between nations in ways that affect all sorts of things in society. In *The Geography of Time*: *The Temporal Misadventures of a Social Psychologist*, Robert Levine explores all the curious ways in which different cultures conceive of time – what it means to be "on time" and how much of a *faux pas* it is to be "late"; how rapidly people on average walk down the street in different countries' metropolises; and how these variant attitudes towards and understandings of punctuality and temporal urgency correlate with broad sociocultural trends like economics, efficiency, health, and so forth. And by no means is this differentiation among cultures limited to concepts of time, its value, and its use. Cultures vary widely in norms concerning many things that most people like to believe are personal choices that they themselves make, as individuals.

Take music, for instance. Most folks have strong opinions about music. Some people in the West even build much of their identities around a musical genre and its attendant sartorial norms (think Goth, Rockabilly, Heavy Metal, Ska, and so on). But even something as superficially subjective as musical taste is, on a deep level, largely a product of culture and upbringing, rather than carefully considered individual choice.

Choice and the Mandates of Music

Western "chromatic" music only has twelve notes that are recognizable (whether consciously or not) to the Western ear; whereas Eastern music is often microtonal, in that it utilizes a wider range of subdivision of tones (*i.e.,* notes that are in-between the notes on the twelve-tone chromatic scale). People who grew up in the West, listening to chromatic nursery rhymes ("Mary Had a Little Lamb," "Twinkle, Twinkle, Little Star," "Old MacDonald Had a Farm," *et cetera*) tend to like other chromatic music that operates in the same scales and uses similar consonant melodies and harmonies – "Johnny B. Goode," "Smells Like Teen Spirit," "Rapper's Delight," "I Want to Hold Your Hand," and so on. Music that is deemed "catchy" in the West appeals to listeners because it's familiar – in a sense, the listener already knows where the music is going to "go," within one of a fixed number of scales, so it's natural for them to like it, effortlessly. Music that deviates from this—say, for example, microtonal Chinese Opera, or Javanese Gamelan music— sounds out of tune, dissonant, atonal, and cacophonous to the Western ear. It doesn't "go" where Western listeners expect it to go, so it's unfamiliar, and therefore not easy to like. Have most Westerners made a conscious, deliberative decision to prefer chromatic music to microtonal music? Of course not. But they all fuckin' act like they did.

Choice and the Leverage of Language

Cultural preferences for certain kinds of music over others may be down to the fact that the cultures that produce microtonal music tend to have languages that (unlike English) are heavily reliant on the fine nuances of tone to express meaning, rather than just vocabulary and syntax. In Mandarin Chinese, for instance, *mā, má, mǎ,* and *mà* all mean different things. In Vietnamese, *ba, bà, bá, bạ, bả,* and *bã* all mean different things (and the variations in tone can depend on whether the speaker is from North or South Vietnam). It all sounds pretty similar to a lumbering English speaker like me – which is probably why I also can't fuckin' stand their music. But that also suggests that I couldn't even really freely "choose" to like their music if I wanted to – I'd have to put effort into it. Which suggests that my own musical preferences are not fully "free" choices as such, but rather have been directed by the culture in which I was raised, and the language that is native to me.

So, it follows that the very language we speak colors our comprehension of the world in ways that we don't—and possibly can't—even distinguish, such as preferences for different types of music. Language probably also has even larger effects on us than just musical taste, however. Apart from different emphasis on tone, different languages also have dissimilar ways of expressing concepts predicated on how sentences are structured in the language. In Spanish it's often not necessary to state who is doing something when constructing a sentence. Businesses don't advertise "We Speak Spanish at This Business," but rather "*Se Habla Español*," which is closer to "Spanish spoken here" (the "*se*" in the sentence doesn't refer to anyone specifically in this context – it can mean "we," "they," "he," "she," *et cetera*). I'm told that Japanese is similar. Many languages (unlike English) also feature entirely different conjugations to connotate formality and informality; deferral and respect or familiarity and insouciance between the speaker and recipient of speech. Languages also often have different phonomimes to denote the sounds that animals make. In English, birds will make sounds like "cluck cluck," "squawk," "coo," "quack," "cock-a-doodle-doo," and "hoot" – but in German it's "*gack gack*," "*krächzen*," "*gurren*," "*quaken*," "*kikeriki*," and "*schreien*" (or "*rufen*"). Why? I have no fuckin' idea, but it sure is weird, given that last I checked, most animals don't speak regional dialects.

Some of the variation amongst human languages is pretty "out there," and differs in more than just sentence construction or emphasis on tone and cadence versus vocabulary. Supposedly, aboriginal Australian speakers of the Kuuk Thaayorre language use cardinal directions to describe space, position, and movement in ways that seem perplexing and counterintuitive to speakers of most other languages (*i.e.*, "Take your north-facing hand and put it on your east-facing leg" would not be an abnormal thing to say). This means that such people are always aware of where they are situated in space in relation to the points of the compass – they possess an acuity for spatial position that the rest of us apparently don't. Which is pretty fuckin' bizarre, given that, in the absence of landmarks, awareness of such spatial relativeness rarely if ever enters the minds of most Anglophones. In other words, aboriginal Australian speakers of the Kuuk Thaayorre language are, to whatever extent, experiencing the world and their place in it differently than speakers of other languages.

How these linguistic distinctions might influence cultures at a meta level – such as whether a language that assigns agency to most actions (like English) versus one that doesn't (like Spanish), may gently push a whole culture towards or away from individualistic governance or communal governance is unknowable, but certainly provocative to consider. And further, if languages can influence how speakers experience, view, or interpret the word (such what kinds of music they like, how they assign agency, the importance they put on relational social hierarchy, how they hear animal sounds, or how they conceive of themselves in relation to points on a compass), then how much can language also influence individual choice in ways that speakers don't even perceive? Probably a fuckin' lot.

Language, society, and culture, then, clearly implicate our individual faculty to make decisions, by framing the context in which we are even able to conceive of a decision being possible. And this phenomenon doesn't stop with the relative variability of place, as in where we happen to have been born and grown up on the globe – it also applies to history in time. Setting aside cultural standards respecting food, music, temporal norms, language, and religion—as influences on our facility and inclination to choose—there's also the fact that many things like social mores, customs, and standards of probity invariably change *within* a culture, dramatically, over time.

Choice and The Myopia of The Moment

In the West, the color pink is associated with girls, and blue with boys. This is, unsurprisingly, mostly random and only arose relatively recently in the early-to-mid twentieth century. It could be the other way around, or just different (orange for boys, brown for girls). It's completely irrelevant and arbitrary, and yet there are major industries affected by it (*e.g.*, Mattel's Barbie toy line). This is just one of innumerable examples of a social convention that haphazardly developed over time and has now become a durable norm. There are many others.

There was a time in the West when it was ordinary for people to "group sleep" and people bifurcated their nightly slumber up into a "first sleep" and "second sleep"; when bathing was considered abnormal; when shitting into bedpans in the presence of others wasn't shameful or odd; when women were seen as property, or at least second-class citizens; when people were burned at the stake or drowned as "witches" after sham trials; when human slavery wasn't regarded as a moral wrong but blowjobs and anal sex were "detestable and abominable crimes against nature" punishable under the law; and so on. In the here and now, these anachronistic practices seem peculiar and crazy to us, but, within the ambit of recorded history, they were once commonplace and quotidian. Unremarkably "normal."

This, too, is odd – that subjectivity and perspectival relativism are present not just between cultures, but within a single culture across time. And yet, as with other received preferences, the norms of the current historical moment tend to be regarded as if they are evergreen and fixed in amber – what is deemed objectionable or "offensive" today in a given culture is generally regarded as if it will always be so, and always should have been so. Such an attitude towards the accepted norms of the moment, common though it may be, makes little sense if one stops to mull it over. Our ancestors would find many of the social norms of our times to be gobsmackingly strange, and vice-versa – yet everyone acts like what's "normal" now is the correct and accurate version of "normal."

How many other things are like this, that we're unaware of, or are dimly aware of but never really stop to think much about? Given the pervasive influence of social and cultural norms that we are acculturated to on account of where and when we happen to be living, how much do we really ostensibly "choose" our own preferences, which each of us likes to believe are a part (to a greater or lesser extent) of our bespoke personality, of who we *are* as individuals?

Choice, Parochial Patriotism, and Permissive Pluralism

Notwithstanding Herodotus' early admonition that having the temerity to question the social norms of one's country makes one a "madman," people on the margins of society have been noting the oddness of sociocultural balkanization for a long time. In the late 1500s, the French philosopher Michel de Montaigne ruminated on the superiority in design of then-contemporary German iron stoves over the French open fireplaces that he was accustomed to; and about how senseless it was that the French hadn't emulated the Germans in this advancement for any reason other than dumb obstinacy interspersed with the chauvinism of provincial pride. Montaigne was, of course, following in the footsteps of Herodotus' gadfly contemporary, Socrates, who is apocryphally credited with having stated *"All I know is that I know nothing"* – and supposedly made a habit of sauntering around ancient Athens wantonly pissing everyone off by asking them obvious-seeming questions like, *Why do you prefer ketchup on your fries instead of mayonnaise?*

But regardless of whether one is more inclined to adopt the Montaigne's Socratic view on the subject of cultural norms over that of Herodotus, the very fact that norms are "normal" by necessity dictates that Herodotus' view is descriptive of reality for most people most of the time, while Montaigne's is merely prescriptive. There is everywhere a pervasiveness of the tautological attitude that foreignness is "incorrect" simply because it's foreign: *We drive on this side of the road because that's normal; abroad, they drive on the other side of the road for some reason because they're just weird that way. Krazy foreigners!* In other words, most people seem to think like Herodotus, not like Montaigne or Socrates.

Unfortunately, attempting to take an at-a-distance, nominally objective view of one's endemic culture *vis-à-vis* other cultures is difficult, and can lead people to kooky extremes. At one end of the cross-cultural analysis spectrum lies stalwart nativist jingoism; a kind of *Love it or leave it!* blustering blowhard patriotism that can seem lazy, moronic, and narrow-minded, if not downright xenophobic and bigoted. At the other antipode is a knee-jerk overbroad repudiation of norms as an exercise in iconoclasm or rebellion, often for its own sake. The latter often manifests modernly in so-called "counterculture" movements – the bohemian jettisoning of the social norms of one's own culture in favor of "transgressive" alternatives (and often, an uncritical embrace of the foreign). Think: Dada, Surrealism, and Situationism; the Beatniks, the Hippies, the Punks; *et al.*

Outside of "counterculture," a rejection of social norms is often expressed nowadays in the increasingly mainstream concept of so-called "cultural relativism" – the slippery nonjudgemental idea that all cultural values are context dependent and relative, so therefore there's no uniform standard by which to compare cultures, and further that it's impossible to arrive at any sort of objective conclusion regarding any part of one culture being "superior" or even "preferable" to any part of another. This is often distilled down into the idea of "multiculturalism" – the feel-good notion (at least in the West) that society ought to embrace the diversity of cultural differences in a spirit of pluralism and tolerance. Which is fine, to an extent. However, coupled with the psychogymnastics of postmodernism, cultural relativism often allows people in the West to shift into moral relativism – which creates absurd problems that belie its nonsensicalness.

Postmodernism and cultural relativism are how we've ended up with the paradox of Western progressive liberals descending into wide-eyed apoplexy over every real or perceived slight against feminism, while simultaneously declining to demur on the topic of forced modesty imposed on women in Islamic countries by way of the burqa – because ostensibly it's "not our place" in the West to judge the norms and practices of non-Western cultures by transposing our values onto nonwestern cultures. It's how we've ended up with self-avowed "anti-racists" who support discrimination against certain disfavored groups ... *on the basis of race* under the claimed moral valence of pursuing "equality." And that's self-refutingly fuckin' idiotic.

Ironically, however, the currently trendy practice of engaging in multiculturalism (and the nonjudgmental blinders that it entails wearing) only seems to be applied towards those from other *places*, not to those from other *times*. In other words, a member of the *bien-pensant* in the modern West may be disposed towards nonjudgmentalism— with respect to the practice of, say, child labor in the developing world, or women's rights under Islamic theocracies—and yet the selfsame person is often less likely to extend *any* modicum of understanding for the cultural practices of the past, engaged in by people who were just a much a product of their times as anyone today is a product of their culture. There is no dearth of moral opprobrium from such people for, say, the slave-owning "Founding Fathers" of the United States who lived in the eighteenth century, when slavery was as much an everyday American reality as eating hamburgers made from bovine flesh is today. It's an odd double standard.

The truth is that—although most people like to imagine that if they'd been alive during some beleaguered and dark time in history, like the antebellum American South, they'd have had the moral fortitude to be intransigent abolitionists—statistically, that's farfetched. Most people, in most places, most of the time, just "go with the flow" about most things that are normal in the culture they're a part of – whether it's french fry dressing, child circumcision, tolerance for homosexuality, or being nonplussed by the legality of slavery. Were it otherwise, there would be no norms, nothing would be regarded as "normal," and the practices of other cultures or other times would not seem so surreally abnormal.

Choice in Pop Psychology and Social Science

Why all of this is interesting, and germane to the issue of choice, is that it clearly implicates the ability of individuals to make decisions in palpable real-world terms; about things both small and large. The capability to decide, as an individual, whether something is "good" or "bad," preferred or dispreferred, requires one to compare the subject of the decision to something else – and that comparison will entail extraneous factors such as what is and isn't "normal" in the context in which the decision is made; which in turn is affected by the time, the place, and circumstances surrounding the decision maker – all of which can be studied, at least in theory.

How people make decisions has, of late, become a subject of increased general interest. PopSci, for uncredentialed laymen like me. Social Science popularizer Malcolm Gladwell, in a much-shared 2004 *TED Talk* video entitled "Choice, happiness and spaghetti sauce," discusses the amusing fact that most people will claim that they prefer dark, robust, full-bodied coffee when queried on the topic; but that their "revealed preferences" (*i.e.* what they actually do, as opposed to what they tell others they do) show that they actually like diluted, milky coffee. And further, that, as Gladwell puts it, there is no "Platonic Ideal" of the perfect spaghetti sauce; only perfect spaghetti sauce(s)— namely, plain, spicy, and extra chunky—because different people have different preferences, but only within a narrow, predetermined range. The takeaway is that the consuming public doesn't know what it wants unless and until it has been presented with a panoply of options to choose from – ideally on offer from a corporation standing to make a profit in the marketplace. This area of study falls within the academic ambits of Decision Theory and Behavioral Economics, and has become a topic of increased general appeal in the last half-decade.

Another darling of The TED Set, *wunderkind* Jonah Lehrer, discusses the same sorts of issues in his much-lauded 2009 book *How We Decide*.[1] Gladwell and Lehrer piggyback on the academic work of behavioral economist Dan Ariely (also a *TED Talk* alumnus), who studies the kinds of peculiar decision-making heuristics that people employ in navigating the world. Ariely and other academic scientists like Roy

---

[1] <u>NOTE</u>: On March 1, 2013, *How We Decide* was taken "off sale" by the publisher after an internal review, following revelations that author Jonah Lehrer had made numerous falsifications in a later-published book. How and whether that affects Lehrer's earlier research that led to *How We Decide*, is not clear.

Baumeister have shown that people often make choices by *not* choosing; they dither, out of overwhelmed indecisiveness or mere laziness. Given too many options, people can experience "decision fatigue" and end up choosing none – which is, itself, a choice (albeit an *in*decisive one). For example, Ariely ascribes differential rates of organ donation between countries to whether citizens must "opt in" or "opt out" of donating their organs (*i.e.* if, when getting one's driver's license, one has to check a box that says "I want to donate my organs if I die in a car crash" in order to donate, versus donation being the default and one having to intentionally check a box stating, "I *don't* want to donate my organs if I die in a car crash"). The act of affirmatively having to check the box—to make a decision—can apparently drastically affect the level of organ donation in a country. That's pretty fuckin' weird, given how much most people like to think that they "make" their decisions, rather than the other way 'round. It means that the American Synth-Pop band Devo appears to have prefigured the academic Decision Theorists by a few decades, with their 1980 refrain, "Freedom of choice is what you got. Freedom from choice is what you want."

Choice and the Dark Side of Deindividuation

Ariely's studies in Behavioral Economics tend to be kind of "quirky" and "amusing." Food for thought, but not necessarily massively life-impacting *per se*. But Ariely's work builds on that of psychologists who've dealt with the darker aspects of human decision making. Somewhat notoriously, Stanley Milgram and Philip Zimbardo both did "offbeat" experiments purportedly showing how tractable and obsequious otherwise psychologically normal people can be made to become under the right conditions.

In the early 1960s, Milgram had subjects administer increasingly severe electric shocks to unseen "learners" under the direction of a Scientist in a lab coat, while the subject could hear the learner's cries of pain. The shocks were fake (the Scientist was an actor, as was the learner), and Milgram's intention was to measure the willingness of the study's participants to obey an authority figure who prompted them to engage in conduct that was at variance with their own morals or conscience. These mock electric jolts gradually increased during the experiments, as prompted by the (pseudo) Scientist to levels that—had the experiments' conditions actually been real—would have fuckin' killed the learner. While the results of Milgram's experiments and what they mean remain subjects of debate, the bottom line is that more than half of participants were willing to administer lethal levels of electric shocks to people they didn't know, on the orders of an authority figure whom they'd just met. So, there's that.

About a decade later, Zimbardo became notorious for having presided over the so-called Stanford Prison Experiment, in which he examined the influence of "situational variables" on participants' behavior. Zimbardo recruited a bunch of male college students to act as "guards" in uniforms who oversaw "prisoners" (also male college students from the same cohort) who were arrested by real cops and then held in an ersatz jail. The experiment was supposed to last for two weeks—and everyone involved knew it was just LARPing for science—but Zimbardo had to shut it down after just six days because the pretend guards were leaning too heavily into the sadism of their roles, and were treating the make-believe prisoners like total shit. The Stanford Prison Experiment gave rise to various ethics grievances, and its methodology has been critiqued as being unscientific; but the bottom line, as with Milgram's work, is that otherwise seemingly normal people are ready to go "off the rails" without a helluva lot of prompting, under the right conditions. (The similarities between the conduct of the students in Zimbardo's experiment and that of U.S. servicemembers in Iraq's Abu Ghraib prison in 2004 have not gone unnoticed.)

The approaches of Milgram and Zimbardo have since received some criticism, and the conclusions about the "dark" side of human nature drawn from their work may be overbroad – but it's probably still fair to say that their work sheds some light on how obedience and dichotomous us-versus-them thinking are hard-wired into human beings. Both Milgram and Zimbardo's work is often discussed in the context of the twentieth century's brutal plethora of state-sponsored violence, which cries out for explanation and rationalization in the modern world; genocides, pogroms, "ethnic cleansing," and other horrors of organized human endeavor in an era of modern mechanization.

Choice, Groceries, and Genocides

What the fuck does any of this have to do with the mayonnaise-ketchup fry-dipping bifurcation between the United States and The Low Countries of Europe? What does consumer preference in the marketplace and "decision fatigue" have to do with ethnic cleansing? Well, they all obviously involve decision making and choice, or the deferral thereof. The Holocaust, The Chinese Cultural Revolution, The Hutu Genocide Against the Tutsi in Rwanda, the oh-so-zany kookiness of Cambodia's Khmer Rouge—*et cetera*—all beggar belief. But what they have in common is rigid group cohesion, obedience to authority, and ... "going with the flow."

If the Scientist in the lab coat insists that it's "normal" to administer electric shocks to the "learner" during the experiment, then the shocks are administered by most subjects to "go with the flow." If all the other college kid "guards" are treating all the college kid "prisoners" in the experiment abusively, then most guards will "go with the flow" and do likewise. If all the other Cambodian villagers are on-board with Pol Pot's program of collectivization, then—heck—one might as well "go with the flow." If all the other Germans seem to be on board with the goal of making *Deutschland* eventually *judenfrei*, then one might as well "go with the flow." You get the idea.

If you're a concentration camp worker at Buchenwald shoveling human cremains out of an oven prior to the next batch; or a Chinese teenager beating the living shit out of your erstwhile math teacher as a member of the intelligentsia in the name of The Great Proletarian Cultural Revolution; or their American equivalents in whatever context might make such a comparison apt (Mai Lai, Haditha, Guantánamo Bay, *et cetera*)—you probably decided at some antecedent point not to "rock the boat" too much and instead to just "go with the flow" of your society on the big questions of life, like *What the fuck am I doing here killing innocent people?* not just the small ones like, *What condiment do I, as an individual, prefer on my french fries?*

Choose Your Own Conclusion

All of this is simply to say that we don't have as much control over our own preferences and choices as we might like to think, and that this can have profound consequences on us without our necessarily even realizing it. As humans, whether we like it or not, and whether we fully realize it or not, we are products of our environments. Our entire cognitive universe is laced with assumptions that we've never even realized we've made. From early childhood, our ears and taste buds are inculcated with the values of "good" and "bad" assigned by our culture, without us ever having been the wiser. Maybe they're sensible and "right," or maybe they're foolish and "wrong." It depends. But if a significant enough proportion of the population complacently sleepwalks through life being placated and blinkered by the comfort of the familiar and "normal"—rarely if ever stopping to analyze their decisions on a case-by-case basis, seldom stopping to think too hard about why they believe what they believe, why they accept some things at face value as being "normal"—then things can "go off the rails" in parts of the culture, or in the culture as a whole.

Perhaps if we all made an effort a bit more often to attempt to look at the world "with fresh eyes," a lot of problems might be averted on both the individual and societal level. Doing this would require trying to stay aware of what one has affirmatively chosen in one's life, versus what may have been covertly prechosen *for* oneself – by one's culture, one's society, one's social class, the language one speaks, the times one lives in, or anything else. It's worth keeping in mind, from time to time, that today's passing trend, which seems "normal," may be regarded as barbaric and backwards in the future; and may already be regarded as such elsewhere in the world today. Of course, questioning the norms of one's culture can be taken too far—and can melt into a morass of cultural and moral relativism that's best given a wide berth—but that doesn't mean that the norms shouldn't be questioned at all, and often.

Who knows? Maybe you'd actually prefer mayonnaise on your fries over ketchup if you gave it a chance, instead of just habitually reaching for the ketchup bottle at the diner; or vice versa? And maybe it makes sense to at least fuckin' look into the pros and cons of having the tip of your kid's dick cut off before just "going with the flow" of whatever is normal in the country the kid happens to have been born in.

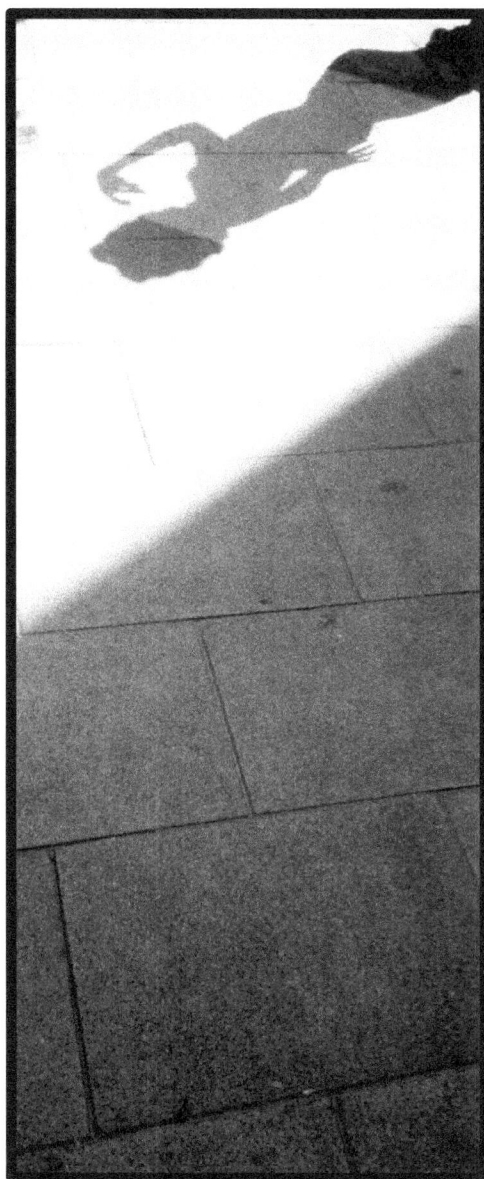

Striiiiiip Cluuuuuub!!!

2013

Unfortunately, I am presently at a strip club on Los Angeles' ("World Famous!") Hollywood Boulevard, on a Saturday night. I'm accompanied by two lesbian couples, a couple'a straight chicks, and one other straight dude. I guess we are here under the conceit that it's "ironic" or whatever. The Bud Lights are, like, ten bucks in bottles. Miley Cyrus is blasting over a distorted and clipping PA system, while a well-endowed "Rubenesque" girl jiggles her butt cheeks onstage. Lecherous losers languidly leer. The bass is too loud.

I am reaffirmed in my view that there's pretty much nowhere I like chillin' less than a strip club. I'd rather have drinks at the morgue, or a Holocaust Museum, or a hospital burn ward. If anyone wants to meet up later for cocktails on an abandoned airport runway littered with decaying coyote carcasses, hit me up.

To who it may concern:

Yo I was just readin thru my old stuffs when i found this litle Dial-A-pirat mailer. I had forgot all about it. it sez on hear June 95 catalog. I dont rightly no what that meens but i ges it meens this heer maler is from 95. thats some time ago. Indeed.

Well, i firstly want yall to now that sum of this records on the mailer is exelant. wes used to listen to ice tray adn da coobs like evry day. Then sheeqwa (thats my bitch thru it out the car window when we was drivin. she get like that sumtimes before i put the bitch down. so i sorely missed that tape. That when is reely bored i like to play nintendo was down. Thats the shit that i think about.

I also liked nic and teh dimonds. My ant and unkle use to be all up into that neel dimond shit. I never liiked it to much so the tape is funy to me. I spect them niggas is making fun and shit.\

I dont take no truck with taht agony shit. thats some fucked up shit jest like the mailer ses. fuck that. I just listen to my bitch wail wen I smack the shit out of her. I aktely put that shit on the tape one time. i shouold send ti to yall to see if you like it. then I can be famus to jest like yall.

One thing i got to tell yall tho is that Rob enbom is one crazy nigga, even if that fool is wite. I gives that crazy foo the upmost props. I dont say no shit like manowarz changd my live and shit butt mayb it come prety close. thats some down shit. yall mite want to tell that nigga that hes alrite in my book.

Yo what yall think of this tipin skilz. I picked this shit up late last nite if yall no what i'm sayin. word.

yo send me the new mailer an shit ya smell me.

out,
Bodyrocker C

███████████ Ave. #G
New Orleans, LA ██████

August 25th, 1999

Dear Bodyrocker C.,

I regret to inform you that Dial-A-Pirate Records has been a wholly defunct entity for quite some time now. The company held out well into 1998, but following a significant lull in sales during the third quarter of that year, and the surprising lack of support for its final release, Dial-A-Pirate Records finally called it quits. Our back catalog of cassettes is still available through special arrangement, but is no longer available for sale to the general public. Should you wish to purchase copies of rare or out of print Dial-A-Pirate releases, you may do so through me personally.

It is with even more regret, and the deepest remorse, that I must inform you that Robert Enbom is no longer with us. Rob parted this world just over three months ago in a fatal head-on collision, at the wheel of his 1975 Duster. I am glad to report, however, that he was not under the influence of drugs or alcohol at the time, and that Rob's untimely death had been a mere case of bad judgment and even worse luck. Luckily for us, however, Rob did leave a legacy. Rob's musical career continued on quite successfully following the demise of Dial-A-Pirate, in the form of a band called Magnum. If you are interested in obtaining a copy of Magnum's self-titled 1998 debut CD from MathLab Records, send $10.00 to:

Shawn Porter
P.O. Box 101
Walnut Creek, CA 94596

I hate to be the bearer of bad news, but I guess sometimes that's just the way it goes. I myself will be leaving the country for Madrid, Spain, in less than a week and won't return to the U.S. until February, but if you have any questions about either Dial-A-Pirate or Rob Enbom, please feel free to email me at Brian@brianMclark.com. For questions regarding Magnum, Shawn Porter can be reached at LazerBoy7@aol.com. Thank you for taking the time to write. My apologies for the sad news.

Sincerely,

– Brian M. Clark

The Epistolatory Enlightenment of One Bodyrocker C.

December 18, 2003

Brian,

So, about three years ago I wrote you a letter inquiring about Rob Enbom, in response to which you told me (pretty eloquently) about his death.

You can imagine my surprise when I got a Friendster message from him last night.

I've evoked brilliant images of the iconic saint of youth that is Rob, and his tragic (albeit stylish) demise, in the minds of every last person I know

What do I tell them now?

You're a kind of scoundrel.

- Bodyrocker C.

Hipsters As a Bellwether of Socioeconomic Health

2009

The term "hipster" is rarely, if ever, self-applied, and almost always used with derision. It implies pretense, falsehood, incuriousness, disingenuousness, inauthenticity, and insincerity. It carries with it the connotations of a postured affectation of jaded indifference and a self-conscious, "ironic" (*i.e.,* insincere) appreciation of culture that is now widely regarded as *passé, démodé, déclassé, bourgeois, louche,* or some other fancy-ass fuckin' French word meaning *decidedly not cool to the average person.* Wink-wink, nudge-nudge inside jokes. Kitsch cool. Studied nonchalance. Sarcasm and spuriousness. Half-hearted, apathetic, plausibly deniable endorsement of niche (*i.e.,* obscure, underground, subcultural, countercultural) interests. Condescension towards popular, "mainstream" culture; or its "ironic" embrace. Hipsters see themselves as a sort of cultural vanguard; the avant-garde, the *cognoscenti,* the *cool.* (But only, like, *sort of,* like ironically. Like, you can't, like, *say* it or, like, explain it, because, like, that like, *ruins* it.)

Free online stock photo of a "hipster"
(real hipsters don't look like this).

You may know them well. They're usually (but certainly not always) white, middle-class, twenty-something young adults living in urban areas. They sport clothing manufactured by American Apparel, ride fixed-gear bicycles, wear once-unfashionable t-shirts and dowdy trucker hats purchased at thrift stores, drink cheap beer, and smoke discount cigarettes. They've got whimsical tattoos in non-cover-up-able places. Most attend or have attended college; many go to art school. They're idiosyncratic as any subculture; some are vegans, others are smokers, some like Noise music while others prefer Indie Rock; some are deejays and others play in bands; many are cokeheads; some eschew television, while others devour pop culture under the auspices of so-bad-it's-good irony. There are straight, gay, and bisexual hipsters (the term "metrosexual" is a hipster phenomenon), and black, Asian, and Hispanic hipsters too.

A hipster is someone who focuses more on being "hip" than on being "authentic," in the eyes of the speaker. What objectively defines hipsters as a cohort is, perhaps, their awareness of fashion and their feigned indifference to the tangible problems of the real world. They consume and incorporate most anything—from Reggae to Rap to Black Metal—and even if what they're consuming is produced with straight-faced sincerity, they *sort of* only *kind of* like it, ironically, anyway, so it doesn't really matter.

What's peculiar about hipsters as a cultural sub-cohort is that virtually nobody self-identifies as a "hipster" – in the same sense, and for the same reasons, as nobody likes to see themselves as a "tourist" abroad. There is a subtext of self-loathing to hipsterism; likely to do with the class-consciousness of generally "privileged" people who'd like to present as one of the "common people," at least in socioeconomic terms anyway. Hipsters often seem to "slum it" and thereby play a part in the gentrification of once-blighted urban areas, a phenomenon that they themselves malign. Accordingly, "hipster" is a largely pejorative term; and a subjective one – hipsterism is always in the eyes of the beholder.

The etymology of the term "hipster" goes back to the Beatniks, and in a roundabout way, modern hipsters are the natural terminus of the postwar prosperity that the original Beats were reacting to. If you trace postwar American counterculture from the Beats, to the Hippies, to the Punks, through the various Post-Punk splintering (Industrial Culture, Heavy Metal, Hip-Hop, Garage, Rave culture, *et cetera*), eventually—like it or not—you'll end up with all of it filtering down modern day hipsters. Hipsterism is really the apotheosis of "postmodernity."

Apart from perhaps lower-and-working-class whites known as "rednecks," "hillbillies," or "hicks," I have trouble thinking of a more reviled group in contemporary American culture than hipsters. I've used the term derogatorily myself, numerous times, over the years. Google "hipster" and you'll find all sorts of online discussion forums lambasting how lame and annoying hipsters are. The website diehipster.com describes itself as "A place to laugh at hipsters. ... You DO NOT make this city more interesting. Stop taking up space and get the fuck out of here." About a year ago, Canada's insufferably preachy, left-slanted, anti-corporate magazine *Adbusters* magazine ran a cover story titled "Hipster: The Dead End of Western Civilization." In Denver, Colorado, there's a band called Hipster Bloodbath. And so on. Americans don't tend to like "hipsters" – but their relevance in America may require looking outside America to fully understand.

Even Mexico has "first world problems" nowadays.

Not long ago, there was a brief imbroglio over the fact that so-called "Emo" culture was being met with violent reaction in Mexico. Apparently, Mexican teenagers from well-to-do families had taken to listening to Emo music, dressing in black, growing their hair out, donning black eyeliner, and generally looking just as ridiculous as their American counterparts.

Being that Mexico is generally poorer and more suffused with machismo than the United States, this kind of foppish and performative *woe-is-me* sad-sack behavior was not received well, and there were several incidents of Mexican Emo teens being publicly beaten by other Mexican teenagers (footage of which is available online). Several of my friends found this spectacle uproariously hilarious (and it is, in a way), but I think that the incursion of a subculture like Emo into Mexico is indicative of something larger. Perhaps hipsters and Emo kids are signs of socioeconomic health?

In Soviet Russia, in the 1950s, rebellious teenagers known as *Stilyagi* publicly flaunted the trappings of Western pop culture as a means of flouting Soviet sociocultural mores and norms. This was a very serious gesture at the time, in an autocratic country where members of the citizenry could be made to literally "disappear" for questioning the Soviet status quo. There is no such corresponding element of dangerousness to contemporary American hipsters. But ... is that a *bad* thing or a *good* thing?

Russian Stilyagi in the Soviet Union, 1950s.

Those on the progressive left who're critical of hipsters tend to lodge their quibbles on the grounds that hipsters are an impotent subculture; that they lack authenticity and display an absence of rebellion and nonconformity; that they are actually conformists who have embraced capitalism instead of properly railing against like the Beats, Hippies, and Punks (ostensibly) did in the past. These are the same leftist progressives who scoff at the standard (or "neoclassical") economic theory of constant growth as being (ostensibly) unsustainable; yet they also seem to demand constant "rebellion" from supposed subcultures. But why should so-called cultural or countercultural "rebellion" proceed *ad infinitum*, irrespective of the conditions in a society, any more than economic growth should? If hipsters represent the ossification of countercultural "rebellion," then maybe that's a propitious sign of sociocultural health and progress, rather than something to bemoan?

When a country is sufficiently stabilized and prosperous that its young people have the time and money to ponder Existentialism and Art; to be picky about fashion and dietary hair splitting; to toy performatively with blithe drug abuse and feigned nihilism; to amass collections of eclectic vintage vinyl phonograph records ... that country is doing *pretty fucking good*. Maybe hipsters are a hallmark of socioeconomic health, rather than a death knell signaling the looming nadir of a Western Civilization as *Adbusters* would have us believe?

In Iran, for example, recalcitrant young people advocating for democracy in (visible, public terms) risk death and imprisonment in the process. In the favelas of Brazil and the barrios of Colombia, young people blast at each other with handguns over drug turf. In Iraq and Afghanistan, young people can't even count on the fact that they'll have a stabilized government in the next few years. In still-troubled parts of Africa like Liberia, Congo, and Somalia (recently dubbed "The worst country on Earth" by *The Economist*), young people face governmental and tribal violence, and struggle with the basic necessities of life. In kleptocratic North Korea, young people seem to have forgotten what "rebellion" even *is* at this point. And so on.

So, when Americans cavil and bitch about how harrying hipsters are, I think they maybe suffer from a paucity of perspective, to say the least. Hipsters are utterly anodyne. You don't see hipster gang brawls. Cabals of hipster smash-n-grab crime rings don't make the news. Hipster drive-by shootings are not subjects of handwringing concern. Yes, hipsters are obnoxious. They're *young*, and that's what young people are supposed to be – obnoxious. Let them have their stupid clothes, ill-conceived tattoos, cheap beer,

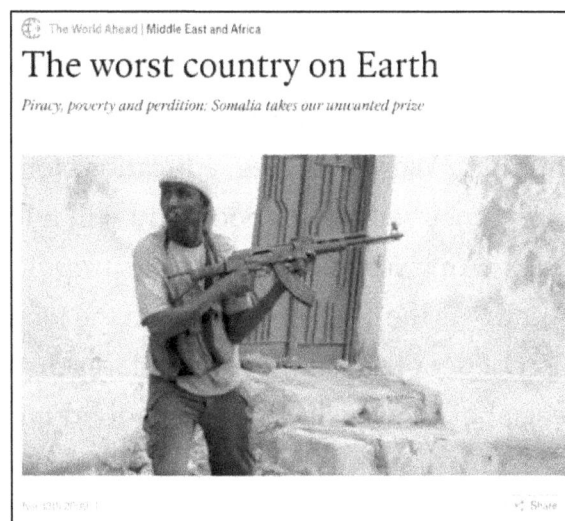

Apparently, the Somali Electroclash scene is weak.

overpriced cocaine, and ironic retro dance parties. They aren't bothering anybody; at least not tangibly. Like every other generation of American postwar young'ns they're just trying to have a good time, and they don't give a fuck about all the stuff that you deem important. And the fact that they *have* that luxury is one of the reasons that America is a pretty decent place to live, in the grand scheme of things.

I think that maybe Americans have a guilty conscience about their own prosperity in the context of perturbing factoids like the cross-country comparisons above. We live in one of the richest countries in the world. Even the poorest of our poor still have luxuries which are unavailable to an appallingly large percentage of the world's population: clean drinking water, access to emergency healthcare, immunizations against communicable diseases, a functioning infrastructure, a reliable power grid, civil rights, and so on.

Thank God Bangladesh hasn't been fuckin' gentrified, yet.

According to the World Health Organization, 1.5 million children under age five die annually of (preventable) diarrhea globally. That is to say, *one-and-a-half million* toddlers literally shit themselves to death yearly; dying of dehydration because they don't have access to basic stuff like Pedialyte or whatever. That is *fucking crazy*. Maybe it puts things in perspective? Homeless people in America certainly have it rough—yes—but there are no bloodthirsty tribal warlords here. People don't often go blind as a result of malnutrition. Children don't typically die of starvation or shit themselves to death in large numbers for lack of immunization. There may be rare exceptions, but there is no systemic comparison between American woes and those of, say, Somalia. Anyone, even someone who lives in a shack, can walk into any library in any town and have free access to books and the Internet. We have free education for citizens' formative years, and basic medical and emergency services to boot. You will not find such things in a great many parts of the world.

Americans consume a disproportionate share of the world's resources. The American military is the biggest and best in the world. And even with our new brown-skinned president, a lot of people in a lot of other places do not like us very much. How Americans feel, or should feel, about this collectively or individually is far beyond the purview of this essay, but the fact of the matter is that the majority of Americans are, at least on some subconscious level, aware of these facts. And they may feel sort of shitty about it, but not really shitty enough to do anything tangible about it; because the scope of such problems is far too vast for anyone to realistically do anything about them anyway. But still ... that gnawing pang of guilt remains. So what do most Americans then do? Find someone richer, more spoiled, more contentiously indifferent, and annoyingly coy about it than they are. Hipsters fit this role perfectly, and that's likely part of why everyone loves to loathe them. Hipsters represent the apogee of how spoiled, entitled, and irritating Americans are in general. Accordingly, hipsters are a suitable scapegoat for Americans generally. They are, in this sense, the "Americans" of America. N' God bless 'em for it.

Boozing With the Band

An Interview with Matt Skiba

2006

Matt Skiba is an American musician, singer, and songwriter, best known as the co-lead vocalist and guitarist of the Punk band Alkaline Trio. Skiba has also recorded albums and performed with side projects including: TheHELL, Lektron, Blink 182, and Heavens; as well as with his backing band, the Sekrets. Apart from music, Skiba is also an avocational visual artist of some note, having exhibited his paintings at galleries throughout the United States, and running his own clothing line, Skiba Clothing. Skiba was interviewed via email for *Modern Drunkard*.

Brian M. Clark: Your first drink – what was it and how did it treat you?

Matt Skiba: Old Style beer; I took a sip off of my dad's 12 oz. can while he was on the phone. I was five or six at the time, but it was the dawning of what would be a long-lasting relationship. I remember it tasting different than I had expected it to, but it was a taste I would grow to love (for a good ten years straight), and I still drink it whenever I go back to Chicago.

BMC: What's your favorite drink?

MS: Bloody Marys in the morning, Blue Hawaiians in the evening.

BMC: Do you have a favorite drinking song?

MS: "Straight Edge" by Minor Threat.

BMC: *Hah.* Do you drink every day?

MS: On tour, I usually just drink when we have a day off the next day (or if we're in Denver). When I'm off I drink pretty much every day. So technically, I guess my answer is, "no."

BMC: Any noteworthy drinking stories while on tour in strange lands with Alkaline Trio?

MS: There is an abundance of drunken Alkaline Trio tour stories, but there's one in particular that always sticks out in my mind, as I still have physical proof burned into my body. ... It was the Summer of 1999 in New Orleans, Louisiana. We were in the middle of a sweltering five-week tour of the U.S. and Canada with a band of fellow Chicagoans called The Blue Meanies. Certain members of their group and certain members of our group (myself included) had, at that point in the tour, developed notorious reputations for getting each other in tremendous amounts of trouble. This "trouble" was absolutely, positively a direct result of excessive alcohol abuse. Much like many other tours in that era of our career, we got completely fucked up every night.

We played just outside of the city in the town of Metairie, and had a show booked in St. Charles the following night, which made for a short drive the next day. We'd decided long before this particular night that we would spend the time between our two Louisiana shows "fuckin' shit up, college style!" in New Orleans.

We were in our vans before we were done playing the last notes of our respective sets, and it seemed that we couldn't get into the city early enough to start the festivities, even though we had already been drinking Miller High Life (in cans) steadily for hours. After the show, we rolled into the city and parked our vans in a public lot just inside the French Quarter section of town. We jumped

Matt Skiba, grumpy in Cleveland.

out of the vans, and us "troublemakers" reunited and vanished into the New Orleans night with warm beers tightly clenched in our fists.

We spent the entire night drunkenly roaming the streets of New Orleans, with the occasional break for "a beer and something to drink" or a lap dance. At one point late in the evening, I remember holding Chas up as he simultaneously pissed and vomited all over himself. We ended up passing out sometime in the early morning hours on some rocks on the shore of the Gulf Coast. Somehow, in my inebriated state, I had the good sense to cover my face with my jacket to avoid getting sunburned. Unfortunately, I removed the jacket from my face in my deep, drunken sleep, leaving my entire head, both arms, and a small portion of my lower mid-section exposed.

I awoke the next early afternoon to a vomit-and-piss-stained Chas berating some "crusty punks" that were camped out on the rocks next to us. "Fucking crusty motherfuckers! I fucking *hate* crusties!" screamed Chas. He then saw a sign attached to a cart advertising Jell-O shots and immediately ran towards it screaming, "*Jelllllo shotssssss!*" Needless to say, I felt like a white raisin soaked in alcohol. Ignoring the "crusties," I slowly got up and followed Chas to the cart for "breakfast."

It wasn't until later that afternoon that I started to realize that I had cooked almost a quarter of the skin off of my body. My entire face started to swell and blister at the same time. I could no longer wear sleeves as it was excruciating to have cloth touch my skin, and the small area of my belly that was left open to the sun felt as if someone had deeply cut me with a scalpel in my sleep. In retrospect, I should've checked myself into the burn victim's ward of a New Orleans area hospital.

The amount of pain I was in was pale in comparison to the atrocity that was my appearance. The looks on people's faces when I entered a room were ones I wouldn't see again until the September 11th attacks on the World Trade Center. ...

We made it to our next show with plenty of time to spare. I stayed in the van trying to drink water (as my esophagus was swollen almost entirely shut) and hiding in shame my appearance. After what seemed like an eternity, I sheepishly made my way into the venue to prepare for the show. I played almost the entire show with my back to the crowd. When I attempted to sing, it sounded like I'd snorted a line of cleanser and washed it back with hydrochloric acid prior to our set.

After the show one of my tour mates, Jerry, suggested I use a diaper rash cream he had with him to soothe my pain (why he had diaper rash cream with him remains a mystery to this day). At that point I was willing to try anything. We went back to the motel and I started to apply the oil-based cream to my wounded face. It felt good at first, but as I continued to apply the thick, white cream the blisters started coming off of my face and began to bleed profusely. Of course I was half in-the-bag once again, and in an effort to make light of the situation I left a negative image of Gene Simmons' "Demon" eye make-up around my eyes with

the dark, sunburned and bleeding skin exposed in lieu of black greasepaint. I passed out with the ointment on my face and wouldn't attempt to remove it again until several days later.

The sunburn took more than a month to heal, and if you look closely you can still see a thin line of "tan" skin stretching across my belly.

Skiba playing with Alkaline Trio at The Warped Tour.

BMC: *Wow. ...* You may have already answered my next question, but here it is anyway: What would you say was your worst, most retardedly regrettable experience with alcohol?

MS: If not the New Orleans incident, I would have to say the time I stayed up all night drinking with my friend Chuck. We were on a U.S. tour together heading down the West coast. We played a show in San Francisco and had an all-nighter to San Diego. There were some people in San Diego that I thought we were going to see that I had a beef with. Since it had been a while since I had been in a fight, and since I was extremely intoxicated, I decided it would be a good idea for Chuck (6', 220 lbs. of muscle) to punch me (6'2", 160 lbs. of cheap beer) as hard as he could in the face. Needless to say, I went down like a sack of potatoes. The long and short of it was we ended up punching/wrestling each other out into the middle of Highway 5 with traffic whizzing by in the far lane. The next day—still awake and drinking—we arrived in San Diego and pulled up to the venue. In bare feet, I jumped out of the bus with my skateboard in hand and proceeded to bomb a nearby hill into the small crowd of people waiting to get into the show. I hit the group head-on, but was the only one bleeding when we all got up. I was forced by my bandmates to "take a time-out." The guys I had my 'beef' with must have not known about it and never showed up. The show that night was the worst I've ever played in my ten years of touring. It was even worse than St. Charles I'm pretty sure.

BMC: Why is alcohol better than drugs?

MS: Alcohol is better than drugs because it's something (if you're good at it) you can ingest a lot of. With most drugs, you will reach your limit much quicker. Alcohol works better if you're socializing, as well. A round of drinks is better for good conversation than a pile of blow. A pile of blow just makes people try to talk over each other rather than with each other.

Alcohol is better than drugs because you have options. If you take a hit of ecstasy, you're most likely going to be on ecstasy for the rest of the night. If you're doing cocaine

it's probably not a mixed bag. If you get bored with what you're drinking, you can always switch it up in the next round. That "beer before liquor" shit is for weekend-warriors and pussies.

Alcohol tastes better and is more fun to do. You can go out to "get a drink." You don't go out to "do some drugs." I don't anyway.

BMC: I understand that you're a fan of Absinthe. What makes absinthe more appealing to you than the other varieties of booze, and what are your thoughts on its illegality?

MS: I do enjoy absinthe quite a bit. It started when we began touring Europe several years ago. At first, I didn't really know the difference between quality absinthe and that garbage they try and pass off on dumb tourists like myself at the time, but after a certain amount of experience and research I feel a bit more knowledgeable.

Initially, it was the taboo of absinthe that was appealing, but when I started to realize the difference in taste and effect is when I feel I actually understood its true purpose. There was a time when absinthe was regarded as a high-class spirit, and when you drink good absinthe you understand why – mostly because it's really expensive. As far as commercial absinthe is

Skiba drinking on the job.

concerned, Edouard from France is widely recognized as top-notch among absintheurs and is one of my favorites. It has an extremely high thujone content and is as smooth and tasty as hell.

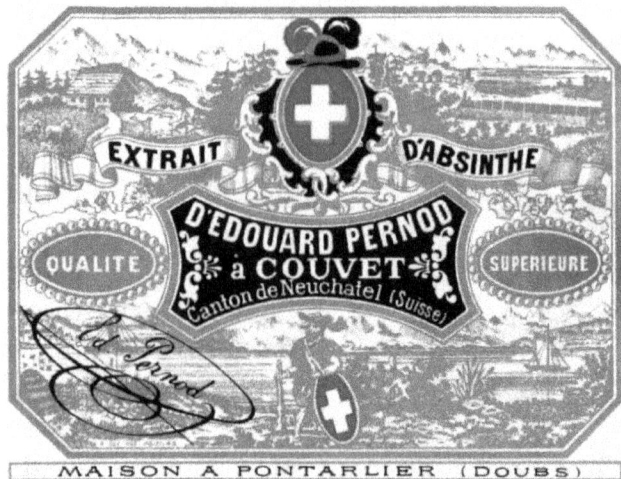

The ritual involved is also very appealing. The Alkaline Trio never go on tour anymore without our fountain glasses and French sugar cubes, made specially for use with absinthe.

BMC: What's the best country to drink in?

MS: I would have to say Japan. When I first went over there years ago, you could buy beer from vending machines on the street. It was perfectly legal to waltz around the city with an open container in your fist. The last time I went into a bar in Osaka, everyone in there told me I looked like Tom Hanks and bought me drinks so that they could laugh at me freely. I don't think that would happen in any other country.

BMC: What's your favorite bar, where is it, and what makes it special?

MS: The Owl Tree at Post and Taylor streets in San Francisco. The sign on the inside of the bar reads "Bobby's Owl Tree" and is owned and operated by a gentleman in his

eighties who tends the bar in traditional white shirt/black bow-tie barkeep attire. The entire inside of the bar is covered in all things owl. Taxidermy, paintings, stained-glass, light fixtures, *et cetera*. It's very dimly lit and 45s of Johnny Cash or Billie Holiday are usually playing softly on the old-school jukebox. It has a very classic, warm feeling to it, especially on a cold and rainy San Francisco night. Bobby cracks jokes and drinks alongside the clientele, which usually consists of a mellow, enlightened drinking crowd. It never gets too crowded and although it's mellow, it's very happening.

The Owl Tree in San Francisco, California.

BMC: Who, in your estimation, were some of history's greatest drunkards, and why?

MS: I've read that Abraham Lincoln was a big drinker. I'm not sure how "great" he was, but I remember reading a quote of his that said something about how drunks are generally more romantic and creative people. Benjamin Franklin was supposedly a lush, which makes me think much more highly of him than I did back in school. Frank Sinatra was great at drinking while maintaining an immense amount of style. He once said, "I feel sorry for people who don't drink. When they wake up in the morning, that's as good as they're going to feel all day.

Those Of Heightened Consciousness

2004

The other night I was drinking and smoking in the dark corner of a local Denver bar, watching a handful of jock-ish guys play pool, drink beer, laugh, and yell; while a chubby, homely, and very plain looking girl sat on a stool playing some of the darkest elegiac dirges I've ever heard, on an acoustic guitar. I really enjoyed her music—it was just really well-written, melancholic, and gloomy singer-songwriter compositions, that would put The Angles of Light and Two Dollar Guitar to shame—and she sang "mellifluously." Perhaps unsurprisingly, everyone in the bar was totally ignoring her, and the guys in question were actually making it difficult to even *hear* her in the first place. I presume that she went home later that evening, deflated and defeated. Maybe I should have said something to her. Complimented her, I don't know. But I didn't. I was minding my own business, drinking and smoking.

The experience got me to thinking though; that it's a shame, a real damned disgrace, that often the most intelligent and creative people are usually also the most shy, asocial, and insecure. I imagine it's because they have the intellectual faculties to be aware of (and hypersensitive to) their own flaws and faults – while often the least intelligent, creative, and talented (the most commonplace) of people are usually the most confident, outgoing, and secure. Riding roughshod over those around them. Presumably because they aren't the slightest bit introspective, and therefore overlook their own, numerous, shortcomings.

I suppose it's the reason that someone like John Kennedy Toole can write a Pulitzer Prize-winning novel, *A Confederacy of Dunces*, leave it unpublished in a trunk in his attic for decades, then commit suicide – remaining unknown and unpublished, until his mother one day discovers the text and has the good sense to send it off to a publisher ... yet there are scores upon scores of unremarkable pedestrian morons, who are just *so* uncomplicatedly sure of themselves, and of how much they deserve to be famous, that they'll appear on television programs like *American Idol*, sing in the most gratingly off-key falsettos imaginable, and then become aghast and offended when they get cut from the show – because they're totally oblivious to just how shitty they really *are*. It's a shame. But then, on the other hand, as Fyodor Dostoevsky put it in his 1864 novella *Notes from Underground*:

> Such a direct, simple man is the true, normal human being, the kind of human being that tender mother nature herself had hoped to see when she was lovingly creating him on earth. I envy such a man to the point of loathing. He is stupid, I admit, but perhaps a normal man should be stupid, how do we know? Perhaps it's even very beautiful that way. And what particularly confirms me in this—if I may call it so—suspicion, is that if you take, for example, the antithesis of the normal man, that is, a man of heightened consciousness ... this retort-man often gives up so completely in the face of his antithesis that he honestly feels himself, with all his heightened consciousness, to be a mouse, not a man ... And the main thing, again, is that it's he, he himself, who considers himself a mouse; nobody else asks him to, and that is the important point.

God Bless The Service Industry

2010

I once had a customer complain to me that my bar's ice was too small. In his view, the drinks were fine, the music was fine, and the ambiance of the bar was fine – but he took umbrage with the size of the ice cubes that I was using in the cocktails. As he was kind enough to educate me, larger cubes have less surface area and don't dilute the drinks as rapidly, so by using small cubes and charging full price for craft cocktails, I was "ripping off" customers. Very edifying, that accusation.

Of course, I hadn't stopped to reflect on that idea like he had, because I was obviously just a knuckle-dragging lunkhead bartender with only a rudimentary layman's grasp of fluid dynamics, unlike him. It sure was a good thing that he deigned to enlighten me on the subject though, because, as a person who made less than minimum wage and worked for tips, I had a *tremendous* amount of sway when it came to the bar owner's ice-machine purchasing decisions.

Naturally, I dutifully brought the matter to the proprietor's attention at the first opportunity, following which the offending ice machine was promptly disposed of and replaced by a new one that produces larger ice cubes, at a cost of several thousand dollars to the bar. The customer is always right, after all.

Customer service is priority number one.

Fuck You and Your Stupid, *Stupid* Cat

Toxoplasmosis and The Selfishness of Pet Ownership

2009

Like many American kids, I grew up with the typical American house pets—a cat and a dog—and I loved them. Back in the mid-to-late 1980s, Scruffy, my family's diminutive, gray-haired German schnauzer, slept at the foot of my bed every single night, well into my adolescent years. Mittens, our tabby cat, wiled away many a quiescent Sunday afternoon atop my stomach while I supinely pored over comic books or played video games on my (then-state-of-the-art) Nintendo gaming system. Not unlike an '80s version of a corny, impossibly idyllic Norman Rockwell painting, I have many fond—I daresay picturesque—childhood memories of time spent with both my cat and my dog.

The author with his cat, 1987.

But that was a long time ago, and things have changed. As an increasingly crotchety adult, I've come to pretty much detest the domesticated cats and dogs so typically cohabitated with by my fellow Americans. Whether they're knocking over my drink at a cocktail party, trying to hump my leg at a friend's house, meowing incessantly outside my bedroom window in the middle of the night, or viciously barking at me from the passenger seat of a redneck's pickup truck; I simply can't fucking stand most of them, most of the time. Increasingly, to me, the term "house pet" seems like it ought to be an oxymoron, because as I see it, animals don't belong inside our houses. It's not that I necessarily have anything "against" animals *per se*—because I don't—it's just that, to my mind, most of them belong either in the wild, in a zoo, or in a university lab somewhere.

Jeeze Louise – why the sourpussed change of heart, Mr. Grumpypants?

138

Well, since you asked; by the time I was a teenager the initial novelty of my own family's cat and dog had long since worn off, and I'd come to appreciate the innumerable downsides to cohabitation with four-legged housemates; like our dog's predilection for depositing runny-yet-gritty diarrhea all over the white living room carpet (which was often my duty to clean up). Or the instances in which I'd wake up in the middle of the night, sleepily shuffle (in the dark) to the fridge for a glass of water, and bare-footedly step in a steaming pool of feculent, chunk-laden cat vomit. By my mid-teens, having thoroughly tired of the acerbic scent of cat urine, as well as of having my personal effects mangled canine-style, I couldn't help but begin to ponder, *Why the hell are my family and I living, 24-7, with these disgusting animals?* And I still don't really get it.

As an adult, willful cohabitation with animals now seems to me like an expensive, time-consuming, unhygienic act of emotionally needy *masochism*. Because—I'm sorry—but I don't care how cute n' cuddly they may be, domesticated dogs and cats are absolutely fucking filthy creatures. They alternately piss, shit, slobber, vomit and shed everywhere. They not only bring fleas, ticks, and mites into their living spaces, but also often destroy furniture, blinds, carpets, and belongings in general. They incessantly annoy houseguests by variously scratching, biting, barking, or sexually assaulting unsuspecting limbs; and if all that weren't already enough, they even surreptitiously assail the hapless allergy suffer whose sinuses are pained by their mere *presence*. Bearing all of this in mind, I'm at a loss to see why such creatures are all-but-universally deemed reasonable housemates for civilized human beings; and by forcing the rest of us to habitually *deal* with their pain-in-the-ass pets, pet-owners are essentially a bunch of selfish, inconsiderate, oblivious dickheads. Moreover—as I will argue in the following paragraphs—the national exuberance for pet-ownership can be pretty easily shown as having some seriously deleterious effects on society at large.

In spite of all of the aforementioned ickiness that comes with pet-ownership, droves—legions—of Americans dump substantial amounts of time, money, and energy into feeding, housing, vaccinating, spaying/neutering, grooming, bathing, medicating, playing with, and otherwise taking care of millions of domesticated animals. A great many such pet-owners view their furry companions as literal "members of the family" and beam with pride over their quadrupedal faux-kin. The ever-snowballing American mania for animals is just that – a form of *mania*, which often enough strays into the realm of near-madness. For instance, I know a girl who recently dropped thousands of dollars on a series of corrective knee surgeries for her pet chihuahua, rather than just putting the poor fucker down and getting another one for free. To me, that seems downright nuts (what's the difference; a chihuahua is a fucking chihuahua, no?), but the fact of the matter is that she is far from alone in her alacrity to shell-out bushels of real cash on a pet. And I imagine that many, if not most, pet owners would probably do likewise.

Which brings me to the subject of the subconscious masochism inherent in pet-ownership. Witnessing a dog owner dutifully following around his pooch with little plastic baggies, picking up Fido's droppings, only to then return home to feed, groom, and otherwise accommodate the freeloading canine's needs, one can't help but wonder just who *owns* whom in such a scenario. ...

Most pet owners would be profoundly insulted by the suggestion that they deign to pick up the bodily waste of their best friends and family members, yet they unhesitatingly play the role of pooper-scooper for their sub-human pets, and get nothing but brainless smiles in return. And so, I ask, is this kind of behavior so often displayed by pet-owners somehow *not* an act of willful masochism, if only subconsciously? It sure as fuck looks like it to me.

Considering this and other innumerable examples of people bending over backwards and oftentimes rearranging their entire lives to accommodate the needs of their pets (not getting a particular no-pets-allowed apartment, for example), I can't help but see most pet-owners as emotionally-impoverished people whose lives are so bereft of real human affection that they seek it out from dumb, high-maintenance sub-humans. The fact that pet-owners consistently seem to view their cognitively deficient non-human pals with the same sort of sentimental attachment that a normal person might assign to other human beings is, well, just *weird* to me. I'd even go so far as to say that it's a veiled sort of closeted defense-mechanism-misanthropy employed by those incapable or unwilling to have healthy relationships with other human beings (*People suck, but at least my doggie still loves me!*).

Underlying this zoophilic defense-mechanism-misanthropy is the assumption on the part of pet-owners that—although people have the capacity to knowingly behave like rotten bastards—animals are somehow innately innocent. This is preposterous. Having at best only the rudiments of infantile intelligence, animals can't be "innocent" or "guilty" of anything – animals exist in an amoral reality to which such distinctions of relative culpability simply do not apply. A cat that kills a mouse isn't "guilty" of rodenticide any more than its distant relative, the lion, is "guilty" of hunting and eating a gazelle – they're just animals, doing what animals do; and that's fine. The other side to this coin, however, is the fact that this doesn't necessarily make them "innocent" either. When a junkyard dog gets loose from some low-rent hovel and rips a neighborhood toddler to shreds, it's not really "guilty" or "innocent" of anything – it's a semi-domesticated descendent of wolves, just doing what Loving Mother Nature intended such feral creatures to do; kill and eat pudgy helpless little things like toddlers. We can hardly blame junkyard dogs for such behavior; after all, they're just being dogs, doing what dogs do. Blame instead lies with the responsible party—the douchebag pet-owner who keeps such an animal in an urban or suburban environment in the first place—and really, that rule ought to apply to all sundry pet-related mishaps; whether it's a dog biting a stranger or a cat pissing on a housemates belongings – in every case, it isn't the animal's fault, but the pet-owner who's to blame. But, of course, it's rare to see pet-owners take any real, substantive responsibility for such all-too-common occurrences – because pet-owners are, by and large, thoughtless, oblivious assholes.

In rebuttal to such insensitive conjecture by rude, presumptuous, over-generalizing jerkoffs like me, dog and cat lovers (and my god there are a fuck of a lot of them) often insist that *their* dog or cat is well-behaved, quiet, clean, (*et cetera*), and the gravamen of my general criticisms of house pets are inapplicable to *their* particular pet. Perhaps. I'm certainly willing to concede that there are exceptions to every rule—sure—but I still want nothing to do with your filthy animal any more than a recovering alcoholic wants to hang out in a bar.

Of course, to buttress and justify their need for sub-human companionship, pet-owners will often cite studies indicating that their kind by-and-large outlive non-zoophiles like myself by a few years. In answer to this argumentative *non sequitur*, I say, *Yeah, so what?* Similar studies indicate that the religious are by-and-large happier and more fulfilled in life than the nonreligious – but does that provide evidence for the existence of God? Nope, it's just another indicator that people generally prefer comforting delusion to unpleasant truth. Likewise—I'm sorry—but a small increase in lifespan isn't much of an argument for supporting the idea that human beings should be intimately cohabitating with germ-infested creatures that clean their hairy, distended wieners and protruding poop-chutes with *their own tongues*.

But let's put all that aside. Never mind the inescapable yuckiness of butt-licking house pets and my personal aversion to them; let's transcend such petty subjective considerations and briefly consider the socioeconomic side of American pet-ownership on a grand scale. The growing pet food industry alone is a multibillion-dollar business in the United States (that's *billion*, with a B). If one excludes all the other money spent on domesticated animals (veterinary services, animal control services, animal shelters, pet toys, pet books, kitty litter, dog houses, corrective chihuahua knee-surgeries, *et cetera*), and only considers pet food—just what the fuckers eat, that's it—that still means that Americans on average spend more on dog n' kitty chow annually than they do on _____ (oh, *anything* can fit in that blank, because almost *anything* has more social import than house pets). Billions of dollars are certainly enough to feed a lot of homeless people. Or insure a lot of poor people. Or send a lot of kids to college. Or fund cancer research. Or fund NASA. Or fund alternative energy research. Or fund *anything* more important and socially relevant than the primped-and-preened daily maintenance of millions of stupid, useless, shitting, pissing, shedding, clawing, vomiting, farting, barking, biting, hairball-coughing-up animals.

Of course, I jest and exaggerate a bit—animals aren't "stupid," they're just "dumb friends"—and I apologize if I've hurt your tender feelings, you needy, maladjusted, affection-starved pet-lover. But, in all seriousness, I write this today, because I recently listened to an episode of *Scientific American* magazine's SciAm podcast, through which I was informed of yet another reason (as if my own personal distaste weren't already enough) why it's utterly fucking dumb to cohabitate with domesticated animals (specifically cats, in this instance): Toxoplasmosis.

You can go ahead and lazily look it up on Wikipedia like I did, but basically here's the gist: Toxoplasmosis is a surprisingly common yet widely ignored ailment caused by an intracellular protozoal parasite called *Toxoplasma gondii*, which is related to the malaria bug. The parasite is capable of infecting most mammals and, like Salmonella, can be contracted from improperly cleaned or undercooked food; but, unlike Salmonella, it is transmitted to humans typically by way of common housecats. Yep, that's right, cuddley-wuddley widdle housecats. As Wikipedia explains, human contraction of the parasite occurs through "ingestion of contaminated cat faeces … through hand-to-mouth contact following gardening, cleaning a cat's litter box, contact with children's sandpits, or touching anything that has come into contact with cat faeces." Which is to say, if you've ever inhaled the airborne poop-dust from a cat's litter box, or played in a sandbox-turned-cat-toilet as a kid—sorry—but you may well be infected with Toxoplasmosis.

In the half-assed, surface-scratching online research that I did on the lovely little *Toxoplasma gondii* parasite, the most alarmist estimation I came across regarding its proliferation in the United States is that roughly half of Americans are infected. Another source gave the figure forty percent. And another quoted thirty percent. Still another dropped its estimate to one quarter of Americans. The most conservative estimation I came across was a rather modest ten percent. In all likelihood, it's probably higher than that, but I'll be conservative and assume it's closest to the latter – one in ten Americans has Toxoplasmosis. Which still means that, at minimum, one in ten people in this country literally has parasitic cat-shit-bugs infesting their brain. Because, you see, that's what Toxoplasmosis literally is; *a fucking brain parasite you get from cat shit.*

Delightful, no?

The way that this totally-uncool-bullshit-in-an-adorably-huggable-package goes down, is like this; the *Toxoplasma gondii* parasite gets into one's system, then up into the gray matter betwixt one's ears, and then creates cysts in the brain which produce an enzyme called tyrosine hydroxylase, which then affects the production and reception of the mood-regulating chemical dopamine. And what's so utterly charming about this parasite is not only its apparent ubiquity (ten-to-fifty percent of the American population as unwitting carriers), but also the sheer ambiguity and subtlety of the symptoms it produces. Essentially, the devious little

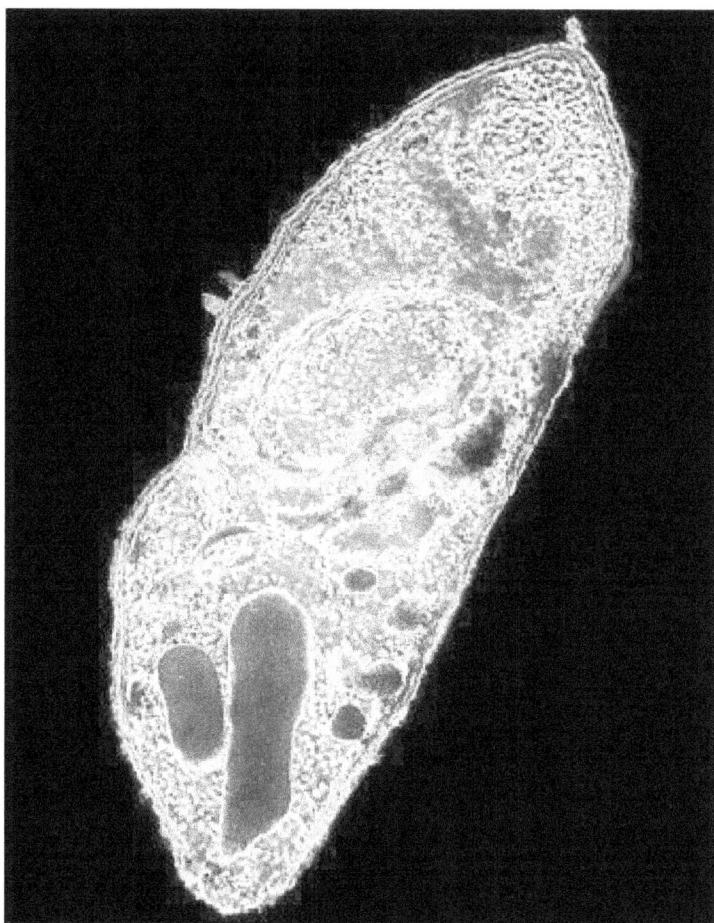

The endearingly cute Toxoplasma Gondii parasite in profile.

skull-fuck buggers nestle up inside your noggin, fiddle 'round with the chemicals in your brain and then (here's the kicker) they don't make you physiologically ill or kill you outright, but instead faintly—indistinctly—affect the way you *behave*. Creepy, no?

The real-world effects of Toxoplasmosis are difficult to determine exactly, since it'd be woefully unethical to knowingly infect people with the bug and then test them afterward to determine subsequent changes in their behavior – and thus it's hard to get a straightforward and unambiguous answer on the subject. Rooting around the web, I came across several conflicting takes as to how seriously the public should be taking this issue. For instance, Joanne Webster (a biologist who studies *Toxoplasma gondii* at the University of Oxford) assured the United Kingdom's *The Guardian* newspaper back in 2003 that for "the vast majority, 99% of people or above, the results [of infection] will be very subtle." Unfortunately, reassuring though it may be, her statement is flatly contradicted by other sources, such as a ScienceDaily.com piece from March of this year, in which the author explains, "The [*Toxoplasma gondii*] parasite may play a role in the development of [mental] disorders by affecting the production of dopamine. ... Dopamine's role in mood, sociability, attention, motivation and sleep patterns are well documented and schizophrenia has long been associated with dopamine, which is the target of all schizophrenia drugs on the market." Said article goes on to quote the unfortunately-surnamed Dr. Glenn McConkey (lead researcher on a team from the United Kingdom's University of Leeds' Faculty of Biological Sciences) who explicates therein:

> Toxoplasmosis changes some of the chemical messages in the brain, and these changes can have an **enormous effect** on behaviour. Studies have shown there is a direct statistical link between incidences of schizophrenia and toxoplasmosis infection. ... [T]oxoplasmosis infection—which is more common than you might think—can impact on the development of the condition in some individuals. (emphasis added)

Wait ... *schizophrenia?* Oh, yes, *fucking schizophrenia.*

Granted, the effects of Toxoplasmosis on human behavior are subtle and not terribly easy to measure—so clearly there's no reason to fret n' fuss about infected people becoming walking cat-shit-brain-parasite zombies—but this isn't to say that the parasite's effects are by any means negligible, either. The 2003 *Guardian* article goes on to report the following:

> Results from studies of students and conscript soldiers in the Czech Republic in the mid-1990s highlighted the fact that infected people showed different personality traits to non-infected people – and that the differences depended on sex. Infected men were more likely to be aggressive, jealous and suspicious, while women became more outgoing and showed signs of higher intelligence.

One of the Czech researchers quoted in this article, Jaroslav Flegr (professor of parasitology involved in research at Charles University in Prague), apparently takes the subject seriously enough, especially when it comes to the effect

Eleanor Abernathy, the paradigmatic "Crazy Cat Lady."

144

that Toxoplasmosis allegedly has in slowing down infected persons' reaction times with regard to driving. Flegr even goes so far as to say that car accidents resulting from Toxoplasmosis infections have resulted in a not-so-insignificant death toll. "If our data are true then about a million people a year die just because they are infected with toxoplasma." User-edited (and thus not entirely reliable) Wikipedia corroborates Flegr's statement, saying:

> Studies have found that toxoplasmosis is associated with an increased car accident rate, roughly doubling or tripling the chance of an accident relative to uninfected people. This may be due to the slowed reaction times that are associated with infection. ... There are claims of toxoplasma causing antisocial attitudes in men and promiscuity in women, and greater susceptibility to schizophrenia and bipolar disorder in all infected persons. ... The possibility that toxoplasmosis is one cause of schizophrenia has been studied by scientists since at least 1953. These studies had attracted little attention from U.S. researchers until they were publicized through the work of prominent psychiatrist and advocate E. Fuller Torrey. In 2003, Torrey published a review of this literature, reporting that almost all the studies had found that schizophrenics have elevated rates of toxoplasma infection.

Ya' know ... every couple of decades or so, a few people get killed in a spate of shark-attack incidents that happen to occur in roughly the same coastal area, in a relatively short timeframe – and the mainstream American media goes into an hysterical fear-mongering frenzy over it, with screaming headlines about shark attack "epidemics" (remember "The Summer Of The Shark"?). Yet, according to researchers, possibly as many as *a fucking million people a year* die as a result of infection from cat-shit-brain-parasites, and nobody in the mainstream media makes nary a goddamned peep. Aside from one 2003 British newspaper article and some field-specific veterinary journals, the issue simply hasn't been on the public's radar at all. Why isn't this a major public health issue that we've all had hammered into our heads since preschool? Because cats are cute, millions of people own and love them, and they don't make for convenient scapegoats like sharks, wolves, spiders, and snakes do. Which, frankly, is downright retarded as fuck, America.

But you pussy-cat-lovers—excuse me, you *cat-loving-pussies*—are skeptical, I know. You adore little Mittens, and you want proof—*irrefutable proof, damn it!*—that I'm not just using this whole Toxoplasmosis thing to rationalize my own obviously tendentious dislike of your beloved pet, and thereby engaging in some of my own baseless fearmongering to suit my personal curmudgeonly ends. Maybe you don't trust user-edited Wikipedia, and heck, who knows if *The Guardian* got it right back in '03? Maybe you think I'm just being a big meanie-pants, animal-hating killjoy, and I'm cherry-picking the most menacing-sounding of quotes from a smattering of articles I found in two seconds on Google. Fine—*touché*—that may all very well indeed be the case. But you can't well plausibly argue with august sources like *Scientific American*, which stated earlier this year that, "In immunosuppressed people, the [Toxoplasmosis] infection can change the brain's levels of dopamine which means a link to Parkinson's, Tourette's, ADD and bipolar disorder in addition to schizophrenia." Moreover, you pussy-whipped sissies certainly wouldn't have the balls to call into question the assessments of ponderous academic, peer-reviewed scientific journals, now would you? And as it so happens, the most damning exposal of how utterly fucking lame your stupid cat is, comes by way of Dr. Milton M. McAllister (professor of pathobiology in the College of Veterinary Medicine at the University of Illinois at Urbana-Champaign), in a 2005 piece published in the journal *Veterinary Parasitology*. Being a dry, medical-literature type thing, I really only had the patience to read through McAllister's introductory abstract, wherein I nevertheless found the following cat-strangulatingly-delightful vindication of my growing animus towards your stupid, *stupid* cat:

> One of the most compelling topics to emerge from the last decade of veterinary protozoology is disease caused by a zoonotic pathogen, *Toxoplasma gondii*, in otherwise healthy people. These findings may catch the health professions by surprise. ... [N]umerous reports in the last decade associate toxoplasmosis with lymphadenopathy, fever, weakness and debilitation, ophthalmitis, and severe multisystemic infections in people who **do not** have immunosuppressive conditions. (emphasis added) ...
>
> Mental aberrations are coming to light in humans; recent studies associate *T. gondii* infection with personality shifts and increased likelihood of reduced intelligence or schizophrenia. These conditions reduce the quality of life of individuals, and may exact a significant economic burden upon society. ... Public health policies should prohibit the practice of allowing pet cats to roam. Organizations and individuals that feed feral cats are unwittingly contributing to the dissemination of *T. gondii*, by sustaining artificially dense populations of a definitive host of this protozoal parasite.

If that weren't kitten-stompingly authoritative enough, Dr. McAllister is quoted elsewhere as saying:

> Our profession needs to come to grip with the accumulating body of evidence about the tremendous burden wrought on society by toxoplasmosis. ... Further research is needed to clarify the association between toxoplasmosis and mental health, but until such time that this association may be refuted, it is my opinion that **the current evidence is strong enough to warrant an assumption of validity**. (emphasis added)

So, there you have it, folks. *Fuck* your stupid, *stupid* cat. Seriously.

While I'm sitting here astride my High Horse of Self-Righteous Reproach—for dramatic effect—allow me to make a brief comparison, if I may, to further illustrate just how inconsiderate and selfish you cat-lovers are:

Ahem.

Cigarettes are a frivolous expense on which Americans waste billions of dollars annually. They shorten lifespans and provide little besides a temporary nicotine fix – they make people *feel better*. Even though they've been demonstrably proven to cause cancer, people still knowingly spend money on 'em and smoke 'em, just because doing so makes them feel good. As a result of considerable scientific research indicating that there's a likely link between cancer and secondhand smoke (thereby also putting nonsmokers at risk for cancer) the general public has become enraged, and over the last several decades we've witnessed overblown awareness campaigns, stigmatization of smokers, and draconian laws forbidding smoking nearly everywhere but on the street corner.

Agreed? Good.

Okay, now consider: even though Toxoplasmosis appears to have been initially identified just as long ago as the dangers of smoking (the mid-twentieth century) have you ever even fucking *heard* of it before? Has there been *any* substantial public awareness campaign advising us of the dangers of cat ownership? Has there been any stigmatization of cat owners whatsoever? Has there been any outrage or lawsuits on the part of those who've contracted the Toxoplasma parasite from the housecats of their neighbors? Of course not. But does that really make sense? Cigarettes are a frivolous indulgence that make people *feel better*, but can probably give them (and those around them) cancer. And housecats are likewise a frivolous indulgence that make people *feel better* but can potentially infect them and those around them with *a fucking brain parasite that demonstrably alters personality and can possibly make you bat-shit crazy.* I realize that the comparison probably seems overwrought to all you emotionally vacuous, feline-dependent ninnies, but is it really such a poor analogy? I'm not so sure. I don't know about you, but

given the choice, I'd sure as fuck take lung cancer over schizophrenia any day of the week.

In closing, I might add that this probable (if not *strongly likely*, goddamn it) correlation between cat-shit-brain-parasites and human mental illness really shouldn't be the least bit surprising. Because the fact is, a wide variety of deadly diseases and lethal parasites that have afflicted humanity for eons initially emerged simply because people started *living around and with animals*. A few examples:

- Measles – to humans via dogs.

- Avian flu – to humans via chickens.

- Influenza – to humans via pigs and ducks.

- Smallpox – to humans via cows.

- Tuberculosis – to humans via cows, again.

- Bubonic plague – to humans via rats and mice.

- Typhus – to humans via rats and mice, again.

- Malaria – to humans via chimpanzees.

- HIV/AIDS – to humans via chimpanzees, again.

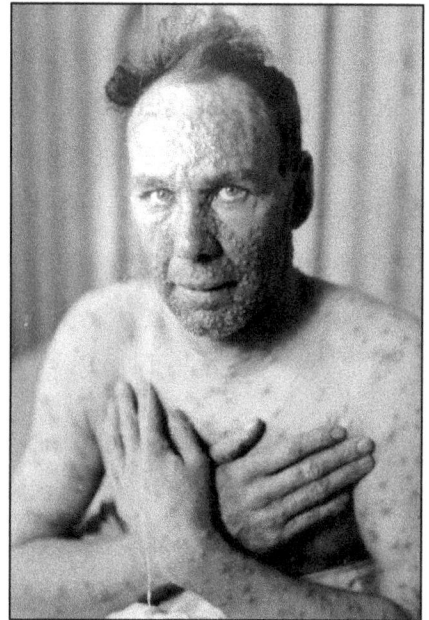

Smallpox, thanks to cows.

So, pet-lovers, as far as I'm concerned, you can all go royally fuck yourselves. As you masochistically coddle and care for filthy animals that eat rotted food out of the trash and use their own tongues as toilet paper, just try to bear in mind that maybe—just possibly—you're blissfully and obliviously sowing the seeds of your own eventual doom. Whether it's schizophrenia from kitty cats or bird influenza from chickens, in my humblest of most humble opinions, *people and animals really shouldn't be living together, assholes.*

Todo El Mundo Es Un Crítico

2004

"La gente maligna ataca a otros en vez de hacer frente a sus propias faltas."
- M. Scott Peck

Desde luego, tú sabes cómo poner a parir cualquier cosa. ¡Oh sí, claro que sí! Por supuesto, todos lo hacemos continuamente. Todo el mundo suelta un montón de mierda, yo incluido. Y naturalmente, no hay nada malo en criticar o poner a parir algo. De hecho, es casi lo más normal.

Para ser justo, mucha de la mierda que sueltas tiene bastante crédito. Claro, se pueden encontrar fallos en prácticamente cualquier cosa. Pero tú no eres un mero crítico, tú eres un *echa pestes*, encuentras fallos en cosas que siendo objetivo no tienen por qué ser criticadas. Destrozas películas, obras de teatro, novelas, grupos, pinturas ... cualquier cosa. Todos hemos escuchado tus explicaciones con detalle del porqué las cosas apestan. Sí, tienes tus opiniones y pueden estar bien formadas, pero he llegado realmente a odiar a gente como tú. Casi no tengo respeto hacia ti. Casi nada en absoluto. Porque tú sólo eres un echa pestes y eso es todo lo que eres. Porque, mira; es mucho más fácil hablar de algo que hacer algo.

Así que antes de abrir tu bocaza, una vez más, trágate tu opinión no solicitada; considera este obvio (aunque muy a menudo ignorado) prerrequisito para poner algo a caer de un burro.

Sí, rajas de mala manera; sí, sí, sí, pero ¿qué has hecho tú en tu vida, eh?

Criticas películas por ser muy "pretenciosas," o muy insustanciales, o muy "arty," o muy hollywoodienses o por cualquier otro motivo. Pero si alguien te pusiera detrás de la lente de una cámara no tendrías ni la más puñetera idea de por dónde empezar.

Criticas a un autor por una serie de razones; el estilo de la prosa, el argumento, su tono, su estilo de vida, *etcétera*. Pero seguramente serías incapaz de expresar algún concepto coherente por escrito, cuanto más un libro entero.

Eres capaz de putear a un grupo por no tener "presencia" en el escenario, pero te cagarías en los pantalones si alguna vez te vieras en un escenario en frente de una audiencia. Pero ¡qué cojones! Si ni siquiera tienes la capacidad de escribir una canción y mucho menos de tocarla. Así que ¿Cuándo pararás de despotricar, eh?

No me malinterpretes. Yo he sido partícipe de este juego. Hay una gran cantidad de cosas y de gente que pienso que son o que hacen mierda, y nunca he tratado de aparentar otra cosa. También puedo alardear mucho de mis opiniones. Supongo, no obstante, que lo que nos diferencia a ti y a mí, no es sólo el hecho de que yo siempre estoy intentando hacer movidas: sino el *porqué* yo pienso que algunas cosas apestan.

Desde mi punto de vista, no sólo porque una banda suene bien significa que sean buenos, pueden ser un cliché hecho de partes saqueadas a otros artistas. Simplemente porque una película tenga un gran presupuesto significa que esté bien hecha. Sólo porque un libro aparezca en la lista de "best seller" del *New York Times* o en el club del libro de Oprah, no significa que sea mejor que alguna pequeña publicación de poca tirada. Algunas veces cosas como el contenido, contexto, intención, innovación, originalidad o riesgo tienen su importancia. Pero tú eres tan corto y estrecho de miras como para darte cuenta de esto ¿no es así? Pues claro que sí.

Sabes, me das mucho asco. Tengo más respeto por unos niñatos de una cochambrosa banda de garage que por ti. Más respeto por un pintor sin talento y sin ningún concepto de la estética que por ti. Más respeto por un aspirante a novelista puerco que por ti. ¿Por qué?

Pues porque, a parte de la habilidad, se necesitan muchas más pelotas para sacar el cuello ahí fuera y, arriesgarte a expresar y crear algo; que para sentarse cómodamente a descuartizar las cosas desde la distancia como hace la gente como tú.

Quiero decir, ¿te has parado por un momento a observarte a ti mismo? ¿qué coño has hecho con tu vida que sea de algún modo envidiable? Tienes un estúpido trabajo sin ninguna diferencia a cualquier otro, te machacas a diario para ganar dinero, que luego te gastas en cosas totalmente predecibles como el resto de la gente. Aún así tienes la audacia para destruir a menudo todas las tentativas de otras personas para hacer algo interesante con sus vidas. ¿Cómo podría respetarte? Eres un clon. Un zángano. Un zombi. No tienes alma, así que jodes las tentativas de otras personas por conectar con las suyas.

Me tienes que perdonar con esto, pero soy un poco escéptico con tus motivaciones por ser un crítico muy informado sin pelos en la lengua. ¿Ves? Pienso que te duele ser tan consciente de tu propia falta de habilidad (y eso te corroe) que todo lo que puedes hacer es poner mal a otra gente. Hablar mal de lo que otra gente hace, porque eso de algún modo te hace parecer un poco menos patético e inútil.

Ahí he metido el dedo en la yaga ¿eh? Lo gracioso es que hasta pareces tener una tendencia a rajar sobre las cosas y la gente que sabes que el que te está escuchando tiene cierta estima. Todo el mundo conoce a alguien como tú y todo el mundo odia a ese alguien.

Imagínate si alguna vez en tu monótona y olvidable vida te arriesgases a exponer tus pensamientos y opiniones en un foro público, dando la posibilidad a otros de criticarte, juzgarte y destrozarte uno detrás de otro. No creo que pudieras hacerlo, eso es algo que tú puedes hacer pero nunca aceptarías que te lo hicieran. Si alguna vez tuvieras la tentativa de sentarte y escribir sobre tu vida, ¿le importaría a alguien lo más mínimo como para leerlo? Los dos sabemos la respuesta ¿verdad? No sólo pienso que no estás por la labor de correr el riesgo de expresarte libremente sino que ni siquiera tienes nada que decir. Sólo puedes encontrar errores, que es mucho más fácil.

A lo que voy con todo esto, miserable criatura, es que todo lo que tú eres es un mero consumidor. Compras las cosas que otras personas hacen. La gente que crea cosas que te gustan los adoras como verdaderos dioses: estrellas de rock, estrellas del cine, directores de Hollywood, artistas aclamados y brillantes escritores. En realidad son sólo gente corriente, pero han sido elevados a celebridades por zánganos como tú, por el mero hecho de que ellos crean cosas parece de alguna manera "mágico" desde que necios como tú sean totalmente incapaces de crear algo por sí mismos. Por otro lado, la gente que crea cosas que a ti no te importan son sólo terribles amateurs sin talento que están desperdiciando sus vidas, sólo hacen basura que te deleitas al criticar.

Por supuesto, lo que no consigues comprender, insípido tarugo, es que la diferencia no está entre las llamadas celebridades y los amateurs, está en la gente que hace algo independientemente del éxito comercial, y miserables, y consumistas críticos negativos como tú. Pero por supuesto, nunca jamás comprenderás esto. Lo que es verdaderamente triste y preocupante es que hay miles, si no millones, de tipos como tú. Hordas de mentes cenagosas que no hacen nada remotamente interesante con sus vidas, que no contribuyen más que a la producción consumismo y a la vez mueven sus labios arrogantemente sobre los defectos de la música, películas, escritos y arte de otros.

Todo el mundo es un crítico. Así que estás en buena compañía, eres exactamente como el resto de la gente. Pero perdóname, soy un poco escéptico, hay una pregunta que sigue carcomiéndome ¿Qué coño has hecho? Oh espera, no me respondas. Es hora de que vuelvas a tu curro.

Annoying, Nerdy, Unpopular, and Insufferably Pretentious Opinions About Music

2011

1. Apart from their eponymous debut album, The Clash were not a Punk band. Songs like "Rock the Casbah," "Should I Stay or Should I Go," and various of their other '80s Pop-Rock numbers could've seamlessly been released during the same era by The Talking Heads, Culture Club, Men at Work, or any other '80s Pop band.

2. The first two Coldplay albums are mostly good.

3. The theme from the 1984 American comedy film *Police Academy* is a better musical march than most countries' national anthems.

4. The best Metallica song is their 1988 cover of Diamondhead's "The Prince."

5. Most IDM or "Intelligent Dance Music" seems technically complicated because the rhythm frequently varies and effects on the tones often modulate or phase – but compositionally it's mostly very simple and repetitive. IDM rarely features any interplay of melody and harmony or musical counterpoint – it's largely just odd electronic sounds, breakbeats, and knob-twiddling of effects. Also, the name for the genre is incredibly fucking idiotic.

6. The Grateful Dead have been unfairly misjudged, maligned, and lampooned, largely as a result of their godawful dirthead fan-base. Assessed objectively on just the music alone, they aren't bad.

7. Social Distortion, The Replacements, and Dinosaur Jr. are tepid, mid-tempo Dad Rock.

8. Ministry started out as a more-than-decent Synth Pop band. They should own it instead of running from it.

9. Henry Mancini was the greatest American composer of Orchestral music to date; far superior to John Phillip Sousa and George Gershwin, both of whom undeservingly persist in overshadowing him.

10. Oasis' cover of Slade's "Cum On Feel the Noize" is the song's finest rendition. Likewise, The Pet Shop Boys' version of "Always on My Mind" is superior to the Elvis and Willie Nelson versions.

11. Lars Ulrich was right about Napster, and nobody in the Arts has done more to devalue intellectual property than Steve Albini.

12. Godflesh's "Like Rats" is the best Mother's Day song ever recorded.

13. If Deke Dickerson had been a contemporary of Bill Haley, he would have been more famous than Haley, because he's much more talented – Dickerson was just born a few decades too late.

14. Blatz was the most original, creative, and interesting Punk band.

15. There's no better example in popular music of Sigmund Freud's "Madonna–whore complex" than the fact that Dion's two biggest hits were "Runaround Sue" and "The Wanderer" – and they were released in the same year, no less.

16. The Foo Fighters are okay.

17. The Nine Inch Nails remix EP *Fixed* is better than the original EP on which it is based, *Broken*; also, their debut album, *Pretty Hate Machine* has aged poorly, given that the synths and production now sound corny and dated.

18. Mötley Crüe are generally awful, but "Kickstart My Heart" fucking rules.

19. The overuse of double-bass drumming and "blast beats" in Death Metal music and related subgenres reduces musical contrast, thereby rendering the music monotonous and tiresome rather than dynamic and engaging.

20. Joy Division's Ian Curtis was a shitty singer.

21. Billy Joel's "My Life" and Weird Al Yankovic's "I'll Be Mellow When I'm Dead" are better angst-ridden teenage rebellion songs than any of their snotty "first wave" Punk contemporaries released around the same time.

22. The second My Chemical Romance album is good.

23. Throbbing Gristle and Nurse With Wound should properly be regarded as Art projects rather than musical projects. Einstürzende Neubauten, The Residents, and Men's Recovery Project straddle the line.

24. Warren G's "Regulate" is superior to Michael McDonald's "I Keep Forgettin' (Every Time You're Near)."

25. The hype surrounding Sonic Youth is misplaced. They mostly look and sound like lethargic junkies.

26. Hank Williams' two-chord Country song "Ramblin' Man" is orders of magnitude better than anything written or recorded by virtuosic guitar shredders like Steve Vai, Yngwie Malmsteen, The Great Kat, Joe Satriani, Stevie Ray Vaughn, *et al*.

27. With rare exception, Blues, Rockabilly, and Surf Rock bands all tend to engage in paint-by-numbers songwriting due to the constraints of the genres and audience expectations, and so rarely, if ever, bring anything new or engaging to music.

28. Thee Headcoatees' cover of The Undertones' song "Teenage Kicks" is superior to the original.

29. American ska music is terrible.

30. The Smiths would have been better with an uninventive bass player who just played root notes.

31. Afficionados of Flamenco music absolutely fucking loathe The Gypsy Kings, but—like it or not—they've done more for the genre than anyone. And some of their stuff is great.

32. Nirvana, The Stooges, The White Stripes, The Pixies, and The Velvet Underground—although perfectly fine, passable, and even "good" as Rock groups—are nonetheless exhaustingly overrated by music critics and the music press.

33. Underrated: The Couch Of Eureka, Scenic, Nový Svět, Grimple, Zen Guerilla, Loop (UK), Hellbillys (US), Superconductor (CA).

34. Chuck Berry would've been bigger than Elvis if he were white.

35. People mock so-called Yacht Rock or only *sort-of* like it "ironically," but most of it is pretty good, and some of it is excellent.

36. Love them or hate them, The Doors exist within their own standalone musical genre.

37. Slayer's rendition of "In-A-Gadda-Da-Vida" is second only to Exodus' version of "Low Rider," when it comes to ill-advised, shitty covers by Thrash bands.

38. Modernist Orchestral music of the early-to-mid twentieth century—by the likes of Igor Stravinsky, George Antheil, and Arnold Schönberg—was more innovative, bold, and risk-taking than anything done later in the century by the sundry progeny of Rock n' Roll.

39. The best music video is Electric Six's "Danger! High Voltage."

40. Setting aside the less-than-compelling Pop Rock direction they took in the 1980s, Cheap Trick's first three albums are great '70s Hard Rock.

41. Moondog's "New Amsterdam" would have been much better as an instrumental.

42. Gabber and Death Metal albums generally start out super—upbeat, fun, invigorating, full of brio, and even catchy—but by the third song they're tedious and boring on account of every song sounding the fucking same.

43. The Eagles' "Hotel California" is very overplayed, but deservedly so.

44. Iron Maiden's first two albums with what's-his-face singing were their best.

45. Noise "music" isn't.

46. The best / worst love song is Momus' "I Want You, But I Don't Need You."

47. U2, The B-52's, and R.E.M. all started out as above-average, interesting, and innovative bands.

48. Pyotr Tchaikovsky's *The Nutcracker* is top-tier Western Classical music; too dang good to be balkanized as a mere "Christmas" thing, trotted out every December and thereafter ignored the rest of the year. Give it a spin in July sometime. It rules ass year-round.

49. Atari Teenage Riot and Digital Hardcore probably deserved to be more of a big deal when they came out, even in spite of their silly politics.

50. Paris Hilton's album is just as good as that of any other saccharine mainstream Pop chanteuse of the contemporary era.

51. "Ride of the Valkyries," from Richard Wagner's leaden opera *Der Ring des Nibelungen*, kind of sucks. Most of Richard Wagner's overwrought music pretty much sucks.

52. The Mummies were the greatest Rock n' Roll band of all time.

53. The majority of acoustic Neofolk music is dreary and wearying. Neofolk is generally an amalgam of: (1) uninventive songwriting that utilizes only standard chords, timeworn and predictable chord progressions, and simplistic strumming patterns; (2) minimal percussion playing very basic time-signatures with little to no changes; and (3) middling vocal melodies.

54. Propagandhi are unintentionally hilarious.

55. As a general rule, bands that have a conceptual schtick are fantastic: Spinal Tap, The Upper Crust, The Go-Nuts, The Ruttles, Man or Astro-man?, Señor Coconut, Steel Panther, Blowfly, Hatebeak, *et al*. It's just a shame that they usually tend to be constrained by the schtick.

56. When he first came out, Little Richard was more "punk" than The Sex Pistols.

57. Dolly Parton is an extremely talented songwriter and singer, and also a decent guitarist. I'd like to think that she would receive more "serious" acclaim if it weren't for the distracting massive tits ... but I'm not sure if that would actually be the case.

58. The second movement of Ludwig van Beethoven's Symphony N°· 7, performed by The Boston Symphony Orchestra as conducted by Leonard Bernstein on August 19, 1990, is the best song. That or The Swingin' Medallions' "Double Shot (Of My Baby's Love)."

59. The following full-length long-player studio albums are, generally speaking, "all killer, no filler":

The Go-Go's – *Beauty and the Beat*

Slayer – *Seasons in the Abyss*

Depeche Mode – *Violator*

The Smashing Pumpkins – *Siamese Dream*

The Ramones – *Ramones*

Satan's Pilgrims – *Satan's Pilgrims*

At the Gates – *Slaughter of the Soul*

Neko Case – *Blacklisted*

Interpol – *Turn On the Bright Lights*

Guns N' Roses – *Appetite for Destruction*

The Cardigans – *Life*

New York Dolls – *New York Dolls*

She Wants Revenge – *She Wants Revenge*

Black Math Horseman – *Wyllt*

T. Rex – *The Slider*

The Rezillos – *Can't Stand the Rezillos*

The Sword – *Age of Winters*

Jesu – *Jesu*

Eydie Gormé y Los Panchos – *Eydie Gorme Canta En Español Con Los Panchos*

Portishead – *Dummy*

Danzig – *Danzig*

The Raveonettes – *Lust, Lust, Lust*

Circle Jerks – *Group Sex*

Amon Tobin – *Supermodified*

The Strokes – *Is This It*

Nikki and The Corvettes – *Nikki and The Corvettes*

Autechre – *Amber*

Screeching Weasel – *My Brain Hurts*

M.Kourie – *The Dreams Of M.Kourie*

Beck – *Sea Change*

Los Bunkers – *Vida de Perros*

Weezer – *Weezer*

Electric Wizard – *Dopethrone*

Plastikman – *Consumed*

Metallica – *Kill 'Em All*

Honorable mention: Radiohead's *OK Computer*, were it not for the fact that the track "Fitter Happier" is the epitome of superfluous "filler."

60. The Beastie Boys are the most obnoxious musical act ever, on multiple levels.

The first cassette tape I ever purchased, in the fourth grade, was the Beastie Boys' 1986 debut studio album, *Licensed to Ill*. Having only owned, maybe, five cassette tapes in the latter half of the 1980s, I must have listened to *Licensed to Ill* hundreds of times before my balls dropped. I unfortunately still probably know every fuckin' word of the lyrics, to this goddamn day. Needless to say, I was a big fan of the Beastie Boys as a kid. Naturally, however, once I left elementary school for middle school, as the 1980s came to a close, I was exposed to much more music, developed my own musical sensibilities, and tried to leave the music of my childhood—The Beastie Boys—behind. I could do no such thing. The Beastie Boys' popularity, acclaim, and influence only grew as I aged through adolescence, my teenage years, and into adulthood. And they seemed to only get more insufferably fucking annoying and inescapable with the passage of time.

Why do I harbor a stunted antipathy towards the Beastie Boys as an adult, even though I adulated them as a kid? Well, first off, whether he's rapping or singing, Adam "Ad-Rock" Horovitz's nasally voice is as grating on the nerves as the warbling of a stray cat giving birth. ("*The King Adroooowwwck that is my naaaaaaaayyyyme.*" Ugh. Fucking awful.) Secondly, while the concept of "cultural appropriation" is generally dubious as a rebuke of artists borrowing from disparate sources, in the case of the Beastie Boys—possibly uniquely—it's apropos. As a band, the Beastie Boys have consistently been overlauded by music critics for ostensibly being "musically diverse" and for "evolving" their sound and style – but I don't see it that way. I regard the Beastie Boys as shrewd, groundless chameleons who are ever ready to pivot to the next trendy thing by purloining aspects underground music and culture; and who then receive undue credit in the mainstream for superficially having been "groundbreaking" by doing something on MTV that'd already been going on outside the mainstream for years.

From what I understand—*despite consciously trying to fucking ignore them for decades as an adult*—the Beastie Boys started out as a run-of-the-mill New York City Hardcore Punk band in the early '80s. They then glommed-on to the nascent local Rap scene and released a novelty Rap song. This, then, secured them a record deal that allowed them to release a full-length album on a major-affiliated record label, just as Rap was blowing up. It bears noting that the Beastie Boys were not progenitors of Rap or Hip-Hop music – rather, it had already been simmering for a while in the early-to-mid-1980s thanks to the likes of The Sugarhill Gang and LL Cool J, but it blew up in the late '80s when Run-DMC made it a national phenomenon. The Beastie Boys' first full-length album came out around the same time, and promptly rocketed them to stardom.

Now, it's been argued—as with Vanilla Ice and Eminem ... and before them, with Elvis Presley, *et al.*—that the Beastie Boys' initial success is largely attributable to the fact that they're white guys who allegedly "ripped off" supposedly black underground music and made it mainstream. Whether or not there's any validity to that argument, I think it's lazy; an artist's race or ethnicity—an immutable characteristic that they have no control over—is a pretty shitty and half-assed basis for critiquing their art. It's also not necessary to resort to such accusations of "theft" when assaying the Beastie Boys' initial success. "Race" issues aside, the Beastie Boys epitomize trend hopping. They are erstwhile Punks who jettisoned Punk, jumped on the Rap Train, and started dressing like B-boys. Whether the transition makes them "posers" or "sellouts" is irrelevant – it reads to me as a decisive and timely marketing ploy, and it worked. In the '80s, the Beastie Boys "got in early on the ground floor" of The Next Big Thing in music – Rap and Hip-Hop. It was the beginning of a pattern in their career.

After my cassette copy of *Licensed to Ill* had long since worn out and I'd moved on to an interest in Hard Rock music, I first re-noticed the Beastie Boys in middle school. They had a new sophomore album out and a new hit song on the radio and MTV, which was harrying as all fuckin' Hell – "Hey Ladies." There was a music video for the tune that featured one of them strutting around dressed like a '70s pimp, rapping to camera. I remember thinking to myself on encountering the video, *Wow, I can't believe that I thought these guys were cool when I was a kid. Sheesh!*

The Beastie Boys then disappeared from my radar for a few years until I was in high school, in the early '90s, and I spotted the cover of their album *Check Your Head*. Thereon, the trio of former bogus B-boys were dressed like the asshole California skater dudes who went to my high school. They'd seemed to have shapeshifted from New York City B-boys, to ironic '70s pimps, to California skater bros ... and I found it irritating. Nobody in my peer group seemed to notice or care, however, and the Beastie Boys were again all over the goddamn radio. *Check Your Head* featured the annoying-as-fuck song "So What'cha Want," which was omnipresent at the time. I hated it. Lots of my peers loved it. Next came the album *Ill Communication*, which was accompanied by another "ironic" music video for the (admittedly catchy) single "Sabotage," in which the band lampooned '70s cop shows. *Ill Communication* also featured the track "Root Down," yet another awful and irritating song that seemed to be played way too often, everywhere. I kept attempting to ignore them, but the Beastie Boys remained omnipresent throughout my time in high school in the first half of the 1990s.

By the time I was in college, the Beastie Boys released the 1998 album *Hello Nasty*, for which the ubiquitous single was "Intergalactic" – a shitty Rap song with yet another concomitant "ironic" music video. Both were annoying. At some point around the same time the Beastie Boys—by this time a longstanding pop cultural fixture—did an album of throwbacks to '70s instrumental porn-funk songs, and somewhere along the line they did an album of Punk songs – and many people I knew loved it all, as did the college press and radio. At the dawn of the new millennium, with proverbial fingers in my ears, I kept trying to ignore the Beastie Boys, which was impossible.

It's still not easy. Lots of people adore the fuck out of the Beastie Boys. They've sold millions of albums. They've gone platinum. In high school and college, people I knew who weren't really "into" music had *all* their albums, loved the Beastie Boys *to death*, and seemed to believe that the Boys had conceived of pathbreaking musical turns that were, in actuality, just shoddy imitations of underground music. Take "Intergalactic" for example – the song is just a looped beat that the Beastie Boys rap over, and there's sort of an intermittent quasi-chorus, in which an effected voice with a vocoder (or whatever) on it says "intergalactic" over and over again. I recall hearing other college kids at the time gush about how brilliant it was that the Beastie Boys had branched out into "Electronic" or "Techno" music on account of that stupid fucking song. My take was ... *Why the fuck is this vapid garbage a hit song on the radio?* It still eludes me.

The shimmering jewel on the crown of my animosity towards the Beastie Boys arrived when, at some point, I learned that one of them had married Kathleen Hannah, frontwoman of the seminal Riot Grrrl band Bikini Kill. It's safe to say that my first in-depth exposure to casual misogyny in pop culture occurred by way of my intimate childhood familiarity with the Beastie Boys' song "Girls" from 1986's *Licensed to Ill* – a trashy, retrograde pean to female domesticity and servility, which has aged as poorly as unpasteurized whole milk in the intervening decades. ("Girls to do the dishes. Girls to clean up my room. Girls to do the laundry. Girls in the bathroom.") It's also safe to say that my first in-depth exposure to "reverse" racist misandry in pop culture was my teenage contact (via my first girlfriend) with Bikini Kill's song "White Boy" from their 1993 split LP, *Yeah Yeah Yeah Yeah*. ("White boy. Don't laugh. Don't cry. Just die.") The fact that the respective singers of these two divisive cross-gender-bashing songs are now collecting music royalties from *each other's* recordings, since they're married, is *pretty fuckin' rich*. That's the music biz for 'ya, I guess.

While I harbor no malice against them as individual people *per se*, the Beastie Boys are nonetheless the most obnoxious musical act ever, because not only are they annoying as fuck ("*So what'cha, what'cha, what'cha, waaaaant?*"), but further, they epitomize the phenomenon of artists proactively leaning into burgeoning cultural trends in an attempt to get ahead of audience expectations, for profit. The Beastie Boys are a band that started out in Punk, hopped trains over to Rap and started dressing like B-boys, got big, then borrowed the aesthetic style and "vibes" from SoCal skate culture, then dipped their toes into shitty electronic music, and then imitative '70s pono-funk, then "retro" Punk again – and at every shamelessly appropriative turn they've been praised as innovative, exploratory, and trailblazing by the music press. But the Beastie Boys' *oeuvre* is largely derivative, not innovative. They are not a weathervane pointing towards where culture is going – they're following a trail of cultural breadcrumbs laid down for them by others, and monetizing it. In short, the Beastie Boys have the effrontery to habitually scoop up components of counterculture, corporatize it in the mainstream, and then get golf claps for having "invented" it. What could be more fuckin' obnoxious than that?

Various Photographs From 'round About the Early Twenty-First Century

Shitty Action at a Distance

On the Faults and Foibles of Online Interaction

2010

The Internet is a fantastic thing. As a fount of breaking news, I love it. I sure as fuck don't subscribe to a daily newspaper or keep up with the TV evening news anymore. When I want to know the forecast, I open a web browser. Likewise, as an informational archive, it's invaluable. As a means of doing away with dictionaries, encyclopedias, thesauri, telephone books, and other hefty paper indexes, it's excellent. And while the decimation of the music industry and the disenfranchisement of travel agents worldwide are both lamentable, I guess I sort of deem them tolerable losses in the grand scheme of things. It's just so nice to shop for ... well, pretty much *everything* ... without leaving one's apartment, and finding said purchases waiting in one's mailbox just days later is great. But I'm highly skeptical of the increasing ubiquity of "virtual communities" online. I realize that this is hardly an unprecedented stance to take on the subject, as plenty a commentator has inveighed against various aspects of Blogs, MySpace, FaceBook, and others – but I think they're a problem.

It's plausible to suggest that there's a proportionally inverse relationship between the ways in which many people conduct themselves online versus how they behave in real life. The intelligent, introverted, contemplative—shall we say "sensitive"—characters of delicate constitution and heightened emotional acuity who populate the shadowy corners of most social settings can easily adopt all those characteristics that they lack in reality, in an online environment. With the added anonymity of usernames, socially maladroit introverts are provided with a safe haven through which to vent their pent-up frustrations and most sublimated desires, online. Blogs, for example, give unassertive people a semblance of having control; if only with respect to how they want to see themselves in digital print. The same seems to increasingly be true of the "virtual communities." I know more than just a couple'a virtual ersatz badasses who've affected a persona online that simply does not parallel their daily realities in the slightest. It's a curious phenomenon, but I don't suppose this is intrinsically any more dysfunctional than role-playing, or any other sort of escapism that's best left behind in adolescence.

The problem, however, is that online it *isn't* generally understood to be role-playing and is instead often taken at face value.

I'm no tough guy, but, working in bars, I've witnessed bone crunching melees suddenly erupt over nothing more than the disyllabic diss "faggot" – and yet, nowadays, perfect strangers who are totally unaware to whom they are addressing denigrating insults will, as a matter of habit, unleash lengthy vitriolic diatribes filled with invectives ... from a distance, at strangers, on the Internet. In online jargon this is called "flaming" – defined by UrbanDictionary.com as "An online argument that becomes nasty or derisive, where insulting a party to the discussion takes precedence over the objective merits of one side or another." This kind of thing rarely happens in tangible "meatspace" reality, where cause and effect relationships play out in real time; but online it's a fairly common occurrence. It's almost as if, as humans, we weren't "designed" to interact with each other online. ...

In the 2007 essay collection *What Is Your Dangerous Idea?*, contributor Daniel Goleman begins his anti-web missive "Cyberdisinhibition" with the statement:

> The Internet undermines the quality of human interaction, allowing destructive emotional impulses freer rein under specific circumstances. The reason is a neural fluke that results in cyberdisinhibition of brain systems that keep our more unruly urges in check. The tech problem: a major disconnect between the ways our brains are wired to connect and the interface offered in online interactions.

Goleman's sentiment is thereafter convincingly fleshed-out in the few pages that follow. It's an intuitive concept. Human beings evolved over millions of years to engage with each other in the context of small social clusters whose interaction was face-to-face and whose behavior was modulated for the benefit of the group by things like social cues, shame, stigma, and ostracization. In normal social contexts, we get all sorts of non-linguistic signals from each other: posture and body language, voice intonation, eye contact and the avoidance thereof, *et cetera*. Being able to intuit the meaning of these non-linguistic indicators allows us to regulate our behavior without our necessarily even being conscious of it. If one is arguing with someone and can see that they're getting upset—maybe their face is getting red and the vein on their forehead is bulging ... or maybe their eyes are welling up with tears and their voice is faltering—one can respond to that real-time feedback and modulate one's own behavior accordingly. Ease up a bit, maybe make a joke, change the subject, alter the inflection of one's speech, smile and avert one's gaze ... whatever. Not so on the Internet, where petty, otherwise forgettable arguments froth up into friendship-annihilating feuds, and where teenagers commit suicide after being subjected to relentless online humiliation and harassment – in a forum that is both fixed and public, and constantly broadcasting 24/7 ... and in which their humiliators and harassers can't see them weeping, alone in their bedrooms.

I've caught myself being "cyber-disinhibited" from time to time, without realizing it or stopping to think too much about it; jotting off some snarky missive online to someone I've never met, after having had a couple of drinks and not really pausing to consider how my text will be received on the screen by its intended recipient. It can be sort of amusing. Fun, even. But, as a result of this sort of thing, I've lost what I thought were friendships over email, and apparently even made nominal "enemies" of people I've never met in person over dumb online text disagreements. So, increasingly as of late, before I hit "post," I ask myself, *Would you say this to a stranger, in person, without even knowing who you're speaking to?* And if the answer is "no," I hit the backspace button and move on with my day. It's a good heuristic for steering clear of headaches, I think. But it requires checking oneself, which is an acquired skill, and often one that doesn't come naturally to young people.

It certainly wasn't always this way. I'm old enough to remember when people unironically employed now-waning neologisms like "the information superhighway," "cyberspace," and "surfing the web." When the Internet was a curious novelty that required explanation in local news fluff pieces. When only *total fucking nerds* went on BBS boards and traded "warez." Things have changed. The cultural transformations wrought by the Internet have come in ways that I would never have predicted at the time, back when the Internet seemed like an amusing novelty for geeks, at most. Nobody seemed to predict the ways it would change things. Perhaps most notoriously, Nobel Prize-winning economist Paul Krugman wrote in 1998, "By 2005 or so, it will become clear that the Internet's impact on the economy has been no greater than the fax machine's." *Oof.* Krugman's oracular flex was obviously way off – but he was only talking about economics, and thus his lack of prescience is itself only half the picture. The Internet has changed more than just the economy – it's changed everything about society and much of human interaction in the West, down to the roots.

I remember when I was finishing high school and starting college—back in the mid-to-late 1990s—how differently the subject of pornography was perceived than it is today. Porn was ghettoized to adult bookstores in rundown areas of town, frequented mostly by solitary men skulking around with their gazes affixed to their shoes. People timidly shuffled in and out of the places, making their magazine and VHS purchases quickly, hoping not to be spotted by their neighbors or coworkers. Women tended not to show their faces around such locales, and the perception (at least in my local community) was that porn was something that only gross boys—perverts—were unrepentantly into. The majority of my teenage male friends and I would have climbed over our own mothers in the mud for access to porn – but few would ever admit to that in the presence of our female peers. It was taboo; frowned on, and looked down on as being regressive, chauvinistic, and trashy.

Fast forward to the Internet age, and porn is instantly accessible in the privacy and seclusion of one's own home; it's become normalized and socially acceptable. Young people of both genders are quite familiar with it and casual about it. To my surprise, the last girl I dated, a "millennial," had a collection of porn DVDs when I met her. This was simply unthinkable in 1996, during my freshman year of college, but now it seems unremarkable. I think that what has facilitated this shift is partly to do with the convenience and ease of access furnished by the Internet; but also the privacy and anonymity—and therefore, dearth of shame and public ostracization—that the Internet has created space for.

It's more than just "flaming" and porn, though. Consider that the average law-abiding middle class American father of two would never in his right mind walk into a record store and make off with a dozen artists' CDs; nor would he try to sneak his family past the ushers at a movie theatre to shirk paying the modest entry fees – but, such behaviors are entirely common in an online context in which pirating copyrighted music and films is nearly effortless and consequence free. Because the elements of ignominy and social excommunication are missing in a digital or "virtual" context – which is the same reason why 21-year-old middle-class women are now unabashedly comfortable with consuming hardcore porn; because they don't need to experience the awkwardness of visiting an adult bookstore frequented by middle-aged creepers, or having their reputations blemished on account of their consumption of porn – because it's been normalized.

Similarly, the Internet has only made it easier for conmen to commit fraud, identity theft, and so on. A criminal can drain a person's bank account remotely nowadays, from the safety of their own home, using however many proxy servers might be necessary to evade detection – and he needn't even have to walk into a bank with a fake ID and some forged checks anymore. The anonymity and detachment of it—the attenuated connection between cause and effect online— make it not only more appealing (and possibly easier), but also attract a *type* of person that, a generation ago, would never dream of committing bank fraud in person in the "real" world. The same bashful, socially inept, "sensitive" introverts who can flex virtually on Blogs, can also be virtual-yet-literal bank robbers nowadays, without leaving their couch, let alone engaging in risk-taking that might subject them to bodily harm.

All this stuff is only becoming more "normal," if not normative. The illegality of minors being able to access (free!) porn, much like the pirating of copyrighted intellectual property online, appears to be mostly irrelevant to most people online, most of the time. It's an accepted online norm. Nobody seems to genuinely care. Lip service is paid to these issues being of some concern, sure, but they persist in a widespread way. And as more and more people become online denizens, they are likely to adopt these norms, despite their offline illegality. Thus, the Internet is—and will increasingly be—the handmaiden of social disharmony and discord in the twenty-first century.

But it would be hackneyed to note that the Internet is "warping" us. Technologically facilitated interaction at a distance and "virtual" remote behavior already *have* warped us. If I were to tell you that my twenty-five year-old cousin sliced the throats of twelve people last month, I assume you'd be horrified to learn that he's not in prison and hasn't even committed a crime; yet if I tell you that my twenty-five year-old cousin killed a dozen people remotely, while sitting in an air-conditioned government office outside Reno, Nevada, while piloting a military drone dropping bombs on people in remote parts of Pakistan – that's fine. So, yeah, we're already *warped*.

I do wonder, though – how much longer until interacting on the Internet becomes the norm—the default way that people interact with one another—and in-person interaction is the novel anomaly? And, what then? We're probably fucked, that's what.

The Lost Weekend in Las Vegas

Half-Remembering the Inaugural Modern Drunkard Convention

2004

Modern Drunkard Magazine is a glossy print periodical run out of Denver, Colorado. It's a publication about the glories of drinking, which attempts to turn back the tide of neo-prohibitionism (which began to appear in the early 1980s, with the inception of anti-drinking organizations such as MADD), and harks back to the golden era of the 1940s and '50s, when, as The Rat Pack taught us, drinking was not only acceptable, trendy, and even ... *fashionable*.

I first heard about *Modern Drunkard* in 2003, while living in San Francisco, California. My girlfriend at the time, (a homebrewing enthusiast) was in charge of ordering and stocking magazines for a small independently-owned "hip" bookstore in the city's Richmond District, and she came home from work one day, raving about how funny this new drinking magazine was, especially its section titled "The Clash Of The Tightest," (a monthly feature pitting historical figures such as Charles Bukowski, Jackie Gleason, Earnest Hemingway, and Dean Martin, against one another in amusing "what if" drinking competitions). She became a regular reader of the magazine, and less than a year later, I got her a subscription for Christmas.

When I moved from San Francisco to Denver, less than a year later, I never would have imagined that I'd actually wind-up meeting the people who run *Modern Drunkard*, but then—big city, small town—when you meet one interesting eccentric in a new place, you usually end-up being introduced to many of the rest. So, I first met *Modern Drunkard* editor, Frank Kelly Rich, at (of all events), his wedding reception. Thankfully, I was quite drunk at the time.

When I heard that *Modern Drunkard* was hosting its first annual convention in Las Vegas, I didn't even consider going – because I had a full-time day job and was somewhat skint at the time. But, only a few days preceding the convention, I found myself at a Denver dive bar with *Modern Drunkard*'s editor and several of its writers, all of whom collectively managed to cajole me into somehow *finding* a way to attend. So, I did ... and it went a little something like this:

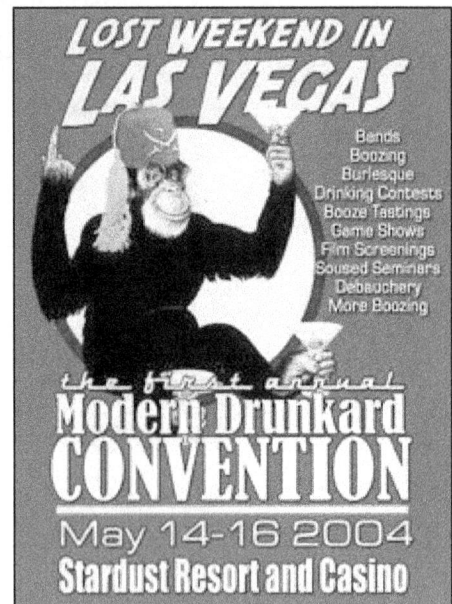

LOST WEEKEND IN LAS VEGAS

Bands
Boozing
Burlesque
Drinking Contests
Booze Tastings
Game Shows
Film Screenings
Soused Seminars
Debauchery
More Boozing

the first annual
Modern Drunkard
CONVENTION
May 14-16 2004
Stardust Resort and Casino

Day Zero – Thursday, May 13, 2004

I get off work at 8:00 p.m., change into my suit jacket, and get on a bus heading toward The Streets of London Pub. Once there, I grab a couple of pieces of pizza across the street and then return to Streets and settle into a couple of pints of Pabst

Blue Ribbon while waiting for the other drunkards to arrive.

By 9:00 everyone is there, and by 9:30, it's time to load up the vehicles and head out to Vegas. Unfortunately, due to technical difficulties beyond the control of the *Drunkard* staff, the planned "Booze Bus" wasn't deemed roadworthy and had to be substituted with a twelve-seater van. Even more disheartening was the fact that the promised Booze Bus Keg had also been cancelled. Not one to be daunted by such an inopportune turn of events, I immediately departed the idling van and dashed to the nearest liquor store to purchase a 32-can "cube" of PBR, as well as a bottle of moderately-priced whiskey. And so, the van departed, and the drinking began in earnest, before we'd even left the parking lot.

The first couple of hours of our journey were quite convivial; everyone was pumped up and in good spirits, and lighthearted small talk was exchanged as flasks of whiskey and cans of PBR circled their way around the van. I don't know about anyone else, but by the time we made our first rest-stop, on the outskirts of Denver, I was fucking pie-eyed. Of course, sitting in the way back of the (poorly-suspended) van, drinking down beers and whiskey, it was only a couple of hours before I turned sallow and suddenly felt the overwhelming need to vomit. Yes, I was officially the first person on the trip to puke (but mind you, I also started drinking over an hour before we even left). Anyway, so, before puking, I hastily emptied the remaining cans of PBR from "the cube," tore the hole agape, and shoved my head inside – just in time to empty my stomach of the semi-liquefied slices of pizza that I'd eaten a few hours earlier (there was a bit of splash-back, and resultantly, I awoke the next day with flecks of vomit on my suit, tie, and shirt). *Woo-hoo*.

After vomiting, I *immediately* passed-out, and slept the entire rest of the journey, awakening just as we pulled into Vegas the next morning. Couldn't have planned it better, actually. Not surprisingly, due to "The Telephone Game" effect, by the next day, people were asking me, "Oh, are you the guy who puked all over himself on the ride down, then passed-out in his own vomit in the back of the van?" – which was of course, a colorful embellishment of what'd actually happened, but they can believe whatever they want.

Day One – Friday, May 14, 2004

Rolling into Vegas, all dozen passengers in our van were fatigued from the twelve-hour alcohol-infused drive across Colorado, Utah, and Nevada, and I was still somewhat tipsy from the night before. As soon as we pulled into the parking lot of The Stardust Resort and Casino, my first mission was to find a bathroom in which to relieve myself, as well as wash off the flecks of vomit that had splashed out of the PBR box and onto my clothing. Others strode straight to the slot machines and bars.

Following our arrival and de-boarding, there was a period of several delirious hours, during which the various *Drunkard* parties wandered around The Stardust and its surrounding environs in a state of sleep-deprived, hungover confusion. There was some minor debacle with the room reservations ... nobody could check-in until 3:30 p.m. ... and everyone was clearly distempered – exhausted, hungover, and fuckin' pissed off. Some of us made our way over to The Peppermill, where I had a couple of non-alcoholic Cokes and a breakfast plate (this was met with some disapproving cluck-clucking from the token surly-sloshed Scotsman in attendance).

Following brunch, about fifteen or so drunkards managed to make it over to The Double Down Saloon (a dank armpit of a Punk Rock bar) for the scheduled opening "meet-and-greet" event, which naturally, involved drinking. My first drink in Vegas (at The Double Down) was a pint of Guinness, sometime around noon on Friday. Apparently, *Modern Drunkard* hosts an online chatroom, and the majority of the people in attendance at The Double Down, were folks who'd flown out from all over the country (and in one case, Europe), and were now meeting each other in person for the first time – this filled the dank, near-dark bar with hoots, yells, and drunken hugs. Not being "in the chatroom club," so to speak, my companions and I left as soon as this nonsense started.

Franklin Bell – the man, the myth, the drunk.

Back at The Stardust, there was more confusion about rooms and how to get them. Frank Bell, our "designated driver" from the previous night, had been up for about thirty hours straight and was beginning to stare off into space with a blank, zombified look in his glazed-over eyes, while intermittently blinking hard and rubbing his temples. While we waited (and waited, and *waited*) for our rooms, there was a lot of wandering around looking for affordable booze. Boyd Rice discovered the $2.99 margaritas over at Westward Ho! that come in fluorescent, foot-long, dumbbell-shaped glasses (with $1.99 refills), and he and a very delirious Frank Bell knocked back a couple of those, while I drank something with far less pizzazz (I dislike margaritas).

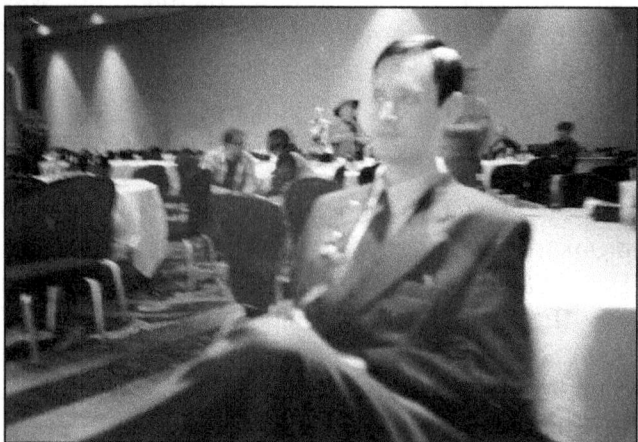

Me doing my best impression of a wax figure, while waiting for the convention to start.

Boyd and Frank, each being staff-writers for *Modern Drunkard*, had been promised free rooms at The Stardust for this event, whereas I'd joined on at the very last minute, and hadn't secured accommodations beforehand; so I made an arrangement with Frank to share his room with him, and just pay him a to-be-determined sum of money for the extra bed that would have otherwise gone unused. This arrangement would have worked out just fine ... except that when it finally came time to check in (somewhere around 4:00 p.m.), it was revealed that Boyd and Frank were supposed to *share* a single room. This, obviously, presented a problem for me, having *no* reservation at a booked-up hotel (during a weekend in which a pool tournament, a NASCAR event, and a drunkard convention were all being held). Now, this would have left a less committed

man "up shit creek," but I resolved to simply sleep on Boyd and Frank's floor and then spend the money that I'd set aside for accommodations on booze, booze, booze and more *booze*.

At 6:00 p.m., the weekend officially kicked-off, in The Stardust's Avalon Ballroom, which I'm told is the very same *classy* venue that Elvis played his 1968 comeback special at. Emceed from the stage by Denver's answer to Lee Press-On, the icy-witted and immaculately-dressed Sid Pink, the event began with an introduction to *Modern Drunkard*'s various writers and staff-members, as well as a series of concise drunken speeches given by the masterminds of both *Modern Drunkard Magazine* and The Lost Weekend In Las Vegas event; the magazine's editor, Mr. Rich and, urm, "Giles Humbert The Third." By this point, I was back in a state of all-but-total inebriation, and hence found all of this very amusing and entertaining.

Sometime shortly after the convention kick-off, a local news crew showed up and filmed interviews with various drunkards in attendance. Luke Schmaltz, singer of the Denver-based Punk band King Rat, gave a spirited performance for the cameras, jumping on top of a table, knocking it over, toppling a chair, spraying his beer all over the place, and immediately receiving a stern and solemn warning from Hotel Security. Boyd gave a lengthy interview, which I caught none of, but apparently made it onto television in almost all of its entirety. Then everyone drank for a while.

Mr. Sid Pink, emcee.

Soon, the embittered drunkard comic Troy Baxley took the stage to perform an event billed as "Falling Down Drunk Stand-Up Comedy," a fitting title, of course. For the most part, I can't stand stand-up comedy, but Baxley was actually pretty funny, and not only had most of the room riotously guffawing at points, but unflappably managed to navigate a surprisingly combative, heckler-addled crowd, with relative ease – turning many of the dumb-dumb hecklers' yelling back on them (Mr. Pink didn't do such a bad job of this either). Meanwhile, everyone drank.

Pabst Blue Ribbon was—yes—*free* at the bar, but throughout most of the weekend I resisted drinking beer in favor of more elegant beverages, namely: White Russians, Bloody Marys, and Gin & Tonics.

Assorted drunks.

An hour or so later, the preliminary round of "The Clash of The Tightest" began. This was a dead serious drinking competition of the highest order. I believe the rules went something like this: everyone pairs off; each contender gets to select their drink of choice, which will be poured at the bar; the contenders each have five seconds to neck down their drinks following the completion of their opponent's drink; after each drink, it is incumbent upon each contender that they complete a dexterity test, by dropping a ping-pong ball through a suspended tube and then catching it at the bottom of the tube; a contender loses the contest if they pass out, vomit, refuse a drink, or fail the dexterity test; winners from round one advance to round two, the following evening.

Naturally, this was an unmitigated fucking fiasco—just an absolute fall-down drunken mess shitshow—which I prudently declined to participate in. If I recall correctly, the highest number of drinks ordered by a pair of competitors was up in the thirties, or something insane like

that. One of the losers (a fashionably disheveled, hipsterish-looking fellow, who donned a tilted baseball cap and aviator glasses *all* weekend) smashed one of the ping-pong ball tubes in a fit of rage, upon losing the contest. All in all, the whole thing was very reminiscent of that scene in *Indiana Jones & The Raiders of The Lost Ark*, in which Indy's girlfriend is going shot-for-shot with some big bruiser in a cabin in the Nepalese frozen wilderness in the middle of nowhere, prior to the Nazis bursting in and shooting-up the place before it burns to the ground. It was, um, *sort of* like that.

At one point, a young, very, *very* crocked couple took the stage and announced their intention to marry, and (apparently) did so. This was absolutely fucking hilarious; they could literally *barely* stand up, and they were both mumbling into the microphone, *"I fuuukkin' love this fukinnn' girl right her! I love yoooouuu!"* and then they made out in the most gratuitous of manners possible ... and this was all captured on film for posterity, of course.

A few hours elapsed, during which my companions and I retired to our room with various bottles of booze and mixers, and hit the liquor *hard*. From here on, my preferred drink was Bloody Marys. Upon returning to The Avalon Ballroom (stumbling drunk at this point), we were witness to a burlesque show, presented by the ladies of Denver's own Ooh La La Burlesque Troupe. Very nice.

Shortly thereafter, none other than Lorin "Partridge" appeared on the scene with a posse of misfit characters from San Jose, California. He and I had been in correspondence for a while and hit it off immediately, and got on more than well throughout the remainder of the weekend. There was more wanton boozing, as only the pros are capable of.

Lorin and I discuss clandestine matters of great import.

There are no "open container" laws in Vegas, nor is there any "last-call." Ergo, around 2:00 a.m., a number of those in attendance at the convention managed to make it over to The Double Down Saloon for a pre-scheduled "Late Night Mixer," which my companions and I passed on, in favor of John Holmes-sized $1.59, three-quarter-pound hot dogs and foot-long margaritas over at Westward Ho!. I can't remember exactly what happened after that because all this stuff blurs together now.

I do remember this however; at some point in the wee hours of the morning, Boyd and Frank retired to the hotel room, while I wandered over to Walgreens 24-hour pharmacy to purchase an air mattress, which I'd planned on using throughout the trip and then giving to Frank when it was all over. Of course, being that we were in Las Vegas—the city where "luck" is everything—naturally, as luck would have it, Walgreens didn't sell air mattresses; they only seemed to sell Hawaiian shirts and cheesy souvenirs. So I returned to the hotel room empty-handed, to find my roommates passed-out cold in their beds. I then decided that the wisest course of action for me would be to just crawl into the closet and pass-

out – the logic of which being that since the sun would be up in a few hours anyway, at least inside the closet I wouldn't be awakened by sunlight. And so, I spent the entire weekend sleeping spartanly; in a hotel room closet, with nothing but a couple of pillows ... but damn it, I slept *in a suit*.

It doesn't matter *where* you sleep; it matters *how* you sleep.

Day Two – Saturday, May 15, 2004

I wake up liquored up, in a closet in a hotel room in Vegas, and the first thing I hear is Frank rousing Boyd in a state of semi-panic regarding my whereabouts, saying things like, "Boyd! All Brian's stuff is here—his boots are here—but he's gone ... oh *fuck*, what if he got arrested? Oh no, this is *really* bad!" So Frank's rummaging around the room, and decides to slide open the closet door – sees my feet, and literally jumps back in shock. Laughter ensues. It's nice to wake up drunk – saves you the trouble of having a hangover.

Anyway, again we pass on the scheduled "Bloody Mary Morning Mixer" at The Double Down Saloon, and instead opt to pick-up Lorin at his nearby hotel, and head-out to the sticks of Vegas to pay a visit to Boyd's longtime friend, cult film director Ray Dennis Steckler. Steckler (director of such Dada-esque films as *The Incredibly Strange Creatures Who Stopped Living and Became Mixed-Up Zombies,* and *Rat Pfink a Boo Boo),* now runs his own video store out in the burbs, which naturally carries all his numerous, far-out films, on both VHS and DVD. Steckler proved to be somehow both outgoingly congenial and aloofly reserved at the same time. He was more than happy to talk about his films, and the book he and Boyd had worked on together back in the '80s, *Incredibly Strange Films.* Boyd had brought him a Denver Broncos baseball cap as a gift, and in turn, walked away with a stack of Steckler VHS tapes. Before leaving, we all took turns snapping photos with him:

Me n' "Cash Flagg."

Following this, we headed out for lunch, to a nearby Steckler-recommended Mexican restaurant, outside of which was this dazzling advertisement:

Anyway, we returned to The Stardust just in time to catch the *Modern Drunkard* film festival, titled "Indie Cinema for Inebriates." This

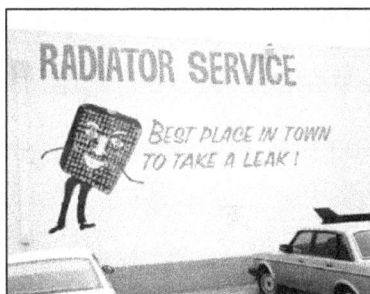

featured a rough cut of the film *Nixing The Twist*, a feature-length production written and directed by *Modern Drunkard* editor Frank Rich. Shot in black-and-white and heavy on the shadow-play, it's a sort of drunkard's film noir about a couple of hit men who start to mentally break down as their hit jobs become more and more fucked up. The whole thing was shot in and around Denver, and most of the cast comprises local musicians and other notables, many of whom were in the audience. Fine film. Dug it. However, I was wasted – so maybe it's actually terrible (who knows?). Apparently, much of the production of *Nixing The Twist* was paid for by various bizarre means possible, while its writer / director was sleeping on the lead actor's couch and eating recently-killed big game out of his refrigerator. God damn.

Then there was a "break for dinner," during which time my companions and I trekked to the liquor store, bought more booze, went back up to our room, and imbibed some more. At 8:00 p.m., there was a scheduled "Modern Drunk Rock

Blow Out" back down in The Avalon Ballroom, which featured the bands King Rat, Barstool Messiah, The Swanks, and The Dead Heaven Cowboys. I remember none of them. Following the live bands, however, I do remember returning to The Avalon Ballroom to bear witness to "The

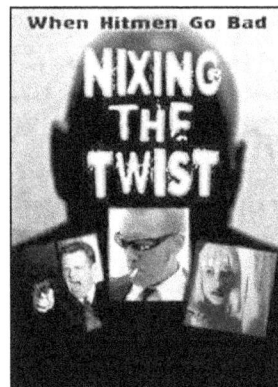

Clash of The Tightest" semi-finals. This featured the use of such ridiculous inventions as the-six-man-beer-bong and was just as disturbing and impressive as the first round.

Actually, come to think of it, the beer bong stuff wasn't part of the drinking competition proper, it was just sort of another over-the-top thing going on in the intervals between rounds, but since I don't have any photos of the actual drinking competitions, you get a photo of the beer bong instead. Deal with it.

The six-man beer bong in action.

So, following this nonsense, we were then coaxed into returning to The Double Down Saloon, which was packed to the gills with Punk Rock types, there to witness the same (now even drunker) bands who'd just played a few hours earlier at the Avalon. Being a bit *too* besotted at this point (yes, it is possible), I made my way over to the nearest 7-Eleven to purchase some— *wince*—water. On my walk there and back, I was fortunate enough pass several overcrowded gay discotheques, whose clientele had a number of flattering things to say in my direction, and once inside 7-Eleven, I was privy to the inner workings of how a pimp handles his ho when she is being intractably uppity and needs to have her stubborn will broken, yet again. *Ahhh, Vegas*.

Back at The Double Down, Boyd and Lorin were completely fed up with Punk Rock, and something resembling a cat fight had broken out betwixt one of the Ooh La La Burlesque Troupe girls and some local female Punk, which resulted in a ripped shirt, and all parties being ejected from the premises. Taking this as our cue, my companions and I were treated (by Lorin's hesher friend) to a breakneck-paced ride back to The Stardust, which was set to the soothing sounds of old-school Death Metal at full volume.

Back at the hotel, we set into some more drinking, of course. Foolishly, Frank decided to immediately pass out stone-cold on his bed ... (ahem) ... so naturally, Lorin took this opportunity to *beautify* him a bit:

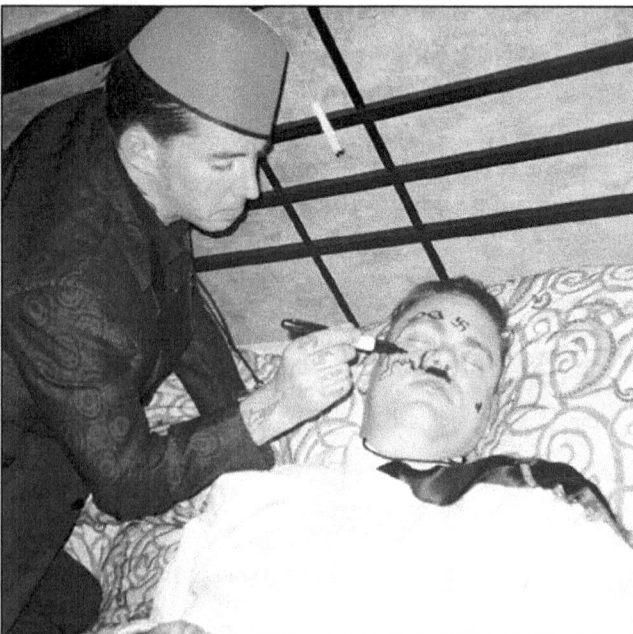

Day Three – Sunday, May 16, 2004

I wake up drunk. The first thing I hear is the sound of running and splashing water that goes on and on and on, and I think to myself, *Ahh, that must be Frank trying to wash all the Sharpie off his face* – when I entered the bathroom afterward, he'd left one of the hotel towels looking not unlike The Shroud of Turin, but in the end, he was quite the good sport about the whole thing.

At this point in the weekend, 11:00 a.m. is *waaaay* too early to make it to the scheduled "Bloody Mary Morning Mixer" at The Double Down, though I did manage to make it to the "Soused Seminars" back in The Avalon Ballroom. This event commenced with Boyd giving a presentation on the birth of post-WWII Tiki Culture in the United States, and its (imitation) "tropical" (made-up) "exotic" alcoholic beverages, which was accompanied by a somewhat elaborate slideshow on a big-screen digital projector. Considering just how much booze he must have still had in his system, and how late he'd stayed up the night before, Boyd gave a commendably coherent lecture. So too did Rich English and Nick Plumber, who followed Boyd with an erudite symposium on the illustrious history of booze, from the time of the ancients, up to the present day. They, too, were surprisingly coherent and articulate, and also used fancy digital slide projections.

At some point in the evening, there was an award ceremony, and I was presented with "The Dorothy Parker Award," formally anointing me as "Most Sarcastic Drunkard."

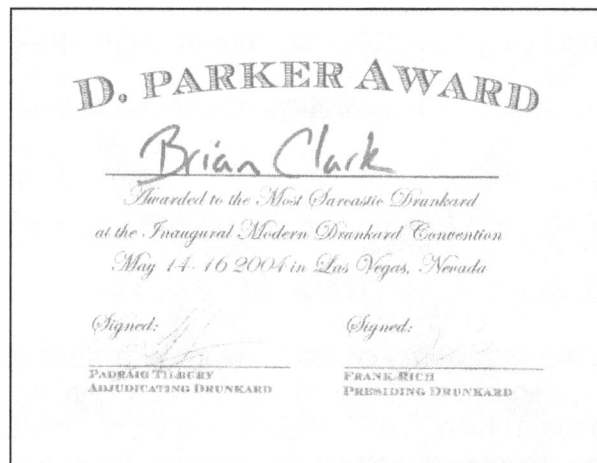

Being, um, *very drunk*, and not expecting to win anything (since I knew only a fraction of the people there), I lumberingly made my way to the stage and gave some lame, slurred acceptance speech that hopefully wasn't recorded.

We were then treated to another performance by the Ooh La La Troupe, and this one was definitely the finest of the weekend, the highlights being: when they did a sort of Scopitone shadow-dance behind big cutouts of liquor glasses; and when they all broke-out the pigtails and Catholic School Girl outfits, while a guy named Eric came out dressed as the Pope and sort of lecherously ogled the lot of them while wandering around the stage.

Sometime late on Sunday night, Lorin and I both made appearances before the event's documentary film crew, in which they asked each of us questions like, "What's your name, where are you from, and why are you a Modern Drunkard?" Lorin gave an impassioned monologue, the content of which I forget, while I only made a quick, vague statement like, "I'm on board with The Dunkard, and I'm here, because this is what people want – it's fun and people want to have fun." Probably going to be on the documentary film – and probably going to be lame and inarticulate. Oh well.

Anyway, of course, the highlight of the evening, the crown jewel of The Lost Weekend In Las Vegas convention, was the final "Clash of The Tightest" bout. This came down to two finalists: a fellow of average build (one of the guys from DrinkingStuff.com), and a behemoth of a man, who went only by the appellation Oggar. In the end, cruel fate left the smaller man vomiting into a large Rubbermaid garbage can, which he then toppled into, head-first. *Nice.* The winner, on the other hand, seemed largely unfazed by the obscene amount of alcohol he'd just consumed. And that was that. Who knows what Oggar won, but he sure could fucking *drink.* Anyway, things

Me and Eric (The Pope).

didn't get, um, "unpleasant" until the very end of Sunday night. Permit me to explain:

First off, I'd been drinking all weekend. I was tanked as all hell. I'd agreed to help load a bunch of the stage audio equipment (monitors, speakers, cables, *et cetera*) onto the vans that were to head back out to Denver the next morning. While walking between the rows of dining tables, over to the stage, to begin doing this, I strolled past a trio of fellows coming in the other direction, whom I'd had virtually no interaction with whatsoever all weekend. One of the three, a hipsterish looking fellow about my age, who was sporting a deftly disheveled bed-head hairdo and a pair of black jeans tucked into his black cowboy boots (something approximating the Jon Spencer look, I suppose), well, I don't know who this guy was, who he was friends with, where he was from, or what his relationship to *Modern Drunkard* was, but somehow he and I had managed to rub each other the wrong way, in what little interaction we'd had.

Well, as I walked past this fellow and his two friends, he says to one of them, while gesturing in my direction, "Well, at least you aren't a total loser like this fucking guy." Hearing this, and being, as I said, piss-potted, I immediately spun on my heel, turned around, and followed them over to the bar. As they stood there at the bar, I stood about ten to fifteen feet away, with my arms crossed, emanating a hostile look in this fellow's direction. Well, he saw me and realized I'd heard him, but pretended not to see me staring right at him; avoiding eye contact and nervously laughing with his friends. So, I stood there, for perhaps ten seconds, then, sufficiently content that this guy knew that I'd heard him, I turned around and set about loading gear into the van.

Upon finishing with the gear-loading, I headed over to the water cooler, and—what do you know?—none other than this same fellow moseys on over and fills up his cup with water.

189

While he's doing so, he says something to me along the lines of, "Hey there, champ." If my recollection serves correctly (which it probably doesn't), I look at him and say something to the effect of, "Do you have a problem?" To which he mutters something along the lines of "Whatever … *champ"* as he turns to walk away. So, as this gentleman is turning to walk off with his glass of water, I simply turn toward him, ever so slightly, extend my foot, and trip him.

Mr. Fashionably-Ironic-Cowboy-Boots goes tumbling to the ground like an old lady tripping over a tree root—flailing his arms in an attempt to keep his balance and not spill his drink—and lands face down on the carpeted floor of The Avalon Ballroom. Despite all the "unpleasantness" to follow this event, it was *totally* worth it, just to see this fucker fall down flailing.

Well, naturally, he jumps to his feet, and is up in my face shouting, red-in-the-face with flecks of spittle flying, "What the fuck motherfucker! These people put on this nice event—this convention—and now you're trying to fucking spoil it by tripping me!" Of course, he knew exactly *why* I'd tripped him—because he'd fucked with me, not once, but *twice* mind you—but that's beside the point for now. So I say to him, "Okay, you know what, you're right. You're totally right. This is a nice convention, and I *don't* want to spoil it, so let's just put aside the fact that you said shit to me, and that I just tripped you, and leave it at …" at which point he socks me in the chin with his right fist. Funny, I guess he wasn't such a grateful conventioneer after all.

So anyway, this guy is hammered and I'm hammered, and he lunges at me too hard, and I lean back to dodge him too much, and so he basically lunges on top of me in the same motion as he punches me. So the next second, we're on the floor rolling around punching each other like a couple of high school kids, and I don't know where or how well I got him, but he managed to hit me square in the temple, as well as the neck.

Of course, within moments, The Stardust's security guards were dragging us off each other, and then few moments later, this fellow and I are sitting in a side room, surrounded by hotel security, deliriously confessing to having violated the terms of our stay in the hotel. They were going to toss us both out of the hotel (I wasn't technically "staying" there, but they didn't know that), but since Lorin had wisely gotten chummy and ingratiated himself with one of the security guards beforehand, they gave us the option of affecting a purely performative reconciliation by shaking hands; and then being immediately escorted to our rooms on the conditional insistence that we stay there for the remainder of the night lest we be kicked out of the hotel. Being reasonable people (at base anyway), we both agreed to this proviso.

Now, I must confess that while I do think the gentleman in question definitely deserved to be tripped, I do feel more than a bit guilty for having been at least fifty percent responsible for having brought the unseemly air of playground-level violence to the Inaugural Modern Drunkard Convention. For this, I am, in all honesty, contrite and embarrassed. I hope I didn't cause any problems for the convention's organizers, because that really *would* be a shame. However, as someone later astutely pointed out, it was a three-day convention that contained *all* the facets of inebriation: drinking contests, sloshed speeches, wasted weddings and inebriated engagements, soused sex (one can assume), plastered Punk bands, buzzed burlesque dancers, and finally, a boozed-up (albeit brief) bar-fight. So, to put a gloss on the incident, at the very least, "the circle was complete," so to speak. And it wasn't a particularly *bad* fight *per se* – no black eyes or broken noses.

Of course, it was also somewhat appropriate that not less than two hours after being presented with the award for "Most Sarcastic Drunkard," I was rolling around on the floor with some other alcohol-addled asshole.

So anyway, following all this, I returned to the quarantine of my room for about half an hour, then disobeyed Security's orders and escaped the hotel for yet another three-quarter-pound mega schlong-dog at Westward Ho!. While Boyd and I split ours, Lorin, intrepid soul that he is, purchased a big-gulp-sized margarita and continued drinking in earnest – and this was late (*late*) Sunday night. I passed out plastered in the closet about an hour later.

Day Four – Monday, May 17, 2004

I wake up woozy, shower, get my stuff together, then totteringly stumble bleary-eyed into the van, for the dozen-hour drive back to Denver. Of course, the drive home was unadulterated *fucking pain*, for everyone. Morale was at rock bottom, and whatever *esprit de corps* that had developed amongst the rabble lot of drunkards heading into Vegas had clearly evaporated. Drowsy though I was, I couldn't sleep because the van bounced *way* too much, and my head and jaw were both aching from a farrago of fists and firewater.

Predictably, we sorry lot of hapless hungover van passengers were subjected to the musical fancy of the drivers, and as a result, I was lucky enough to get to hear Madonna's techno album in its entirety, as well as a number of other sappy and cloying girlie musical selections. During one Tori Amos or Natalie Merchant song (or whoever the fuck it was), Boyd yelled from the back of the van, "Wow, this is the longest commercial for tampons I've ever heard!" which was my favorite part of the whole journey back.

Frank, powering through a brutal hangover.

All in all, it was a dreary, protracted, nauseous daylong odyssey through the desolate, barren, extra-terrestrial-lookin' arid badlands of Nevada, Utah, and western Colorado – which I would prefer not to recollect any more than I already have.

And that was it, The Lost Weekend In Las Vegas. I got home at 1:45 a.m. Monday night, sober (mostly), but then again not really. To be honest, as I write this, it's been a full day and a half, and I still don't feel completely sober.

Perhaps the best part of the whole trip is the fact that while I spent about three and a half days in Las Vegas, I didn't spend so much as *a single cent* on gambling – not a penny. No, all my money went to booze and cheap cigarillos. Gambling is for experts and suckers – I'm no expert, so I didn't want to be a sucker.

Anyway, maybe it was the three solid days of hard drinking; maybe it was the fact that I smoked probably, oh let's say six or seven packs of cut-rate cigarillos throughout the weekend; maybe it was the three days of eating naught but $1.59 three-quarter pound hot dogs and items from the McDonald's "value menu"; maybe it was the three nights of sleeping with no blankets on the floor of a hotel room closet; or maybe, just maybe, it was the mild concussion that I sustained from being punched in the side of the head; regardless, now, back here in Denver, my present sodden state cannot sufficiently be summed-up with the simple idiom, "hung over"—it's much, *much* more than that— more akin to withdrawal, or radiation sickness perhaps, but prodigious enduring pain, nonetheless. I worked eight hours today, and it was like ... *fuck*, somehow I managed to be coherent and not fuck things up at my job, but it took a lot of effort and sheer willpower, to say the very least.

Now, youngsters, I want to tell you something, in all seriousness; I survived this event, but it wasn't by serendipity alone. There was a method to the madness. I made sure to drink ice water intermittently, between every five or six drinks; I made sure to eat regularly, but *in moderation* (so as to keep sustenance in the stomach, while not providing excessive vomit-fodder); every morning I downed a multivitamin horse-pill, and every night before I went comatose I swallowed a B-complex supplement and a couple'a Advil PMs. These are the tricks of the trade, whippersnappers. Use them wisely. ...

The Inversion of Cool

2007

When I was a kid and an adolescent—in the 1980s and early '90s— it wasn't "cool" to be poor. It was decidedly *un*-cool, in fact. Poverty was something that children and adolescents were ashamed of, and attempted to conceal as best they could. In elementary school, the cool kids invariably came from money; they had tons of new toys, Nintendo video game systems with lots of games, top-end BMX bikes or skateboards, and their parents threw them decadent and ostentatious birthday parties. By middle school, the signifiers of "coolness" had changed, but they were still mostly based on affluence: Sony Walkmans or "boombox" stereos and lots of store-bought cassette tapes; expensive Nike Air shoes, state-of-the-art Nintendo Gameboys, new and seasonably in-fashion name-brand clothes, and so on. Poor kids didn't have most of this stuff, and were often therefore taunted simply for being poor; for wearing hand-me-down clothes; for not having "hot" new expensive athletic shoes, or toys, or nascent digital gaming tech. Schoolyard interclass ridicule was a thing. Sneering laughter was had. Humiliating tears were shed.

As an adult, I can't help but notice that this socioeconomic desirability dynamic has pretty much completely inverted; at least in The United States, anyway. Having come from wealth is now something that American grown-ups tend to obfuscate and are ashamed of. To be deemed a "trust fund kid" or having been "born with a silver spoon in one's mouth" via intergenerational wealth, are essentially mild slurs, aimed at cutting a person's accomplishments down; as a way of saying, "You didn't *earn* what you have, you inherited it; and even if you did earn it, you still 'had a leg up' on the rest of us."

In the world of adulthood, having had any kind of perceived advantage in one's upbringing is treated as a species of "cheating" in The Game of Life; whereas coming up working class and having "pulled oneself up" by the proverbial bootstraps is a basis for beaming pride, if not smug haughtiness. This is owing to the fact that, as adults, we all like to believe (or at least pretend) that we live in a "meritocracy" – a sociocultural system in which everyone should be allowed to compete fairly in the capitalist marketplace "on a level playing field" – and that following such ostensibly fair competition, one's socioeconomic status is determined by individual talent, achievement, and performance—in a word, *merit*—rather than by familial social class or arbitrary immutable traits. It's an aspect of the so-called "American Dream" – the archetype of the "self-made man" in a meritocratic nation of equals under the law, with a parity of access and opportunity, competing in the "rat race" to "make it" in America. Accordingly, to attain social acceptance and respect in the world of contemporary adult Americans, one must claim to have "earned" one's socioeconomic stature out of whole cloth, as a grownup.

Ergo, as an adult, I've heard many a braggadocious slurred rant at bars about how the speaker claims to have been "dirt poor" as a kid, and "worked their way up" to where they are now, as a comfortable homeowning and fully employed respectable member of adult society. ("I *worked* for *my* money, buddy!") What I find odd about this attitude is that people who claim to have grown up poor and "pulled themselves up by their bootstraps" often seem to be simultaneously complaining about all the adversity they had to undergo, and yet also concurrently bragging about the fact that they surmounted it and came out the other end as a fully actualized and functional adult. They'll harangue the listener with yarns of youthful deprivation and hardship, as a pretext for the predictable self-congratulatory culmination of, " ... *and look at me now!"* Life's surmountable challenges are overcome, and humble, ostensibly plebeian beginnings are cashed in for prideful, eminent endings.

Which begs the question: would such allegedly scrappy and tenacious people actually prefer to have traded places with the childhoods of pampered "rich kids" who had everything handed to them "on a silver platter" and "never had to work a day in their lives"? It would seem that the answer is, by implication, a resounding *"no."* After all, rich kids—having never had their mettle tested by adversity and lack—cannot have pulled themselves up by their ignoble bootstraps – and, more importantly, can't boast about supposedly having done so after a few drinks at the bar.

The Argument from Celebrity Authority

The Most Regrettably American of Logical Fallacies

2009

Henry Rollins. The name evokes images of shirtless, muscle-bound, tattooed, shaven-headed, testosterone-fueled, amped-up Hard Rock. As well it should; as the frontman to his eponymous Rollins Band, the man successfully plugged away at sweaty stomp-rock for many years. But unlike the vast majority of Hard Rock singers out there, Rollins is something of a polymath; an orator, actor, TV presenter, radio deejay, publisher, and published writer as well. Partly as a result of this suite of varied talents, Rollins is one of those anomalous public figures who somehow manage to retain underground Punk/Hardcore credibility, while concurrently achieving mainstream notoriety.

Rollins first made his mark as the vocalist to the seminal early '80s hardcore band Black Flag, following the demise of which he founded the more Metal-ish Rollins Band, for which he is now probably best known. Being a charismatic fellow comfortable in front of both the camera and the microphone, a passionate performer, and (apparently) a generally hardworking guy, by the end of the '80s Rollins had become one of those recognizable underground music personas with a distinct ideological bent, whose names and visages are (to one degree or another) synonymous with a particular worldview. Unlike similar underground-music-scene mainstays, however, Rollins is notable in the sense that by the mid-1990s, he'd managed to break into the commercial music mainstream. He became an overground celebrity while still somehow staying "indie."

I first noticed Henry Rollins in my teens, back in the mid-1990s. While idly watching MTV in my parents' suburban living room, I was mildly befuddled by Rollins Band's "Liar" video (on regular rotation at the time), for which Rollins alternately donned a cop uniform, a Superman outfit, a "square" white-collar getup, and was painted bright red. Throughout the video, he grinned psychotically at the camera while lip-synch-screaming the song's lyrics. I later spotted him hosting an episode of *MTV Sports*, following which I recognized him again, playing bit parts in hip films like David Lynch's *Lost Highway*.

Rollins Band's Liar/Disconnect *single, 1994.*

As a teenager, I was very into bands like Dead Kennedys, Big Black, Melvins, The Dwarves, and other ostensibly "underground" acts that occasionally drew the same fans as Rollins Band. And of course, circulating in that sort of social milieu, I soon became aware of Black Flag, and eventually picked up a copy of their *Damaged* album, on which Rollins delivers some pretty catchy paeans to violence and angst. But to be honest, that's really the extent of my exposure to the work of Henry Rollins. I've seen his face grace the covers of magazines and noticed his name on the spines of books on friends' bookshelves for years now, but I just haven't paid him a lot of attention in the decade-and-a-half since I first became aware of him as the Superman-outfit-wearing singer of "Liar."

About a week ago, however, I finally read a piece of Rollins' writing; one installment of a column he regularly contributes to the website of the internationally distributed, glossy magazine *Vanity Fair* (I don't know whether or not the piece appears in the actual print version). The column in question is titled "Change You Don't Have To Believe In, Just Deal With," and is but one of an ongoing series of op-ed pieces from "VanityFair.com's resident straight talker" (a cartoon caricature of a stern-looking Rollins appears next to this title). It's a fairly succinct screed, wherein Rollins attacks those he disagrees with and defends those he does agree with regarding the issue of President Barack Obama's recent visit to Great Britain.[2]

Henry Rollins is VF.com's resident straight talker.

Happening across this particular installment of Rollins' column while sitting at my computer, sipping on a cold can of beer, I was shocked—*yes, shocked!*—at how mind-bogglingly terrible it was. How poorly written. How intellectually lazy and misguided. How directionless and pointless. How utterly juvenile. Most importantly, how undeserving of the imprimatur of legitimacy that comes with being a columnist for a magazine like *Vanity Fair*, having one's work presented alongside that of real writers like Christopher Hitchens. Rollins' piece was so bad that after I finished it, I put down my beer and read it again, just to make sure I hadn't missed something the first time around (nope – it was still terrible). On the second reading, however, I realized that this particular piece of writing is salient, not for its content or ideas, of course, but as an instructional tool. Although brief (it's just a few short paragraphs), it's worth discussing because it is absolutely chock-full of flawed logic—a smorgasbord of bad argumentation—and thus it inadvertently serves as an almost point-by-point exemplar of how *not* to make a convincing argument. As I will illustrate in the following paragraphs, every single point Rollins attempts to make in "Change You Don't Have To Believe In, Just Deal With" is not supported using straightforward reason or solid logic, but rather, by his employment of a range of torpid argumentative shortcuts – that is to say, logical fallacies. Foremost among these logical fallacies—and overarching Rollins' piece as a whole—is a quintessentially American cultural affliction that I've been increasingly annoyed with as of late (and the reason I decided to write this essay); celebrity status as a stand-in for aptitude, or what is otherwise known as The Argument From (Celebrity) Authority.

Rollins begins "Change You Don't Have To Believe In, Just Deal With" by informing his readers that he's been "reading material at conservative sites" (he doesn't say which) and that the "content contributors" to those sites (he doesn't name who) are "sub-literates," who're bent out of shape over the fact that Britain is "in love" with President Barack Obama and the First Lady, Michelle. Rollins then goes on to refer to these unnamed conservatives as "mouth-breathers" and "knuckle-draggers," who he asserts must be frustrated by the fact that "Obama will be received exceedingly well all over the world and perhaps help the entire planet become a more peaceful and prosperous place" – and that in so doing, President Obama will get in the way of all the "disaster" these unnamed conservatives had planned.

---

[2] Rollins, Henry, "Change You Don't Have To Believe In, Just Deal With," *Vanity Fair*, April 3, 2009, web.archive.org/web/2009040800425l/http://www.vanityfair.com/online/politics/2009/04/change-you-dont-have-to-believe-in-just-deal-with.html

By not naming which writers at which conservative sites he's been reading, Rollins gives himself the opportunity to simply ascribe whatever vague reactionary hysteria to them that he finds suits his argument; and in so doing make himself appear reasonable in tearing that hysteria down. With no quoted statements, no names named, and no sites cited, Rollins can say whatever he likes about these nameless "conservatives," and can't be proven wrong. He then (needlessly) attempts to invalidate the opinions held by said "conservatives" by simply insulting them like a kid on the playground ("mouth-breathers," *et cetera*). This is just petty name-calling—hardly objective, reasonable, writing for grownups—but Rollins wants us to take him seriously.

Having already contrasted President Obama with his predecessor the "born-again Texan," Rollins then devotes a paragraph to pointlessly speculating that, were a hypothetical President John McCain to arrive on British shores for an official visit, "The Queen might have all of a sudden been unavoidably detained for an indefinite period and sent an assistant to apologize. The protests on the streets may have resulted in even more destruction and arrests." He bases this conjecture about *what might have been* on nothing, of course. But it doesn't matter, because he's already moved on to discussing the actual violent protests that accompanied President Obama's real visit to Great Britain.

Being VanityFair.com's "resident straight talker," Rollins now levels with us and starts givin' it to us straight, saying, "So, let's talk about those protests. Some of the protestors did a fair bit of destruction but they were only a fraction of the huge amount of people on the streets in London. If you read some articles, the protestors were nothing but agitators. They were characterized as 'anarchists,' 'anti-capitalists,' and 'environmentalists,' out to end the existence of money. I'm not buying it." Again, Rollins refers to "some articles" which impugn the character of the London protestors, but doesn't bother citing them.[3] Nor does he bother to explain to us why he isn't "buying it" – but the implication is that (*sans* evidence either way) we shouldn't buy it either.

G20 protesters in London, 2009. Imagine the smell....

Rollins then goes on to assure us that he personally does not condone the destruction of property, but that, nevertheless, "the anger expressed speaks to a very real, global ailment that is having catastrophic effects on people everywhere. It could very well be that many British folks know what's at stake and are so alarmed by what they feel is an impending disaster that they took to the streets to let their voices be heard." This statement leaves me wondering; if this "global ailment" is so "very real," then why can't Rollins just come out and simply say what it is? If

---

[3] I didn't follow this particular tidbit of news at all, but I'm willing to cede to Rollins on this particular bit of conjecture. Most of the protestors who did damage in London probably weren't ideologically-driven anarchists, anti-capitalists, or environmentalists with some sort of cohesive political goal – like most smash-happy protestors in most places they were likely just a bunch of misguided malcontents with a seething contempt for that nebulous, vaguely-defined entity known as "the man."

he thinks that British folks "know what's at stake," and it's as serious as he seems to believe it is, then perhaps—just perhaps—it might be worth sharing with the rest of us as well, no? If Rollins feels that there's something out there which he alleges "is having catastrophic effects on people everywhere," then why doesn't he give it a name already? Is it poverty in the "developing world"? Is it the specter of total global economic collapse? Is it impending food shortages? Is it the threat of epidemic disease? Is it overpopulation? Is it war? He sure makes it sound important, but apparently it's not important enough to elucidate upon, so we're left to conjecture as to what this "impending disaster" might be.[4]

Rollins' doomsday omissions aside, there are also a couple of glaring inconsistencies that pop out midway into his column. Although he has no problem whatsoever characterizing conservatives as "sub-literates," "mouth-breathers," and "knuckle-draggers," Rollins nonetheless balks at the idea that those Britons who "took to the streets to let their voices be heard" are characterized unfairly as mere "agitators" and "anarchists" who want to destroy the monetary system. Likewise, while Rollins initially deplores "all the disaster" that he feels conservatives "had planned" for a McCain presidency, he nevertheless offhandedly excuses as justified the real, tangible destruction attendant to Obama's visit to Great Britain. These are two, rather blatant, internal inconsistencies – and we're only midway through his piece.

Moving on, Rollins then speculates, "Why you don't see street scenes like this in America is perhaps due to the fact that many Americans don't seem all that bothered by endless war, corporate greed, and a potentially ruined future. We go along with stuff, even when it's totally destructive and insane." All of Rollins' other indefensible nonsense aside, this statement in particular is downright surreal to me – because I don't know what "America" Henry Rollins has been living in for the last eight years, but in my own anecdotal experience, the Bush years were nothing if not politically volatile. Everyone I know was pissed off about

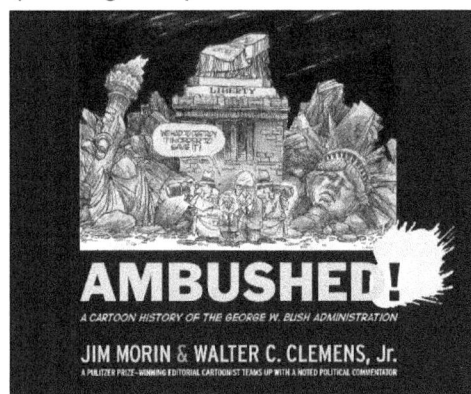

One of many anti-Bush books.

something, all the time. People protested repeatedly throughout Bush's entire presidency. Innumerable

One of many anti-Bush films.

books, magazine articles, documentary films, and other articulations of collective frustration and impotence were produced. The country was bitterly polarized. The media became split between the pro-Bush Right of Fox News and the anti-Bush Left of MSNBC, *et al.* Moreover, as Bush's presidency was drawing to its end, Americans went out to the polls and overwhelmingly elected a liberal, anti-war candidate whose platform was centered on the idea of "change," with regard to the policies of the previous administration. So, I find the idea that many Americans "don't seem all that bothered

---

[4] Here I'd like to point out that while it's a bit specious—albeit common—to complain about a problem for which one can't offer up a feasible solution, it's another thing entirely to complain about a problem of global doom-n-gloom proportions and *not even attempt to articulate what the fucking problem is*. This is Rollins' crowning achievement in intellectually lazy, bad, *bad* writing.

Anti-Bush music compilation, Vol 1.

by endless war, corporate greed, and a potentially ruined future" to be delusional at best, and downright patronizing at worst. (Bear in mind, these are not comments that Rollins made off-the-cuff in an interview; they're something that he actually sat down and wrote, and then submitted to an editor.)

From here, Rollins' sophism veers toward the precognizant. Like a TV psychic making vague, open-ended predictions of future events, he dourly warns us, "You can call the protestors in London any damn thing you want, but one thing is for sure: change is coming. It can be rational and beneficial to all or it can go another way. You might not dig those stats." Well golly, with parameters that fuzzy and open-ended, I guess Rollins will invariably be right in his predictions – "change" will come, but if it doesn't benefit everyone then it will go "another way." I find it difficult to come up with a more asinine statement to make in print, excepting perhaps the axiom "shit happens, dude." Yes, "change" will indeed come – and if it doesn't go one way, then you can put your money on the fact that it'll go "another way." Yeesh.

Still, Rollins continues irrationally slogging along, "The world is wanting to have a talk with America. I hope we can listen now. Eight years of arrogant deafness has done America no favors at all." Reading this I ask myself, *What in The Name Of Fuck is this guy even talking about at this point?* To whom, exactly, is he referring when he says that "America" needs to listen to "The World"? Does he mean the British? The European Union? The Russians? North Korea? Iran? The Islamic world as a whole? We're left scratching our heads because this aimless, hyperbolic statement, like the column as a whole, is essentially pointless. Moving on from hyperbole to complete *non sequitur*, Rollins then inexplicably states, "The Queen of England has an iPod. John McCain doesn't know how one works." Again, a totally pointless comparison and indicative of nothing whatsoever (especially considering that The Queen isn't an elected British official, The Prime Minister is).

Finally closing out this meandering installment of "straight talk"—in lieu of making anything resembling a cogent argument—Rollins opts to leave his readers with yet some more playground-level insults, saying, "Oh, before I forget, I had an idea for you Glenn Beck fans. Get your pal Chuck Norris to send you a pair of his sweaty boxers, post *Total Gym* workout, drop them into a large pot of freshly boiled water, allow them to steep for several minutes and then serve at your next Tea Party, you crazy kids! Please stop breeding." (For all intents and purposes, a simple "go eat your own poop, you big dummies!" would have sufficed, no?)

So that's internationally-recognizable Rock persona, published author, and "VanityFair.com's resident straight talker," Henry Rollins for you – driving home his closing argument with the suggestion that those he disagrees with should just go drink some sweaty-boxer-shorts-tea and "stop breeding." After years of seeing this guy's name on the spines of books, his hardboiled "tough guy" mug on the cover of magazines, his albums in barroom jukeboxes, and his big, self-confident grin on national TV, I'm now confronted with the realization that this—*this*—is the adolescent level of discourse he's capable of mustering on matters of international politics. Ridiculous. Just completely *fucking ridiculous*.

Regardless of what one may think of President Obama, Former President Bush, Senator McCain, The Queen of England, Glenn Beck, Chuck Norris, Rollins Band, or Black Flag, I'm gonna' go way out on a limb here and contend that this installment of Henry Rollins' column for *Vanity Fair* is some pretty undeniably terrible writing. At best, it reads like an unfocused, angst-filled rant from a high school student; and that's being charitable. More importantly—to reiterate, for the purposes of this essay—it is an exercise in sloppy sophistry that contains either directly or by implication, the following lethargic, argumentative copouts commonly known as logical fallacies:

- "Poisoning The Well" (Before I tell you what position I'm opposed to, you should know that the people supporting that position are "sub-literates.")

- "Straw Man" ("Conservatives" have whatever crazy, extreme opinions I want to ascribe to them, but I'm not going to quote them because it's easier for me to attack the exaggerated, proverbial "straw man" position that I've erected to suit my argument.)

- "False Dichotomy" (A McCain presidency would be full of "disaster," but "Obama will be received exceedingly well all over the world and perhaps help the entire planet become a more peaceful and prosperous place." *I.e.,* there is no middle ground between disaster and peace.)

- "False Analogy" (A McCain visit to Great Britain would essentially be synonymous with a Bush visit because even though they're different people, they both represent "conservatives.")

- "*Ad Hominem*" (The conservative commentators I disagree with are just mouth-breathing knuckle-draggers. It's easier for me to insult them as people than it would be to mount an actual argument against their position.)

- "Inconsistency" (It's fair for me to insult and generalize my opponents and their views, but unfair when people whom I agree with are likewise insulted and generalized.)

- "Circular Logic" (Protestors sensing an "impending disaster" are causing damage to property, which is justified because a "global ailment" is having "catastrophic effects," which is causing protestors to sense an "impending disaster" and damage property.)

- "Begging The Question" ("Change" is coming, but if it doesn't benefit everyone, it will go "another way.")

- "Appeal To Popularity" (President Bush was disliked by "The World" and Britain is "in love" with President Obama; therefore, President Obama is somehow "better" than President Bush, simply because he is more well-liked by Britons.)

The Queen has an iPod!

- "Hasty Generalization" (British protestors can sense "impending disaster" and are therefore protesting. Americans aren't protesting, so therefore Americans don't care about "endless war, corporate greed, and a potentially ruined future.")

- "*Non-sequitur*" (The Queen has an iPod, but John McCain doesn't know how one works.)

- "Unstated Major Premise" (Americans should care about how their President is received overseas because the U.S. President is synonymous with "America." *I.e.,* "Eight years of arrogant deafness has done America no favors at all," but now "America" is ready to listen to "The World," because the world likes President Barack Obama.)

It's impressive, really, that Rollins somehow managed to cram that many logical fallacies into such a short piece – especially a piece which really has no central argument to it (and there are probably even more, subtle fallacies that I likely missed).

I've got nothing to say one way or the other about Rollins' abilities as a singer, actor, orator, TV presenter, or deejay (I've managed to mostly ignore him in all of these capacities), but I will say that in my humblest of most humble

Not John McCain.

Not George W. Bush.

opinions, his "Change You Don't Have To Believe In, Just Deal With" is absolutely, mind-bogglingly ineptly written. Irrespective of whether or not one agrees with Rollins' basic political sentiments or feels that his heart is or isn't "in the right place," the fact remains that (at least in this particular example), the man cannot effectively articulate his ideas or communicate his views in a compelling way that sways readers. He tries, but even with the manifold crutches of logical fallacy, he still fails miserably.

So, if I may engage in my own conjecture about *what might have been*, I would argue that, were the text "Change You Don't Have To Believe In, Just Deal With" submitted by an unknown essayist, it would have been flatly rejected by any even moderately respectable magazine not published on a copy machine. But it wasn't rejected. There it is, somehow having passed muster at *Vanity Fair* – and on the surface, that doesn't make a lot of sense. So, the question we have to ask ourselves is: why?

And the answer is, in itself, the most overarching logical fallacy of all: "The Argument From Authority." Henry Rollins' political commentary is presumed worth reading simply because he is a celebrity. That's it. Rollins is a public figure well-schooled in being in the public eye, and in America, that makes him notable. It makes him respected by default. It gives his opinions and political views a weight that they, in truth, have not earned and simply do not deserve. Thus, the fallacious "Argument From Authority" here is the unstated implication on the part of *Vanity Fair* that what Rollins is saying should be accepted by readers as true and worth reading—not because he's done a good job of arguing his case by presenting reasonable arguments and backing them up—but simply because he's famous and *he's the one saying it*. The emphasis is not on the veracity of arguments presented to support the case being made, but is instead on *who* is making them – in this case, the former singer to a Hard Rock band turned TV persona.

This is germane (it prompted me to write this essay, anyway) because this particular isolated little example of a mediocre political column penned by a Rock celebrity is unfortunately indicative of a much larger problem in American culture. I wish that Henry Rollins' poorly-argued text were just a fluke—an isolated example of the connection between celebrity status and The Argument From Authority in

America—but it isn't. In fact, Rollins is just the tip of the hubristic Argument From Celebrity Authority Iceberg; and, to be fair, he isn't even really one of the more egregious examples. Consider the following:

Actress Jenny McCarthy and her even-more-famous boyfriend Jim Carrey are ardent anti-vaccination activists who argue that, despite the weight of evidence and the consensus of the scientific community, vaccines are the likely cause of autism in children. Actor and comedian Joe Rogan believes that NASA's moon landing was a hoax; that Apollo astronauts never actually set foot on the moon. Actor Tom Cruise—an adherent of that most curious of organized religions, Scientology—denies the efficacy of psychiatry and the pharmacological treatment of mental disorders. Actor and born-again Christian Kirk Cameron rejects evolution as a scientific theory, instead positing that human origins are explainable solely by way of the creation story described in The Old Testament's "Book of Genesis."

Fuck off, Immunologists, Virologists, and Epidemiologists – we're actors!

So does Chuck Norris – and similarly-minded actor Ben Stein felt strongly enough to make the faux-documentary film *Expelled*, arguing that quasi-scientific "creationist" ideas are being unfairly muscled out of the American education system by "Darwinism." And so on, and so forth.

All of the aforementioned celebrities use their celebrity status to *actively promote* the dissemination of whatever madcap flavor of crackpot nonsense they happen to subscribe to – and the credulous public, unfortunately, often falls for the Argument From Celebrity Authority, and occasionally actually listens to them.[5]

As Americans, we as a culture put celebrities on a pedestal for having achieved something notable that we respect, but the problem here is that we then go on to make the mistake of thinking that the

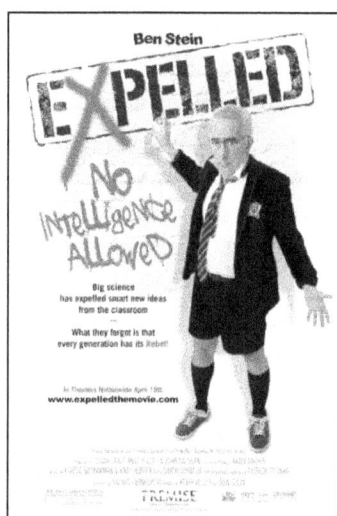

(Angus Young wears it better.)

respect that they have earned from us for their accomplishment should also be extended to everything else they say and do – and they know that, and they exploit it.

The Chinese have an adage (or so I'm told – I don't speak Chinese) that I came across a long time ago, which I've always been very fond of. It goes something along the lines of, "Being on the right side of an argument does not involve having the loudest voice." In our culture, celebrities have some of the loudest proverbial voices, and some of them choose to use those voices to shout down Doctors, Researchers, Economists, Scientists, Analysts, and other people who've devoted their lives to studying some particular topic of social import. But what's stupid isn't that celebrities opine on subjects about which they aren't experts (after all, everyone does); what's stupid is that the public often *actually listens to them.*

---

[5] Note that this is not the same thing as celebrity endorsement. If people want to buy Paul Newman's salad dressing, Francis Ford Coppola's wine, or George Foreman's grill—simply because those particular celebrities have leant their names to such products—then fine. But when Tom Cruise and Jim Carrey think they're qualified to dispense medical advice, the needle on my Bullshit Detector starts bouncing all over the place.

Henry Rollins' status as a celebrity by no means qualifies him to comment on international politics any more than anyone else—he's not a political analyst, Sociologist, Economist, or an expert on international relations—but that doesn't matter. *Vanity Fair* doesn't give him a regular column predicated on his caliber as a competent political commentator or his ability to make a convincing rational argument – they do it because there is a significant number of people out there who will see his name and the little cartoon portrait of him beside it, and they'll think to themselves, *Oh, cool, a column by Henry Rollins, that guy rocks pretty hard. I wonder what he thinks about President Obama's visit to Great Britain?* And—my God, people— that is a moronic, foolhardy way to think.

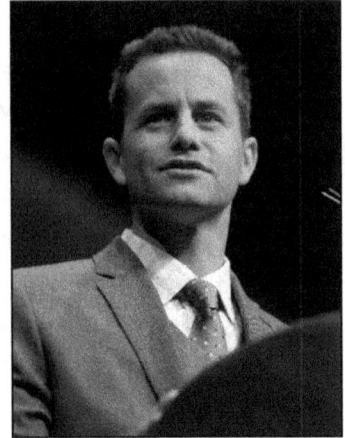

Kirk Cameron – Grown Pain.

Joe Rogan – comedian, actor, martial artist, podcaster, and moon-landing-denier.

Consider, for a moment, if you will; maybe most astronomers aren't as funny or self-assured as Joe Rogan is (and he certainly is both). Maybe they get awkward in front of the camera, or experience nervous brain-freeze and have trouble summarizing decades of research and observation into a single soundbite; but perhaps—just maybe—their collective body of accumulated knowledge and scientific consensus ought to be given way, *way* more credence than Rogan's fringe conspiracy theory that the Apollo moon landing was a hoax. And consider that—yeah, probably most of the employees over at The Centers for Disease Control aren't even close to as fuckable as Jenny McCarthy—but perhaps, just maybe, their collective research deserves to be taken far, *far* more seriously than her misplaced maternal instincts with respect to the idea that vaccines are the likely culprit behind her son's autism. And perhaps (again, just a maybe here), Tom Cruise, Chuck Norris, Kirk Cameron, and Ben Stein are all so completely immersed in their religious views that they just can't be objective about the subjects against which they've set themselves in opposition. Maybe, rather than being given airtime by mainstream media outlets simply because they're famous (as is often enough the case), all of these people simply ought to be *ignored.*

Members of bands like U2, Radiohead, and Coldplay have strong opinions on issues of international trade, international banking, human rights, *et cetera.* Actors like Sean Penn, Tim Robbins, Susan Sarandon, Alec Baldwin, and Martin Sheen are all vociferous critics of U.S. foreign policy. Pamela Anderson is a spokesperson for People for the Ethical Treatment of Animals (PETA). And there are many others like them. Now, mind you, I'm not saying that any of these people are necessarily "wrong" *per se*—that's a subjective judgment, and isn't what's at issue here—what I am saying is that just because they're celebrities doesn't make them "right." If any of these individuals have a case to make, and they can present compelling arguments in favor of that case—just like anyone else advocating a particular position—then fine, by all means, let them present evidence to back up their arguments in public fora.

World-renowned Economists, Coldplay.

This fuckin' guy. ...

However, whether or not one accepts those arguments should be based on the strength of the evidence presented, *not* whether or not one happens to like U2's music or Pamela Anderson's movies. Because it's silly—just plain goddamned silly—to think that celebrities are more in touch with reality or somehow more privy to "the truth" than anyone else. In fact, it's not unreasonable to argue that precisely because celebrities are often surrounded by fulsome sycophants ("yes men" and other assorted hangers-on), they're actually probably *less* in touch with reality than the average person; less able to be objective and to question the premises of their own conclusions.

Bearing this in mind, it's odd to me that as a culture Americans are (rightly) indifferent to what Scientists, Doctors, Researchers, and other specialists think about the subjective merit of music, movies, art or other forms of creative expression – yet so many of us put some level of significance on what musicians, actors, artists, and other celebrities think about science, medicine, or other areas of empirical knowledge. This seems all but insane to me. Celebrity status by no means nullifies one's opinions—I'm not arguing that at all—but it doesn't validate those opinions, either. That's the point. That's the problem with the Argument From Celebrity Authority; what should matter to the public is the validity of a case being made and how well it's argued and supported, *not who's making it*.

The prevalence of this phenomenon—The Argument From Celebrity Authority—to me, is a far more damning exposal of the shortcomings of American culture than any hyperbolic indictments someone like Henry Rollins might make about our supposed deafness to the outside world. Certainly, "America" would do well to listen to "The World" in a metaphorical sense ... but in a literal sense, it may also be a good idea for Americans to stop listening to what celebrities like Rollins think about anything other than what they're famous for – especially when they can't even backup their arguments without resorting to a host of logically fallacious argumentative copouts.

As a caveat, I'm obliged to add that I'm not saying that I've never been swayed by the Argument From Celebrity Authority. Of course I have – most of us have at one time or another. But I am saying that there's no time like the present to simply stop and say, *You know what, you famous, overpaid, unqualified blowhard – I don't give a shit what you think about anything other than what you're already famous for, because you're anything but an expert. Show me the evidence, make a convincing argument using solid logic and reason, or just <u>shut the fuck up already</u>.* I sincerely wish that we, as a culture, could do this – although unfortunately I don't see it happening any time soon.

As for Rollins specifically ... just prior to finishing this piece, I emailed a draft to a friend whose opinion I respect, and who also happens to be a pretty big fan of Rollins' various creative endeavors. I wanted to get an objective, outside take on what I'd written about the

This fuckin' guy. ...

guy — to make sure my criticism wasn't too overbroad, unfair, off-base, or just plain wrong. My friend's emailed response included the following:

> I was a big Black Flag fan in high school and I thought the better Rollins Band stuff was amazing. I've been to several of his spoken word shows and enjoyed them thoroughly. ... I've read a lot of his books, and he's good when he follows that age-old rule that all writers should follow: write what you know. He's a good storyteller when writing about his travels or touring with bands. He's also an entertaining music writer, if somewhat absolutist ... but he kind of writes about politics in the same way he writes about bands: in a black-and-white, absolutist voice.

Okay, fine. Assuming that my friend's statements are true, Rollins is a compelling storyteller who makes entertaining commentary about music, delivers enjoyable spoken word performances, and used to put on great live shows back when he was performing. That's all super. No argument from me there. Unfortunately, none of that has any bearing whatsoever on his qualifications (or lack thereof) to write about politics. In the case of his piece "Change You Don't Have To Believe In, Just Deal With," Rollins manages to stumble his way through the perilous realm of Logic Land and somehow step on nearly every

No argument that Mr. Rollins can properly rock.

Logical Fallacy Landmine along the way. His piece never should have made it past an editor, but it did, precisely *because of* all the other (irrelevant) aspects of his career. *That's the problem.*

My friend goes on to say, "I'm not sure where you're publishing/submitting this, but ... Rollins himself — he is known for directly replying to his critics." *Hmm* ... Well, if this is also true, then it actually only further supports my argument. Because again, what's at issue here is the strength and validity of arguments themselves, *not who's making them* — and that goes both ways. It's childish to respond to "critics" — the substance of the criticism itself is what's at issue. Bottom line; if someone is wrong and is using bad, sloppy argumentation, then *they're just plain fucking wrong* — irrespective of who they are, and without regard to who happens to be pointing it out. The idea that a muscle-bound celebrity like Henry Rollins would obliquely dissuade criticism of his work through his being "known for directly replying to his critics" only implies that the work being criticized probably isn't really durable enough to stand on its own in the first place.

If Rollins wants to be taken seriously as a political commentator (at least by me, anyway), then he'd do well to learn from criticism, and to devote the same sort of uncompromising discipline that he applies in his workout regimen to honing his critical thinking skills and vetting his ideas before publishing them. Because the simple fact of the matter is that calling one's opponents "knuckle-draggers" and citing "some articles" as evidence to backup inarticulate political views doesn't come even close to approximating a legitimate argument for or against anything — it's listless writing supported by the crutch that its author happens to be famous. That's just downright silly — and *Vanity Fair* should know better.

On the Tedium of Teenage Tutelage

2003

A lot of people prefer to look back on their adolescent and teenage years with wistful fondness, but in my experience, they're usually confabulating or just kidding themselves. Contrary to the smug, self-assured chuckles of most adults, I think it's really a lot tougher being a teenager than most care to recall or admit to. In my case, however, I'd like to at least get the story straight: I spent most of my teen years miserable and alone; at least that's what it *felt* like anyway.

What I recall most about my adolescent and teenage years was an overwhelming feeling of powerlessness—that I had no control over almost any element of my own life—yet control was what I wanted, and needed, more than anything else. I surveyed my life and found that I detested nearly every element of my existence, yet I had the power to change practically none of it. Some of that may have just been delusional teenage paranoia that was divorced from tangible reality; but the truth is that a lot of it wasn't.

Essentially, high school for me was partly about being a warm body in a seat for an allotted period of time, partly about half-heartedly submitting to teachers' pedagogical mental gymnastics while pacifying their sense of innate infallibility, and partly an exercise in surviving adolescent social Darwinism. In a nutshell, it was a dreary daily crucible, compartmentalized into smaller ordeals, all held together with the implicit, ominous warning of, *Do what you're told—do what you're supposed to do now—or you're going to fuck-up your life forever.* I suspect that it was probably the same for a lot of people.

I, for one, loathed high school for a number of reasons. It wasn't so much that I feared failing my classes, social pressures, or even violence (though those were all factors), but that it just seemed like such a monumental and time-consuming *pain in the ass*, on so many levels. Every stupid little fucking thing was just a pointless, aggravating nuisance and little else; from going to bed early, to getting up early, to riding my bike in the rain, to the drudgery and monotony of one unedifying class after another, to the hours of mind-numbing busywork done under the false pretense of "learning," to constantly reporting everything back to the judgmental scrutiny of my parents, to the ceaseless droves of innumerable teenage assholes that I had to deal with on a daily basis.

Of course, like any other socially maladroit teenager, I would have much preferred to just stay at home in my room reading, drawing, or playing video games, but alas, this was an impossibility. Instead, not only did I have to wrench myself out of bed every day at 7:00 a.m. and waste the better part of the afternoon listening to some has-been-who-never-was bloviator rattle on about American History or Geometry, but to top it all off, the real "kicker" was dealing with the other students. I did not like the other students.

There were the adult upperclassmen who knocked me down merely for their own amusement; the geeky little troll-snitches who'd rat out anyone for anything so that they might fleetingly feel important; the jocks whose brittle egos needed constant gratification at someone else's expense; the shameless kowtowing brown-nosers with college tunnel-vision and a total paucity of integrity; the catty bitch-princesses who lived for the rumor-mill and delighted in calling attention to even the most minuscule personal flaws of anyone they came into contact with; and so on and so forth. I detested them all.

Above all else, it was the petty, underhanded, and often downright vicious nature of most people's behavior that irked me the most. Their propensity to scrutinize and judge each other in every imaginable way—from physical flaws like acne, overbite, posture, and weight, to economic shortcomings from non-mall-bought clothing and shoes, to cars, to even where one lived—everything was fair game in the churning social hierarchy which I found myself forced to be a part of at the wee age of fourteen. After a few months, I just got tired of dealing with it all, because I had no desire to be there in the first place.

I tried to avoid people in general most of the time, and spent the majority of my first year of high school by myself whenever possible. In fact, most days I ate lunch alone – by choice. Lunch was the only time I could find real solitude and was therefore always the best part of any given day throughout my freshman year. I'd slip off to the side of the school, to a little nook where nobody but the sneakiest of lunchtime-smokers ventured, and I'd have a thirty-minute respite from the rest of the herd, in which to read a book and daydream about massacring them all.

Remember the Columbine High "incident" a few years back? Were you surprised or shocked by that? I wasn't. I wasn't surprised at all. When I first heard news of the killings, I remember thinking, *Well shoot, somebody's finally gone and done what we all used to fantasize about. It's finally actually happened.*

My friends and I always used to kid around about how great it would be to do something like put nerve gas in the ventilation ducts, or switch-out the drinking fountains with flame-throwers, or just blow the whole place to bits ... but of course, we were just joking around and talking big, because we were quite small, and all we could do was talk. It never would have occurred to us that eventually kids actually *would* start bringing guns to school and firing off indiscriminately at their classmates. We never had that kind of conviction ... but I for one can sort of see where they were coming from, in a roundabout kind of way. Kids – they sure can be a *handful* sometimes, eh?

I think that young people, in a certain sense, function as a sort of social barometer, because they haven't yet sunk into the benumbing habituation and self-absorbed routine of adulthood. Analogously to how some animals can supposedly sense earthquakes before they happen, young people seem to be aware of social changes long before their ossified parents ever are.[6] After all, teenage computer geeks were "Internet savvy" long before their corporate dads had ever even heard the term "dot com," let alone bought stock in one.

Maybe, when children and teens start bringing guns to school *all over the country*, that's emblematic of a larger social sickness, which adults are just too oblivious and out-of-touch to comprehend? Maybe it isn't as simple as, *Johnny's mommy didn't love him enough, so he hated the world.* Maybe it's never that simple?

It's odd how most high schools have chosen to react to the Columbine incident and others like it – they've installed new security measures and treat every student like a dormant murderer in waiting, instead of meaningfully probing as to *why* the students might be disgruntled in the first place. It's sadly ironic, really – the nature of the institution itself dehumanizes those it's supposed to serve, and when they act out their pent-up frustrations, the institution responds by only becoming *more* invasive, oppressive, and demeaning. Further proof of the inherent stupidity of bureaucracy in action.

Here's an outlandish idea: maybe, instead of making school feel even *more* like a prison, all campuses should be "open" campuses? Maybe by trusting teenagers, they become more trustworthy? Maybe, rather than treating teenagers like overgrown children or petty criminals, they should be treated like people? They certainly have enough sense in their heads to use semiautomatic assault weapons and build bombs, so perhaps they ought to be given just a tad bit more respect, lest they seek to *assert* themselves upon those around them for lack of it. Just a thought.

I graduated from high school in 1995, and was fortunate enough to have made it out before the introduction of corporate sponsorship, metal detectors, and surveillance cameras – just before "school shootings" were all the rage. I imagine it's an even more repressive institution these days than it was when I was a teenager, which is a disturbing notion indeed.

---

[6] The whole "animals can predict earthquakes" thing is, apparently, a pervasive myth that's unsupported by good science.

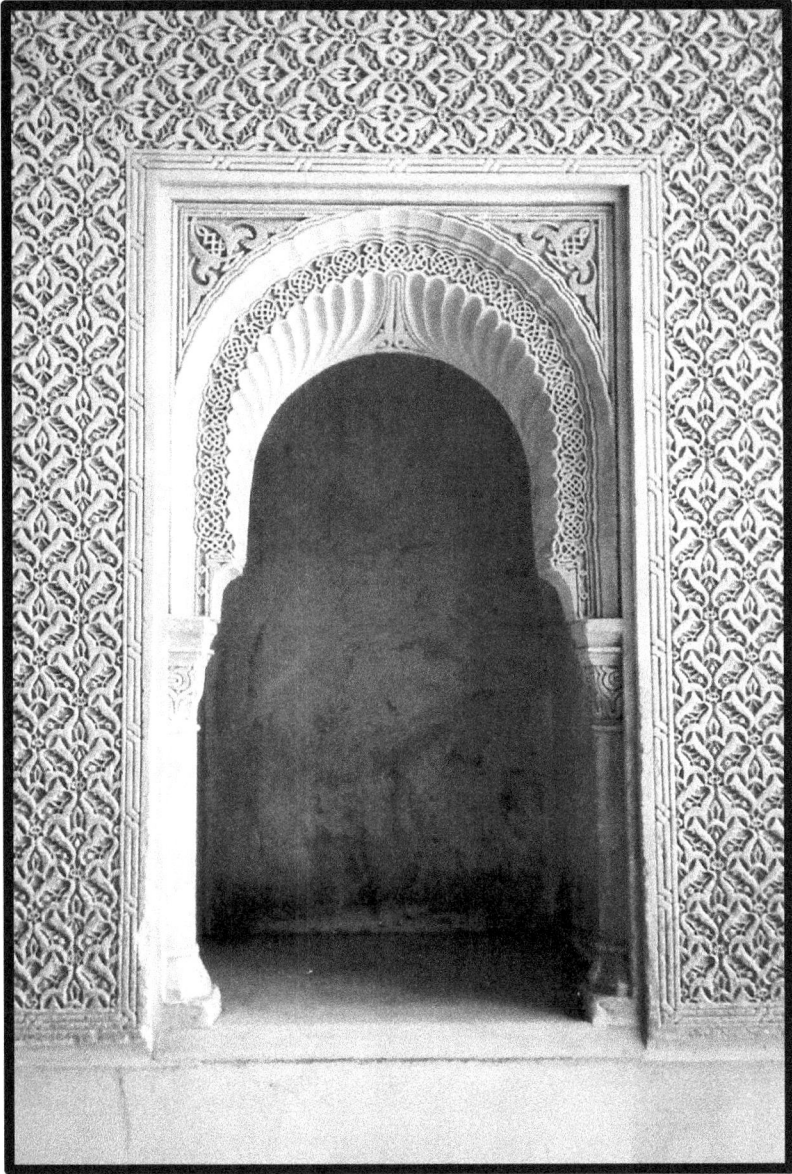

El Museo de Cera

Madrid's Macabre Museum of Meretricious Mimicry

2002

Every major city in the world has a wax museum, the most famous being London's Madame Tussauds and The London Dungeon. Sure, fine, terrific. Lame tourist traps to be sure. I can't say I've spent much time in any of them, and I suppose I could be wrong, but I think Madrid's wax museum, located in the humongous Plaza de Colón, is something special – because it's totally ridiculous.

One of the nice things about Spain is that the Spanish have yet to really grasp the concept of "*kitsch*" – campy, cheesy, tacky, hokey ... whatever you want to call it. When people here sing love songs or give Hallmark greeting cards, they really mean it. There is a certain degree of sincerity, earnestness, and *naïveté* that abounds, and which is really, just plain weird to the tetchy "politically correct" sensibility of Americans (I hear it's even worse in Italy, though I find that kind of hard to believe).

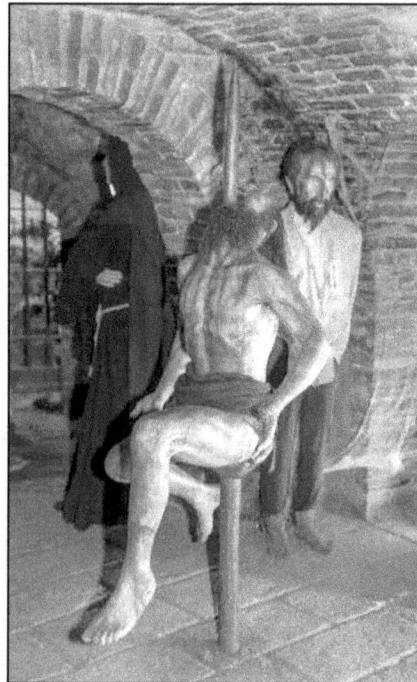

Right up the you-know-what.

For instance, they have this brand of candy here called Conguitos (little Congo-boys), which are like chocolate-covered peanuts or something, but whose mascot is a little caricature of an African tribesman, complete with big red lips and a spear. Stuff like that would never fly in The States (for obvious reasons), but to the Spanish, it's like,

Yanqui Jessica and some French politician.

What? What's so "ofensivo" about that? Why the hell not? They are just so literal about everything, that it's just beyond them to read anything pejorative into that at all. But I digress.

So anyway, Madrid's wax museum – it's great. And the reason it's great is that these people just don't realize just how completely silly it all is. A lot of the museum is just like any other dumb wax museum in any other dumb city (famous actors, rockstars, sports figures, *et al.*), but what makes Madrid's wax museum special are incongruous things like the fact that The Beatles only have three members. Screwy stuff like that.

Other highlights of Madrid's Museo de Cera include:

#1. The "medieval times" (read as, The Spanish Inquisition) exhibit, which features bare-breasted women being whipped to death, and people impaled on posts (one guy has the post going right up his ass, and out his open mouth);

#2. Famous "political figures" such as: Napoleon Bonaparte, Joseph Stalin, Francisco Franco, Benito Mussolini, and Adolph Hitler;

#3. Reenacted famous "murder scenes" from Spanish history and the busts of famous serial killers from around the world;

#4. Late '70s era Animatronic "monsters" whose movements are so erratic and jerky that they actually *are* scary;

#5. An Animatronic Louie Armstrong who sings "What a Wonderful World" and looks like a black version of Yoda with a trumpet;

#6. And the undisputed highlight of El Museo de Cera; an animatronic Dracula who makes a long "scary" speech about sucking blood and hunting the living (in Spanish, but in a Transylvanian accent), and who then bursts into a lip-synched rendition (in English) of "I Want to Marry a Lighthouse Keeper," which, incidentally, is sung by a woman.

And you get all of this for the equivalent of around four bucks. Screw El Museo del Prado.

Fun for the whole family!

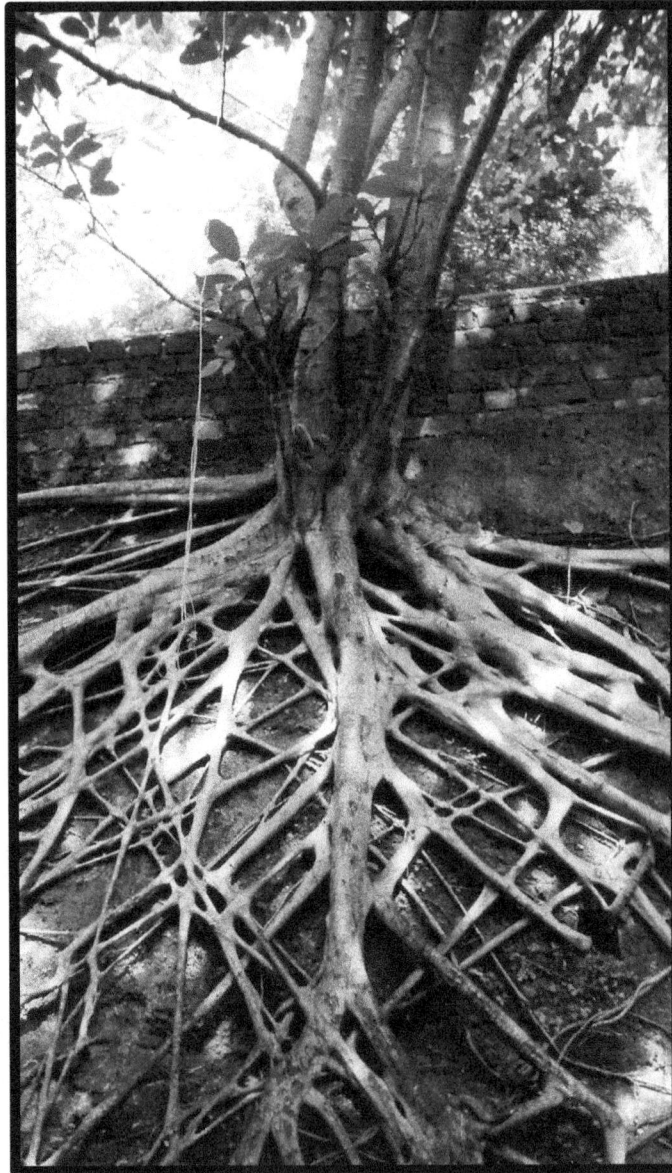

It's Different When We Do It

2013

A few months ago, I reconnected with an ex-girlfriend from college. We hadn't spoken in about fifteen years, but briefly—strangely—we floated the idea of getting back together again, in our mid-30s. It was a misguided aspiration produced by both of us being single and in shitty places in our respective lives. Despite numerous hours-long cross-country phone calls reminiscing about our college days in the late 1990s, the contemplated reconnection didn't work out, and we again went our separate ways. During the course of our communications, however, she mentioned that her most recent boyfriend was Korean-American, and that this fact had pleased her parents. She was born in China, and her family had come to the United States sometime in the late 1970s, when she was a toddler. Apparently, her mom had disapproved of her dating white guys like me, and was delighted at the idea that "at least" the Korean-American guy was Asian. I found the comment odd and mildly insulting, but it wasn't the first time that I'd heard this kind of odd talk from an ex's immigrant parents. I once dated a Nicaraguan-American girl whose parents had fled the Sandinistas and relocated to Florida, where she was later born in the early '80s. Apparently, when she and I broke up, circa 2001, her mother opined to her that it was all for the best, because "white people have no souls." What a very strange way to see the world, having moved by choice to a majority "white" country. ...

I was recently reminded of this retrograde attitude *vis-à-vis* dating and "race" by a black guy that I'm connected to on Facebook, whom I've never met before in real life. He's in some branch of the military, studying law in Texas. His Facebook posts are unintentionally revelatory and informative, at least to me, anyway. He often shares memes about black pride stuff; a lot of it is either innocuous, cliché, or just reasonable – along the lines of Martin Luther King's "I Have a Dream" speech. But from time to time, he'll post some kooky thing about protecting the integrity of the black race; *i.e.,* a tongue-clucking admonition about "race-mixing," advising black men against being "traitors" to their race by dating white women. It's illuminating to read the comments below these posts, which comprise various of his black friends wholeheartedly agreeing with him about the risks of diluting the purity of "the race."

What the hell is wrong with people?

I have yet to hear an intellectually consistent explanation as to how this dubious "racial purity" sentiment is, or should be, deemed socially acceptable when it's unidirectionally aimed at the alabaster majority, and yet remains contemptibly regressive and bigoted in the inverse. I get that tribalism and xenophobia are hardwired into human nature; but if you're going to be a racist asshole, at least be fucking consistent about it across the board.

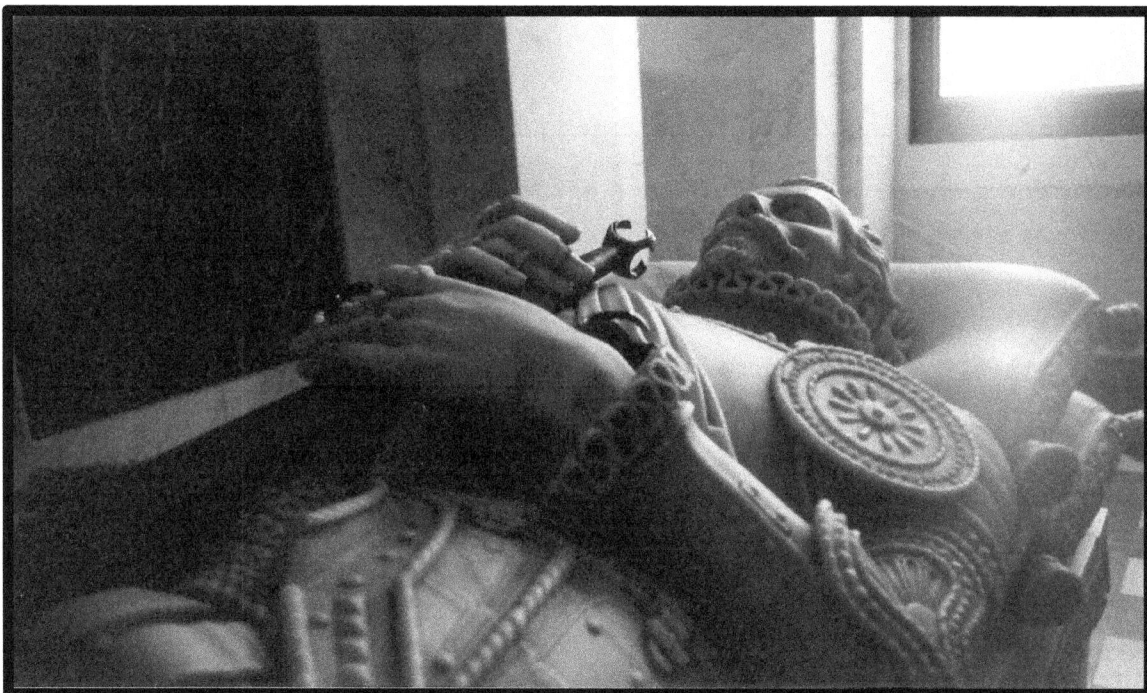

The Mimes

The Mimes were a short-lived performance art troupe (masterminded by Adam "Don Pie" Gross) that was active in Long Beach, California, in 2011. The group put on several concerts of pantomimed rock performances on stage, at music and variety shows held at Long Beach venues such as Fern's Cocktails and The Que Sera, as well as an impromptu concert at the restaurant/bar of The House of Blues, in Hollywood. The Mimes' live shows consisted of all six members soundlessly simulating the act of setting up invisible musical equipment on stage, and then mutely "playing" songs for several awkward silent minutes, until eventually being booed off stage by the unamused crowd. Stupidly, The Mimes were generally neither well-liked nor well-received.

218

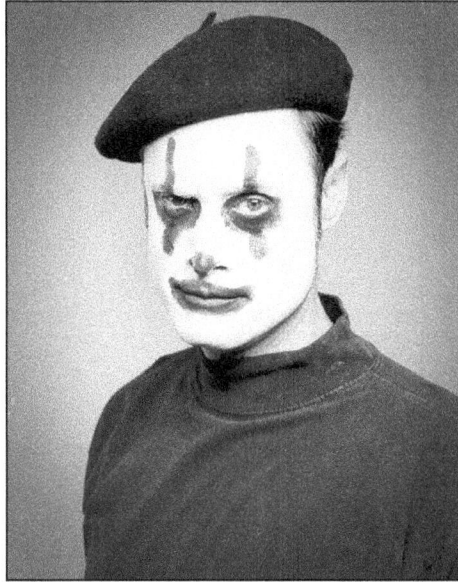

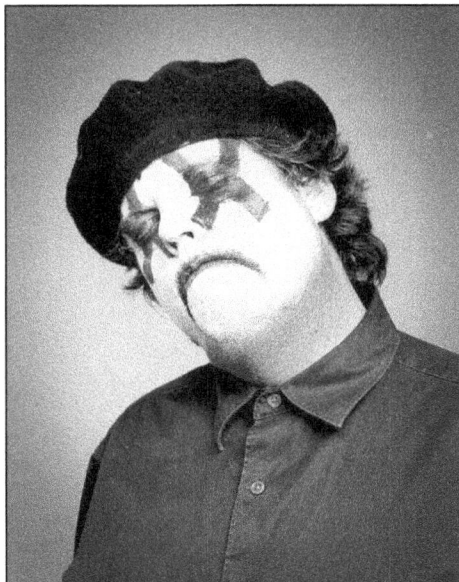
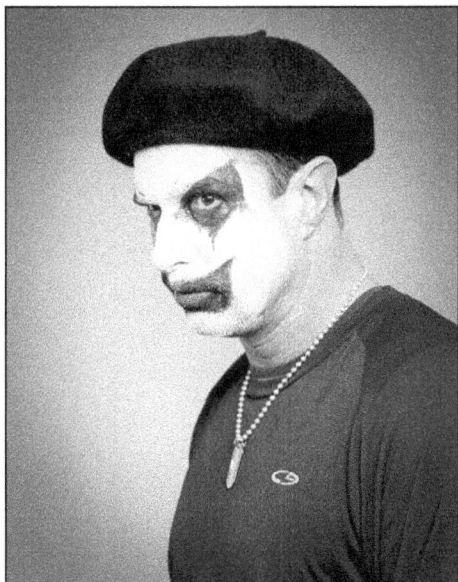

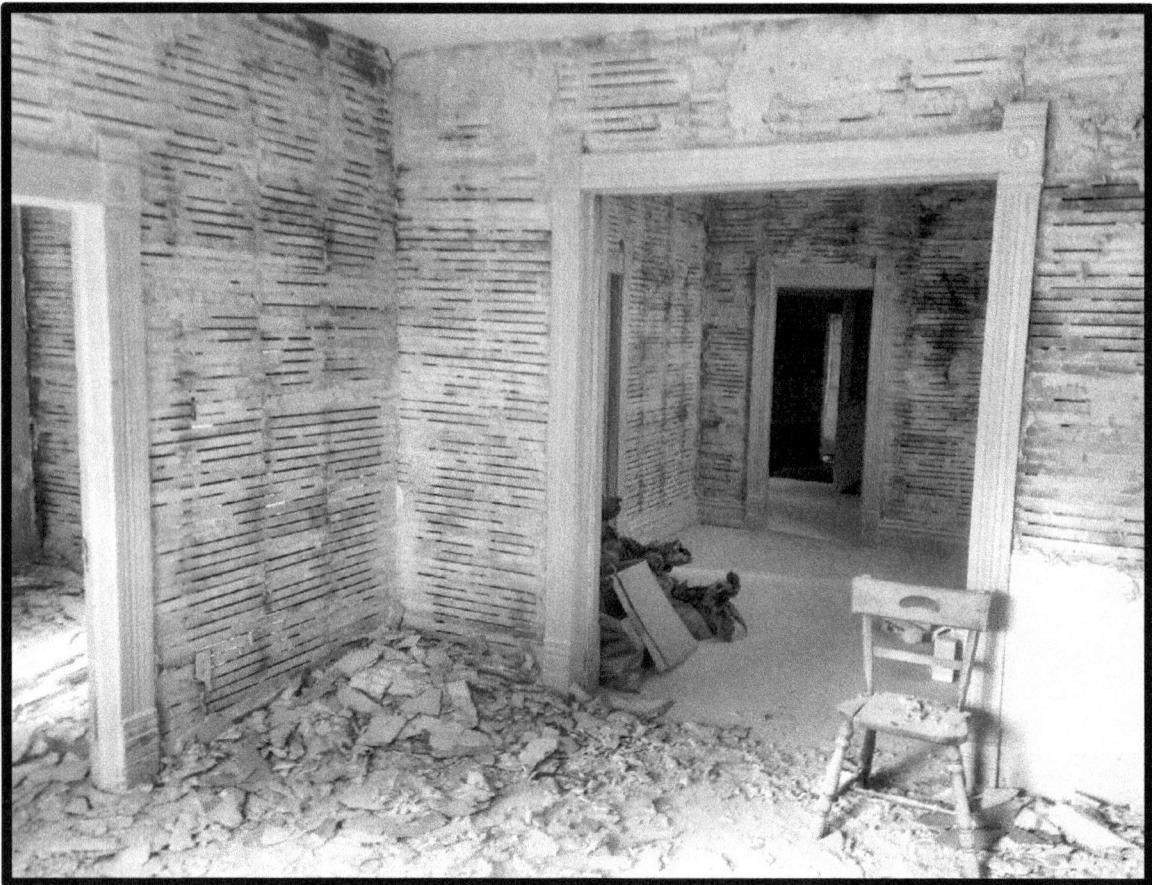

Notes from Underground Monkey Mania

A Blog from Beneath Denver

2003 – 2004

In the early Fall of 2003, I moved from California's San Francisco Bay area to the rarified air of "The Mile High City" – Denver, Colorado. When initially planning my relocation, I came across a listing on CraigsList.org advertising a dirt-cheap room for rent in a shared space located right in downtown Denver. So, I dialed the number listed in the ad and spoke for a bit with one of the renters, Amy. She explained the basic dimensions of the room and the common living areas, the space's amenities, the number of housemates, and so on – and I agreed to rent the room, sight unseen. What Amy neglected to mention on the phone was that the shared place was an under-the-radar Punk warehouse showspace called Monkey Mania, where raucous bands played just about every weekend, fireworks were intermittently detonated inside, and underage mohawked teenagers guzzled smuggled-in booze in the bathroom. (A trivial detail that must have slipped her mind, I guess.)

Anyway, it was fucking awesome. I showed up in Denver not knowing a soul, but by happenstance I'd moved into a spot that basically had a wild party and a show every weekend; so in no time I was introduced to all the most interesting weirdo personages in Denver, and I got to see all sorts of great touring bands for free. I only lived at Monkey Mania for just over nine months or so before I decided that I needed to get a "real" apartment, but there was a lot of madness and fun packed into the ten-months-and-change that I resided there; and I look back on it now as a stroke of fortuitous luck that I got to be a Monkey Mania denizen when I did. National bands capable of selling out shows at proper venues played every couple'a months in my pad, and it was like, just another weekend "whatever" thing that I spectated for all of ten minutes before going back to my room. I should have appreciated all of it more at the time.

The following is an online journal kept on an intermittently regular-ish basis from October of 2003 through June of 2004; while I was living in the basement of Monkey Mania and working as an

Monkey Mania on Arapahoe Street (upper floors condemned), Denver, Colorado.

Administrative Assistant in the "document service center" of a large corporate law firm's downtown Denver office. The other residents of Monkey Mania at the time of this writing were: Josh Taylor (of the band Friends Forever), Amy Szychowski (of Rainbow Sugar), Claudine Rousseau (of Sin Desires Marie), and Ben Brunton (of R.O.C.K.). Most of the photographs accompanying the text were shot on film on automatic cameras, and later digitally scanned.

October 1, 2003, 10:07 p.m.

Hello again. So, as of about a month ago, I've been living in Denver, Colorado, in a living space called Monkey Mania. The house has a name, because it's also a venue – the only all-ages venue in town, as a matter of fact. I suppose it's sort of what one might call a "Punk" house, though that term isn't entirely accurate, since we have DSL internet, all bathe fairly regularly, and are generally too old to give a shit about "Punk" anymore. Anyway, it's a place where people live and shows happen, so call it whatever you like. There's one bathroom for six people, and the "kitchen" consists of: a sink, a hotplate-burner, a toaster oven, and a microwave.

I live in the basement, literally. The state my room was in when I moved in was, shall we say ... *sub*-par. Prior to unpacking my things, I wet-vac'd the carpet, sealed all the fissures and cracks in the walls with sprayfoam, painted the walls and ceiling, and installed fiberglass insulation, a threshold, and a fan-powered ventilation system. Being paranoid about radon and fifty-year-old basement dust, I also purchased a fancy air filter / ionizer (which, judging by the buildup on its filter, has already paid for itself). Perhaps the most noteworthy thing about my room, however, is that a heroin addict overdosed and expired in it, some five or six years ago. Isn't *that* cute?

My basement bedroom / closet.

Anyway, once upon a time, this place was an ink factory, maybe fifty, sixty years ago; but it's been a venue since the 1980s. Supposedly once-indie bands like Nirvana used to play here, but that could just be bullshit hearsay – not that it really matters either way. Nowadays, I assume that Monkey Mania's main claim to fame would be that Josh of the oft-lauded band Friends Forever and Nothing Gets Worse Than This (N.G.W.T.T.) record label lives here. He organizes the majority of the shows, and from what I can tell, seems like a pretty swell guy all around, as do my three other housemates. The unfortunate thing about Monkey Mania, however, is that even though it's only about a five-minute walk from downtown, the location is hardly convenient—no supermarkets or laundromats anywhere in the vicinity—so I've been ambulatin' like Wagner these days.

Monkey Mania's showspace.

As for the city of Denver itself, there's nothing much to say about it, really. It's a mid-sized American city, more or less like any other, and has most of the things one might expect of a city its size. The city limits include a pseudo-bohemian neighborhood, an ostensibly "black" area, a couple Hispanic neighborhoods, several "nice" enclaves, and so forth. The downtown mall is full of comfortable places to spend money, roving cops, outspoken beggars, and the occasional foreign tourist. I'm sure there's more, but I've only been here a month, so ... we'll see. Anyway, the important thing now is that I find a job ... always a joy.

October 4, 2003, 4:05 a.m.

The band Lightning Bolt performed at my house tonight. They sounded pretty good, though I couldn't actually see them, since there were about two hundred people in the way.

Lightning Bolt, live at Monkey Mania.

Overflow seating for Lightning Bolt.

It's funny, initially I really liked the idea of having shows in my house, but though having two hundred drunk "Indie" teenagers in one's living room may sound like fun, it does have its downsides. For instance, tonight I was reminded of just how much I don't care for so-called "crust punks," or "crusties." I really, really don't care for crusties.

Now, don't get me wrong; I'm all for people thinking and saying whatever they want, but see, okay, there was this table set up in my living room all evening, right ... and at said table, some "enlightened" folks were distributing some literature, tee-shirts, and flyers having to do with the alleged "injustices" of celebrating Columbus Day, and well, I just thought it was kind of silly. Their motto went something along the lines of, *No More Racism! Take a stand against racism,*

slavery, and genocide – protest against this year's Columbus Day celebration!

Ok, now, as much as I do feel that it is of urgent, vital importance to "take a stand" against slavery and genocide (serious problems in this day and age), I'm a bit skeptical as to how protesting the celebration of an event that transpired hundreds of years ago, is somehow supposed to change anything at all. It's like protesting Christmas or Easter because the crucifixion was "wrong" – it's so redundant that it's funny. Personally, I couldn't give a shit either way about the issue. However, the plain, simple fact is that if it were not for Mr. Columbus, I would probably not be sitting here typing this right now – so it's a bit silly to protest his having "discovered" the continent we all take for granted. However, the real issue here, is that whether or not one chooses to celebrate or protest the man's "discovery" of the continent in question, changes absolutely fucking nothing. Getting upset about it, or attempting to "enlighten" people about how wrong it is (especially in my living room), is really just a self-serving, vainglorious act of toothless performative altruism; a flaccid gesture of preaching to the converted, affecting nothing but needless guilt-freighted emotion from people who just want to watch some Rock bands play. The past—like much of life—is often very, very ugly, and no amount of retrospective guilt will ever raise the dead, so ... what's the point?

Yes, I must concede, celebrating Columbus Day is a bit stupid – but not nearly as stupid as actively trying to prevent other people from celebrating Columbus Day. (One can't really be a moral bulwark against something that fuckin' transpired more than half a millennium ago. ... right?) Moreover, why is that that the vast majority of those people who seem so terribly concerned with "fighting" racism are white kids? 'Cause, see, when I left my house after the show and wandered around town looking for a late-night snack, I crossed paths with quite a few African-Americans, all of whom were far too occupied with having a fun night out on the town, to concern themselves with disabusing anybody of wrongthink notions about "racism" related to Columbus. Seems to me that these black folk were too "enlightened" to waste their time "educating" people about something that doesn't matter. But, of course, that's just my interpretation. You, like the crusties, are entitled to your own.

October 8, 2003, 2:09 a.m.

The instrumental Norwegian band Noxagt performed at my house tonight. They have sort of a Sludgy/Doom Rock sound, consisting of a heavily distorted bass, a violin (with various effects), and heavy drumming. I liked them enough to shell-out ten bucks for a CD, so if you're into that kind of thing, I'd recommend checking them out. The various opening bands (both local, and of the Providence, Rhode Island, variety), didn't elicit my interest enough to warrant sticking around the showspace, so I retired to my underground bunker to listen to Mozart's "Requiem," followed by his "25th Symphony in G Minor," while drinking some Chamomile tea. T'was delightful. At the end of the evening, I chatted briefly with the fellow who runs Load Records, an affable gentleman from Rhode Island who's put out quite a few albums by bands I like, and seems to have a pretty good head on his shoulders.

Anyway, this entourage of Norwegians and Rhode-Islanders will be making its way out West in the next few days, so I'd recommend that anyone living in the San Francisco Bay Area go see them at the Grandma's House venue, whenever it is that they're playing.

October 23, 2003, 8:03 p.m.

Yesterday, around dusk, Oakland, California's Hale Zukas rolled into town to play a show here at Monkey Mania. Being that they're friends of mine, we promptly drove out to Casa Bonita for some pleasure and pain. Our waitress was about as enthusiastic and cheerful as a mortician, the performers / actors were, for some reason, in very bad form, and Hale Zukas' singer, Rob Enbom, declared that the food was not merely unpalatable, but "the second worst meal I've ever eaten in my entire life." I'd been to Casa Bonita a couple times prior, and this time around, I made the prudent decision of going with the cheese enchiladas rather than the chicken, and also had

the foresight to bring along some Tapatío hot sauce to augment the sub-elementary-school-cafeteria-grade food. As a result of this, not only was I able to eat two full plates of Casa Bonita fare this time around, but I didn't experience traumatic, gut-wrenching bowel pain until much later in the night (around 3:00 a.m., to be precise). So, all in all, it was a successful expedition.

Hale Zukas, live at Monkey Mania.

Upon returning home, Hale Zukas performed a couple hours later, along with some local acts, as well as a fun Grind / Death / Black Metal band from Providence called Necronomitron (who sparked a small, yet thoroughly aggro mosh pit, as well as some late-'80s-Florida-style head banging / swinging). I liked them so much that I bought their CD – this in spite of the fact that the three sweethearts who comprise Necronomitron all but refused to take my money since I live at the showspace. I ended up just taking a CD and dumping my money in their CD box.

So, it was a pretty good show / evening, aside from the fact that this particular show was actually intended to be a birthday party. Josh went out and bought a cake and a keg, and everyone had a merry time

*Necronomitron,
Load Records, 2003.*

... except that the asshole whose birthday it was never even showed up. I suggested that we egg his house—at the very least—but nobody seemed up for the idea (especially considering that he lives in an apartment). At the end of the night, Rob crashed on my floor, and then Hale Zukas disappeared early this morning, heading out towards Lincoln, Nebraska. They'll be back here in a few weeks, on the return leg of their tour.

Tonight, there was some kind of scheduling mix-up (two shows being booked for the same night), so now there are going to be eight bands—yes *eight* bands—playing upstairs, throughout the course of the evening. In order to save on setup time, some of them will be playing in the kitchen. It's a good thing that I like loud live music, because if I was one of those people who didn't like loud live music, I'd be just *fucked*.

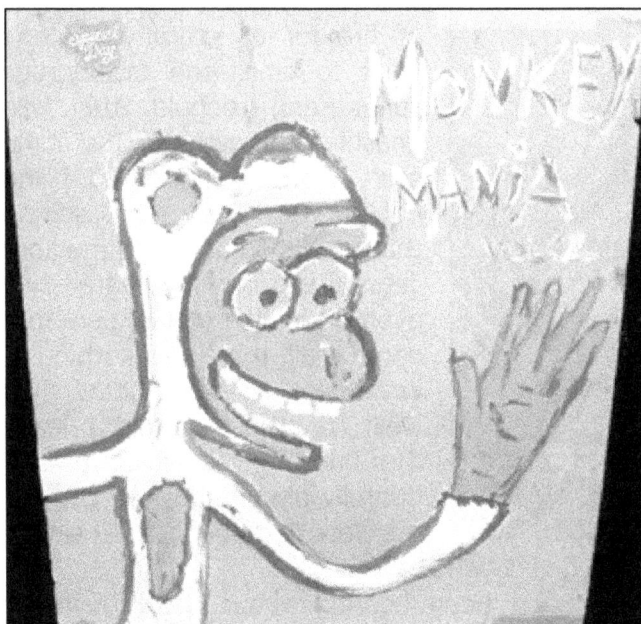

The sign in Monkey Mania's front window.

October 24, 2003, 11:37 p.m.

Tonight, myself and a handful of housemates and acquaintances drove out to the suburban Colorado town of Thornton, to check out a performance of Hell House. Thornton, from my passing impression of it, is a no-frills working-class suburb. A place where culture appears to be frozen *circa* 1988. A 'burb where white guys with mullets drive Cameros and blast Metallica, without the slightest redolence of irony. Above all, it's the kind of place where "born again" Christians still have some degree of clout. So, we drove out to a strip mall in Thornton, coughed-up six bucks, and waited in line for about half an hour to see Hell House.

Curiously, the security for the evening was provided by a Christian bike gang called Righteous Thunder or something. They were big, fat, hairy, bearded bikers just like The Hell's Angels, except that they had backpatches on their jackets that read, "Satan Is A Punk," and all wore ostentatious crucifixes. Obviously, these were men who'd lived rather unsavory lives at some point, and much like Norbert Knox, tried to overcompensate by becoming outwardly pious loud-n'-proud "born again" Christians. I avoided eye contact with the lot of them.

After being warned that if we were to cause any trouble the bikers would throw us out, my companions and I were let into the small auditorium where the Hell House performance was to be held, along with about seventy or so other sinners similarly lacking in moral rectitude.

Now, in the past, I understand that Hell House used to be a Christian fundamentalist haunted house (and there's been a documentary film made about it), but this year, for whatever reasons, they've switched over to a stage production, complete with smoke, strobe-lights, and a projection screen. All in all, the performance of Hell House was very much on the same wavelength as most entertainment that's geared towards the lowest common denominator: overstated, obvious, and very dumbed-down, in the vein of professional wrestling; or evocative of Jerry Bruckheimer films, *American Idol*, and similar Christian fundamentalist infotainment such as The Power Team and Chick Tracts. So, of course, it was totally great, and well worth my six dollars.

The hour-long Hell House performance was hosted by two grimacing demons from Hell, who pranced around the hallowed ground of the strip mall stage, shouting all the time and ostensibly trying to act wicked and mischievous. They were occasionally accompanied by Satan—a thirty-ish guy with sleazy facial hair—who was dressed in a red suit and a long leather jacket. He was, I guess, supposed to look dapper or "rakish" or whatever, but he just looked like a sleazy loser. The man's hammy overacting was unnerving in and of itself – as was his eye makeup. So I guess he succeeded on some level, anyway.

So anyway: First off, we witnessed the iniquitous influence of our demonic hosts upon the breakup of an American family; dad was drinkin', mom was yellin', the kids were cryin', and the demons were lovin' it. In the end, our hosts were delighted when mom uttered the big "D word" – *divorce*. Thereafter, in similar fashion, throughout the course of the hour, we were shown the horrors of: teen suicide, drunk driving, attending raves, abortion, and homosexuality, as well as a few others. They were all great, so I have trouble deciding which was my favorite. The homosexuality bit involved a gay marriage, followed by the inevitable AIDS-infected-hospital-bedside death scene. That was pretty nice. But the abortion bit was better. This entailed a young woebegone aborter seeing visions of how her aborted fetus's life would have been, as she wept and regretted, and moaned and lamented. It trudged on, and on ... and on.

All of these skits were punctuated by the two demons gallivanting around the stage, shouting about how delighted they were at causing so much mischief with their sinister machinations. The pair also reminded all of us in the audience—several times—that we were each and every one of us, sinners. In the end, an embodied Death came out to bellow at us about eternal damnation, following which all the cast came out dressed up as zombies in Hell, and caterwauled and moaned for far too long. Then Satan, or Lucifer, or The Devil (not to be confused with the guy in the red suit) came out to take his turn yelling at us some more about how we're all sinners, and how much he's looking forward to seeing us in The Big Pit of Fire. Oh, the terror of it all.

Then, in a sudden change of plot, the name of God was invoked (not "Yahweh" or "Jehovah," just plain ol' "God"). This utterance was anathema to all the baddies, and the demons and damned all abruptly decamped the stage, only

to be replaced by a dozen or so effeminate and/or overweight angels, and a man with a big plastered-on forced smile, who was supposed to be Jesus Christ. Mr. Christ beneficently explained that if each of us obdurate sinners were only to accept him into our hearts, then all of our sins would be forgiven; that we would be given a "clean slate" with which to begin our lives anew. Following this, the house lights came on, and the Pastor who'd sponsored the whole event came out and took the stage to speak to us about saving our souls from eternal damnation.

Sitting there sheepishly, amongst my fellow *hopelessly flawed* human beings, I began to ponder my life, and all the indiscretions and blunders I've made. ... I am an incorrigible sinner. ... A reprobate. ... I have done wrong. ... I don't want to burn in a lake of fire for all eternity. I don't want to smell the malodorous sulfur and behold the vile gnashing of teeth. ... It's some scary stuff! I considered filling out the provided form stating that I too, had accepted the Lord Jesus Christ into my heart—they even supplied the pen—but damn it all, there was nothing to write on, so I didn't bother. Oh well. We were then told to leave the building, at which time I dutifully obtained a free copy of the New Testament, titled simply *The Great News!*

I'd been hearing about Hell House for years. It was sort of notorious. In college I briefly dated an *über*-liberal pro-choice chick who proudly protested Hell House somewhere in California's Bay Area. I was expecting it to be nominally "offensive" on some level. Meh. I can't speak for my companions, but I wasn't the slightest bit offended by anything about Hell House, other than the fact that there was too much wailing involved. Really, I wasn't. All the issues they deal with are simply ugly aspects of reality that most people choose not to think too much about. Of course, I don't agree with the ridiculous Christian take on why those unpleasant elements of reality are important, but I do like it

this church wants to scare the Hell out of you

HELL HOUSE

when people—regardless of their take—are actually acknowledging the distasteful things everyone else is sweeping under the carpet. It's refreshing.

Anyway, despite all that, I couldn't help but notice a few key inaccuracies in Hell House's little story. First off, the Devil is supposed to appear beautiful to the eye, disguised as "an angel of light" (it says so in the Bible). He wasn't, he just looked like some schmuck who attends the DeVry Institute while working part-time at Circuit City. He was a total fucking loser. I was profoundly disappointed with the Devil. Secondly, Jesus was not a cracker. He was a brother, or at least an Arab. Okay, well, he was a Jew, but he was Middle Eastern, so I presume he would've had dark skin. They fucked up this detail completely. Also, why did the aborted fetus show up at the end, in Heaven, as a young girl? If all aborted fetuses gain ascension to Elysium by default, then what's the big deal about abortion? I mean, the rest of us have to fuckin' slog on *suffering* down here on Earth, but apparently the aborted get to skip the line to Paradise, so ... where's the problem exactly? Unfortunately, there was no Q-&-A session following the performance, so my questions will have to remain unanswered.

November 1, 2003, 11:48 p.m.

Yesterday was Halloween. I dressed up as a bum—sorry, "mendicant," sorry ... no ... "homeless person"—and it may have been one of my best costumes ever. The costume consisted of the following: I didn't shave for three days, put on a pair of old pants, an old shirt, an old hoodie, an old beanie, and one tattered glove. Additionally, I lugged around a duffel bag, a sleeping bag, a Styrofoam cup, and a cardboard sign which read, "Homeless. Hungry. Cold. Anything helps. God bless. ...☺..." What made the whole package believable, of course, was the fact that I'd removed my dentures, and spent the majority of the evening with no front teeth. My standard line for the night was, "I'm just tryin' to keep things on an even keel right now." Which worked quite well, actually.

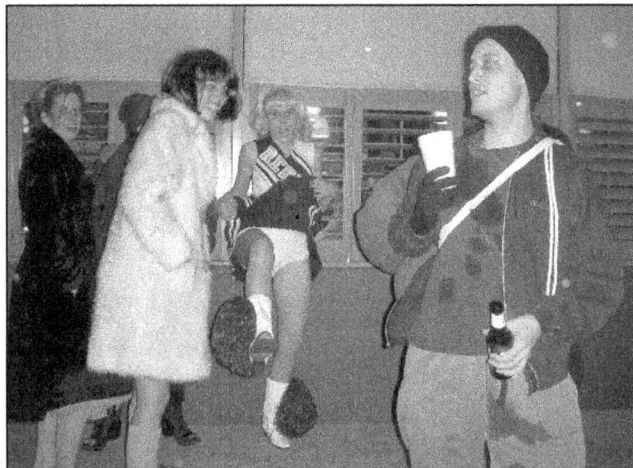

Girls gone wild, a cheerleader, and a bum.

Anyway, the evening started out at a party at a sushi bar that my housemate Claudine's Japanese girlfriend works at. Josh, Amy, and myself drove way the fuck out into South (?) Denver for some free sushi, free sake, and free Kirin beer. As soon as I walked into the place, the drunk, Japanese proprietress immediately mistook me for a vagrant, but was kind enough to offer me some food anyway. Once she discovered that I wasn't really homeless, she let out a big laughing hoot, and throughout the evening kept saying things like, "Oh, you blow me up big time!" My housemates who'd also attended this party were variously dressed up as: a cheerleader, a beaver, and a couple of "girls gone wild." The proprietor of the place had a great inflatable sumo wrestler suit, which all the kids got a kick out of punching and kicking. So, we hung out at the nice sushi bar, with the nice Japanese people, and drank, and were regaled with good food for about forty-five minutes. They were very nice people.

At one point, everyone ventured outside to take some photos, and I stumbled into the sandwich shop next door to test out my costume. I came out with half a loaf of free sourdough bread. Shortly thereafter, Josh drove Amy to the rave she was supposed to bartend at (which was busted by the police by 10:30 p.m.), then he dropped me off at a bar called The Lion's Lair for a performance by a musical duo called Little Fyodor & Babushka.

I paid the five bucks entrance fee, and—in spite of my costume—made it inside. Then I wandered around the bar begging for spare change. Most of the patrons ignored me and my awkward beseeching, but one fellow (a chap dressed as a Mexican *bandito*) took me aside, gave me a long speech about "staying on the right track," and then deposited *five dollars* in my Styrofoam cup. As soon as he left, I used this money to purchase beer.

Total asshole.

I made another round or two of spare-changing, but nobody was biting. I spare-changed the star of the night, Little Fyodor, but he only gave me his business card. Sometime around this point, the Lion's Lair doorman informed me that I couldn't spare-change in the bar, even though I'd paid five dollars to get inside. I explained that it was part of my costume. He told me that yeah, he

knew that, and that it wasn't funny and it wasn't cool. "But what do you care? All the money's just going to your bar anyway." He replied with: "You know, man, you're a real asshole." And that was that.

Little Fyodor & Babushka then took the stage; a peculiar guitar / keyboard duo with rather amusing lyrics and a genuinely psychotic stage presence.

As the show was winding down, a slightly tubby lesbian took a shine to me. See, she'd been homeless for a while too, and—with no petitioning on my part whatsoever—she put three dollars in my Styrofoam cup. We made some small talk about livin' the hard life, and then went our separate ways. And that was Halloween. As Halloweens tend to go, it wasn't a bad one. Not at all. In fact, as a homeless person, I made a total of eight dollars and also got a bunch of free sushi and sake.

And to think that my dentist tried to convince me to get permanent implants drilled into my skull, so as to eliminate the need for dentures. Where's the fun in that?

November 4, 2003, 11:56 p.m.

Tonight, Nels Cline was supposed to headline a show at my house, but he and his crew canceled at the last minute. So, in an attempt at filling the vacant slot in the evening's lineup, Josh, Nate Hayden, and myself formed a band called The Taylor-Clark-Hayden Free-Jazz Ensemble. This was inspired by a band I saw open for Vholtz at The Hemlock Tavern in San Francisco, about six months ago. I don't know what they were called, but they were terrible: an absurd-yet-stoic spastic "Jazz" drummer and a guitarist who frenetically fretted for about forty minutes.

So, in similar fashion, The Taylor-Clark-Hayden Free-Jazz Ensemble consisted of myself playing spastic "Jazz" drums, Josh fretting on his bass, and Nate reading selections from *The Portable Nietzsche*, *The Tao Te Ching* and some other book. The stage was illuminated by candles and a single spotlight, the three of us were all drinking tea and wearing turtlenecks, Josh and I were smoking cigarettes, and I was sporting a pair of sunglasses. We performed three "songs" for about twenty minutes, to a crowd of about fifteen to twenty people, some of whom halfheartedly clapped. The gesture was so obvious that I hope they all "got it."

Then some other bands from New York played, and two of them were pretty good, but I forget their names, so fuck it.

November 10, 2003, 11:50 p.m.

So, this evening, Josh, Amy, and myself broke into the abandoned building next to ours (Josh did the actual "breaking in," but I supplied the flashlights). It was gross. Very *Blair Witch Project*; crumbling walls, floors, and ceiling. Josh pried open the door leading to the second-floor staircase, and the entire staircase was strewn with the fetid, rotting, and putrefied carcasses of pigeons, as was much of the first floor. I snapped some photos, but there wasn't much to do in the place, so we left after only a few minutes. Josh has vague plans to venture up to the second floor at some point—in goggles and a facemask—but I don't suspect that I'll be joining him. I'd hate to fall through the second-story floor of an abandoned building that's more than a century old, and break a limb landing on a pile of decomposing pigeons – but hey, to each their own.

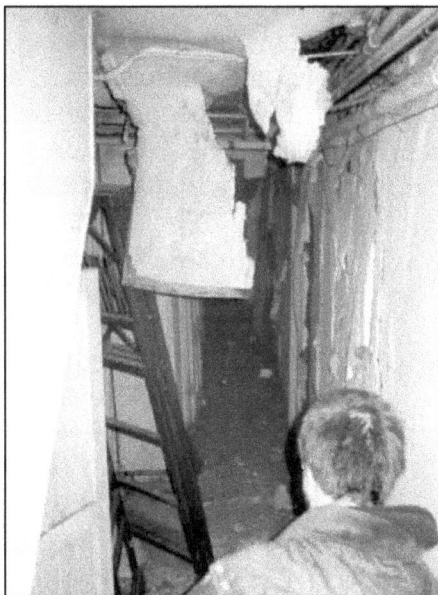
The back of Josh's head.

November 12, 2003, 2:37 a.m.

So, tonight I witnessed a couple of noteworthy performances here at Monkey Mania. I missed the first band because I was listening to records and drinking beer in my room. Following this, however, was Andrew Novick's one-man lip-synch act, Get Your Going. This featured Andrew singin' and a dancin' along with old Manson Family recordings, while a television broadcast footage from Manson's trial. It was an entertaining performance, and Andrew (ex-vocalist for Warlock Pinchers) is much-beloved in this town, so the crowd emphatically cheered him on, and everyone seemed to really enjoy it. I missed the third act because I was drinking at a nearby bar.

The main event for the night was, as promised beforehand, a "porno-social-ritual-opera," titled "Holy Virgin Cult," as performed by touring Frenchman Jean-Louis Costes, a second Frenchman, and a French girl of, perhaps, twenty-one. Mr. Costes has been staying at Monkey Mania for a couple of days now, but it wasn't until earlier this evening (before the performance) that I actually got a chance to talk to him. We discussed my experiences in Spain and France, the stupidity of the concept of foreign "work visas," and some other things. He was a very taciturn, humble, well-mannered man of small stature, with an intermediate grasp of the English language. Once on stage, however, Mr. Costes transformed into a writhing forty-nine-year-old toddler.

His show was essentially a "performance art" piece dealing with heretical Catholic themes, as enacted by, um ... three "performance artists." The show basically went like this: for about fifteen minutes, you have Costes and this other French guy, both wearing suits and dancing around the stage and singing along to a backing tape. At some point, they start to sort of attack each other, and the performance becomes increasingly more belligerent. Both men don face-masks that cover their mouths; Costes' is a vagina, and the other fellow's is a penis. They begin to "fuck," ramming their heads together, jamming the penis into the vagina. Shortly thereafter, the shaven-headed French girl runs onto the stage and joins in the fray. The three of them are all yelling/singing, dancing around, careening into each other, employing a number of various props, and occasionally stumbling out into the audience. Soon, their clothes begin to come off, and things start to get, er ... *wacky*. At the height of the show, both Costes and the other Frenchman are stark naked, and the girl is wearing only a bra (incidentally, her crotch was just as bald as her head). Meanwhile, the shrieking / singing / prancing continued, and the props grew larger and more involved.

Throughout the performance the following transpired: Costes and the other Frenchman each induced themselves to vomit by sticking their fingers down their own throats, Costes and the other Frenchman briefly took turns sucking each other's flaccid cocks; the girl pissed into Costes' open mouth; Costes and the other Frenchman pissed into goblets, which all three of them drank from; various objects were inserted into the men's assholes; the trio took turns dry-humping each other, as well as an inflatable doll ("The Virgin"); candles were lit, then used to singe the performers' genitals; ketchup, chocolate pudding, and urine found their way onto the performers' bodies; and as the show progressed, the three of them became increasingly aggressive with the audience, rolling around on the ground, grabbing people and dry-humping them, and so forth – meanwhile, they're all singing operatically about The Virgin Mary and dancing around the stage area. At one point, Costes and the girl came out into the audience with the inflatable female fuck-doll, inciting people to, "Fuck zee virgin! Fuck zee virgin! Fuck zee virgin!" with their fingers. For the record, there was no *bona fide* shitting (it was just chocolate pudding), and there was no actual literal fucking – if that's what you've been hearing, then you heard wrong, bucko. So there you have it – "performance art." French performance art, at that.

Later, I got the idea into my head to go into the kitchen and retrieve the leftover slice of

Relax – it's just chocolate pudding.

Self-induced upchucking ... for "art."

carrot cake sitting on the kitchen table. My intention, initially, was to throw this at the performers, but once I was back at the front of the crowd, I realized that I was hungry and started eating it instead (I had been drinking, and was craving the sugar). Later, Josh told me that that was one of his favorite parts of the evening – that while all the naked, food-smeared ass-interpolation and piss-drinking was going on, I was standing there eating a piece of carrot cake. (Perchance ... that makes *me* a performance artist too?) Anyway, the show carried on for over an hour, but I eventually got bored of it and returned to the bar around the corner with Andrew and Nate, and drank until last call. And that was that.

Anyway, I have to say that all in all, it was a pretty entertaining maelstrom of a show; floppy French cocks, a shaved French pussy, attempted oral sex, vomiting, piss drinking, anal insertions, condiments, and Catholicism ... all rolled into one act. Sure it's all been done before—yes—and I don't presume to that I can deduce exactly what "concept" they were attempting to express (aside from working out their personal issues) but nonetheless, it was far more entertaining than the usual Rock band fare we have here at Monkey Mania. As far as I know, everyone in attendance seems to have had a pretty fun time.

As for Costes being "the French G.G. Allin" – I wouldn't necessarily say so. Yes, his show was completely chaotic and frenzied, but it was a controlled, scripted sort of welter, directed more at the performers themselves than at the audience *per se*. It seems to me that G.G. Allen was more about attacking people than he was about

230

performing. G.G. threw punches at the audience and genuinely hurt himself onstage; Costes (while he did seem to incite some degree of panic in certain members of the audience), rarely touched anyone, and he certainly didn't "attack" anyone. Those spectators who were dry-humped were clearly into it and agog about it.

... still just chocolate pudding.

I don't reckon anyone in the crowd was upset by his roiling performance – most people seemed bemused and genuinely entertained. I'd actually put Jean-Louis Costes in pretty much the same league of performative bedlam as eXtreme Elvis, which is neither a compliment nor an insult – they're both just doing their thing. That's fine with me – their thing just isn't really *my* thing, that's all.

Anyway, right now, Costes and his retinue are sleeping just on the other side of the wall from me, curled up like little French puppy dogs in snuggly French sleeping bags. Onstage, they may indeed be the terror or the French bourgeoisie, but offstage, they're as gracious as one could ever possibly expect from houseguests. They even cleaned up their mess and showered – many of the bands that stay here don't even have the decency to do that.

November 15, 2003, 12:32 a.m.

Last night we had another show here at Monkey Mania. The drummer of the opening band, Majestic Sunbeast, cancelled at the last minute, so Josh and I decided to fill in for him, and the band then became Josh Taylor's Majestic Sunbeast Orchestra. This was actually a lot of fun – Josh and I both played drums, a couple of members of Zombie Zombie did keyboards / noise, and three other guys (whose names I don't remember) did vocals, guitar, and bass. We busted out the fog machine, some psychedelic lights, and jammed on one song, for a total of fifty minutes (think Crash Worship meets Hawkwind). It was pretty *far out.* "Concept art," really.

Over the course of about an hour, the sunbeast rose up from the pit of Hell, ascended through the depths of the ocean, burst to the surface, and finally—resplendently—lifted up toward the heavenly firmament. This was all, in fact, *so epic* that the twenty or so audience members who'd witnessed the song's beginning shrank to two, who actually witnessed its end. I suppose it's pretty rude for the house joke band to make the evening into a travesty by spending an hour "jamming" on *one* extemporaneous Prog Rock improv track, but fuck it – I had fun.

Anyway, following this, a two-man band called Less Than Human played, and their drummer was so proficient that it didn't matter that the other guy was just noodling around with a keyboard and some effects pedals. Then there was some art-student bullshit that I won't validate by even describing. That was last night.

Today, my housemates and I were invited to co-host the "locals only" radio show at the college station in Boulder, Radio 1190 (part of me went because I wanted to play music, and part of me went because I wanted to check out Boulder). Anyway, this was a two-hour show featuring only local artists' recordings.

Amy, Josh, and Claudine on the mic.

Over the course of about two hours, we played a number of discs, including: Marbles, Sparkles, Friends Forever, Ralph Gean, BioBitch,

Little Fyodor, Cindy Wonderful, and some other stuff that I've either forgotten or had never heard of.

November 16, 2003, 5:55 p.m.

Last night six bands played at my house: The Ultra Boys, Zombie Zombie, Kindercide, Not To Be Eaten, Wives, and Hale Zukas. For, I think, the first time since I moved in here, I actually watched all of them.

Wives, live at Monkey Mania.

Generally speaking, they were all pretty good ... or at least decent anyway (though I really could have done without Kindercide, a Grindcore joke band, and Not To Be Eaten, a Florida-style Death Metal band that could still use some work).

Hale Zukas, live at Monkey Mania.

The evening's attendance wasn't half bad either, and the kids seemed to dig most of the bands, which was nice. There was an odd mix of people at the show – in addition to the Monkey Mania regulars, there were also some seventeen-year-old "Street Punks," a few would be Indie-Rock hipsters, some understated Death Metal folk, and a very "Industrial" looking guy in a black latex shirt, who had a miniature black obelisk sticking out of his lower lip. I liked the teenage Street Punks the best – they were as cute as buttons!

November 23, 2003, 2:08 a.m.

Denver became a winter wonderland today; icy roads, slippery sidewalks, booger-freezing winds, and a two-inch thick white snow-blanket enrobing everything. It's absolutely fucking freezing. Anyway, around nightfall, I found myself briefly at an art gallery (where I commandeered a beer), then at a show at an anarchist "collective" called The Breakdown, then at Bar Bar, and finally at Denver's finest 24-hour diner, The Breakfast King.

On two separate and unrelated occasions throughout the evening, there was more talk of my room being haunted. Oh yeah, everyone says my room is haunted. Luke Fairchild, the guy who used to live here, apparently always slept with the lights on, because of a baleful "dark presence" lurking in the corner opposite my bed. Claudine and her girlfriend, Toshimi (both of whom slept in here on several occasions), claim to have seen some sort of apparitions mutely gliding around the room. Nora Keyes, of the band The Centimeters, slept in here while coming through town on tour, and reports having had similar creepy supernatural experiences (she mentioned this to me with no prompting on my part whatsoever). Anyway, so some guy whom I'd never met before tonight says to me, "Oh, so you're the guy who moved into the haunted room, eh?" And I guess I am. I suppose anything is theoretically possible ... after all, this building is over a hundred years old and is fairly dilapidated (the top two floors have been condemned). Nonetheless, I remain skeptical 'bout ghosts. As of yet, I ain't seen shit.

Tonight, however, tonight—a cold, snowy eventide when the stars and moon are occluded behind the clouds ... just like the night when little Victoria was savagely murdered and hurriedly buried 'neath the floorboards back in 1891—would be the perfect gloaming for something *interesting* to happen. ...

November 26, 2003, 11:58 p.m.

Last night I played bass in a Yoko Ono cover band – Yoko Oh-No! This was some kooky concept-joke-project that Josh had conceived, and for some reason, he actually put on the flyer for the Kites show. Strangely, a young hippie-ish couple showed up to the show just to see this non-existent Yoko Ono cover band (?). And so, with about fifteen minutes' notice, Josh, Claudine, and myself prepared the *high concept Art Rock project* that was to be Yoko Oh-No! – and we executed it, in spite of the fact that neither Claudine nor I had ever actually heard Yoko Ono's music. Josh played some up-tempo drums, I played three-stringed-bass-power-cords through a phase / flange / distortion effect, and Claudine (dressed as a ladybug and wearing a long black wig) assembled a homemade light fixture while screaming, nay—shrieking—a single phrase in Japanese, over and over and over again. We played for as long as it took her to assemble the light fixture (about ten minutes), and the set ended with her plugging it in, turning it on, and me falling to my knees in psychedelic ecstasy while noodling on the bass. It was *high-concept* Art. You probably wouldn't comprehend it, actually. Neither did the six people in the audience. But that's why *true artists*—like Yoko Ono—suffer as much as they do for their art. Because you'll never understand. ...

Anyway, today I got my hair cut by the Mexican-American war veteran down the block. This guy is very special. See, I used to get my hair cut in my hometown, by this old fucker named Paul, whose barber shop hadn't changed since the mid-sixties; same wallpaper, same mirrors, same TV set, same dogeared copies of *Playboy*, and so on. I was the only non-geriatric member of his clientele, as far as I know. I used to think this was pretty neat.

But this guy here in Denver, he's way more "special" than Paul – because he's older, he's nicer, he's Mexican, and he's a vet of the Second World War. His shop, much like Paul's, seems to be stuck in a time warp. The major differences between the two being that, instead of *Playboy*, this guy has copies of *Disabled American Veterans*, and instead of faded '60s kitsch, he has a mix of old Americana and Mexicana. And perhaps strangest of all; in the back room of the barbershop, there is a full weight room, complete with faded, tattered girlie posters from the early '80s. And he's even older than Paul. This guy is so old, that not only does he constantly make little hissing / wheezing noises while he cuts your hair ... and not only does he go to the trouble of busting out the old straight-razor to shave your neck and behind your ears ... but this guy ... he's so old, that he only charges *three dollars* for a haircut. I shit you not; three dollars. He's cut my hair three times now, and I give him a fiver every time, but I still feel like I'm stiffing him. I can't even imagine paying fifteen bucks plus tip to have my hair cut by some twenty-one-year-old chick at Supercuts.

December 1, 2003, 1:59 a.m.

Tonight my home hosted a benefit for Wesley Willis (R.I.P.). Mr. Willis, even though he was a (*ahem*), er ... "Rock Star," has been buried *sans* headstone. A couple of my Monkey Mania housemates were close personal friends of Mr. Willis', so tonight my home hosted a benefit to raise money to buy him a headstone. It was something of a potlatch. Our living room was turned into a makeshift art gallery, wherein locals who'd been collecting Willis' artworks put them up for sale, and then donated the profits to the headstone fund. Footage from an unreleased documentary about Willis was shown, as was some never-before-seen animation he'd done. His records were played, and there was even a raffle to raise further funds, for which the Boulder-based record store, Black & Read, was magnanimous enough to donate a bunch of gift certificates (as well as about $200). And, of course, there were bands.

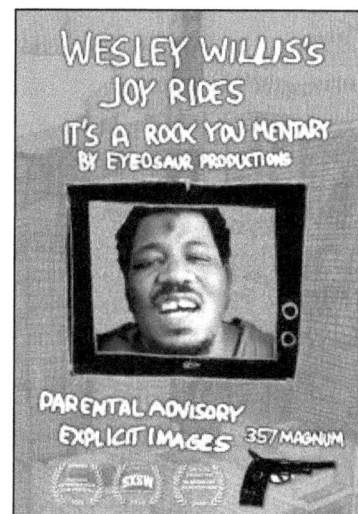

WESLEY WILLIS'S JOY RIDES

IT'S A ROCK YOU MENTARY BY EYEOSAUR PRODUCTIONS

PARENTAL ADVISORY EXPLICIT IMAGES 357 MAGNUM

The show began with a touring Power-Pop-Punk band. I forget their name ... I think it might have been The Queers #201, or maybe it was NOFX #608 ... I don't recall. Something that's been done for the umpteenth time, anyway. What I do recall is that the bassist had tattoos on his neck. *Hard.* They were followed by Andrew Novick's Get Your Going. For this installment of Get Your Going, Andrew explored the concept of Waffle House. He dressed up as a Waffle House employee and did karaoke versions of Waffle House songs in front of a monitor showing footage of people working at Waffle House. Throughout the performance, his lovely assistant (the spitting image of a younger Debbie Harry), who was also dressed as a Waffle House employee, prepared coffee and syrup-covered waffles, which were then handed out to the audience. As usual, the kids loved it completely.

Then there was Nightshark, an instrumental guitar-and-drums combo. I liked them – their drummer blew my socks off, without acting like a big shot about it. This was followed by Organz, who I didn't watch, because the last time I saw them, they irritated me, and I wasn't in the mood for that sort of thing tonight. The star of the show was Mr. Pacman, who seem to be a pretty big deal to a lot of people around here. Apparently, Mr. Pacman is usually a three-piece, and do a lot of intricate stuff, but for some reason tonight Mr. Pacman was just a guy in a fat guy suit and a helmet, singing along to a Casio. He started his set by eating fifteen hot dogs, which was impressive in its own right, but other than that, it didn't really grab me. Maybe the full band is better though.

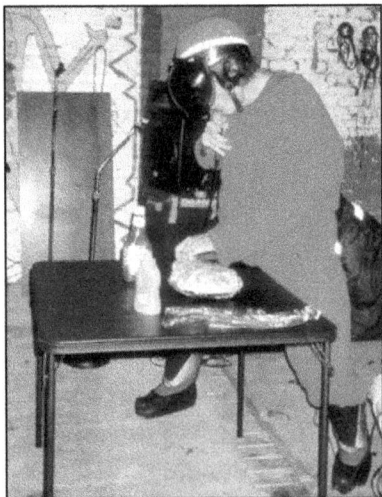
Mr. Pacman eating hot dogs.

Of course, throughout the evening, I've been drinking calimochos with Mike and Zack from Zombie Zombie, so I'm sort of drunk right now. Anyway, all in all, it was a pretty mellow, unremarkable night, though I found it curious that two people—neither of whom I know very well—decided to confide personal secrets to me tonight, *tête-à-tête*. Both prefaced their admissions with the phrase, "Ok, now, you have to swear not to tell anyone this, but ... " Having learned the hard way, I rarely make statements (or admissions) like that anymore. Somehow, no matter how much people "swear" to maintain their silence, such things almost always end up becoming public knowledge. But I won't spill their beans, I swear.

December 3, 2003, 12:19 p.m.

My old friend Joe C. flew into town for a visit, arriving around 10:00 p.m. last night. The first thing we did was amble over to a bar to get food and booze. He was kind enough to have brought me a gift – a bottle of Smirnoff Vodka. As soon as we got back to my house, we set into drinking it with my housemates Claudine and Amy, and a fellow by the name of Ian. Once we were sufficiently liquored-up, Claudine, Ian, Joe, and myself headed out to a cowboy-themed gay karaoke bar called Charlie's, where we met up with Ian's co-worker, Mila, and continued drinking in earnest.

Though it was a karaoke bar, nobody sang, since the karaoke slots were all filled up 'til closing (which was unfortunate, since Joe seemed to be really itching to belt-out some tunes). Nor did any of us dance, as the music was predictably garish gay bar music ("It's Raining Men," *et cetera*), and the dance floor was all but dominated by a muscled African-American fellow, who seems to have believed himself to be the vivacious reincarnation of some ballerina-dancing-queen-princess.

After Charlie's closed at 2:00 a.m., we all headed back to my room, wherein the five of us polished off the rest of the bottle of vodka and had an "after-hours" drunken party. People started getting silly. Joe drunkenly knocked over my stereo. There came a point, at about three or four in the morning, at which there was no booze left, and everyone was thirsty and desperate – so *someone* produced an alternative intoxicant, which temporarily satiated the substance-lust for some of those in attendance. I myself didn't partake, as booze is really my only "jam," so to speak. So anyway, we all decided to "party" *all night long*, and made a pact to be at Bar Bar when it opened at 7:00 in the morning.

Before aiming to open up Bar Bar, there was some brief "chill out" time, during which everyone lay around in the dark, gazing at my lava lamp in a state of benumbed repose, while we listened to Aphex Twin's *Selected Ambient Works Volume II*.

Drunk Joe didn't want photo evidence of this fuckery.

We made it to Bar Bar just after they opened their doors at 7:00 a.m., and promptly resumed drinking in earnest. Joe kept pumping money into the jukebox and insisting that people dance to Frank Sinatra songs with him. I played Van Halen's "Panama" and ZZ Top's "Legs" in an attempt to keep the "party" vibe going. We finally left Bar Bar at about 9:30, stopped momentarily at various people's homes to get cash, then headed out towards Casa Bonita for breakfast. Those among us who were employed stopped to call in "sick" before continuing onward into the depths of delirious decadence.

We arrived at Casa Bonita at about 10:45 – fifteen minutes before they're open for business. So, while waiting for The Pretty House to open its doors to the public, there was some drunken, sleep-deprived wandering around The Dollar Store, where Claudine bought everyone chintzy award ribbons that bore messages like "I Can Count to Ten!"

Once we got inside Casa Bonita, at 11:00 a.m., everyone ordered the all-you-can-eat plate of chicken enchiladas, and everyone, save myself, got pitchers of margaritas *(yuck)*. The place was a veritable graveyard. We were basically the only ones there. And so, we sat there at Casa Bonita, eating chicken enchiladas, while watching our own private cliff-diver shows, and acquitting ourselves poorly. Claudine couldn't stop laughing, Mila felt compelled to heckle the performers, Joe spilled strawberry margarita all over the table, and Ian somehow managed to eat a second plate of food. Eventually, we finished our meals and made a half-hearted attempt at showing Joe around the restaurant, though he was too exhausted and drunk to really appreciate any of it. Eventually, we finally left and headed back home.

Driving back home in the midday sun, through a bustling Denver, I felt like total shit – like I always do when I stay up all night. The brain-and-gut-busting combo of drinking for hours on end, not sleeping, and eating Casa Bonita food at noon felt not unlike how I imagine a "bad trip"; teetering just on the edge of becoming a horrible nightmare, but never quite getting there.

Once home, I slept from about 2:00 p.m. to 8:00 p.m. and woke up feeling as warbly and foul as would be expected following such a night. The evening has been spent lackadaisically lounging around, watching movies, drinking hot cocoa, and trying not to move too much. Rock n' Roll, *dude*.

December 7, 2003, 6:30 p.m.

Today, my friend Joe and I stumbled into consciousness late in the afternoon. We'd been drinking late into the morning last night, as with the night before – in fact, as with most of the week. We both felt like complete shit, and were in no capacity to do anything much aside from drink coffee and eat. After ingesting some cheap diner food, I decided to take him to a café located a few blocks from my house, called The Mercury. The Mercury Café is an amusing cliché – a set of by-the-book stereotypes actualized as though by the art director of a cheesy 1980s teen film.

It's a hippie café – the kind one might find in Portland, Eugene, Berkeley, Madison, or any other progressive college town. It's dimly lit, the ceiling is latticed by deep red Christmas lights, all the lamps are decorative and exotic, there are indoor bike racks, racks of free weekly papers, the wait staff is composed of cute, twenty-something baristas of varying ethnicities, and the clientele includes a disproportionate number of gray-haired men sporting ponytails. They make their own bread and desserts, brew their own beer, feature a wide variety of vegan menu selections, and probably have a policy of "celebrating diversity" (whatever that means). The best part, of course, is that there is a curtained-off section of The Mercury Café which houses a stage, on which one can observe performances of "Free Jazz," spoken word, "poetry slams," feminist performance art, singer/songwriter solo guitarists, and various other progressive partisan art garbage. It's a trope. There's probably one in every town, but the one in Denver happens to be only a couple blocks from my basement bunker / hideout / fortress / lair. So anyway, I took Joe there for a cup of coffee, and we sat at the bar.

Within minutes of being served, a pair of barrel-chested, working-class fellows strode through the door, sauntered up to the bar, and planted themselves next to us. Both were middle-aged white males, wearing baseball hats and pro-sports sweatshirts. Before they'd even sat down, they were hooting "Yeah Broncos!" and asking for Budweiser. These gentlemen were, shall we say ... rednecks. Not to be confused with "bumpkins," "hicks" or "hillbillies," but *rednecks*, in the defiantly proud sense of what that term conveys. Seems they'd driven all the way from Ohio to see the Broncos, and they were pumped, 'cause the Broncos had just kicked some serious ass on the field. They'd been drinking, but they weren't quite drunk. So anyway, they wanted a couple'a Budweisers.

The hippie bartendress informed them that The Mercury only serves local microbrews, but that the closest they had to Budweiser was some beer that neither the rednecks nor I had ever heard of. In spite of this, the rednecks ordered a couple of these. They then proceeded to attempt to make small talk with my friend Joe and me. They asked us if we were Broncos fans, and we replied "no." They asked us where we were from, and Joe said, "San Francisco." They asked us if we were football fans, and we replied "no." This shocked and offended both of them immensely.

They became very vocal. ... How could we not *like* football? Naturally, they then asked us if we were gay. I laughed and asked what had given them that impression. Rather than answering my question, the portlier of the two rednecks reassured us that it was "fine" if we were gay. We assured him that we weren't gay. Their beer arrived. They tasted it, and informed the bartendress that it tasted "like shit." The bartendress informed them that the beers were four dollars each. They were both horrified and completely taken aback by this. *What the hell kind of bar was this, where they don't have Budweiser, the beer they do have costs four dollars and tastes "like shit," and the guys sitting at the bar don't even like football? Has the whole world gone mad?*

So anyway, it was blatantly obvious that these rednecks felt unwelcome and out-of-place. Of course, being rednecks, they couldn't simply keep this to themselves and drink their beers. No, they had to make sure that everyone in the joint knew how disgusted they were. They had to be loud. They continued to make small talk with Joe and me. Even though they'd pejoratively insinuated that we were both gay, neither of us was offended or annoyed. After all, I was wearing all black and sporting an admittedly faggyish beard—looking like an urbane asshole—and Joe, a trim Korean man with aerodynamic glasses would make for a fine piece of tail anytime. We continued to humor them. We remained polite, as we understood that these were a couple of guys from Ohio who were out of their element, bewildered and slightly threatened by their surroundings. They just kept getting surlier.

I was just trying to enjoy my coffee, shake off my hangover, and wake up a bit. I informed them that they might feel "more at home" a couple miles north, in LoDo, where all the sports bars, pickup joints, and Hooters are. They complained again to the waitress that the beer tasted "like shit." Then, one of them inquired of a passing waiter as to whether or not this was a gay bar. The waiter, blushing, informed him that it wasn't. They both declared that—no—it *is* a gay bar, and informed Joe and I that—yes—we were faggots. We just stared blankly at them. The rednecks then proceeded to storm out of the faggot bar, leaving their shitty-tasting, four-dollar beers all but untouched. This was a truly beautiful moment. It was beautiful, because while all this was going on, a black girl with dreads was "slammin" some freestyle poetry/rap on stage with something resembling a band. The whole situation was just surreal.

December 22, 2003, 4:25 a.m.

Okay, so I set up my first show at Monkey Mania. Tis' as follows: Ralph Gean! Little Fyodor! Get Your Going! (with more to be announced). If you live in Denver and you're reading this, please be nice and print out the flyer:

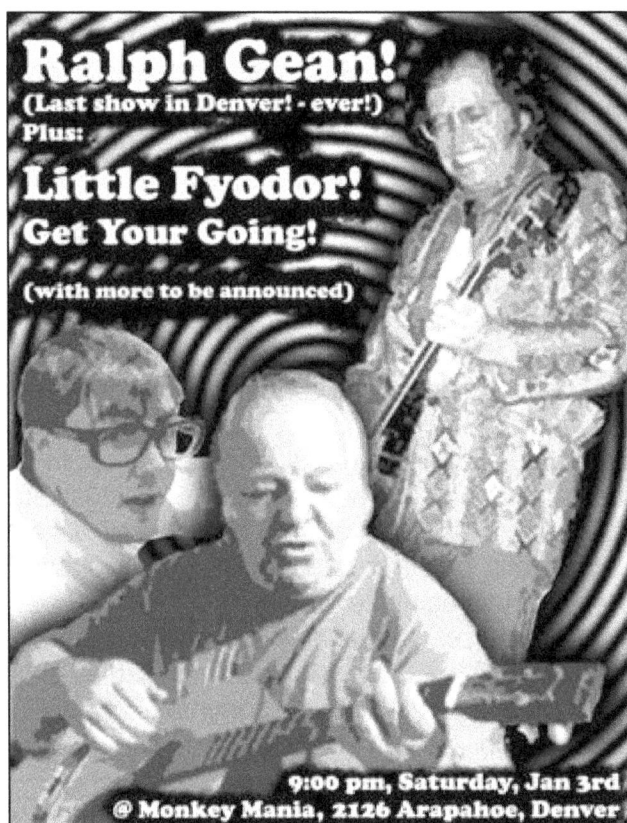

... make hundreds of copies of it, and plaster them all over town. Thank you.

January 3, 2004, 11:23 a.m.

Last night, seven Punk / Hardcore / Grind / Glam bands played at my house. *Seven*. The kitchen / living room area was filled throughout the evening with all sorts of sloppily-dressed Punk and crustie rabble.

To balance out the *feng shui*, I wore my suit jacket, and as is often the case, was the sharpest-dressed person I saw all evening. But I didn't watch any of the bands. Instead, I sat in my room drinking Absolut Vodka and Vanilla Coke, while watching a Japanese anime with Claudine – a film in which, whenever anyone gets any of their limbs sliced off, blood shoots out as though from a high-pressure sprinkler valve, people can revivify after they've been decapitated, and poisonous snakes sneak out of women's pussies to assassinate people. It was pretty good.

Tonight: Ralph Gean, Little Fyodor, Get Your Going, and Majestic Sunbeast. I guess I'm supposed to be "in charge" of this shit. ...

January 4, 2004, 10:54 p.m.

So, the show last night went off pretty well. Andrew Novick opened up as Get Your Going, and for this installment, he did a bunch of Morton Downey Jr. songs and dressed up as a boxer.

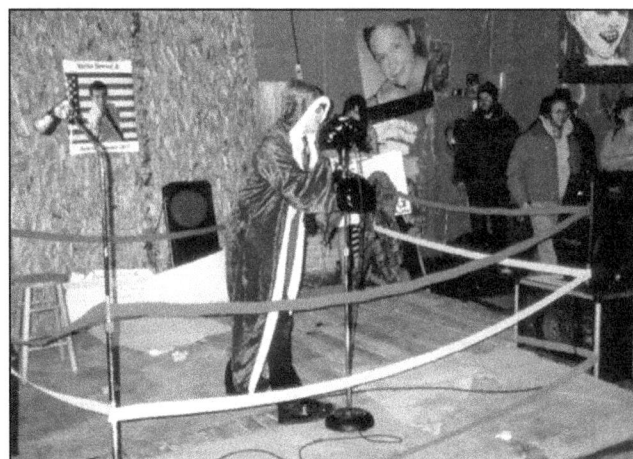

Get Your Going, live at Monkey Mania.

I only caught the tail end of it because I was working the door, but what I observed was pretty amusing. Get Your Going was followed by Majestic Sunbeast (not to be confused with Josh Taylor's Majestic Sunbeast Orchestra). I didn't see any of their set, because again, I was working the door, but I could hear their clamorous psychedelic Free Jazz noise jamz well enough anyway. They seem to have gathered a few new devotees as a result of their performance. Then there was Little

Fyodor, whom I also missed, because again, I was working the door.

Finally, Ralph Gean, star of the show, put on what I considered was a pretty superb performance. This big, round guy in his sixties, who is still on the mend from shoulder surgery, came out on stage with only a crummy little cheapo acoustic guitar, and played for like—shit—an hour and a half or something, and he rocked it pretty hard. He was getting requests for both originals and covers late into the night, and had everyone in the place singing along to "The Asshole Song" in one of those beautiful perfect-show-moments that happens every once-in-a-blue-moon. I think he had a lot of fun playing, and everyone had fun watching him.

Ralph Gean, live at Monkey Mania.

Ralph received the lion's share of the door, and a bit went to Little Fyodor, but Monkey Mania didn't profit from the evening. I figured that since Ralph is in his sixties, unemployed, and now, technically homeless, he needs the money more than Andrew and the Majestic Sunbeast guys.

January 25, 2004, 1:04 p.m.

Last night I did something stupid; I mixed several kinds of alcohol, and as a result, I got way too drunk ... so now today, I'm hungover and feeling like total shit. Anyway, so I finally got to see Denver's answer to Heavenly, Dressy Bessy, play at The Hi-Dive. Apparently, their big claim to fame (or so I'm told) is that they were featured on the *But I'm A Cheerleader* soundtrack, and as if that weren't enough, they're huge in Japan. Huzzah. I actually kind of liked them – they reminded me of the things I like about sugary twee girlie Pop like Go Sailor. If I'd had any cash, I might have bought a CD, but all I had was plastic, so I left the show empty-handed. After the show, I ended up at Dressy Bessy's bassist's house, with my housemate Claudine and three of her friends, where we remained until like four in the morning or something.

Nothing against the people who live there or anything, but—*fucking hell*—they easily have the most hipsterfied home I've ever seen (and I've lived in both San Francisco and the Pacific Northwest). So, so, *so* much thought, time, and energy must have gone into beautifying this homestead; the rooms were all painted different colors to match the furniture, the lights were colored to match the hue of the walls, and everything that wasn't nailed down was some kind of vintage, thrift-stored kitsch, or was otherwise somehow art-related. The place was curatorially decorated with knickknacks, doodads, tchotchkes, curios, and bric-a-brac from the '50s, '60s, and '70s, and, I swear, they had dozens and dozens and dozens of different kinds of groovy lighters from every imaginable time an

d place. As much as I usually pooh-pooh magpie stuff like that, I have to admit that all in all, it was actually a fairly admirable display of years upon years of assiduous collecting – probably pre-eBay too ...

Anyway, I'd begun the evening drinking Bloody Marys and Vodka-n-Cokes at home, switched to various kinds of beer once at The Hi-Dive, then guzzled some more beer furnished by Claudine's friend Owen, so by the time I was sitting in the Hipster House, I was pretty well soused out of my head. Unfortunately, by then I'd reached a state in which if I closed my eyes, my head spun about jarringly (at least it felt that way, anyway), and I suddenly felt the need to stand outside in the bracing cold – which I did. I haven't felt that uncontrollably, nauseatingly, fucked-up in quite some time – which is unsettling, because it wasn't the kind of fun, "goofy" fucked-up I usually so enjoy, but rather the somber, *Don't-touch-me-I'm-going-to-vomit* fucked up that I dread and usually manage to evade. Anyway, today, I woke up, sipped some coffee, and spent some quality time sitting next to the garbage can, just in case. ...

February 10, 2004, 2:25 p.m.

According to a recent opinion piece that I read online, my housemates and I are "first wave gentrifiers" because we ignore building codes, and could be characterized as "artists, students, or gays." However, it could also be said that I personally am a "second wave gentrifier" since I'm among the "individuals who affect the bohemian lifestyle while holding secure jobs." It's true. I confess. I affect the bohemian lifestyle while holding a secure job; by day I work a "straight" job in a downtown office – by night I throw paint at canvases in candlelight, while drinking wine, smoking imported cigarettes, and listening to Yo La Tengo at full volume. I'm so, so, *so* sorry.

Josh and Amy's dog, T-man, at Monkey Mania's door.

February 19, 2004, 9:21 p.m.

Last night I went to the Climax Lounge with Claudine and Andrew for their "free pinball" night. How do you take a shitty bar in a crappy neighborhood and make people actually show up on a Wednesday night? – free pinball. Brilliant.

While I was standing there playing the pinball interpretation of the '90s rendition of the film *Dracula*, I noticed some very "special" human behavior from the very "special" human standing next to me; a twenty-something guy wearing a Plaid Retina t-shirt and a trucker hat, and sporting massive mutton chops and too many arm tattoos. This guy was so into pinball – he cared so, *so* much, that whenever he bungled a ball, he had to curse at the machine, take off his hat, slap it against the side of the machine, take a step back, stomp his foot, and then curse some more. It was pretty *special* behavior, considering that the pinball was *free*, and no matter how many times he botched a play, all he had to do was hit the "start" button, and—*lo*—another ball would appear. Idiot. But maybe that's just me applying my own unrealistic standards of "reasonable" behavior on someone who is obviously an aficionado of a game I could never possibly master.

March 22, 2004, 8:41 p.m.

As it turns out, Ralph Gean's last Denver show wasn't last January's performance at Monkey Mania – he played Greg Ego's birthday party this last Saturday night. As usual, Ralph put on quite a show for a sixty-two-year-old man – he played three solo sets, and walked away with about $100 worth of tips, plus a $35.00 comp tab. The best part of the Ralph Gean show was when (while on my way to the services) Tom Lundin said to me, "Watch out for the midget in the bathroom..." Assuming he was just kidding, I was somewhat surprised to find a drunk Latino midget in the bathroom, who proceeded to heckle me in Spanglish, while I pissed.

The "funny" thing about that evening, however, was that, while drunk, I told Ralph Gean that if he needed a place to stay, he could always crash at Monkey Mania. He'd been lamenting his impending ejection from his friend Donna's house, and naturally, I told him that if he had nowhere else to go, he could stay with me. Being drunk and distracted with other things, I promptly forgot all about this ... until Ralph showed up at my doorstep last night, with all his stuff, ready to stay at my abode for a week or so. I guess it never occurred to him to call ahead or anything. ...

Now, as much as the prospect of Ralph's presence might thrill my housemates (with whom I never consulted regarding this matter, since I'd forgotten about it), I told Ralph that he could stay with us for a few days, but that he might want to look into other arrangements, if at all possible. Hopefully, this won't be a problem, and hopefully, he'll be able to get hooked-up with a free room within the next couple of days or so. ...

March 23, 2004, 8:44 p.m.

Got to "jam" (forgive the term) with Ralph Gean last night – him on guitar, myself on bass. We played his songs "Electricity," "Goddess of Love," "You're Drivin' Me Crazy," and a few others, as well as various Elvis covers. This was good fun. Ralph, even at age sixty-two, is easily one of the most energetic people I've ever "jammed" with. He was jumping around and singing at the top of his lungs, to an audience consisting of ... me.

Ralph hanging out in my basement bedroom.

Following this, we spent hours *(hours)* going through his files of personal memorabilia. The man is an obsessive archivist – on par with the serial killer villain from the film *SE7EN*. Though he's "between residences," he carries with him a thick stack of four file folders—the equivalent of a college student's book bag—and this is in addition to his clothing, personal effects, and guitar. These file folders constitute what Ralph refers to as "the small file" (not to be conflated with the *large* file, in storage out in Broomfield) and contain *everything* relating to his bizarre life: photocopies of high school photos, letters, receipts, checks, notes, flyers, *et cetera*. In many cases, not only does he have a copy of the original document in question, but also carries with him a series of several enlargements of that document, tailored to suit his deteriorating eyesight.

Now, a lot of this stuff is really neat and genuinely interesting—like Ralph's high school music club photos, in which he's standing with Janis Joplin (a teen buddy of his, apparently)—but a lot of it is extraneous to his career to the point that it's tedious; like his photocopies of checks he cashed in 1983, or his assorted tidbits of Elvis or *Xena*-related fan material. Ralph, naturally, makes no distinction whatsoever between the curious and the mundane. The comical and the mind-bogglingly dreary. The enthralling and the unedifying. And I kid you not when I say that he has absolutely, positively *everything* pertaining to his life and career. If he was mentioned briefly in a 1987 article about Rockabilly music, he has it. If he played a show in 1991, and the show was advertised in the newspaper, he has the advertisement (and the next week's, and the next week's, and the next week's). If he was billed on a big show in 1979, and his name appeared on the marquee, he has several photos of it. If his CD is mentioned in a list of titles distributed by a music distribution company, he has a copy of that list. In fact, it seems the only thing he doesn't have (and this vexes him horribly), is a copy of a *Xena: Warrior Princess* fan newsletter in which he is supposedly mentioned somewhere (his song "Goddess Of Love" was inspired by Xena, and the folks at the fanzine probably heard about it). If you have a copy of this document, for God's sake, I implore you, make a photocopied enlargement for Ralph.

Anyway, the point is; to the indomitably loquacious Ralph Gean, all these things are perennially absorbing, and worth lugging around all the time; from Denver to Texas, and back. And so, I spent hours last night listening to Ralph wax lyrical, recounting stories relating to all the various documents in his files that detail his curious life and career, and every twenty pages or so, I scanned-in a kooky fake photo of him riding a giant bunny rabbit; or wearing a shiny, pink, silk shirt, posing like Adonis somewhere in suburban Texas, in the 1960's. One might presume that Ralph is (or should be) entering his dotage and struggling with senescence, given his age – far from it. He is absolutely *compos mentis*, and remembers every granular detail with surprising fidelity – dates, names, locations, and the surrounding minutiae; to the extent that he verges on being a savant. It was a long night.

Oh, and I almost forgot; the folder-viewing was preceded by me waiting outside my house for ten minutes, banging on the door and yelling. See, I'd given Ralph my housekey, so that he'd be able to come and go without leaving the door unlocked … and when I got home, nobody was there to let me in. I dialed the house telephone, but it just rang and rang and rang … normally the machine picks up, but it was just ringing and ringing and ringing. … I looked through the holes in our blinds, and I thought I could see someone sitting there, talking on the phone. … Of course, it was Ralph, oblivious to my knocking on the door and ignoring the call-waiting. So I kept banging on the door, my housemates' dogs were freaking out, and he was still ignoring me. This went on for several minutes, until finally, I got down on my hands and knees, stuck my face in the mail slot, and shouted, "Ralph! Let me in!" … "Oops – Sorry there, Brian, I didn't realize that was you."

Anyway, last night we made it through three folders of his magnum-opus-photocopy-autobiography – which means tonight I have one left. I see the light at the end of the tunnel. Notable fact about Ralph Gean: he claims that he's related to Richard Wagner.

March 25, 2004, 8:48 p.m.

There was a show at Monkey Mania last night. Good stuff too. Josh and Amy opened the show as Fistie, their current project, which consists of Josh on drums/bass-effects, and Amy on vocals, violin-effects, bass, and more effects. For a two-piece, they put on quite a varied and voluminous show – though I only caught their first song (I was at the door for most of their set), everyone seemed to really dig them. I later overheard various folks fawningly oohing and awing over Amy's bass-playing, which I also, unfortunately, missed. Fistie was followed by local pretty-boy darlings, Zombie Zombie, who were, in my opinion, particularly good last night. I'm a sucker for organ, and I've always liked Zombie Zombie's music, but I was quite pleased with the fact that their singer has apparently ceased his Coalesce-style screech-screaming, and has actually started *singing* – a major improvement. The sky's the limit, boys.

Zombie Zombie, live at Monkey Mania.

Following Zombie Zombie, the touring band, Old Time Relijon, played. I didn't watch them. Everyone had been ranting and raving about how amazing they are, and how they sound like Captain Beefheart or something, but at that point in the night I just really didn't care. I just didn't feel like watching them. So instead, I went to Bar Bar with Shannon Dickey and got drunk.

As soon as we sat down at the bar, the bartender said to us, "Whoa, you guys look dressed to kill – just come from a club or something?" Hardly. Most of the folks at the place we'd just come from were dressed like aspirant "street people" – lots of skin-tight, faded tee-shirts, unkempt beards, and even a few dreads, *brah*. You know, the sort of Indie-Rock chic that screams, *I'm not a middle-class white kid from the suburbs! No, really, I'm not, I swear!* Anyway, all of these people (including myself) had been completely upstaged by Shannon, who was wearing a suit-jacket, a rhinestone-covered skinny tie, and a pair of slim, early-90's porno-star sunglasses, all of which was topped off by his jelled-up "flat-top" hair. He looked like a debonair Texas oil man; a cross between J.R. Ewing and a late '80s WWF wrestler, or as the bartender put it, simply "Dressed to kill."

March 26, 2004, 11:24 p.m.

Ralph lost my house key. Perfect. Just *perfect*.

March 27, 2004, 4:07 a.m.

Okay, so Claudine made two copies of her house key; one for me and one for Ralph. Ralph lost his (second) key within a day, I shit you not. Tonight he plays at The Zephyr Lounge. I plan to attend.

March 30, 2004, 9:08 p.m.

Further reports of my basement bedroom being haunted. Yesterday, I was at work all day, yet my housemates claim to have distinctly heard footsteps coming up and down the basement stairs all morning, yet they were alone in the house. I dunno what to make of it. Ex-occupants of my room are said to have slept with the lights on, because of the "dark presence" in the corner; couples who've slept down there to escape the summer heat have reported seeing apparitions; touring bands who've stayed down there have mentioned "bad vibes" and "evil presences"; housemates have reported seeing or hearing "ghosts" in both the basement and the showspace ... I ain't seen or heard shit. Maybe I watched too much *Scooby-Doo* as a kid, but until I do actually see, hear, or feel something in the basement, I'll remain skeptically amused and dismissively

cavalier with respect to the idea that it's "haunted."

April 3, 2004, 11:44 p.m.

I've been enjoying some much-needed "alone time" as of late. Since Monday, Josh and Amy have been on tour as Fistie, and Claudine is out in New Joisey dealing with family stuff, so for the last few days, I've been strutting around bare-ass naked, and drinking milk out of the carton. Ben doesn't seem to mind too much, when I see him. (Kidding.)

Tonight I saw Little Fyodor & Babushka perform at The Mercury Café, and finally got to witness "The Dance Of The Salted Slug," an interpretive dance which is to Little Fyodor as "The Moonwalk" was to Michael Jackson, back when he was human. Pretty goddamn special indeed. ...

Dance of the Salted Slug.

April 12, 2004, 3:03 p.m.

Easter Sunday. Headed out to The Gothic Theater to see Mr. Pacman, Little Fyodor, and Robot Mandala. I only caught the last half of Robot Mandala's last song, so I can't really comment on their performance. I can, however, say that Little Fyodor was in great form. The particularly great thing about Little Fyodor's show was that he was playing in front of a colossal projection screen, which was filled with the live close-up image of his head and upper torso, psychedelicized with various cheesy effects.

Then there was Mr. Pacman – they were pretty special indeed. Mr. Pacman is perhaps best described as a fusion of early '80s New Wave, late-'80s Stadium Rock, and Miami Booty Bass. They consisted of three guys in form-fitting bodysuits (ski suits), with matching moon-boots and motorcycle helmets; each member being a different primary color. The fourth member was wearing what appeared to be a giant cockroach costume, very much along the lines of what one might see in an old Godzilla film. Add to this a drum set, a Casio keyboard, a guitar, a keytar, and a hearty helping of MIDI, and pump it all through a hellacious P.A. system, and you have Mr. Pacman. Oh yeah, and they had hoes – as in choreographed dancing / backup singing booty hoes (always a plus). To top all this off, the end of their set, the singer / keytar player took off everything but his helmet and a codpiece, which was amusing.

Of particular interest was that I got to observe Mr. Pacman member Jim Compton playing his own personal invented instrument; a computer-keyboard hooked-up to a Commodore 64 and programmed in such a way that the top two rows of keyboard keys correspond to piano keys. It's amusing to watch him play it, as he's basically typing, but since it's monophonic, and can only produce one bassy square-wave at any given time, he pecks at it with one finger at a time, but fast enough to play a bassline. Jim is amazing. I've heard so many great stories about this guy; like that he once lived in his office, *à la* the film *Bartleby*, but for real ... or how he used to go around hitting on girls at bars who were with guys – to see how obnoxious he could be before the guys attacked him ... or the phony bald-guy haircut he had for a while ... *et cetera*. Definitely a "good egg."

So that was the oft-lauded Mr. Pacman – a thoroughly entertaining spectacle, whether or not one cares for their music.

April 22, 2004, 9:17 p.m.

There was a show at my house last night, most of which I missed. I missed The Corndawg and some other opening band, but caught most of Zombie Zombie, who were in good form, as usual. They were followed by The USA Is A Monster ... now, as much as I absolutely abhor their band name,

and I find it particularly silly to play a show for teenagers at a warehouse, and close it by saying, "Vote Democrat!" (all zero of the Republicans in the audience were totally offended, I'm sure), I must, however, concede that The USA Is A Monster are a pretty fucking amazing band. I mean, they're really, really good at what they do. They were followed by a dreadlocked white guy from the Czech Republic who was calling himself Koonda Holla, and who was basically doing what Tyondai Braxton does, though not as well, and with a comical Czech accent. I watched his first song, and then had to politely skedaddle after he kept annoyingly mispronouncing English words like "mother" and "father," while maintaining his ever-so-solemn "artist face" and playing a bongo drum through effects processors (*sweeeeet*, dude).

At some point, everyone was suddenly stoned, and it was sort of amusing to witness. Corndawg, for instance (a solo musician from Virginia), is a funny motherfuckin' guy. After talking to him for all of two minutes, I regretted having missed his set, as he's one of those people who just exudes effortless comedic charisma – hopefully I'll see him next time. The guy from The USA Is A Monster is also quite an amusing fellow, whose company I found very agreeable. Then I had the misfortune of being introduced to Koonda Holla, the Czech guy ... what a prick.

So, Josh put Yoko Oh-No! on the flyer for an upcoming show, so that means I have to figure out something to play.

May 1, 2004, 8:41 p.m.

Played a show at Monkey Mania last night, as part of the sort-of-impromptu postmodern performance troupe, Yoko Oh-No!. For this performance, Josh laid down a cymbal-heavy beat, I played some Boredeoms-esqe riffage on the distorted bass, and Claudine hurled Ginsu knives at the back wall, while screaming into a microphone – we all wore those black, mesh masks that conceal one's face without totally obstructing one's vision (sort of). Our original plan for this Yoko Oh-No! performance, was to set up all of Josh's twenty or so keyboards in a circle on stage, tape down a single note on each one, and then go from there – but when it came time to set them up, it was revealed that the majority of them were busted, so we scrapped the idea.

So anyway, we got up on stage and did this phony performance art gag that didn't really work. Though we were wearing masks, everyone in the crowd obviously knew it was us, and the general impression I got was that they either presumed that we were being serious, and trying to be a "real" band, or that they realized that it was an ill-conceived, unplanned farce, which wasn't actually the slightest bit funny or clever. Anyhow, I was on my knees, headbanging to some Sludge Rock, which I kept ruining by attempting to insert noodly bass solos (which I fumbled every time, because I couldn't see my hands through the goddamned mask). All in all, an entirely forgettable incident, though maybe some of the photos will come out okay. After us, Will Sartan of Red Tape played, and I missed him because I was at the bar. Then Zombie Zombie played, and the kids danced like lunatics.

Important lesson learned from the evening; any female who identifies herself as a "bitch" whether literally, sarcastically, satirically, or in jest, is, indeed, a bitch.

May 3, 2004, 11:38 p.m.

Ralph Gean showed up at my house last night. He'll be staying with us for the next few days. He treated me to a private performance in my kitchen, in which he played numerous covers, including "A Teenager in Love," "Rock n' Roll Music," and (upon my request) "Ring of Fire." He also informed me that he wants to make music videos for all of the songs on his forthcoming album. This, of course, would be a high-concept project; most of the videos would consist of Ralph-scripted skits in which he himself played no part. After some discussion, I got him to entertain the idea that it would be better to make *one* really good video for one good song, than thirty crappy videos for thirty good songs. He agreed,

considering "Cowboy Convention" as a possibility, when I suggested that he could cast all his friends as the different cowboys.

June 9, 2004, 12:31 a.m.

Touring band, The Yellow Swans, from Portland, Oregon, sleep in the Monkey Mania basement, outside my room. They report seeing ghosts; two girls. As always, I see nothing.

June 11, 2004, 7:43 p.m.

Those who know him should be pleased to learn that Mr. Ralph Gean has finally ended his six-plus-month couch-surfing tour of the homes of friends, family, and hotels, and now resides permanently in an assisted-living community for senior citizens, retirees, and the disabled, located in Broomfield, Colorado. At his age, and with dwindling vision, this is long, long overdue indeed.

June 13, 2004, 2:22 p.m.

The band Glass Candy, from Portland, Oregon, played at my house on Saturday night. Apparently, they're something of a "big deal," what with their female singer being listed among *Playboy* magazine's list of the hottest Indie Rock girls (or something like that). They had originally been booked to play at the (proper) venue, Rollerama, which has since been closed, so for some bizarre reason, the booker moved the show to our house. So, unlike the standard Monkey Mania flyer fare, this show was promoted to the point of obnoxiousness; unlike the usual hand-drawn and xeroxed flyers, the promotional flyer (which ended up all over town) looked somewhat like a rave flyer.

Apparently, Glass Candy had been promised quite a hefty "guarantee" by the promoter, whom I met briefly, before he rushed off to pick them up from their hotel while the opening band was finishing its set. All told, I'm sure they were just *thrilled* to find themselves performing at our house.

There were some opening bands, but I missed them. That is, except for the unfortunate spectacle which is Houston Bernard. Houston's shtick is that he's a bisexual white guy from New York City, who, like Peaches, is as nasty as he wanna' be. He ended his one-man karaoke performance in nothing but his Speedo. Meh. Anyway, I spent most of the evening drinking. Sooner or later, a bunch of people ended up boozin' it up in my room (Monkey Mania's V.I.P. lounge, from now on), and drunk-ass silliness ensued. Eventually, Adam "Partridge" and Terry Campbell were wrestling on my floor, shirtless, in front of an audience of scooter girls (one of whom, incidentally, was ostensibly once engaged to one of the guys in Celtic Frost, who apparently now lives in a castle – no foolin'). This was all documented on video and film, for the embarrassment of posterity.

Drunks.

After everyone got sick of fucking around in my room, I wandered upstairs, plastered out of my gourd, and strode onto the dance floor, while Glass Candy was playing, whereupon I variously assaulted Andrew, Amy, Germaine, and some others on the ersatz dance floor, and then proceeded to dance around smoking a cigarillo like a total asshole.

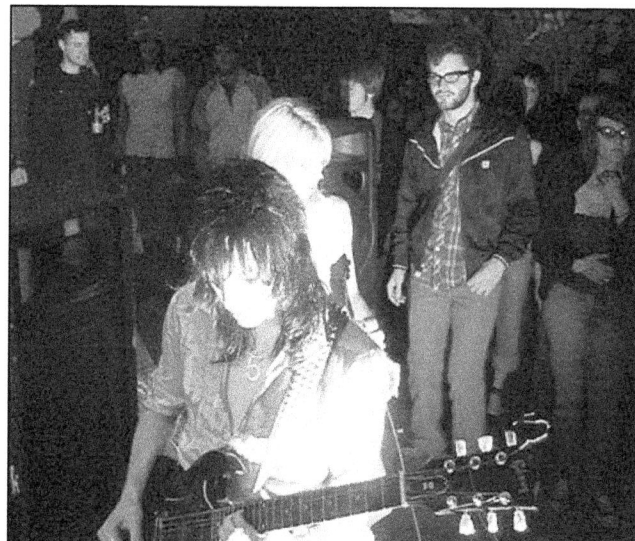
Glass Candy, live at Monkey Mania.

Glass Candy, from what I recall, are a sort of two-person psychedelic glam-rock band, consisting of a statuesque barefoot blonde chick in a dress, and a long-haired guy who looks like a chick, playing space-rock riffs over a drum machine, the beats of which were slightly more sophisticated than those of Suicide, but still simpler than those of Big Black. Not really my thing.

June 21, 2004, 11:51 p.m.

Had a beer last night with Robie, of the band Weather. She used to be in a band called Milemarker, which I've never heard, but have always viscerally harbored a mild disdain for – for no reason other than their arty, sweaty album cover, on which she's prominently featured:

Ugh. Awful.

But, contrary to my assumptions, Robie was actually a very nice, unpretentious girl, and her new band Weather (who later played at our house) was pretty impressive, even though they aren't my particular cup of tea.

Weather, live at Monkey Mania.

I'm sure she totally cares what I think, just like everybody else. *Right*.

June 29, 2004, 10:39 p.m.

Last night a bunch of local darling bands played at my house. The two that I witnessed were:

The Hot Rock: facetious faux-gay disco side-project of Mr. Pacman frontman, Avery; spandex bodysuits, underpants, jumping around singing to pre-recorded disco.

The Hot Rock, live at Monkey Mania.

Magic Cyclops: the alter ego a mild-mannered local gadabout, who upon donning an '80s jogging-suit, a wig, some cop glasses and a headband, is transformed into a mouthy British cheeseball entertainer.

Magic Cyclops, live at Monkey Mania.

It was an evening of inside jokes, and everyone laughing heartily at them.

July 8, 2004, 10:47 p.m.

Well, it looks as though my simian stay here at Monkey Mania is about to come to an end; I recently quit my dismal office job as an Administrative Assistant working in the "document service center" of a law firm up in a downtown skyscraper, and a secured new job as a live-in Apartment Complex Manager in the Governor's Park area of Denver. This means I'll be moving into a one-bedroom apartment (with a proper kitchen and bathroom), in a somewhat more residential neighborhood; in exchange for my rent and utilities I'll have to collect the rent each month, rent-out any of the other fifteen apartments that become vacant, and do assorted odd jobs when necessary (change light-bulbs, vacuum hallways, mow the lawn, trim hedges, *et cetera*). This, I imagine, will be a very suitable arrangement for me; I get "free" rent and utilities, in exchange for about ten to fifteen hours a week of work – thus, presumably, I'll have much more time to work on other things. Of course, I'll have to get a part-time job somewhere in the proximity of my pad, so that I'll have spending cash for food, transportation, the cellphone bill, and booze n' whatnot, but I'm hoping that won't be too difficult. (We shall see. ...)

So, I'm leaving Monkey Mania. It's been a good run; September of '03 to July of '04. Living here, I've witnessed numerous great shows, been introduced to numerous fun people, and generally benefited from being immersed in what might constitute a local "scene" of sorts. It's been a lot of fun, and I will definitely miss certain parts of it ... but it will be good to move on. The fun of living in a "Punk" warehouse has lost its luster, if it ever had any. I won't miss my housemates' dogs or their hair. I won't miss Amy's caged bird and its incessant screeching. I won't miss waiting to use the one bathroom while it's being occupied by one of the other four residents, or members of various touring bands. I won't miss having to cook all my meals using either a single functioning hotplate-burner, a toaster oven, or a microwave. I won't

miss trekking about a mile to do my laundry or go to the grocery store. I won't miss coming home to shows I don't want to see. I won't miss the drunken bums wandering around outside. ...

Anyway, while I have enjoyed the last ten months of living here, I am also looking forward to having my own space, in a new neighborhood, with on-site laundry facilities and nearby shopping – and knowing that it's paid for by my simply being there most of the time and keeping the place up.

So, I suppose my life at this junction is going to take on a markedly more solitary turn. Now that I'll be living alone, across town, in a proper apartment, I think I'm going to take on a somewhat more antisocial, private approach to living in Denver. I'm thinking I'll make the place sort of *nice*, and like to envision myself spending afternoons lounging about in a smoking jacket, idly puffing on a pipe, sipping cocktails, and listening to Lounge Music, while entertaining lady-callers – an idealized glamorization, of course, but worth shooting for, nonetheless. But I am thinking of making this new apartment my *sanctum sanctorum* – disallowing all but the rarest of individuals from coming inside. We'll see. ...

Postscript

2025

Monkey Mania carried on with its raucous ruckus after I moved out in the summer of 2004, continuing to hold shows and other wacky happenings for another year and a half or so. Following my departure, I occasionally showed up to attend events there and was usually let in for free, which was nice. Josh and Amy then decided to leave Denver in 2005, and moved to Los Angeles, California – where Josh would later join the band Foot Village, Amy would play in the band Ground Unicorn Horn, and where the two of them were somehow involved with the downtown L.A. venue The Smell.

Monkey Mania's final show was held on December 3, 2005. The venue was then handed over to a group of new young tenants: Denver "Punk" kids who rechristened it as Kingdom of

Smash Club, performing at Monkey Mania.

The Microphones, live at Monkey Mania.

Doom ... and from what I understand, summarily trashed it. The space probably stopped being a venue sometime in 2006, and I believe was condemned entirely at some point thereafter, standing vacant for some years. The brick building that housed Monkey Mania was finally demolished in 2019, and in its footprint a nondescript multi-unit, multi-purpose imposing corporate skyscraper was erected – one of many that have since sprung up in downtown Denver.

During the time that I was a resident at Monkey Mania, unauthorized all-ages "underground" showspaces like it were not uncommon in most decent-sized American cities, and had been since probably the early-to-mid 1980s. They were places where teenagers and under-21 adults could go see local and touring "Indie" bands, for a modest entry fee – and maybe engage in some underage intoxication outside the adult "bar scene." There was even a pre-Internet 'zine-esque periodical directory to such venues, *Book Your Own Fucking Life*, which assisted in the planning of frugal low-budget touring across the United States and internationally, by broke young musicians willing to perform at warehouses and sleep on couches.

That all changed somewhat drastically at the end of 2016, however, when an "artists' collective" and all-ages underground venue in Oakland, California—called the Ghost Ship—went up in flames during a show at which some 80 to 100 people were in attendance. The inferno took the lives of 36 attendees and left many of the survivors with lifelong injuries. The Ghost Ship warehouse fire was, apparently, the deadliest building fire in California since the 1906 San

Francisco earthquake, making national and international news, and leading to felony involuntary manslaughter charges for a couple of the venue's organizers, as well as an eventual multimillion dollar settlement from the city of Oakland to survivors and families of the victims. Following the cautionary tale of the infamous Ghost Ship fire, cities and municipalities across the United States pretty much stopped looking the other way when it came to under-the-radar showspaces like Monkey Mania, and began clamping down on the enforcement of zoning codes, housing laws, noise ordinances, cabaret and alcohol licenses, and any and all other legal means of rendering the operation of such live-in showspaces impractical and unfeasible, if not downright impossible.

It's hard to argue with the notion of enforcing safety laws—let alone contend with 36 corpses and millions of

Sonic Youth, live at Monkey Mania.

dollars in legal settlements—but the loss of underground showspaces like Monkey Mania nonetheless comes at a cost. Independent music and the chaotic culture surrounding it were fun and invigorating – an experience. Music that's recorded, produced, mixed, mastered, and distributed globally online, all from a laptop in an apartment ... *meh*, not so much.

Planes Mistaken for Stars, live at Monkey Mania.

Contagious Alcoholism Infection!

2008

I find it deplorable when former alcoholics refer to their intemperate drinking as a "disease," as if they are the victims of some nefarious external agent beyond their control. It's such piffling nonsense. AIDS is a disease – the mechanism of contagion is bodily fluids, whereby the virus that causes HIV enters the victim's body and wreaks havoc upon his or her immune system. Similarly, the maladies that we call Cholera, Malaria, Smallpox, Diphtheria, Guinea Worm Disease, and Whooping Cough are all varieties infectious diseases; in each case, the mechanism of contagion is that a pathogen—an infectious agent—like a virus, bacterium, or parasite that enters sufferers' bodies and then *fucks them the fuck up* from the inside. They're debilitating, agonizing, and also often fatal afflictions. Scourges of humanity from time immemorial, responsible for suffering on a scale that dwarfs that of armed conflict.

There are also diseases that aren't so easily transmissible and don't require anything from the outside coming into the body to cause harm. Parkinson's is a neurodegenerative disease that slowly erodes the sufferer's central nervous system until they tremble and shake to such an extent that they can't function anymore – its causes are unknown, but in some cases the origin appears to be genetic. Cystic Fibrosis is another horrific genetic disease that causes the inflicted to eventually drown on mucous inside their own fucking lungs. Awful. Tae-Sachs and Sickle Cell Anemia are other examples of inherited diseases that leave their sufferers living lives riven by constant, crippling physical pain. There are many other terrible examples like these. But "alcoholism" isn't on the fuckin' list.

Drinking too much and fucking up your life is not a goddamned "disease" – it is a dearth of willpower and an inability to control yourself. Alcoholism may have a tangible somatic basis in the body absorbing a foreign intoxicant—sure—but alcoholism is psychosomatic in that it's a *behavior pattern* caused by a response to a feeling produced as a result of the body taking in the intoxicant. With rare exceptions like Tourette's Syndrome and compulsive disorders, behavior patterns are, largely, alterable for most people, a lot of the time. Alcoholics can, if they truly desire to do so, *choose* to stop drinking ... whereas sufferers of diseases proper—AIDS, cancer, malaria, and other horrid maladies—cannot simply *choose* to change their behavior in such a way that they can escape the disease or its effects on them. Often, they're just plain fucked. Alcoholics, on the other hand, have options. They can stop drinking, difficult though it may be to do so.

So, the malingering, self-pitying pining for sympathy bullshit that "alcoholics" drone on about—how they suffer from a "disease"—should be met with eye-rolling and derision. There may be valid, or at least understandable, reasons for drinking too much too often (depression, post-traumatic stress disorder, *et cetera*), and sympathy ought to be extended to those who've screwed up their lives as a result of such – but calling that phenomenon a "disease" with a straight face is an oblique insult to people who suffer from *actual diseases*. Rather than garnering sympathy for being victims of the "disease" of alcoholism, alcoholics who blame the booze instead of taking responsibility for themselves deserve to be summarily dismissed as the unserious people they are.

Oh, you're an alcoholic plagued by the "disease" of "alcoholism"? Try telling that to a kid dying of Leukemia, you fuckin' prick.

The March of Man's True Destiny

An Interview with Douglas P.

2006

Douglas Pearce (known professionally as "Douglas P.") is a British-Australian musician, singer, and songwriter, best known as the vocalist and guitarist of the seminal Neofolk band Death In June. Since the early 1980s, Death In June has drawn considerable controversy and intermittent pillorying for dealing with the subjects, iconography, and imagery relating to Europe's war-torn history, and often specifically to Nazi Germany – making the group something of a pariah within underground counterculture and the music industry generally. Despite this, Pearce has not bowed to criticism and rarely explained himself publicly, even when his concerts have been protested and cancelled due to pressure from far-left activist groups. What many are unaware of, however, is that prior to forming Death In June, during his late teenage years, Pearce founded one of England's most ardently left-leaning Punk Rock bands of the late 1970s – Crisis. Pearce was interviewed via email for *Occidental Congress*, following the release of the retrospective Crisis compilation album, *Holocaust Hymns*.

Brian M. Clark: In the late 1970s, Crisis marked your first appearance on the music scene as one of the band's two main songwriters. In the years since, your music has evolved drastically; your current project of the last two and a half decades, Death In June, is markedly dissimilar to your work with Crisis, musically, visually, and politically. That said, why a retrospective "complete discography" Crisis CD now?

Douglas P.: First of all, I don't believe that in retrospect Crisis and Death In June were that dissimilar on any of those levels. Certainly not musically towards the end of Crisis in 1980 and, the yet to be, birth in 1981 of Death In June. Visually we also had from the very

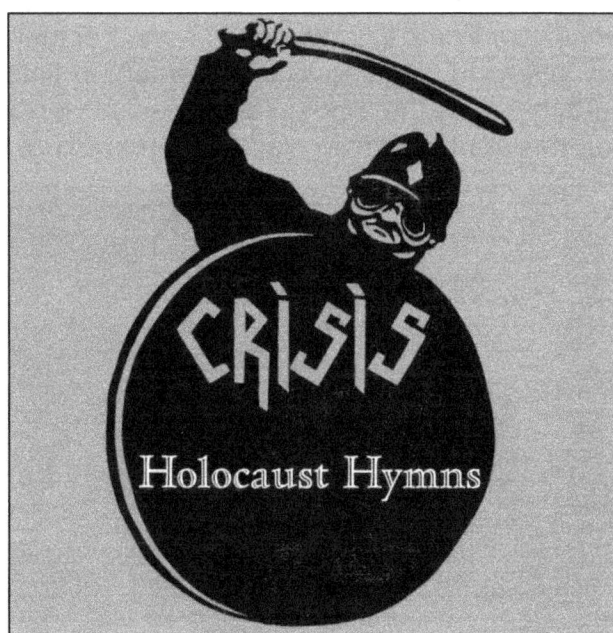

Crisis' Holocaust Hymns, Apop Records, 2005.

253

beginning a look that could have easily blended into latter day DIJ with camouflage and black clothing being '*de rigeur.*' We saw ourselves as 'Music to March To' and so did the British mainstream press and our followers – whatever side of the political spectrum they came from. And, despite being 'obviously' Left wing we had many far-Right followers which gave birth to a whole gamut of interesting liaisons and conversations and mutual agreements, and perhaps even respect. Nothing was ever straightforward, no matter how much we might have even liked it to be. If you were a punk or a skinhead—regardless of your colour, political stance or sexual orientation—in the UK in the late 1970s that was enough to blur all and every prejudice and boundary.

Whether I like it or not, Crisis forms a very important part of my personal and musical contribution to history and after six years since the last readily available compilation I thought it was now time to issue another, better thought-out, retrospective. *Holocaust Hymns* effectively replaces the *We Are All Jews And Germans* compilation that was put out by the now defunct World Serpent Distribution. And, it's a lot better than that one, after being remastered and with more accurate track information, exclusive photos, *et cetera*. For the first time in years, I actually am enjoying listening to this moment in time. And, going by the amount of requests I've had for this material over recent years, so will

Early Crisis photo.

many other good folk. Basically, there was a demand and hopefully I've met it.

BMC: Crisis seems to have appeared fairly early on in the whole Punk "movement" of the late 1970s; what initially drew you to Punk Rock, and what inspired you to form your own band?

DP: Very simply everything on all levels was horrible in England in the mid-late 1970s. When I see newsreel footage of the UK during that period I can't believe quite how dour it all looked—and was—especially if you were from white working class backgrounds like Tony Wakeford and myself! Something had to happen and it did culturally, and had a continuing significant effect on youth culture and society as a whole. I had hair down to my waist until late 1975 when I realised that wasn't for me—that was another time—cut all my hair off and wandered around being pissed off, looking like a runaway from Francois Truffaut's *400 Blows*. Then one day on the Tube in London I noticed someone else looking like this and then I saw a poster for a Sex Pistols gig showing two cowboys greeting each other but whose cocks were also exposed and touching, and then I heard about The Clash, and then I saw in late 1976 The Sex Pistols on an English TV show called *So It Goes*, hosted by Tony Wilson (later of Factory Records fame), and then Tony Wakeford telephoned me and asked if I had heard of Punk Rock and if I wanted to form a group. I said "yes" to both those questions and the rest is hysterical. It was a series of events that led me to Punk early on, but in comparison to the trailblazers, we took our time. Crisis came in the wake of those events and people.

BMC: Many reviewers have compared Crisis to the far-left UK band Crass, due to the two bands' heavy use of politics as lyrical and visual subject matter within the context of Punk Rock. One reviewer wrote,

[Crass and Crisis] both signaled the end of punk as fun, spontaneity, massiveness and anarchy (as a way of feeling). In this new "new wave" of punk, punk was seen as a tool of protest ... Crass, Crisis and the bands they bred became the new puritans. [The Crisis track] PC1984 might as well have stood for politically correct 1984 as they told us the truth about the world and what our part should be in it according to their rules. The truth was black and white ... the enemy obvious ... the police were the fascistic army to dominate the workers.

Do you think this is a fair criticism, and does it reflect your actual aims for the band at the time, or more of how the band was perceived by the press and fans? Do you look back on your time with Crisis as being "fun," or was it something else, as the above quote alleges?

DP: Crisis and my experience of Punk Rock in Britain/Europe was anything and everything but 'fun,' and this sort of idea comes from people who were either not there at the time, or were and have an axe of some kind or another to grind about their own experiences with Crisis. The years between 1977 and 1980 were some of the hardest of my Life and they certainly contributed to Tony and I wanting to destroy the group in 1980 and head for sunnier pastures artistically, culturally, and whatever else we could find. However, we couldn't deny our cultural imperative at the time. We were in Crisis unashamedly left wing or, at least trying to be, and wanted to be taken seriously politically. Which we were! So seriously in fact that when celebrities found out we were part of the Anti-Nazi League or Rock Against Racism benefits they withdrew their support. Names like the author Keith Waterhouse, TV compare Michael Parkinson and Football coach Brian Clough immediately spring to mind. They publicly withdrew their

support because of Crisis! Crisis were referred to as "Red Fascists" almost from the outset, which seemed to confuse and upset some folk and also endear us to others. They were 'interesting times.'

Douglas P. performing live with Crisis.

And as regards any comparisons to Crass: They were not contemporaries of ours, I don't remember any comparisons at the time and I think we only became aware of them after the demise of Crisis and at the beginning of Death In June in the early 1980s. Certainly to us then they seemed like the guys at free festivals dishing out lentils and orange juice to those on a bad trip when they realised they had been left behind, there was no one left at the festival anymore and in order to catch up with 'the kids,' cropped their hair, wore black and decided to form what was I think akin to the Hari Krishnas; a caricature of a punk group, and do their bit for those who weren't there in the first place. I'm sure their hearts were in the right place, and I love lentils and orange juice, and they did indeed invent their own particular version of Punk but ... 'Do they owe us a living?' Of course they fucking DON'T!

Crisis' songwriters, Tony Wakeford and Douglas P.

BMC: Following the dissolution of Crisis, members of the band went on to form or join acts such as Theatre of Hate, Sol Invictus, Sex Gang Children, and of course your own Death In June. Are you still in touch with any of these other ex-Crisis members, and if so, what is your perception of their post-Crisis work?

DP: Even before the end Luke Rendall, the last drummer in Crisis, was basically headhunted by Kirk Brandon who was then in a group called The Pack. They went onto to form Theatre Of Hate which I quite liked and I saw a few of their early shows in the London area. I think my best memory was being backstage when Boy George was having a fit about some bloke giving Kirk the eye and how he was going to beat the shit out of him! This was before Culture Club and I have to say I think fame really became Boy George, who seemed more like a transvestite psychopath that night than a Karma Kamelion. It also evidently made him lose interest in Kirk! I heard a few years ago that Luke had been murdered.

Lester, the lead guitarist of Crisis, went on to form a group called Car Crash International with members of the Sex Gang Children, but I can't recall what they were like and am only aware of one 12" single that they put out. Our two roadies Martin and Flea went on to work with The Clash and Big Audio Dynamite; and Flea (who designed some of the original Crisis record sleeves) was even in several Big Audio Dynamite videos. I don't know how much input he had in their creation, but he was a very talented artist and all-round interesting guy. Sol Invictus, of course, came out of Death In June not Crisis. With the exception of Tony Wakeford, I'm not in contact with anyone from those Punk days.

BMC: In the years since Crisis, you seem to have moved from the realm of politics to that of aesthetics. Conceptually, Crisis seems to have been a very direct, literal and "instructive" project in nature, in the sense that the songs were clearly about (and commenting upon), something specific, and urging the listener to think and feel about things in certain ways. Because of this, Crisis could really only be interpreted one way— literally and at face value—while your subsequent work with Death In June seems to me as being almost the opposite of that sort of approach; it's rife with vague allusions, double meanings, and open-ended readings. In short, Crisis was a very matter-of-fact thing, while Death In June is a much more nebulous and poetic project. Assuming such an interpretation of your work is accurate, was this shift in approach a conscious decision on your part, or did it happen as a part of a gradual process?

Tony Wakeford, Douglas P., and Crisis fans.

DP: Even though we might have thought what we were writing/singing about was 'specific' and 'straightforward' it was soon interpreted as anything but. The song "White Youth" is a prime example. We performed several times on the back of a lorry on demonstrations throughout the South of England / London that were organized by The Right To Work campaign. Crisis would play for up to seven or eight hours, with a few breaks in between, entertaining the people who had been marching in protest to their unemployment which was then rife in the UK. It was our equivalent to The Beatles slogging their way through similar set lengths in some sleaze pit in Hamburg in the early 1960s. Whilst they had their happy memories of the Reeperbahn, I have happy memories of stopping traffic crossing Tower Bridge in London playing "UK

79" and "Holocaust." We wrote (with that marching rhythm in mind) the song "White Youth," which we thought was about 'unity and brotherhood,' but much to my surprise some smartarse in the *New Musical Express* was soon saying that it was a white supremacist anthem.[7] There's no pleasing some folk is there! That was key in realising that no matter what you wrote, if it was any good it could be interpreted anyway, anyhow, anywhere. A Death In June prime directive!

BMC: The obvious question, of course, is why Crisis was so concerned with anti-Nazism, and played so many shows for Rock Against Racism, and why Death In June has repeatedly dealt with the same themes, but from what would often appear to be the opposite angle. Many have noted the paradox that Crisis performed at anti-racist shows and wrote anti-fascist lyrics, while Death In June is often accused of being racist and fascist – it's a very polarized transition between the two projects, and I imagine that fans of one project may often be diametrically opposed to fans of the other. What are your thoughts on this, and more specifically, on the irony that the people who most disturb and disrupt your current shows are often members of some of the very same sorts of organizations that you used to belong to and perform for?

DP: Britain was a very strange place to be living in the mid-late 1970s. There was a definite radicalisation of political and cultural thought taking place. We, as young men, got very much caught up in that. Tony and I have probably spent the rest of our Lives trying to disentangle ourselves from that past. There are bound to be contradictions and naturally the irony isn't lost on me. So? Personally, I think the people involved in such organisations today are barking completely up the wrong tree. But, it's an easy tree to bark at and it fulfils their inner need to think they are doing something 'good.' When you look at The

---

[7] The song ends with the repeated verse, "We are black, we are white! Together we are dynamite!"

World as it stands in 2006, they are obviously pissing in the wind. Why should I stand in their way?

BMC: One undercurrent that I personally see in your work with both bands is the handling of the theme of the ugly side of human nature. In Crisis, this was presented literally and at face value; the listener was presented with some statement about a particular state of affairs, and essentially urged to feel outraged by it. With Death In June, the handling of human ugliness is much more alchemical. As I interpret Death In June, there's a degree of ugliness subtly interwoven with harmony and beauty; acoustic folk songs are calmly intoned about war atrocities and then presented in lavishly designed, embossed, glossy packages that bear symbols most often associated with death and destruction. Again, it's quite a departure from the confrontational directness of Crisis. As you've progressed from Crisis to Death In June, how has your view on human nature or "the human condition" changed, or remained the same? Is it only your approach to dealing with these subjects that's changed, or has your outlook changed as well?

DP: I don't feel my overall outlook has changed at all. I was right when I was young as I am right as I'm middle-aged. Depressingly so. In fact, now I realise I no longer have any optimism. That's gone and I'm speechless at how pessimistic I am. We got it right! It is how it should be. Sadly, being correct doesn't leave me feeling warm and fuzzy inside.

BMC: There's been much speculation over the years as to the origin of the name Death In June, most of it being attributed to political events that transpired in that month, during either the First or Second World Wars. As I understand it, the true origin of the name had something to do with you mishearing something one of the other original band members had said to you over the phone, thinking he'd said, "Death in June."

Considering the tendency of people to take innocuous things like this and choose to view them as being sinister, has this sort of misinterpretation been something that you've since incorporated into the imagery and content of Death In June—something you've consciously manipulated—or something you've simply ignored?

Douglas P. in the mid-1980s (Death In June).

DP: As I've already alluded to, there is no need to consciously 'manipulate' anything. People do that for you in the blink of an eye. Whatever you do, once you've attained a certain position in the public eye, people will either interpret or misinterpret in whatever way they see fit. There is nothing I can do about that. Even if I wanted to, it is far too late.

BMC: I've read some pretty harsh criticism of Death In June as being merely a scam through which you flirt with Nazi imagery and ideology, yet buttress this with what is actually an underlying leftist agenda; and that ultimately the project's flirtation with such taboo ideas is just a means of creating controversy so that you can sell more records. One critic alleged that your work with Death In June is about commodifying twentieth century fascism as "pornography," further saying, "Pearce is a businessman and it is a matter of indifference to him if his fans join far-Right groups such as White Aryan Resistance or Green Anarchist – all that interests him is making money." While I disagree with this oversimplification of your career, I'm nonetheless curious to know how you'd respond to such criticism as the idea that you're, "only in it for the money."

DP: They are absolutely right! I am definitely 'only in it for the money.' All the money that is still owed to us by different left-wing organizations like Rock Against Racism, who said the 'cheque would be in the post.' All the money that's owed to us by fuck-wit promoters who forgot to hire P.A. systems, which we then had to do ourselves at the drop of a hat and never be recompensed for. All the music distributors that have ripped off Crisis and Death In June over the years. Yep! I'm definitely only in it for the money! But, what are these people who write such things 'in it' for?

BMC: I'm of the opinion that the desire to censor is "fascistic" in nature, so it's particularly ironic to me that self-styled "Anti-Fascist" groups have made such a concerted effort to censor you and prevent you from performing, on that grounds that your work is "fascistic," – in my view their behavior is ultimately what's fascistic. What are your thoughts on the anti-fascist protests that turned violent at your scheduled show in Chicago in 2003? Likewise, what are your thoughts regarding the 1996 show in Switzerland that was cancelled by the Swiss authorities? Do such instances of organized antagonism frustrate and discourage you, or do they harden your resolve?

DP: I think you're wrong. I think censorship is essentially 'Communistic' and left wing. Censorship was one of the first things that happened in Russia after the Revolution in 1917 and continued until it fell to bits decades later. The way I understand it is that, to paraphrase Mussolini, the Fascists are the real anarchists for they truly did do exactly what they wanted. Libertarianism and Fascism are bedfellows no matter how some people might find that repugnant. They are definitely not mutually exclusive.

People like the Mayor of Lausanne and the street people with a cause outside the club in Chicago are an irrelevance to me. The Mayor didn't survive the next election in Switzerland and is no longer and the types of people protesting around that club that night in Chicago have now realised that they were duped by a far right Xtian group into acting against Death In June or have probably been found dead from an O.D. in a heroin shooting gallery. Both of those types were so ill-informed and ignorant that they neither discourage me nor make me harden any resolve. They are nothing more than a momentary inconvenience and can't stand in the way of the inevitable March of Man's True Destiny.

Douglas P. performing live as Death In June.

BMC: Although I'm perhaps not as familiar with your work as I could be, in the commentary that I have read on Death In June, I've found that many critics feel compelled to bring up the fact that you're a homosexual, and to interpret your work though the tinted lens of sexuality, yet I'm unaware of any references to your sexuality in the actual content of Death In June. I have, however, noticed that Crisis did have a track about homosexuality, "Alienation." Do references to your sexuality in reviews of your work as Death In June frustrate you, or do you feel that they're relevant? Does the same hold true for your work with Crisis?

DP: Being gay is fundamental to Death In June since it became my solo project in 1985 and even before in the songs I wrote/co-wrote. I don't think the homosexual side in my canon of work is explored enough in reviews. In fact, I've rarely ever seen it mentioned, which I find incredulous!

I remember doing some of my first interviews for Crisis in Gay bars on Sunset Strip or Hollywood Boulevard in December 1977, for *Search & Destroy* and *Slash* magazines, *et cetera*. Vale from *Search & Destroy* (now RE/Search) made this classic comment to me as I ranted and preached about how huge Billy Idol / Generation X was going to be and how Crisis was going to reinvent the music scene;

"Do you know this is a gay bar?"

Duuh ... thank you Vale for the warning!

Of course I did, and I introduced him to my 58-year-old partner who had also travelled with me to Los Angeles that Xmas pretty much on the invite of *Slash* magazine after they saw our first performance in England.

I appreciate the work and Lives of people like Jean Genet and Yukio Mishima not only because their work was brilliant but that they were also gay. It adds so much. Like it adds so much to me that The Beatles were

basically surrounded by a gay mafia, three of whom I've had the good fortune to have slept with. Crisis' first manager was a gay London gangster who eventually ended up being murdered and fished out of the River Thames. Most of the first Punk shows were held in gay bars and clubs, *et cetera*. I don't believe it stops str8 people from appreciating my work, but I certainly think being gay also adds to the appreciation of Crisis and Death In June. It gives it a certain little push in the right direction. "The Jews Weren't The Only Ones," after all!

BMC: How has your work with Crisis / Death In June been received by the various gay communities in the countries in which you've toured and lived? Would you like Death In June to be regarded as more of a "gay band" by the international gay community than it presently is, and if so, how would that be of any relevance to your work?

DP: With the exception of a large feature in France's main Gay magazine, *Gai Pied*, in 1984, I don't think Death In June has been received by any gay community – anywhere. I really think DIJ has slipped underneath the gaydar.

BMC: Being that you feel that a listener's awareness of your sexuality contributes to a more accurate and informed understanding of your work with Death In June, do you feel that an awareness of your past involvement with Crisis is equally important? Are fans who're unaware of your sexuality and/or your history in Punk Rock therefore missing a key part of what Death In June is about?

DP: No, not particularly. But like with anything that has proven to have longevity, any aspect of the past will have an attraction to some of those who have an interest in the present.

BMC: I understand that you recently gave a performance in Israel. Would you like to share any thoughts on that experience?

DP: It was brilliant and long overdue! There are some fantastic people there and God knows how they cope with that situation day in and day out. But, I'm sure the rest of the Western World will find out soon enough as it gradually is, and this is a Crisis interview, anyway.

BMC: Here in the United States, our national identity is very heavily centered around the abstract notion of "freedom." America as, "the land of the free and the home of the brave," is an idea that's ingrained in our national consciousness from early childhood; yet my view is that politically, the United States is a nation that's obsessed with control. That said, it's ironic to me that as a European, you've experienced so much criticism from Americans for being a "fascist" and for using ancient European symbols such as the Life Rune, because in

Douglas P. in 2006.

deed, it seems to me that Americans tend to be obsessed with total control—both at home and abroad—much more than they are "freedom." Being that Death In June is such an intrinsically European project in nature, what are your thoughts on such American criticisms? How do you respond to Americans who seem to feel that they're entitled to tell you which ancient European symbols you can and can't use in relation to your music and art, simply because they perceive those symbols to be in opposition to their cherished notions of "freedom" and democracy?

DP: In comparison to the rest of the 'Free World' America still does have a lot more 'Freedom' than most. I'd rather be onside with the greatest Industrial Military Complex the World has ever known, despite some of its more hokey faults, than be against it. Society in America has been based upon European

guidelines in terms of culture, *et cetera*. It is a European society albeit many non-Europeans live there. Pretty much like Europe, in fact! Ignorance regarding my heritage isn't confined to America, so it doesn't faze me any more than anyone else with an axe of ignorance to grind. The Americans I know and most of those I meet, regardless of ethnic backgrounds, all appear to be very well informed about most things that matter to me.

BMC: One of the things I find very frustrating about the way Western society functions is the fact that people are usually judged by their words and beliefs rather than their actions. Someone who commits wholesale murder in the name of Christ, democracy, the proletariat, "freedom," or what have you, can often escape accountability and dispel criticism because they've justified unethical actions with conventional morality, whereas someone who espouses what is perceived at base to be an "immoral" ideology—yet who's done nothing the slightest bit unethical—is endlessly criticized and attacked, and essentially functions as a scapegoat. Do you agree with this sentiment, and if so, do you see that applying to you and your post-Crisis work with Death In June?

DP: Post-Crisis or otherwise, I've always seen that sentiment applying. But, luckily, for five years between 1967-72 I stood in my High School Hall during morning assembly staring at a gold lamp with the inscription: "Deeds Not Words" written underneath, painted above the stage where the teachers sat. It must have had some effect upon me.

Look It Up for Yourself

2005

When I was a kid, I once asked my mother what the word "mack-a-bray" meant. I had kept seeing it reappear in horror comic books, and I knew that it meant something bad, but I didn't understand quite what. In response to my query, my mother brusquely informed me that "mack-a-bray" wasn't a real word, and further that I should stop making things up.

The word was *macabre*. I looked it up in the dictionary and it means, "Grownups are full of shit."

Mr. Romance

Why Modern Art is Complete and Total Bullshit

2003

Whenever I walk into a modern Art gallery, I usually find myself struck by an impulse to set the entire place ablaze, though so far I've, of course, always managed to stop myself. Aside from the obvious criminal repercussions of such an act, one of the main reasons that I do stop myself (and that I go into such places in the first place) is that people-watching in modern Art galleries is of the finest variety imaginable. It's amusing to observe would-be "cultured" types try to outdo each other in their wordy analyses of the light, tone, and ostensible emotion or meaning that they claim to be uncovering in the works around them. I get a mild kick out of listening to someone who's supposedly "in the know" relate what a work of Art is purportedly "about" to awed companions who are gullible enough to listen. Or a parent's attempt to explain all the surrounding grown-up nonsense to an understandably confused and flustered child. It's mildly entertaining, but—fuck the art—I'm interested in the people.

Above all, I'm inevitably amused when I'm fortunate enough to witness a philistine yokel standing there gawking at some lame abstract or conceptual piece and saying to his wife, "It's just a *black* painting! Well shit, honey, I could frick'n do that!'" Naturally, in such altogether common instances of postmodernism run amok, your average Joe Schmoe on the street is justifiably irritated and insulted by the tomfoolery which he feels is being foisted upon him by the snobs of the Art World – and of course the art snobs themselves love it, either because they think that the artistic "statement" of color-field paintings and their abstract ilk—the "gesture" if you will—is an adroit reference to some long-dead precedent, or because they misinterpret the artist's intentions and think they're actually finding aesthetic *beauty* in a black canvas. Either way, it's pretty goddamned pretentious, and that's a big part of why modern art is complete and total bullshit.

There are a lot of problems with modern "Art." *A lot.* To begin with, the term "Art" can refer to everything from the cheesy Disney-esque paintings of Thomas Kincade; to the apocalyptic hyperdetailed paintings of Joe Coleman; to Damien Hirst's so-called "instillations" that are easily mistaken for out-of-place everyday objects; to the transgressive "performance pieces" of Carolee Schneemann and Herman Nitsch. Which therefore presents an obvious problem; that "Art," in the contemporary sense of the term, is so multi-faceted and so all-encompassing that it becomes difficult to even *define*, let alone begin to discuss or critique. In fact, it's all but a complete waste of time getting into discussions regarding what is or isn't "Art," as it's all been covered many, *many* times over, and anyone who ever seriously studied the subject is, I guarantee you, thoroughly sick and tired of hearing about it – as am I. Naturally, this never seems to stop art critics, and certainly hasn't deterred the publication of innumerable, heady essays on postmodern Art Theory, so I'm certainly not about to let it stop me either!

In my own humble and moderately informed opinion, Art in its traditional academic sense is pretty much *dead*. It is all but totally irrelevant as a modern-day social force. In fact, I'd wager that a larger portion of the population invests in the stock market than keeps up with the doings of the Art World – and they're probably a lot of the same people anyway.

A hundred years ago, or even fifty years ago, Art was a vibrant social and political catalyst, at times even capable of starting riots – but *now*? Does *anyone* care about the Art World except for the Art World itself? Is modern (excuse me, *post*-modern) Art salient to anyone aside from those with the leisure time and wealth to concern themselves with such things (*i.e.,* the upper classes, college kids, and academics)? And really, does postmodern Art serve *any* social function whatsoever aside from: giving university Art Departments a justification for existence; providing college kids with an unfalsifiable basis for snooty pretentiousness; proffering the wealthy a means by which to engage in "cultured" conspicuous consumption; and supplying the art gallery and museum world with a basis for income? The answer to all of these questions is, of course, a resounding "no." Contrary to what many a bright-eyed college student may want to believe, Saturday morning cartoons and music videos have more of an effect on world events than modern Art does. Art, as a salient social force, is pretty much moribund, if not already dead. Of course, it may at some point come lurching back to life like an undead zombie and start affecting culture at large again, but I, for one, am not holding my breath.

Obviously, I'm hardly the first to draw such conclusions – cultural critics outside the ambit of the Art World have been writing Art's obituary for decades, and many of them have done so far better than I ever could.[8] But I still intend to anyway. Now, is it hypocritical for me to side with these Art-bashers, after having been an Art student and producing a number of "works of Art" myself? Perhaps. But then, I don't really have a problem with anyone *making* art, that is, for the self-fulfilling enjoyment of doing so. There's nothing necessarily wrong with that. No, what perturbs me are a lot of the attitudes and assumptions that go along with the term "Artist." Like the idea that the Artist is somehow elevated above the rest of the herd and that his or her deeds are in some way more relevant or noteworthy than others', simply by virtue of the appellation "Artist" – because, really, that's very rarely true, if ever.

It irks me that Pablo Picasso's absent-minded doodles fetch obscene amounts of money the world over, simply because they bear his signature. It bugs me that Joan Miró's infantile inkblots are regarded with enough gravitas to hang in major Art galleries from California to Europe, and back. It frustrates me that so-called "performance artist" Karen Finley has been made an art-martyr, merely because American tax dollars, by way of National Endowment for the Arts, no longer go toward funding her baloney "artistic pursuits" of (literally) shoving yams up her ass. It bothers me when I go into a gallery and see a price-tag of $5,000 on a piece of "artwork" which consists of an old American flag soaked in blood and encased in Plexiglas – not because of its supposed political "statement," but because of its lack of originality, talent, and artistry. Because it's just plain fucking *dumb* and obvious, and certainly isn't worth freakin' $5,000! I just think it's all a bit insulting, that's all.

---

[8] *See, e.g.,* John Zerzan's essay "The Case Against Art," Thomas McEvilley's essay "Art in The Dark," and Adam Parfrey's essay "Aesthetic Terrorism."

However, the thing that annoys me the most about Art is not the desperate *outré* extremes or the high price tags associated with the Art World, but how contemporary Art is just so consistently self-referential and predictably repetitive, repetitive, repetitive, repetitive. That nearly *every* Artist spends years (if not decades) refining his or her own respective *modus operandi* or "shtick," which is then repeated over and over and over and over and over again, with *minor* variations; Jackson Pollock with his splatter paintings, Roy Lichtenstein with his oversized comic book reproductions, Georgia O'Keefe with her vaginal flowers, Fernando Botero with his balloon-cheeked portly people, Piet Mondrian with his colored squares, and so on and so forth. Originality? Creativity? Artistry? Art? Ha! – I'd say they're all a bunch of overrated, one-trick ponies.

Even worse than all of this, is the fact that for some bizarre reason, contemporary artists *still* find it imperative to make coy, not-so-subtle artistic references to Warhol, Velásquez, Rauschenberg, Van Gough, Dalí, Renoir, Goya, and yes, of course, DaVinci's *Mona Lisa* – and are even lauded by their peers for having done so. It's ridiculous. You just don't see the same degree of circle-jerk aping so much in other fields of expression. Not *every* Rock band feels obligated to cover "Louie Louie" or "My Generation," so why should so many Artists feel compelled to find some pseudo-clever means by which to "reference" their work with equally played-out predecessors? I, for one, am most definitely not impressed.

Often cited as an example of modern Art's decadence, is that of Italian Artist, Piero Manzoni, who in 1961, produced ninety signed and numbered tin cans filled with his own excrement, and titled the piece *Merda d'artista* ("Artist's Shit"), then sold them for their weight in gold. This "Art statement" called attention to the fact that *anything* made by a distinguished "Artist" inherently becomes coveted by the public—clever indeed—except that those cans of aged Italian shit go for considerable amounts of money these days, and that the rubes of the Art-buying public only succeeded in proving Manzoni correct in his assumptions about their gullibility.

That's modern Art for you, in a nutshell (or in a can).

There are few professions more deserving of scorn than that of "Artist." I, for one, find it difficult to stomach the presence of anyone who sincerely refers to themselves as an "Artist" for more than a few minutes (though there are occasional exceptions). It's not that I have a problem with intellectuals, or genuinely intelligent people, or confident people, or even *arrogant* people for that matter – I just think it's tedious and wearying to be in the presence of people overflowing with *unfounded* self-importance and arrogance, that's all. I don't care for people who've convinced themselves, and each other, that they're special simply because they can spout off convoluted exegeses for why they deserve to be recognized for creating aesthetic or conceptual *nonsense* – and most so-called "Artists" *definitely* fall into that category.

Of course, all of this is horribly over-generalized and stereotyped, but then, so what? It's still fuckin' true! Yes, of course, there are exceptions, but generalizations exist because they function, and stereotypes exist because they're accurate more often than not. I assure you, the archetypal bromide of the turtle-necked, wire-rimmed-glasses-wearing, coffee-drinking, cigarette-smoking, nebbish Art-snob dilettante didn't simply arise out of thin air; I know I've certainly met my share of real-life stereotypes. I've also seen my fair share of talentless, mediocre, jejune garbage touted as "High Art." So, forgive me if I'm lumping the entirety of "Artistic expression" into a handful of negative generalizations, but that has been my experience with the matter, and I believe it to be both a valid and commonplace one.

Not that any of this really matters though. As far as I'm concerned, you can think whatever you want about Art, postmodernism, and the Art World – it makes no real difference to me. My opinions are merely my own, and are based only on my personal experience with "the Arts" and "Artists" – which brings us to the point of all this rattling on about Art. The point is that I went to college, and while I was at college, I majored in Art. I was ... an *Art Student*, and naturally, being an Art Student engendered in me a deep-rooted acrimony towards, and distrust of "Art," as well as so-called "Artists." Slightly hypocritical, I suppose, considering that at times I've been quite guilty of all those things I criticize.

Fine – I'm a hypocrite. I would beg your forgiveness, but then who isn't, to some extent, hypocritical? After all, one has to make mistakes and stumble through cocky, sophomoric assumptions in order to understand the folly of such actions in the first place, right? In fact, if anyone has the authority with which to deride "Art," it is *not* the Art critic, magazine columnist, or museum curator, but rather, one such as myself – a one-time "Artist" who's stormed off the field in disgust before ever having actually accomplished anything. So no, I have no problems with talking shit about Art – none at all. So, without further ado.
...

I Was a College Art Student

Art fag with "Meat Clock," 1997.

As a middle-class, white, male, suburbanite fresh out of high school in the mid-1990s, I did what was expected of me – I went to college. Not because I wanted to, really, for I certainly wasn't mature enough at the time to appreciate the importance of such things, but because it was expected of me; because my parents had set aside the money for it, and because I had no better ideas or plans at the time.

That might sound callous and insensitive to those who didn't have the opportunity or funding to pursue higher education, but you'll have to forgive me if I don't feign guilt or remorse on your behalf. As they say, "it's a dog-eat-dog world," "life isn't fair," and bla, bla, bla – in other words, when opportunities come one's way, it's usually best to take them, even if someone somewhere probably deserves them more. So, even though I by no means "deserved" it and would have much rather continued hanging out and playing music with my friends, I attended college, albeit halfheartedly and with no particular academic interests or career aspirations.

I began my college career at The University of Oregon, located in *über*-liberal Eugene, Oregon – hippie bastion of The Green Party's presidential campaign for Ralph Nader and the largest internal "Anarchist" threat to American National Security (or so its residents like to believe). Upon my arrival as a freshman in 1996, I couldn't see myself lasting long in any of the more sensible pre-career majors like Business, Journalism, or Marketing, and I didn't have a particularly strong interest in English or History ... so I decided to major in Art, and remained an Art major throughout my college years. Ergo, for several stupid fucking years, I was a member of one of the world's more contemptable cohorts – I was a college Art Student.

Art students are an oft-maligned bunch, and deservingly so. They can basically be divided into two categories: those who want to make pretty things, and those who want everyone to pay attention to them. The former group often think they have some talent, and occasionally they actually do. They can usually draw, or paint, or sculpt, and the stuff they make occasionally turns out the way they'd like it to. These individuals usually have some favorite artistic movement, period, or artist, which they shamelessly emulate to no end, totally oblivious to the fact that it's just so fucking *over*, daddy-o.

Then there are the Art students who want to get attention. Talent and ability are of no concern to these individuals, as their Art operates on more of a "conceptual" echelon, *dig*? These folks rarely exhibit any more originality than their pretty-picture-painting counterparts; they just ape and copy more obscure and ostensibly avant-garde precursors, and are full of more complicated and long-winded explanations as to why what they're doing is supposedly important or relevant. This subset includes the "Performance Artists," "Conceptual Artists," and their ilk. These people are *in your face,* especially those with political or social agendas. Their Art is either utterly tangential, abstract, nebulous, open-ended "Art for Art's sake," or some form of so-called agitprop, in which case, it deals with "issues" – issues, *maaaaan*, pressing *issues* that need to be grappled with as soon as possible! Gender-issues, race-issues, class-issues, environmental

269

issues, animal rights issues, and so forth – you know, stuff that absolutely *nobody* is aware of or already thinking about in the first place, and which most certainly isn't so complex or nuanced that it can't be neatly summed up in a single painting or collage ... right?

Sigh.

These people can *really* fucking grate on one's nerves. Being notorious loudmouths, they're usually so preoccupied with *talking* about fighting racism, sexism, homophobia, or the military-industrial complex that they never seem to notice what conceited and humorless drips they themselves are most of the time. Nor do they ever seem to realize that what was revolutionary and "shocking" in 1920 isn't even worth stopping to look at now – it's a hackneyed trope ... and an outdated one at that.

I've found that these folks most often drown themselves in a whirlwind of literature and politics, often seesawing between conflicting ideologies without even realizing it. They conspicuously overuse (and often misuse) obscurantist academic terms like "hegemony," "dialectic," "recapitulation," "praxis," and "intersectional" – and will happily pontificate on and on about how important it is to "subvert the dominant paradigm" by way of "deliberative *détournement*." They like to name-drop abstruse and contrarian thinkers like Noam Chomsky, Michel Foucault, Jean-Paul Sartre, Marshall McLuhan, Franz Kafka, Frederich Nietzsche, and Jürgen Habermas (*et al.*) – but as to whether or not they actually *read* these authors is doubtful.

Members of this bunch incessantly hop the fences of satire and sarcasm, wholeheartedly embracing irony one day and then declaring it "dead" the next. They smoke cigarettes. They listen to Indie Rock or avant-garde free-form Jazz, or Japanese Noise, or "Experimental" music, or some other suitably cryptic sub-cultural variant. (They're totally "over" stuff like Punk, Metal, and Goth, naturally.) After all, they're hip. They're stylish. They're serious. They're tortured. They're "Artists." They're cloistered and mollycoddled children brazenly dealing with "issues" that they've never experienced and don't yet fully understand.

Anyway, as much as I am loath to admit it, I would probably to some extent fall into the latter category, and I'd be lying if I claimed I wasn't guilty of my own weird variations on a lot of the same bullshit in college. I was enamored of all things Dada while I was a college Art Student. Everything Dada was purported to stand for seemed so hugely in accordance with both the immature goofiness I'd always clung to and the anti-everything politics that I'd come to develop in my teenage years, that it and myself seemed like a perfect fit. Dada was all that which was supposedly great about Punk, minus all the angsty political crap and with more absurdity. It was a pre-WWII ideological resonance with a worldview that I'd held dear since childhood, not to mention an academically-sanctioned excuse to have obnoxious fun and get college credit for it to boot. I loved it. Dada became the filter through which I tried to turn anything and everything into *fun*, and occasionally succeeded. That was the main reason I'd majored in Art in the first place – because I imagined that it might be *fun*. Often, however, I found that a lot of people involved in Art were very hostile to the concept of fun; that is, unless it fit within their pre-established conceptions of what was and wasn't "acceptable." Let me give you an example:

Once, just for shits and giggles, I took a graduate-level seminar on Performance Art while I was studying at the University of Oregon. This consisted of about fifteen or so graduate Art Students, all of whom were working on the conceptual texts to "performance pieces." Typically, spoken word rants or quasi-thespian soliloquies for the stage. There were several dealing with "women's issues," some dealing with "sexuality," and one or two concerned with "race issues." (All very endearing stuff, I assure you.) Of this cadre of fifteen or so graduate students, at least ten took it all *very* seriously; the remainder being either confused or apathetic about what they were supposed to be doing with their "Art." I, for one, found it nearly impossible to take it seriously at all. I just couldn't – after all, it was fuckin' Performance Art.

Our first assignment was to write up a proposal regarding what conceptual direction we would be pursuing throughout the course, with the eventual intention of enacting a "performance" at its terminus. Trying to have "fun" with the class, I wrote-up a proposal for a Rap Opera, the plot of which involved the West Coast crew of Tupac Shakur and the East Coast crew of the Notorious B.I.G. which epically battled it out as modern-day Capulets and Montagues (this was just after they had both been killed). The original text of my "Performance Art" graduate-level course proposal of April 14, 1997, is as follows:

Thug Life
A Rap Opera

By Brian M. Clark

My main objective in authoring *Thug Life* is to bring true peace and harmony to the black and white races once and for all. My strategy is really quite simple, yet curiously ingenious: the juxtaposition of exclusively black culture and language with exclusively white musical form and tradition. All black people listen to Rap music and all white people enjoy and identify with Opera, therefore the coupling of black music with white musical form, and the telling of a black story using black language, yet sung in the traditionally white operatic style, can only lead to ultimate harmonious unity between these two races. The tale I hope to tell is that of the East-West Gangsta Rap conflict, which recently came to a head with the deaths of rappers Tupac Shakur and The Notorious B.I.G. This is indeed an epic story of warring "families" (Death Row Records and Bad Boy Entertainment), which is extremely well-suited for an Opera, and can easily be adapted to fit conventional operatic form.

Conventional Operatic Form and Conventional Operatic Devices:

Acts: The conventional Opera is always divided into acts (scenes).

Leitmotiv: Each character has a "theme song" called a Leitmotiv (motif) which accompanies his/her presence in an act.

Overture: The conventional opera usually begins with the overture, which contains every character's motif.

Orchestral Interludes: These separate the acts.

Protagonist: The protagonist (Tupac Shakur) is usually a tenor.

Antagonist: The antagonist (The Notorious B.I.G.) is usually a basso (baritone).

Now, you see, I even though I knew next to nothing about either Opera or contemporary Rap music at the time, I still thought analyzing it and dealing with its "issues" was pretty goddamned *funny*. I laughed a lot while I was writing the proposal anyway. I mean, with statements like: "All black people listen to Rap music and all white people enjoy and identify with Opera," it seemed unlikely that anyone could be so thick-headed as to take my proposal literally; but naturally, I'd overestimated my classmates in assuming this. Upon submitting my proposal to the class, I found myself defensively arguing with several inordinately furious and red-faced—*white*—graduate students about whether or not I even had the "right" to be dealing with issues affecting "black culture," and I was even at one point accused of being an outright racist, simply for finding *any* humor in the subject at all. I remember one round-faced, cherubic little white girl adamantly exclaiming, "Those were *real* people who suffered and *died*, and it's *not* funny! It's *not* a joke!"

Sigh.

I can only speculate as to whether or not Tupac and Biggie would have so adamantly railed against a similar satirizing of "white culture," or wrestled with themselves as to whether or not black people have the "right" to make light of white people's various quirks and foibles. Then again, considering what a couple of upstanding guys they were, it's probably safe to assume that they'd be just as incensed at the notion of a black person poking fun at "white culture" as my white classmates were at my little lampoon of "black culture," right? *Right.*

The reaction that I received from my fellow classmates in response to my proposal was nuts. Histrionic. Deranged. Unhinged. Really extreme, and unreasonably so. I thought that a couple of them were liable to start fuckin' crying, right there in the classroom. I found it very odd. And you know what else is odd? Queerly enough, much of the assigned reading for this Performance Art class was culled from the pages of the 1992 Re/Search publication *Angry Women*, which (among other logical, rational, objective, evenhanded, fair-minded, and completely unbiased feminist diatribes), includes an interview with irascible Greek-American musician and performance artist, Diamanda Galás, in which she declares:

> I want to fuck a man in the ass (so far I haven't had any volunteers; I always ask them and they get nervous and say no) but I want to ... Really, I wanna fuck men in the ass—I want to **break the flesh**, too—and exorcise my violence on them to show them just how **much** I love them! ... I think women should have an "ideal": the only people you treat as equals are other women. And when you want **subordinates**, you can fuck a man in the ass!

Of course, none of my classmates so much as raised an eyebrow over *that*. Oh no. *Tout au contraire*, they fucking loved it. They ate that kind'a shit up! It was strong and empowering, brave and groundbreakingly unconventional. Why? Because the prevalent left-wing attitude at the time (especially amongst college kids in places like Eugene, Oregon), was that it was fine for minorities to make fun of Caucasians (but not the other way around), and it was fine for gays to belittle straights (but not the other way around), and that it was fine for women to disparage men (but not the other way around). What's the expression I'm looking for? ... *double standard*. Oh yeah, that's it. Seem hypocritical? I sure as fuck thought so. But that's college for you.

I never ended up making the Rap Opera (it was far too ambitious a project anyway), so at the course's completion, as the other students submitted their videos of themselves being artsy-fartsy, or gave effusive readings of poetry or dramatic recitations of childhood memories, I submitted some music that I'd done with my friend Doug. It was pretty anticlimactic, considering how much arguing I'd done about how I had every "right" to make a Rap Opera about Tupac and Biggie, but ... oh well. The idea was amusing, but its actualization and execution would have been just too much of a pain in the ass to actually follow through with. Anyway, the reason I'm relating this experience isn't that I'm particularly proud of the Rap Opera proposal, but that the experience was fairly typical and representative of the social climate at the University of Oregon while I was a student there. The entire city was a fucking killjoy.

Everyone I knew in Eugene was antagonistically forthright and open concerning their status as a "marginalized" vegetarian, vegan, homosexual, lesbian, or bisexual; and most were somehow involved in some aspect of either activism and/or communal living. Even though they were overwhelmingly in the majority, everybody still saw themselves as an alienated victim of "societal intolerance," and had any number of "causes" that they were overtly championing, about which they'd hector you for *hours,* if you'd only let them.

Being gay wasn't simply a sexual preference like being straight was – no, it was a powerful, revolutionary, anti-globalization statement! Eco-feminism taught the ladies that not only were they ostensibly being shorted pay for equal work, but their very bodies were battlefields! (To your battle stations, ladies!) Poseurs got involved with the Green Party and Greenpeace – if you wanted to be taken seriously, you'd get involved with Earth First!, and Anarchism. Rusted Root, The Grateful Dead, 10,000 Maniacs, Bob Dylan, and Phish ruled the airwaves, "kind herb" was to be had everywhere; and all the while, Gaia, The Earth Mother Goddess, smiled down upon us. That was Eugene, Oregon, in the mid-to-late 1990s. The Hippiest Place on Earth!

It never ceased to amaze me just how fucking *dumb* some of the college kids in that town were. I was always coming across these upper-middle-class suburban kids from California, who'd be sitting in some tea house organizing a collective meeting for the Wobblies (that is, the Industrial Workers of the World), and talking about "solidarity," and I'd be sitting there thinking, *You've never worked a day in your fucking life, and you're preaching to each other (loud enough so that everyone else in the place can hear), about the oppression of the working classes and the need to organize labor. That's just ... sick.* Silly me, I was under the impression that, in order for one to consider oneself an industrial worker—a wobblie—one must actually *work,* and I seriously doubt that the occupation of University-educated Organizer qualifies. Idiots.

I actually heard my peers in Eugene bloviate quixotically about how they wanted to hitchhike down to Nicaragua and join the Sandinista "freedom fighters" in the "righteous" struggle against their U.S.-backed "oppressors." Big talk—big, *big* talk indeed—but that's all it ever was ... talk. I'm going to go ahead and conjecture that Sandinista rebels aren't crossing their fingers waiting around for the unsolicited "aid" of middle-class American college kids. In fact, if I were a Nicaraguan peasant, fighting tooth-and-nail to establish Communism in my war-torn homeland, there would be few things *more* odious to me than affluent, pampered, performative, loud-mouthed hypocrites who go to college in Eugene, Oregon.

They lacked any sense of self-awareness, and were tin-eared to the actual problems faced by the "workers" they purported to speak for; and their beliefs, and their values. I wish some of those so-called "Anarchist" kids actually *had* hitchhiked down to Nicaragua – they probably would have been taken hostage by whichever side got hold of them first and then been used as a political bargaining tool. An effete, feckless little pawn in a big, nasty game of geopolitical chess. It's a nice notion, but none of them ever put their money where their mouths were, so of course it was never going to happen.

Sigh.

Anyway, as per my experience in Performance Art class, I found that practically nobody in Eugene seemed to find any humor in anything even mildly controversial like "race," unless of course that meant making fun of the "white trash" rednecks in Springfield, the next town over (made briefly infamous by school-shooter Kip Kinkle). Nor did anyone seem to see the irony in being so militantly liberal and intolerantly "politically correct" that it occasionally bordered on ideological thought-policing and censorious fascism – or that for all their grandiose speech-making about the glories of "empowerment" and "diversity," Eugene's young residents were nonetheless completely oblivious to their own propensity for debasement when it came to people who didn't fall on their side of their illusory good/bad, us/them political and social dichotomy. If you disagreed with them, they saw you as *shit*—a fascist fucking pig— and weren't interested in the "diversity" that your divergent opinion brought to the table. But hey, those are all minor technicalities, after all ... right?

Now, in all fairness, I was demographically pretty similar to everyone else at the University of Oregon, at least superficially; I was a middle-class white kid from the suburbs, whose parents were putting him through college – but at least I wasn't in fucking *denial* about it. At least I wasn't *pretending* to be something else, or "slumming it" as they say. At least I wasn't throwing proverbial rocks at the institution that I was paying to attend.

So anyway, on the whole, that was Eugene, Oregon; there was lots of extremist left-wing ideology being tossed around, most of which was just hot air, and that which wasn't was merely tiresome and dispiriting. But it was exhausting to be immersed in that. Though I lasted almost three full years at the University of Oregon, the place and its inhabitants eventually succeeded in breaking me down. The gloomy wet weather, the insufferably sanctimonious people, the uptight and preachy leftist politics, the shitty jam-band hippy music – everything about Eugene was not *my* thing. And so, partway through, I dropped out of college in Eugene, moved back in with my parents in Northern California.

Fucking loser, right?

But, a few months later, upon the insistent prompting of my father, I reentered school at Saint Mary's College, back in sunny Moraga, California. This was an entirely different experience altogether. The University of Oregon was a big state school full of throngs of galvanized liberal kids, where everything revolting about "Art" rears its grotesque head unchecked. In contrast, Saint Mary's College is a small, expensive, very conservative Catholic school snuggled up in the hills of Moraga, California, in the San Francisco Bay Area. The two are as different as night and day.

Nestled up in the hills, away from the troubles of the world—much like a gated community—Saint Mary's College is a glorified high school for rich kids. A place of inherited privilege and "I'll-scratch-your-back-if-you-scratch-mine" politics, openly displayed in all their perverse grandeur. Therein, hundreds of sheltered young minds spend four years perfecting the arts of Business and Marketing, and occasionally a few other things like drinking, fucking, and inhaling overpriced cocaine. Aside from a contingent of Catholic minorities (Latino and Filipino mostly, if I remember correctly), the student body while I was enrolled there was mostly composed of people who—regardless of whatever their *real* names might have been—were all named Brad, Chad, Buffy, and Brandi; and all of whom were either from Orange County or the Oakland hills. Basically, being on campus at Saint Mary's felt like being in an episode of *Beverly Hills 90210*, all the time.

As one might imagine, the Art Department at Saint Mary's was an underwhelming, middling thing indeed. Despite having a relatively small student-body, the school appears to have had enormous amounts of funding (due, I imagine, to its downright pushy solicitation of alumni donations), and having but a handful of perfunctory Art majors, it appears that the college needed an Art Department merely so that its overwhelming mass of Business students could receive a well-rounded, "Lasallian" education (and so that it could include Art as a major in its promotional brochures). There were only three Art Professors on the faculty; two of whom were total space-cadet '60s burnouts, and the third being swell enough to give me whatever materials and supplies I wanted, for whatever purpose I wanted (he once even gave me course credit for building life-size robot sculptures out of material I found in dumpsters).

As much as I've bad-mouthed Saint Mary's College above, the truth is that I really enjoyed being a student there. The student body was mostly composed of people that I had nothing whatsoever in common with, but the professors were intelligent, well-paid, and actually *wanted* to talk to you about what you were interested in – which was something I'd never experienced before. I especially liked being an Art Student—there were so *few* other Art students—it was great. Unlike the University of Oregon, there were no hipsters, no Art-snobs, no hippies, no Indie-rockers, no Crusties, and absolutely *nobody* had dreadlocks or scruffy, stinky, disgusting on-campus dogs. There was a very small contingent of kids who were attempting to be "underground" or "sub-cultural" or whatever you wanna' call it, but they were just so awkwardly bad at it, and so totally out of touch, that it was sort of cute and refreshing. Like "Punk" kids who been living away from mommy n' daddy for all of six months, and had freshly dyed hair, a shiny new nose-piercing, a brand new Minor Threat patch on their backpack and an Operation Ivy sticker on the back of their SUV – far from being jaded and cynical, to say the very least. They were genuinely endearing (and no, I'm not saying that sarcastically). After all, it's far more of an accomplishment to be one of a handful of still-green, pampered poseur Punks in Moraga than one of thousands of pompous, pseudo-bohemian wannabes just over the hills in Berkeley.

Anyway, so those were the two institutions of "higher learning" that matriculated me as a young adult in the second half of the 1990s; The University of Oregon (suffocatingly liberal and annoying as fuck) and Saint Mary's College (underwhelmingly conservative and banal). So now, let me return to the point: Art. More specifically, *my* art. To be perfectly honest, I never really thought I was much of an artist. I always preferred the Art History Courses in the curriculum to the Studio Art classes. I hadn't any real talent to speak of in any particular discipline or "field" as such, but regardless – I tried to have *fun* with my Art *all* the time, which was something that I very rarely witnessed any of my fellow students doing at either of the schools I studied at. They were usually either trying really hard to be "deep," or viewed everything they were doing at school as being merely practice for the "real" Art they were going to start making once they became "real" artists (yeah, right). Either way, I can't say that I saw anyone even so much as *try* to put something of their own personality into their in-class work. They'd be painting a "study" for something, like a still-life with flowers, and that would be *it* – just a soulless study of light and tone, and nothing *else*. Or conversely, they'd be doing some generic, nominally "political" collage about this-

or-that abstract social injustice (using bold text on black and white photos from the '50s, of course), but which conveyed absolutely nothing about the person who'd made it. Actually, that's not true; their Art was insipid, and so were they. Most of these people were as soulless as oatmeal-flavored granola dentist office waiting room music for pacifist vegans who put their lentils in a blender to circumvent the implied violence of having to chew. So I guess their drab Art was usually a pretty accurate reflection of their personalities after all.

I could be wrong, of course, but I'd like to think that, for whatever I lacked in ability, at least the stuff I was doing had more personality to it somehow. Unlike most of my classmates, who acquitted themselves as if their Art were supposed to exist in some kind of unalloyed "pure" Platonic Art vacuum beyond space and time, at least the art that I made in class was usually in some way directed at getting a reaction out of the professor or the other students. At least it was fun, or funny, or obnoxious.

Generally speaking, I got a pretty big kick out of painting dicks. Because it was *funny*, that's why. I mean, how can you *not* find that hilarious? What the hell is wrong with you people anyway?

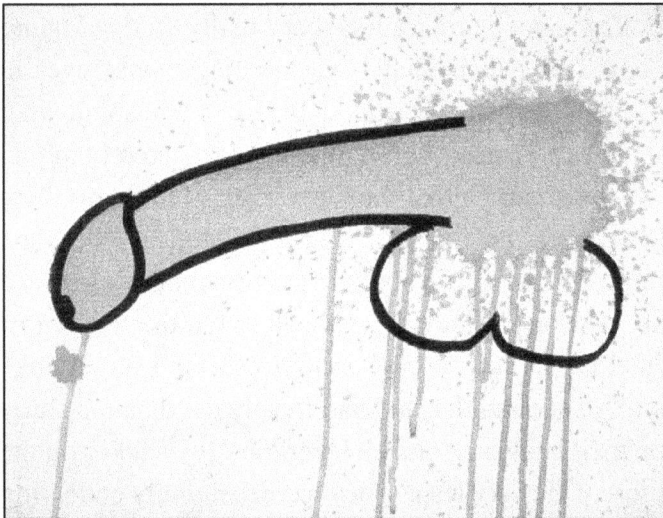

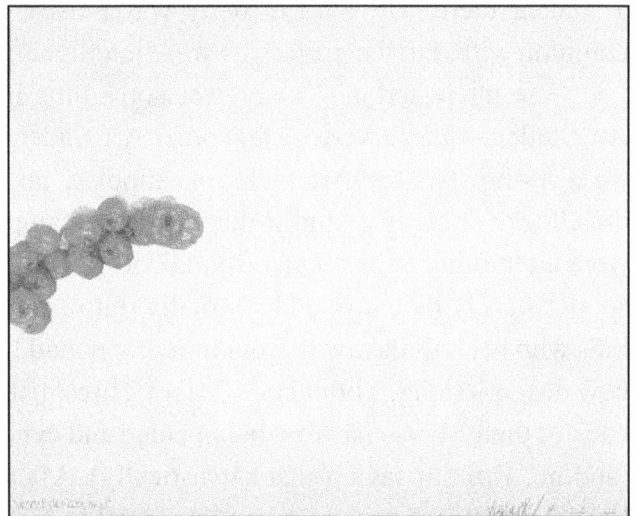

In addition to dicks, I also painted naked devil-women in hell, robots, people having stop-motion sex; public *dis*service messages, and other random shit, *e.g.*:

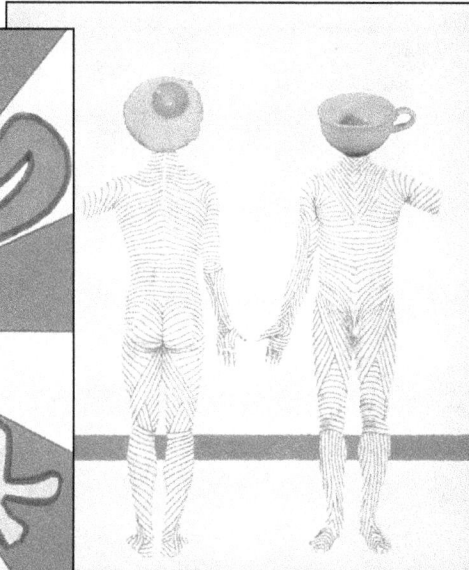

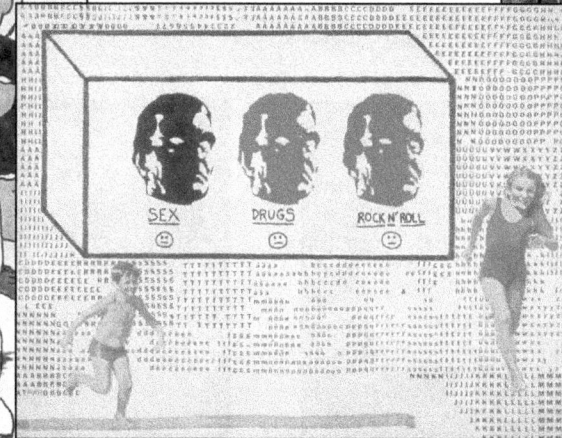

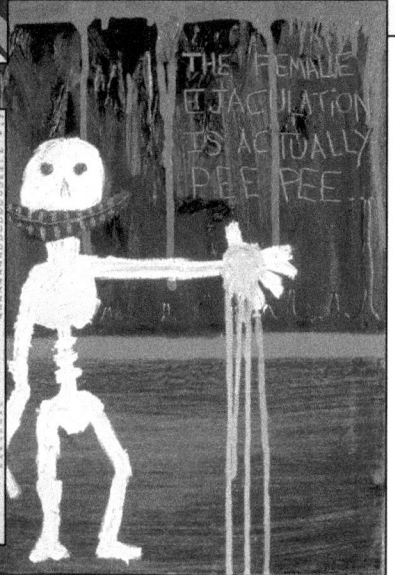

I also created stupid sculptures, such as a life-size working armature lamp, transhuman space-genitals, a working meat clock, goofy pottery, and other dumb tactile creations:

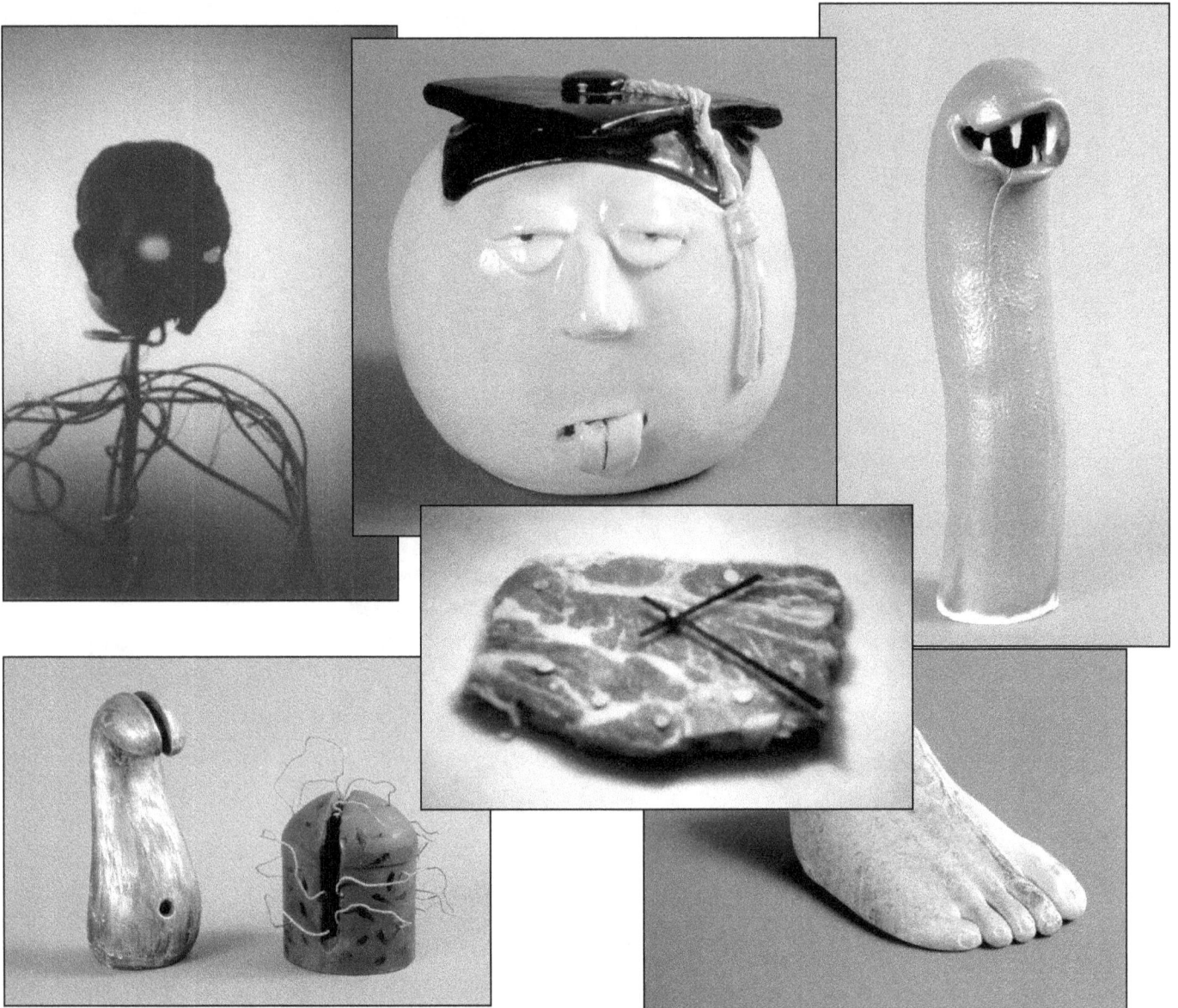

... and made even *dumber* shit like short films that sampled VHS porno tapes showing doggie-style penetration set to mariachi music behind weird filters:

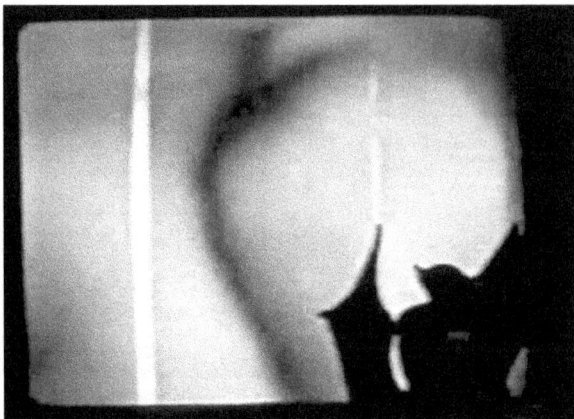

For whatever it's worth, or lack thereof, that was my "Art." Juvenile and petulant thought it may have been, I thought most of it was really funny, because damn it – it fucking was.

Of course, not everybody else thought so. I would occasionally come into class and find my canvases had been turned around on their easels – my work scuffed and smeared, because someone in a class following mine didn't want to *look at it*. I always found this strange, considering that college is supposed to be all about the "free exchange of ideas" and whatnot, but of course it isn't strange – it's entirely predictable. After all, "open-minded" college students are some of the most easily offended and morally outraged folks out there.

As for the "free exchange of ideas," well, Art class rarely had anything to do with "ideas" at all. No, most of the Art classes I attended usually went like this; three times a week, for three hours straight, I sat in a room with twenty or so people who were on the whole, insufferably full of themselves and yet, claiming to be "Artists," were nonetheless abysmally bland, totally conventional and lacking in *any* real creativity whatsoever. People who were often so dreary and downright dull that they imagined that they were being "bohemian" in painting Impressionist or Cubist compositions in the late 1990s, or even worse, "trippy" phony-Surrealist landscapes populated with pot-smoking aliens. Now, you can think whatever the hell you want, but as far as I'm concerned, my booby-monsters and donkey-dicks were echelons above it all – but again, as I said, not everybody else thought so.

For instance, there was the time I wasn't allowed to show my short film *The Big Secret* on the day of the final, because the professor feared it would upset some of the other students – which, of course, to me, meant that the piece was a smashing success! Because, yes, I confess ... in addition to amusing myself, I figured it was an extra added bonus if my peers were "offended" by my work. I know you're not supposed to admit that you were ever trying to "offend" anyone (none of the worst "offenders" ever do)—you're supposed to claim that you just do what you do because you want to, and if it offends people, well then so be it—but I'm not going to say that because, well, it just isn't true, and I really see no point in being deceitful about it.

As much of a self-indictment as it may be to admit any of this now, as regards my own maturity, I actually quite liked the idea of offending people when I was a college Art Student. I liked the idea of confusing them with ambiguous enmity. I wasn't chiefly interested in being "offensive," mind you, or in symbolically saying "fuck you," or anything like that, but I did like the idea of using inanimate objects to produce some kind of negative reaction in strangers. I liked the idea of throwing someone off with a seemingly insolent "statement" that didn't make any apparent sense, no matter how long they analyzed it. I liked the concept of making people uneasy—and possibly even unnerved or irate—by something as innocuous as a painting. It felt like alchemy to me. I liked the idea of using an unpleasant concept to ruin the afternoon of someone I'd never even met, and never would. I thought it was all really *funny*, and to be completely honest, I still do.

The artistic merits of "shock value" may indeed be long gone, but that doesn't mean it isn't still fun to annoy people who repulse you, and most of my fellow students repulsed me. That was my internal apologia for virtually everything I did as an Art Student – that most people *deserved* to be offended, because *I* was offended by most people, and Art just happened to be a facile means of returning the favor. Everything about *them* made me sick in ways that they could never fathom, and I was glad to be having the same effect on them for once, albeit passively.

Now, you may think such behavior base, craven, and pointless, and yes, it most certainly is—in a very literal-minded and short-sighted sense—but in the larger purview of things, actually, no, in fact I think it isn't. You can go ahead and make whatever criticisms or judgments you want —you are as entitled to them as I am to my own—but keep in mind, that if nothing else, at least my Art brought a small measure of *dissonance* into the otherwise pleasant afternoons of either preachy college hippies or well-to-do young Catholics, and in doing so forced them to actually think about something they'd probably avoided thinking about for a few seconds – which I still see as valid.

The funny thing, however, is that even though certain individuals found reasons to get upset about it, most of my Art wasn't really all that "offensive" anyway. Most of it was actually quite tame, especially when considered alongside the work of people like Hans Belmer, Trevor Brown, the Chapman brothers, Stu Mead, or Bella Hoffman (most of whom I'd never even heard of back then). By comparison to these purveyors of the genuinely "taboo," my own work seems almost quaint and even ... *wholesome* in a way – which I actually find unexpectedly comforting. I'm glad that someone is out there being disgusting, fucked-up, transgressive, and genuinely offensive – and I'm even gladder that that someone *isn't* me.

As for whether or not you want to call something "offensive," "subversive," or "taboo," I think it's really quite irrelevant (and usually very silly too). It *always* depends on the context – always. I exhibited my work at a private catholic college. My shit was consistently *the* most bad-ass shit there, hands down. In the larger scope of things, yes, I realize that most of it isn't all that "shocking" or "extreme," or whatever, but in context, it was walking a much finer line than one might at first assume. In context, it was far more effective at accomplishing my aims than something more excessive would or could have been. If I'd ever actually implemented any of my more *amusing* ideas at the time (like big dayglo pink swastikas covered in smiley faces and pot leaves), I would have been quickly disposed of – expelled for being a "hatemonger" or a "bigot" (or whatever they call having a decent sense of humor nowadays). If I'd gone so far as to present anything even remotely similar to the work of Trevor Brown or Stu Mead, then The Brothers of The Cloth who ran the college would have surely delighted in publicly displaying their moral indignation and opprobrium by having me expelled as a problematic thought criminal. No, anything more subversive than what I was already producing would have been akin to flushing money down the toilet, and leaving myself up shit creek (though in certain respects, I fail to see the difference anyway). Anyway, it doesn't really matter, because I never cared about being "subversive" – as I said, my main concerns were in amusing myself, and rarely did I fail at that.

In making any admissions about my artworks, however, I do not wish to suggest that I don't still find humor or value in a good deal of that which I produced as a college student. In fact, to the contrary, I actually think most of it is superior to that which often passes for "real" Art in museums and galleries the world over. I can only assume that most "real" Artists would in all likelihood scoff at my work, to which I say: let them scoff! – after all they're just *Artists*, and who gives a shit what fucking *Artists* think? Regardless, any and all criticism is, of course, certainly valid, but for my part, I still think that attempting to make people recoil in disgust or confusion is far more of a worthy aspiration than just painting pretty pictures or (even worse), self-indulgent abstract nonsense. So there.

Anyway, wrapping things up: After a good deal of time, energy, and (most importantly) money, I now hold a Bachelor of Arts degree in Art, and yet (surprise!) I have almost *no* desire whatsoever to pursue Art any further than I already have, which was too far. All told, over the course of four years "studying" Art, I produced, I dunno, seventy or so pieces of "Art," including paintings, collages, sculptures, short videos, and a short film. After having it photographed, I gave most of my work away to friends and acquaintances. I burned everything that wasn't up to par ... and I gotta' say, it felt good to do so.

I still can't stand having the all-too-common conversations that begin with, "So what did you study?" and naturally include, "So what are you going to do with that?"– because it's just depressing. I was always guileless enough to believe that upon graduation, everything would fall into place, something magical would happen, and I'd know what to do with myself; but as of yet, this simply has not happened. I'm a twenty-five-year-old college graduate, and the last job I had was as menial and mind-numbing as sitting through a high school math class for forty hours a week. I'm sure my next "career move" will be similarly un-glamorous, but fuck it, I don't care. I have my dignity. I have my integrity. After all, *I'm an Artist!*

Sigh.

* * *

Recently, while walking home from a liquor store at night, I passed by an Art opening at a small gallery. The entire front face of this gallery was windowed plate glass, such that while walking outside—in the dark—one can see everything and everyone inside quite well. And, as yet another bad cliché in a world full of bad clichés, this Art opening was everything heinous, ugly, and pathetic about Art. It was a room full of mid-sized abstract paintings and "color field" works, which were being "appreciated" by about fifty or so upper-middle-class, middle-aged white people who were drinking wine and eating cheese.

The Art, of course, was of the worst variety. I swear, I've seen it a thousand times if I've seen it once. Color fields, patterns, splatters, abstract shapes, *et cetera*. No content. No ideas. No commentary. No emotion. No soul. No talent. No ability. No finesse. No risk. Just frivolous, cookie-cutter-esque, self-congratulatory drivel. I'd take a thousand Thomas Kinkade lithographs before I'd let one of these fucking worthless Jackson Pollack or Mark Rothko rip-offs into my home.

Of course, whenever one sees talentless garbage which displays neither aesthetics, ability, nor conceptualism—as in this instance—the best part of it is typically the price tag. I'd wager that all of the so-called "Art" featured in this gallery goes for at least three grand, if not more. Awesome. *Très chic!*

Stuff like that used to piss me off, but now, my attitude is simply ... *terrific. If you can con some upwardly-mobile dope from the 'burbs into paying three grand for your crappy, boring piece of masturbatory "Art," then that's super – all the more power to you.* If only I'd been that shrewd – instead, I gave away or immolated all my art. Not because of some masochistic Marxist impulse towards "sharing" or whatever, but because I just don't think "Art" has any intrinsic value. I don't think most art—including my own—is really worth anything. This isn't to say that I think all Art is shit – because I don't. But I think that if Art isn't stimulating, either technically or conceptually, then it's worse than shit. At least shit smells. At least that's a sensation. At least that's something.

As I stood there for a minute or so, in the cold, in the dark, I just watched this one guy in particular. This one pear-shaped, middle-aged, bespectacled guy with a grizzled ponytail – he was holding a glass of wine in one hand and gesticulating exaggeratedly with the other, to a couple of art-fag-hags who were lapping it up and laughing at his clever quipping. A stereotype embodied in the flesh.

Sigh.

Art doesn't really piss me off anymore. It used to, but now it just seems predictable. It has no meaning anymore, and something without meaning can't really be bothersome. But the people involved with Art will always piss me off. They want to see themselves as part of some sort of cultural "elite" or vanguard, when in fact they couldn't be further from it. They have absolutely no idea. The "Art World" has achieved a state of stagnated entropy. Inert stasis. Heat death. There is a part of me that wants to grab each and every one of them by the collar, and scream into their faces—*"It's not 1922 anymore! It's been done!"*—but then there is another, wiser, part of me that realizes that the worst thing I could possibly ever do to these people is simply ignore them, and keep right on walking down the street. ...

A coterie of contemporary high-ranking Christian American faith leaders—consisting of a Southern Baptist, a Mainline Protestant Evangelical, a Catholic, a Mormon, a Methodist, and a Unitarian—are given a divinely-inspired visionary mandate straight from The Lord God on High, instructing them that they must intercede in history and forestall the crucifixion of Jesus of Nazareth. Members of the group are each given copies of their respective Holy Books, a pocketful of *denarii*, and a flask of water; and are then transported through spacetime in defiance of the inviolable laws of physics, back to Calvary, Judea, just outside the walls of ancient Jerusalem. There, they encounter Jesus himself, being processioned to the cross by Roman soldiers. None of them speaks Latin or Aramaic, but through a mix of moxie, gumption, and sheer pluckiness, each must attempt to save Jesus from being crucified by the Romans.

(SPOILER: They all die.)

SCREAM THE QUESTIONS, not the answers

1999

SCREAM THE QUESTIONS, not the answers, is a short experimental student film shot on black-and-white Super 8, and first screened in 1999. It was selected for the film screenings: "A Moment in Time," April 7, 2000 (Filmhouse Café, Hearst Art Gallery, Moraga, California); "Alternative Requirements," October 3, 2000 (Pacific Film Archive, Berkely, California); and "The International Experimental Cinema Exposition," September 21-25, 2005 (Museum of Contemporary Art, Denver, Colorado). Like the overwhelming majority of "experimental" films, SCREAM THE QUESTIONS, not the answers is mediocre – as in, not particularly engaging, interesting, well-made, or ... good.

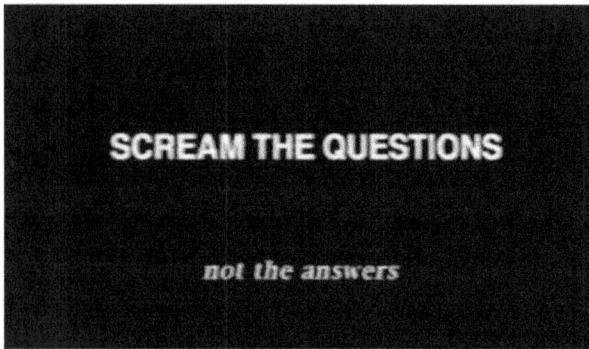

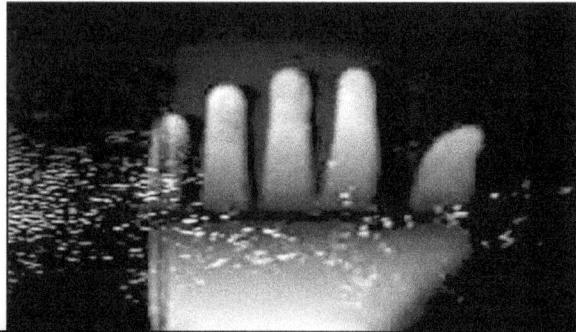

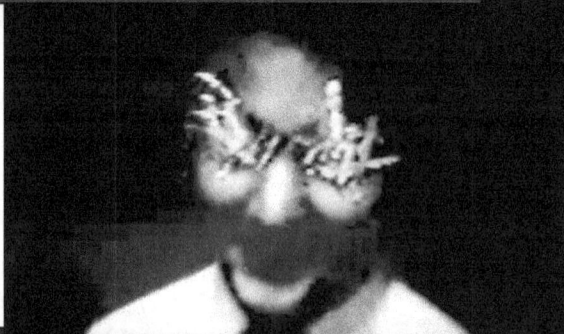

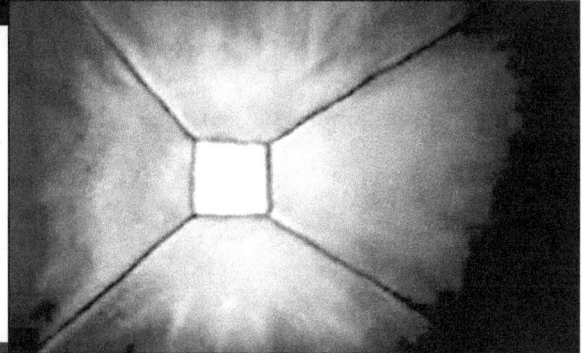

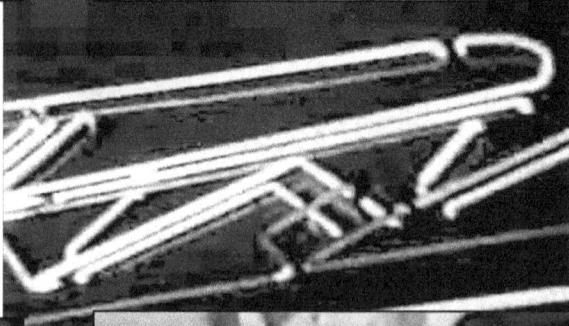

art department and

F I L M H O U S E

present

a moment in time

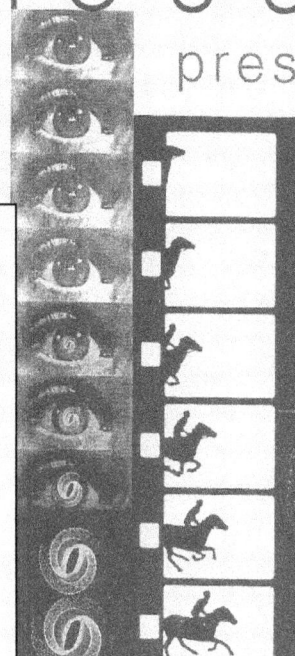

SCREAM THE QUESTIONS *not the answers*
brian clark St. Mary's College (b/w, 4 min)

A sexy, fun-filled romp through suburban teenage wasteland! Sex-crazed young hussies run wild to out-of-this-world sounds, amid the howls of drug-crazed biker boys! Wall-to-wall hilarity that will leave your stomach bleeding and your eyes on fire!

pacific film archive presents

alternative 2000 requirements

7:30 | tuesday october 3

TIE | The International Experimental Cinema Exposition

July 7, 2005

Brian Clark
P.O. Box 1434
Denver, CO 80201
USA

Dear Brian Clark,

On behalf of TIE, I would like to congratulate you. Your marvelous film, *Scream the Questions, not the answers*, has been chosen for official selection in The International Experimental Cinema Exposition's upcoming festival, September 21-25, 2005. This particular round has been highly competitive. Literally hundreds of submissions were carefully reviewed. Thus, we are very pleased to inform you that your work is part of the representative omnibus.

Please consider this letter a formal invitation to attend and participate in this year's festival. You will be contacted shortly via email with further information.

Thank you for your interest in TIE. We are very honored to present your film and look forward to your participation.

Sincerely,

Christopher May
Director
TIE, The International Experimental Cinema Exposition

849 Humboldt Street · #2, Denver, Colorado 80218, U.S.A.
Phone: 303.832.2387
www.experimentalcinema.org

Tuesday October 3

A project of The Time of Your Life: Enhancing Student Engagement with the Arts, supported by a grant from The Pew Charitable Trusts.

Alternative Requirements 2000: Works from Bay Area Film and Video Schools 7:30

Artists in Person

This annual program celebrates experimental films and videos made by students in the Bay Area. These unique works meditate on, provoke questions about, and help to expand the boundaries of the film medium. The show highlights work in numerous formats (16mm, Super 8, MDV, Digital Video, BetaSP, and VHS), experimental styles (documentary, narrative, abstract, found-footage), and subject matter (death, love, kinship). Tonight also includes a Q&A discussion with the artists.

This year's selected works come from students attending California College of Arts and Crafts, De Anza College, Saint Mary's College, San Francisco Art Institute, San Francisco State University, and University of California, Berkeley.

Curated by Jennifer Ammann, Jill Meredith Borut, Huy Chau, Natalia Fidelholtz, Chris Gridley, Kari Hattner, Oscar Huerta, Justin Maradiegue, Dennise Moon, Rebecca Payne, Lola Popovac, Samuel Tomfohr, Jessica Tscha, and Marvella Villaseñor, with the assistance of Tania Haddad. This program is part of a curatorial internship offered by PFA and the UC Berkeley Film Studies Program.

Part 1: **Flip Flim** (Ellen H. Uglestad, Alfonso Alvarez, 70 sec, B&W, 16mm). **Colorized** (Deborah Shubert, 4 mins, VHS). **Jungle Dye** (Nefertiti Kelley-Farias, 2000, 4 mins, Super 8). **A Film for My Unborn Supermodel** (Brett Simon, 2000, 8 mins, MDV). **SCREAM THE QUES-TIONS not the Answers** (Brian Clark, 4 mins, B&W, VHS). **Eighty Layers of Me (that you'll have to survive)** (Tricia Creason Valencia, 2000, 11 mins, 16mm). **Topsy Turvy** (Lisa A. Perez, 2000, 3 mins, DV). **Unbound** (Andrew Denman, 8 mins, B&W/Color, VHS. **&** (Dan Janos, 3 mins, BetaSP).

Part 2: **Degree Zero** (Te-Shun Tseng, 3 mins, double projection, 16mm). **In Collaboration** (Mary Wilson, North Pitney, 2000, 5 mins, VHS). **Heavy Metal Memories** (Peter Glover, 7 mins, 16mm). **Stars, Paper** (Travis, 4 mins, MDV). **Six Hours** (Marcy Saude, 6 mins, Silent, Super 8). **Two Upbuilding Discourses** (John Davis, 14 mins, BetaSP).

* (Total running time: 85 mins plus Q&A, 1999, Color except as noted. From the artists)

On Immutability and Indolence

2011

All my adult life I've been told that I've had it easy and can't relate to or understand people with "real" problems—namely, women, ethnic minorities, and The Gays—on account of the fact that I'm a straight white guy. It's a pretty common thing for most American straight white guys to encounter in the current era, I suspect. And, to an extent, it stands to reason, in the broad context of history.

In the American public education system, starting in around middle school, one begins learning about the dark procession of humanity's pockmarked past, and how different groups of people have grievously mistreated each other across time. One is taught about disquieting things like the colonization and uninvited settling of much of the world by white Europeans; how the Spanish conquistadors brutalized indigenous Central and South Americans; how Anglo-American settlers took possession of North America by foisting pox-riddled blankets on the Native Americans, breaching treaties, or by simply engaging in outright warfare under the aegis of "manifest destiny." Then, at some point, one learns about shocking stuff like the inhuman barbarism of the transatlantic slave trade, the Middle Passage, postbellum lynching, Jim Crow laws, redlining, and other egregious moral transgressions of American slavery and its racist aftermath. And one discovers the history of American eugenics and the internment of Japanese Americans during the Second World War. One also invariably studies the Holocaust as the ghastly apotheosis of insane "Aryan" European ethnocentrism in the twentieth century. One further learns at some point about the concepts of "patriarchy" and "rape culture," and the history of women's social and legal subjugation in the Western world until surprisingly recently. And one can't help but become aware of homosexuality's not-so-distant-in-time criminalization, formal classification as a mental illness, and all-around socially acceptable shunning until the (very recent) current historical moment.

The takeaway from this suite of sociohistorical lessons, often (whether implied or overt), is that all the sundry woes of the world rest at the feet of The Straight White Man. At least it can seem that way. It's a heavy scene for a straight white boy to grok as an adolescent and teenager, coming up in a society that aspires to the overarching ideals of equality and fairness for all; a sort of inherited secular "original sin" that one must grapple with, in one way or another, as part of the process of maturation.

I tend to think that most straight white guys respond to this deluge of less-than-flattering historical facts about their racial-gender cohort in a pretty limited and predictable set of ways. Some of them become spineless, meek, apologetic, self-flagellating "soy boys" who can't bend over backwards quickly enough to deracinate themselves from supposedly pestilential "whiteness" and to denounce the noxiousness of maleness in tandem. They loudly go vegetarian, wring their hands about global warming, aspire to drive an electric car, dutifully disaggregate their recyclables, and wear genuflecting t-shirts emblazoned with the slogan "THIS IS WHAT A FEMINIST LOOKS LIKE" (proverbially, if not literally). Other straight white guys, conversely, reject with insufferable bloviating stridency any insinuation whatsoever of guilt-by-association that may be imputed to them on account of their race and gender. They adopt an unapologetically brash and dismissive attitude towards "political correctness" in the vein of chauvinistic TV buffoons like Archie Bunker and Al Bundy, or Andrew Dice Clay's "The Dice Man" character; deriding and mocking as schoolmarmish any suggestion that they modulate their language and not use the so-called "n-word" or refrain from calling things "gay." If I'm honest, I went through a version of both variants of this, over time, in the process of growing up and sorting out my place in the world. As a teenager I was a self-effacing "PC" apologist. As a young adult I was an indifferent, if not intentionally obnoxious, consciously *un*-PC asshole.

Nowadays I just find the topic tedious and worn out. History is long, and dark, and mostly awful, *everywhere* across the globe – but it's also in the past. We live in the twenty-first century. It ought to go without saying in the here and now that immutable characteristics shouldn't be much of a basis for making predetermined assumptions about a person based on generalizations. It should also go without saying in the modern world that holding an individual somehow vicariously responsible for the misdeeds of others in the past who happen to share some of the individual's immutable inherited characteristics is, well, just silly. The problems faced by humans in the modern world necessitate a frequent reframing of various issues in society, and that should include an assessment of the relative advantages and disadvantages in the *current* moment, not just the past ... right?

Do straight white men still "hold all the cards" in the West nowadays? Maybe. Maybe not. Maybe it depends on the context. Given that "the leader of the free world" is currently a black guy; that single women are starting to out-earn their male counterparts in the West; and that gay marriage is becoming increasingly recognized by both society and the law ... one would think that *some* progress has been made on these fronts, and things are going in the right direction ... no? That we can perhaps move past old-fashioned overemphasis on immutable, unchosen things like "race" and gender, and start looking at people as individuals?

Apparently not. Increasingly, I seem to encounter the argument—especially online from so-called "social justice" activists—that the opinions of "straight white males" ought to be dismissed out of hand because of the "privilege" that they are alleged to uniformly enjoy; with reference to the unpleasantness of history, stereotypes, and statistics, rather than individual circumstances or current sociocultural and economic trends. It's an oafish *ad hominem* line of reasoning—a logical fallacy—but a nonetheless increasingly common one.

I've always found this type of argument both tenuous and pernicious; that, as a straight white dude, one should defer to others on most sociocultural issues, simply because of who one *is*. It seems like a myopically narrow and stupid lens through which to view the entirety of the human experience. I've also had difficulty in dealing with it on a personal level. Being dismissed and told to "shut up and listen" on account of the assumption that I've had a life of ease is condescending at the very least. Not to mention insulting, rude, and half-assed. It's also of dubious accuracy.

When I was a kid, I was in a fairly serious accident – at age nine, while riding my bike across a street, prepubescent me was run down by a car driven by a lady who wasn't paying close enough attention to the road. From what I'm told, I did a face-plant into my bike's handlebars, the hood of the lady's car, and/or the asphalt-paved street. As a result, my jaw was broken in three places, I lost my four upper front permanent teeth, and some of the bone under my nose went bye-bye. I also broke my pelvis, a leg, and an arm. I then spent what felt like a decent chunk of my late childhood bedridden with my jaw wired shut and two of my limbs in casts; "eating" a liquid diet through wired-up chompers, pissing through a catheter tube, and shitting into a bedpan. For a while I literally couldn't even wipe my own ass – so it wasn't exactly a "fun" period in my life. This was followed by some time in a wheelchair, then crutches, physical therapy rehabilitation, and decades of wearing pearly white dentures with fabricated pink plastic gums affixed to them. Some of this immiserating experience I was unconscious for; some of it I was supposedly conscious for, and yet can't remember; and some of it I unfortunately do indeed indelibly recall.

What I can call to memory about my late childhood is not exactly pleasant – and it's a little hard to square with the idea that I couldn't *possibly* have *any* fucking insight *whatsoever* into the "real" problems that ostensibly marginalized and disenfranchised people struggle with, simply owing to the happenstance of my race and gender. So, I'm sort of dumbfounded by the increasingly prevalent across-the-board argument that I should "shut up and listen," because I'm "privileged" ... since women didn't have the right to vote until 1920, or because of the inequities of redlining, or on account of some unconscionable thing that some dead white guy did before I was born (or whatever other dumb *non sequitur* argument is being made). It would seem to me that if your argument is that someone who had their mouth smashed in couldn't possibly fathom the unpleasantness of being cat-called or had a racial epithet directed at them, then you don't know what unpleasantness is in the first place.

I realize that merely mentioning this aspect of my own personal backstory will be regarded by some readers as "whining" – and that's fine. I need no sympathy, empathy, or understanding on the topic from anyone. My raising of the subject in the first place could also be regarded as its own flavor of logical fallacy – the "argument from authority" (You think *you've* had it bad? Nah, let me tell you about how *I've* had it bad!). I make no such claim. But I do think it serves as an example, if only anecdotally, of how half-assed and indurate people tend to be when making hasty generalizations about others based on immutable characteristics, and using such in a lazy attempt to invalidate other people's opinions.

Life sucks. Everyone has a shitty sob-story. Everyone. Out in the world, dealing with people, one often doesn't know what the backdrop of their life is. The absentminded Starbucks Barista who botched one's drink order may have been finger-fucked by her uncle for years before he was hauled off to prison and she started therapy. The impatient co-worker one has to put up with may spend every miserable night wiping his invalid Alzheimer's-stricken mother's gloppy ass and changing her drool-cup. The bitchy old lady sitting next to one on the bus may have watched her sister get hit by a truck and bleed-out on the blacktop. The stunning hot chick at the bar who seems cold and aloof may have had a psychotic stalker ex-boyfriend who destroyed her car and threatened to kill her at knifepoint. The goody-two-shoes Mormon missionary irritatingly seeking to convert one at the doorstep may have been raised by abusive junkies prior to running away from home as a preteen. The rulebound Meter Maid, disinterestedly handing out parking tickets, may have had a child who recently died of sudden infant death syndrome. The dudebro driving like an impatient dick may have just gotten back from an overseas deployment during which he witnessed his best friend's head get blown clean off by an IED, and is late for post-traumatic stress disorder treatment. Who fuckin' knows? There are near-infinite possibilities for the fucked-up suffering scenarios that weave the tragicomic tapestry that is human life. Life sucks. Everyone has a shitty sob-story. The fact that someone may happen to be a member of some group that had some historic (or even current) advantage, does not *per se* mean that their life is all buttercups and dandelions; and the fact that your sob-story, or your ancestors' sob-story happens to be in line with acceptable public opinion at the moment doesn't *per se* invalidate other people's opinions on account of something about them that they have no control over.

Treating people as an undifferentiated mass of uniform groupthink drones who've all had the same backstory, merely on account of their immutable characteristics, is stupid and half-assed. It's lazy, and it's invariably inaccurate most of the time. It assumes, for example, that Danny DeVito has had a cushier life than Halle Berry, merely because he's a white boy and she's a black girl. Maybe that's true? Maybe it's not? I don't know, and neither do you. DeVito and Berry are idiosyncratic individuals, and it's silly to assume much about them merely based on a couple of immutable characteristics about each of them. That's the point.

If you're going to make an argument about something, just make the fucking argument on its merits – don't resort to dismissing those who disagree with you based on their immutable characteristics, or some shitty thing that happened before either of you were even fucking born. If, instead of defending your argument on its merits, you have to call-out the immutable characteristics of the person arguing against it as a means of invalidating their opinion, then your argument has failed. Further, if you have to rely on broad, facile, notions of "privilege"—and hew to them even when the person you're accusing of being "privileged" grew up with some individualized disadvantage (poverty, abuse, physical faults, *et cetera*)—then the concept of "privilege" is unfalsifiable and you aren't making an argument, you're stating a position on faith. Worse, if you're incapable of assaying that individual person's circumstances, and can only see them as a member of a group—regardless of the group—then you're a lazy, prejudiced asshole. In other words, a bigot. And nobody likes a bigot, so stop it already, dummy.

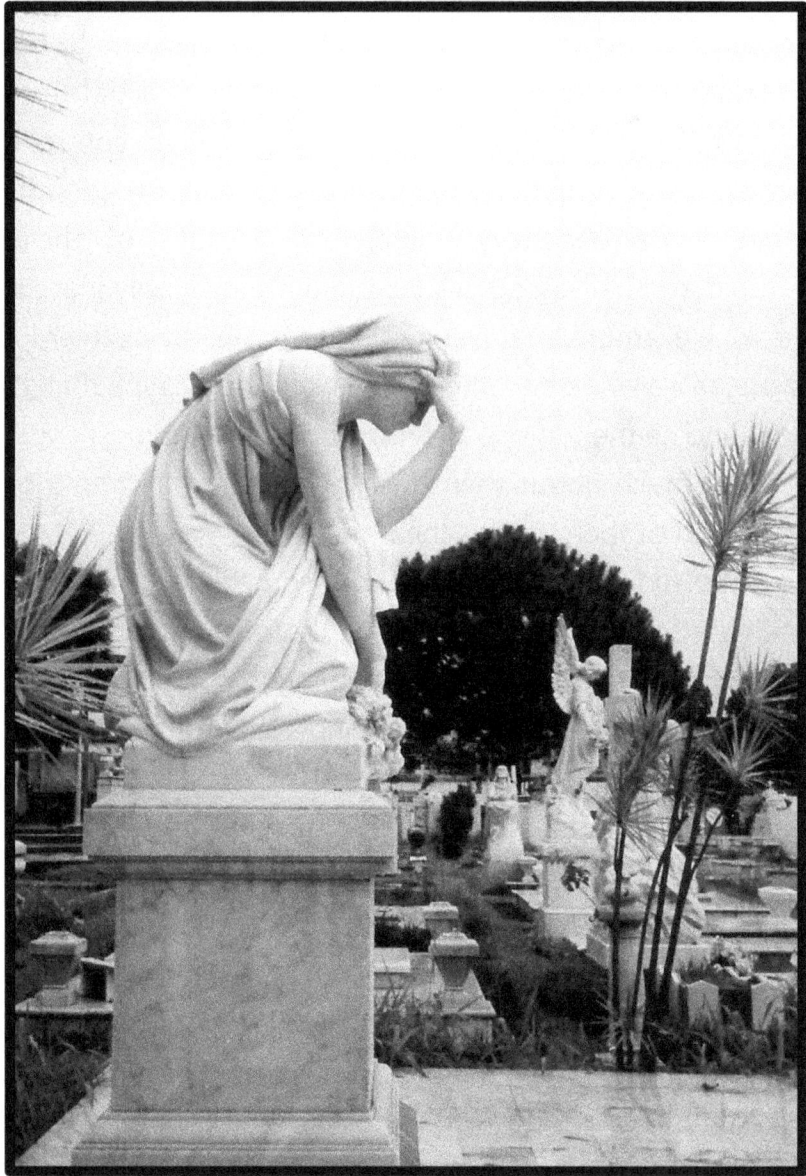

King Con – Scamming Free Drinks as An Art Form

An Interview with Brian Brushwood

2009

Brian Brushwood is an American magician, podcaster, author, lecturer, YouTuber, and comedian who practices a trade that could perhaps best be described as "benevolent deception." As the writer and host of the show *Scam Nation* (previously *Scam School*), Brushwood roams the United States using clever bar tricks to score free drinks. Each episode of *Scam Nation* ("the only show dedicated to social engineering at the bar and on the street") involves the gregarious Brushwood convincing a group of unwitting bar patrons to agree to a seemingly straightforward challenge – the outcome of which invariably results in the participants being duped (usually by their own assumptions and expectations) and begrudgingly buying Brushwood a beer. Brushwood's prestidigitation is all in good fun, however, as at the end of each *Scam Nation* episode, he reveals to the conned drinkers just how he managed to deceive them, and how they too—as well as the show's audience—can make use of these same facile tricks to score free drinks.

Apart from *Scam Nation*, Brushwood performs his "Bizarre Magic" stage show across the United States, co-hosts the podcasts *Weird Things*, *Cordkillers*, and *Great Night*, and has appeared on mainstream network television numerous times. Brushwood is the author of six books, including *The Professional's Guide to Fire Eating* and *Cheats, Cons, Swindles, and Tricks: 57 Ways to Scam a Free Drink*. Brushwood was interviewed via email for *Modern Drunkard*.

<u>Brian M. Clark</u>: Where did the concept for *Scam School* come from, and how did you manage to convince a production company to get behind the idea of a show about using simple tricks to weasel free rounds at bars?

<u>Brian Brushwood</u>: I noticed that bar tricks were extremely popular on YouTube, with views well into the millions, yet the quality of both the tricks and production seemed pretty awful to me. Those revealing the tricks often wouldn't even speak or show their faces, so I figured that some well-produced tutorials, shot out on location and hosted by someone with personality might be a success. Originally, I was going to shoot and produce them myself, but at the last minute thought maybe someone would actually pay for this kind of thing. After

shopping it to a few online networks, Revision3 bit first.

BMC: In all the episodes I've seen online, bar-goers seem to be pretty good sports about being deceived; even when you've managed to get them slamming their skulls on tables to knock imaginary quarters off their foreheads. Has anyone ever reacted poorly to one of your scams? Any drunken louts swinging fists or anything like that?

BB: Not yet, but that's part of the challenge: picking your targets wisely.

BMC: Have you caught any flak for teaching drinkers how to break out of handcuffs and slip out of zip ties? Or for likewise bypassing various types of locks? Those seem like invaluable skills, to be sure, but I could see The Man frowning upon your passing on of such tricks to legions of drinkers.

BB: Strangely, I found out that some of NYPD's finest are fans of the show! When we did the "break out of handcuffs" episode, I knew the folks over in the cyber-crimes division would be watching. Fortunately, they seemed to only be mildly annoyed.

BMC: Which *Scam School* trick is your favorite, and why?

BB: Tough question, but I think I'm most proud of the "Mind Control Scam" from Episode 28 — mainly because it was a totally original idea of mine that nobody understood when I tried to explain it. It was only after a full week of tedious filming, editing, post-production, and uploading 104 videos, that the trick actually worked. It's now become my favorite stunt to pull on people.

BMC: What percentage of the *Scam School* tricks are your own creations, and what percentage are variations on older tricks that newer generations of drinkers just aren't generally aware of yet?

BB: The "Mind Control Scam" is 100% original, but some of the other bits are based on concepts that are hundreds of years old. For those, my job is to try to find new, relevant presentations that would actually play at the bar. Other scams are actual street hustles still being used by criminals to this day.

BMC: A lot of people are very critical of alcohol for an assortment of reasons, but—their various grievances aside—I see a lot of positives to be found in bar culture. Do you think that part of the reason your show works so well has to do with the kind of amenable social environment that only bars can provide? Do you think that people would likely be more or less receptive in a different context?

BB: That's an interesting question. I'm certain that the human element we get from shooting in the bars is a big part of what has made *Scam School* successful: we grab real people, perform the tricks for/on them and get honest reactions. The response is usually positive and fun to watch, but there have been a couple of train wrecks, tricks I thought were home runs, but when we tried to shoot them at the bar, discovered that they just wouldn't work in real life.

BMC: I understand that, aside from bars, you also do a lot of shows at colleges. Do you find that the university-educated folks are generally more, or less, susceptible to falling for simple, real-world dissimulation than Average Joe bar-goers?

BB: Depends on the student, but as a group, you have a lot of confident young adults who really feel like they're smart (or getting there) and that's pretty much the perfect situation for someone looking to scam a few free drinks at the bar. As long as you keep them entertained, college students will keep hooking you up with free booze all night long.

BMC: It seems like a lot of the effectiveness of magic tricks is hinged on exploiting the flaws in people's perception, and their expectations and assumptions about the world. Since alcohol alters perception (and often enough, expectations and assumptions related to one's own abilities), does that change the equation for a magician? In other words, is it easier to

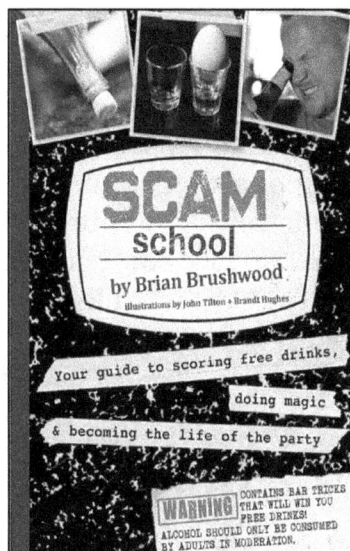

deceive drunks because they're distracted and thus aren't really paying attention to all the details of what you're doing; or is it easier to deceive sober people because they're actively trying to pay attention to all the details, and thus are convinced that they can't be fooled?

BB: The latter is absolutely true for the first two to three drinks; then the alcohol loosens people up, makes them more willing to take risks, and generally more interested in participating in a new experience (the impaired judgment doesn't hurt, either). But once someone's had too much to drink, they become unable to focus and prone to interrupting your performance or trying to flat-out ruin your work. Once they cross over that line, it's usually time to turn your crowd against them with gags like "The Funnel" or "Quarter On Forehead."

BMC: Like a number of magicians (James Randi, Penn & Teller, Banacheck, *et al.*), you're sort of tangentially involved with the modern Skeptical Movement. The correlations between the deception underlying magic and the applied critical

297

thinking of skepticism are pretty direct and obvious – but what about the correlations between inebriation and critical thinking? What I mean by that is; do you see any value in drinking as a means of sharpening one's critical thinking skills and thereby generally avoiding self-deception while sober?

BB: I went to James Randi's annual skepticism convention "The Amazing Meeting" last summer and discovered an entire culture of skeptics who promote meeting at bars and "drinking skeptically." I thought it was a great way to combat the skeptic's image of being a stick-in-the-mud and make critical thinking a fun, social experience. They even have a website up to find local groups. [9]

BMC: Any thoughts on why the vast majority of regional skeptical meet-up groups congregate as Skeptics In The Pub, rather than Skeptics In The Café?

BB: Maybe it's because pubs are traditionally the home of good-natured arguments? Sometimes it takes a drink or two for people to get the courage to honestly speak their minds.

BMC: Tell us a bit about your book, *Cheats, Cons, Swindles, and Tricks: 57 Ways to Scam a Free Drink*. What inspired you to write it, how does it differ from the *Scam School* show, and what is the impetus behind your overarching compulsion to never pay for your own goddamned drinks?

BB: *Cheats, Cons, Swindles, and Tricks* was the original basis for *Scam School*, and as of now, I think a little more than half of the tricks in the book have been made into *Scam School* episodes. Originally, I just wrote the book so I could look like an expert at something (collecting my favorite bar tricks into a short book wasn't exactly rocket science), but I've been really surprised and thrilled by the response it's gotten. To this day, I'll still send out a free copy to anyone who asks for one, as long as they'll cover shipping. As for my insistence on not paying for my own drinks: come on, it's the principle of the thing! It's the thrill of the hunt, a little real-life drama to see if I can really trick someone into hooking me up for free. It's a helluva fun game to play.

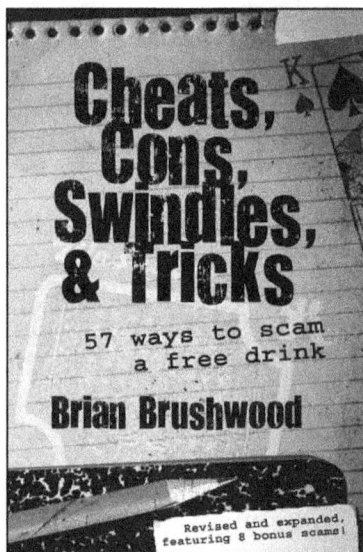

Cheats, Cons, Swindles, & Tricks
57 ways to scam a free drink
Brian Brushwood
Revised and expanded, featuring 8 bonus scams!

---

[9] *See, e.g.,* SkepticsInThePub.org and meetup.com/topics/drinking-skeptically/.

Ugly American Pig

2010

When I lived in Spain, 'round about a decade ago, I shared a flat in Madrid with a bunch of other foreigners, one of whom was a German guy named Mikhail who categorically disliked Americans. His Grandfather had been a wealthy druggist who lost everything when the U.S. bombed Dresden at the end of the Second World War, and Mikhail was somehow still bitter about it in 2001. He was an engineering student who played the violin, had the perfect physique of an Adonis ... and *zero* sense of humor whatsoever, at least that I could discern. Mikhail was always sort of aloof and dismissive toward me and one of my American flatmate friends, for no other reason than that we were Yanks living in Europe. We gave him the nickname "Sieg Heil Mikhail" when he wasn't around.

I tried to keep things copacetic with Mikhail initially, but soon gave up—since he treated me like an uncouth boor for no reason—and so I resolved to just have fun with him disliking me. Ergo, when he was around, I occasionally went out of my way to annoy or disgust him by acting like as much of an unrefined "ugly American abroad" as possible. When he and I were both in the kitchen, I'd leave the kitchen faucet running ... and running ... and running, and I'd throw away perfectly good food and try to produce as much needless waste as possible (all sacrilege to the *über* eco-conscious Germans, I presumed). I once cooked up an entire box of spaghetti (enough to last one person, say, a week) and dumped it all in a large glass mixing bowl with marinara sauce, and then plopped myself down in front of the flat's television set, watching whatever happened to be on in English (with Spanish subtitles), eating spaghetti directly from this comically oversized bowl, getting marinara sauce on my face, and guffawing oafishly at the TV with my mouth full. Mikhail was predictably repulsed. I also recall a conversation with him in which I stated that I'd never been to Germany and had no desire to visit because I had no interest in seeing "Eastern Europe" – which really seemed to irk him.

Most importantly, I occasionally found ways to somehow bring up the subject of The Holocaust when Mikhail was around, *apropos* of nothing. That really got under his skin. Like, the flatmates from various countries would all be in the living room talking about some innocuous thing like shoes or whatever, and I'd find some weird way to drag in The Holocaust. "Ah, so, speaking of shoes, did you guys know that they collected all the shoes from the Jews at Auschwitz before gassing them? It's true. There's photos of the big piles of Jew-shoes. Terrible. Just terrible." God, how Mikhail disliked me. Good times.

Americans are horrible, odious vulgarians. They really are.

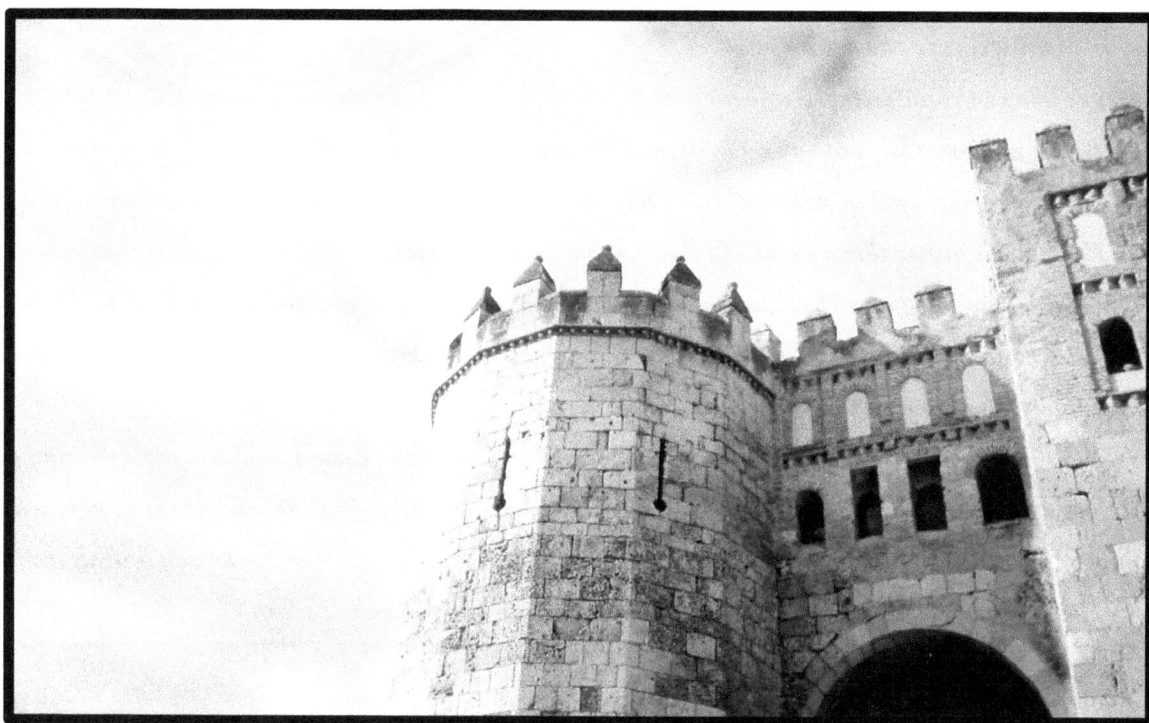

The Denver Gentlemen's Pipe Smoking League was a political activist group founded in 2006 by Frank Kelly Rich and Brian M. Clark for the purpose of combating Colorado's then-pending law to ban indoor smoking. Stupidly, the proposed legislation was crafted to prohibit smoking in indoor areas throughout the state – including in bars. As inveterate bar-smokers, Rich and Clark stridently opposed the ban and formed The League in an effort to thwart its passage.

In addition to clandestinely wheat-pasting agitprop pro-smoking posters on disused billboards and abandoned buildings throughout Denver, the League routinely engaged in political consciousness raising by donning suits and felted beaver fur top hats, then going barhopping throughout the Denver metro area, smoking tobacco pipes inside various drinking establishments. Given the League's members' propensity for getting riotously drunk and playing classical music on bars' early digital jukeboxes, the League tended to be met with a mix of bemusement, irritation, and hostility from both bar proprietors and patrons alike.

There is no evidence that The Denver Gentlemen's Pipe Smoking League's pro-smoking efforts had any effect whatsoever on the Colorado legislature's consideration of its idiotic smoking ban, which was unfortunately passed into law by The Colorado General Assembly as "The Colorado Clean Indoor Air Act of 2006," and remains in force throughout the state of Colorado today.

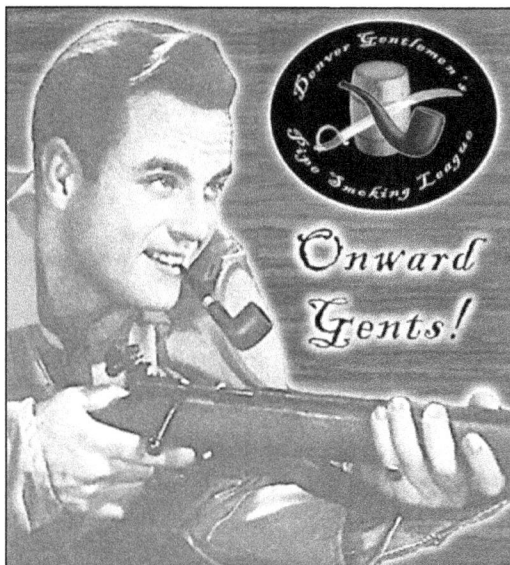

Onward Gents!

Damn straight!

Kill With Kindness

Psychopathy, "Niceness," and The Perils of Arrogance

2012

There's this quotation that I keep seeing online of late, attributed to the rapper Eminem. It goes, "I don't care if you're black, white, straight, bisexual, gay, lesbian, short, tall, fat, skinny, rich or poor. If you're nice to me, I'll be nice to you. Simple as that!" I guess it's supposed to be an "inclusive" credo and feel-good platitude about the importance of civility, kindness, and being "nice," as better indicators of character than immutable characteristics like race, sexuality, body type, or socioeconomic status. This notion is, of course, so self-evidently obvious and well-subscribed nowadays that pointing it out as a laudable ethos is banal. *Of course* one should prioritize civility and basic common decency in others over superficialities like skin pigmentation or social class. *Duh.* Why people seem to feel the need to share and reshare this trite observation online as though it's quote-worthy is beyond me. But the recent online prevalence of this shopworn sentiment raises other issues that I do think bear mulling over.

Civility and a patina of "niceness" are social lubricants routinely used by exploitative psychopaths to take advantage of naïve, trusting people who accept the world at face value. À *la* the character Eddie Haskell from the bygone TV show *Leave It to Beaver*, insincere, mendacious psychopaths can be the most convincingly charming, funny, respectful, entertaining, and "nice" people that one can come across out in the day-to-day social world. Of course, while they're being so "nice" to everyone—exemplifying good manners, genially dishing out compliments, smiling solicitously at every old lady, and making young girls giggle—they might also be draining your bank account; or clandestinely raping your kids. But dang, they sure are nice! Maybe assigning weight to easy superficial displays of amity as a gauge of character isn't actually the best idea in the real world? ...

The flipside to this, perhaps obviously, is that assholes tend to often be trustworthy, but widely disliked and deprecated. Churlish, arrogant, condescending, patronizing, snide contrarian jerks may indeed be *jerks*; but they probably aren't smarmy duplicitous manipulators trying to con or deceive you, at least. Noting that isn't to say that civility ought to be ditched in favor of supercilious rudeness, but it's something to keep in mind when extolling the virtues of mere surface "niceness." It's a nuanced issue.

When I was in my mid-twenties, I had a weirdly solipsistic way of looking at the world and how I should interact with others in it. My own idiosyncratic worldview, I guess. I had been particularly damaged, psychologically, by infidelity in my early twenties on account of what I believed (correctly or incorrectly) was me being too much of an all-around "nice" guy. It was the deception and dishonesty that bothered me, profoundly; and a staunch aversion to such became sort of a lodestar for me afterwards. And so, I refined an odd overcompensatory philosophy roughly akin to "radical honesty," that prioritized inelegantly direct, callous, and occasionally scathing bluntness. In enacting this worldview, I put a lot of import on integrity, trustworthiness, and fairness, to the exclusion of ... well ... almost everything else – including civility and "niceness." At times, I even went out of my way to make a bad first impression on others; on the odd theory that if someone didn't like me, I wanted to preemptively see how they acted on that dislike sooner rather than later. As a result, I was, in retrospect, a fairly obnoxious and probably irritating person in my mid-twenties. I wore suits to Punk Rock shows, smoked cigars, inveterately drank too much too often, blithely dismissed people's serious concerns and hangups with levity, and routinely said and did things that predictably provoked offense and upset in others. A touch pathological, perhaps, but "fun" nonetheless.

At the time, this made sense to me and seemed eminently logical, in that I felt that I lived by a personal code of ethics that was focused on concrete deeds over intangible things like "feelings" and subjective "morality." I never ripped anyone off, always paid back any money I owed anyone, I never cheated on anyone I dated, and so on. I felt, at the time, that this sort of upstanding "ethical integrity in deeds" (or whatever) somehow gave me license to be a rude jerk. And I was. I was stridently self-righteous about being an asshole. And a lot of people disliked me. Some regarded me with outright enmity. And I was pleased by that.

In retrospect, having had to subsequently deal with some often very disagreeable ramifications of a half-dozen or so years of living out that philosophy, there's a quotation from (of all people) Maya Angelou, that rings particularly true to me nowadays – "People will forget what you said, people will forget what you did, but people will never forget how you made them feel."[10] It's true. It's a sentiment that is perhaps worth holding in mind concurrently alongside the disconcerting fact that some percentage of the "nice" and superficially conscientious people out there in the world are actually predatory psychopaths who use civility, superficial pleasantness, and charisma to prey on unsuspecting others. There's a median "sweet spot" to be found in the gulf between these two antipodes somewhere, someday, I presume; but for now, I'll probably still tend to err on the side of being an asshole.

---

[10] The common online attribution of this quotation to Maya Angelou is apocryphal and may be incorrect. A similar quotation ("They may forget what you said – but they will never forget how you made them feel.") is attributed to Carl W. Buehner in the 1971 collection, *Richard Evans' Quote Book.*

Brian M. Clark's Spicy-as-Fuck Vegan (or Vegetarian) Bean Dip

Ingredients:

2 – 16-ounce cans Vegetarian Refried Beans

1 – 16-ounce can Black Beans

1 – 16-ounce can Pinto Beans

1 – 7-ounce can Diced Jalapeño Peppers

1 – 7-ounce can Chipotle Peppers in Adobo Sauce

1 – Large White or Yellow Onion

1 – Large Tomato

1 – Red Bell Pepper

1 – Green Bell Pepper

1 – Yellow Bell Pepper

1 – Orange Bell Pepper

1 – Tablespoon Garlic Powder

1 – Tablespoon Cayenne Pepper

1 – Tablespoon Black Pepper

2 – Tablespoons Olive Oil

1 – 16-ounce bag Shredded Mexican Cheese (optional)

Required Equipment:

- Medium Stovetop Pot with lid
- Slow Cooker (or Large Stovetop Pot with lid)
- Cutting Board
- Strainer
- Kitchen Knife
- Kitchen Scissors
- Large Kitchen Spoon

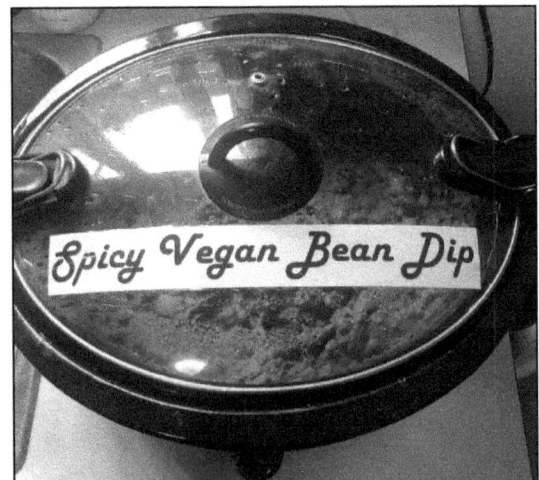

Process:

1. Preheat the slow cooker on "high" until fully heated. Drain the black beans and pinto beans over the sink. Add the strained beans and refried beans to the slow cooker, mix thoroughly, and cover.

2. On the stovetop, heat the olive oil in a medium stovetop pot on "medium" heat. Dice the onion and add to the heated olive oil in the medium pot. While the onion is caramelizing, wash and dice the tomato and bell peppers.

3. Strain the chipotle peppers in adobo sauce over the slow cooker so that the adobo sauce drains into the warming beans. In the strainer, cut the tops off of the chipotle peppers with kitchen scissors and dispose, then cut up the chipotle peppers into small pieces with the kitchen scissors.

4. Add the diced tomato, bell peppers, jalapeño peppers, and the cut chipotle peppers to the medium pot, then stir the mix. Partially cover the medium pot so that water vapor can escape, then let the mix of diced vegetables and peppers simmer on "medium" heat for around thirty minutes, stirring intermittently (the idea is to cook off the water in the tomato and peppers without burning them, so avoid "high" heat and remember to stir every few minutes).

5. Add the garlic powder, cayenne pepper, and black pepper to the beans in the slow cooker, then stir thoroughly. If desired, shredded cheese can be added to the slow cooker at this point (although that makes the dish vegetarian rather than vegan). Cover the slow cooker and allow the beans, adobo sauce, and spices to heat (and the cheese to melt), stirring occasionally.

6. Once the diced vegetable and peppers mix is cooked to the point that it is mushy and most of the water has evaporated, add the cooked mix to the slow cooker, then stir everything thoroughly. Let the mixture sit in the slow cooker on "low" or "warm" until ready to serve.

Yum!

Brian M. Clark's Highbrow-as-Fuck Cocktail Recipes

The following highfalutin libations were concocted by the author on the job, while working as a bartender at a literary-themed, ersatz "craft" cocktail bar in Los Angeles, California.

Heart of Darkness

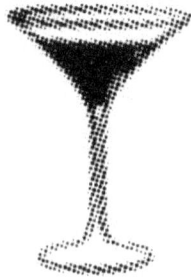

Served:

Martini glass, chilled.

Ingredients:

2 oz. Black rum
1 oz. Lemon juice
1 oz. Honey mix
 (equal parts honey and water)
2 dashes Angostura bitters
1 splash Soda

Garnish:

Cherry with stem intact.

Process:

Add all ingredients except for the soda to a cocktail shaker, add ice, and shake. After shaking, add the splash of soda, then strain into a chilled cocktail glass with a cherry garnish.

Notes From Underground

Served:

Rocks glass.

Ingredients:

1 oz. Dark rum
1 oz. Coffee liqueur
0.2 oz. Lemon juice
2 oz. Honey mix
 (equal parts honey and water)

Garnish:

Lime wheel.

Process:

Add all ingredients to a cocktail shaker, add ice, and shake. Strain into a chilled rocks glass with a lime wheel garnish.

— Original Publication Information —

An abridged version of "El Museo de Cera" was originally published as "The World's Most Bizarre Wax Museum" in *International Living*, Volume 23, Number 5, September 2003. Edited by Laura Sheridan. Waterford, Ireland.

"Todo El Mundo Es Un Crítico" was originally published in *Extremaduro*, Issue 3, 2004. Translated and edited by Luis Sánchez de Ybargüen. Madrid, Spain.

An abridged version of "Boozing With the Band" was originally published in *Modern Drunkard Magazine*, Volume 5, Number 8, March/April 2006. Edited by Frank Kelly Rich. Denver, Colorado, United States.

"The March of Man's True Destiny" was originally published by *Occidental Congress*, online at OccidentalCongress.com, 2006. Edited by Max Ribaric. Trieste, Italy.

"True Alcohol Action!" was originally published in *Modern Drunkard Magazine*, Volume 5, Number 10, September/October 2006. Edited by Frank Kelly Rich. Denver, Colorado, United States.

"The Amazing Ralph Gean" was originally published by Discriminate Audio as CD liner notes, 2007. Edited by Brian M. Clark. Denver, Colorado, United States.

"The Argument from Celebrity Authority" was originally published as "Henry Rollins, The Problem Of Argument From Celebrity Authority & Other Stupid-Yet-Common Logical Fallacies" by *Denver Syntax*, online at DenverSyntax.com, 2009. Edited by Jonathan Bitz. Denver, Colorado, United States.

"Fuck You and Your Stupid, *Stupid* Cat" was originally published by *Unpop Art*, online at UnpopArt.org, 2009. Edited by Brian M. Clark. Long Beach, California, United States.

An abridged version of "Why I Drink" was originally published in *Modern Drunkard Magazine*, Volume 6, Number 6, Issue Number 56, 2011. Edited by Frank Kelly Rich. Denver, Colorado, United States.

"King Con" was originally published in *Modern Drunkard Magazine*, Volume 6, Number 6, Issue Number 56, 2011. Edited by Frank Kelly Rich.

All other texts published herein were either originally self-published online as social media posts, blog posts, or standalone essays on BrianMclark.com, or are previously unpublished and appear here for the first time in print.

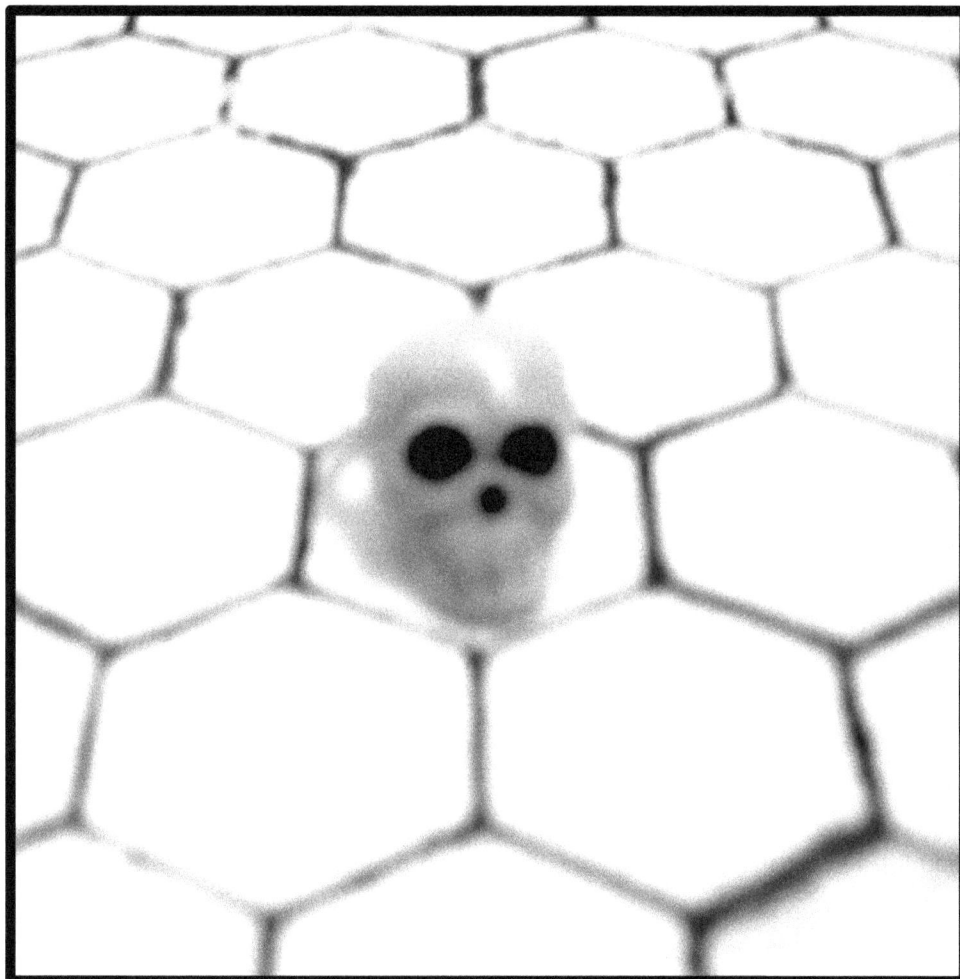

— Image Credits —

Pg. *i*. Office Complex. Dublin, California, USA, 1998. Photograph by Brian Clark.

Pg. 1. Metro Station. Madrid, Spain, 2001. Photograph by Brian Clark.

Pg. 2. Niki Smith and Brian Clark. Eugene, Oregon, USA, 1996. Photograph by Joe Bunik.

Pg. 3. Brian Clark. Hollywood, California, USA, 2009. Photograph by Christopher "Coop" Cooper.

Pg. 4. Brian Clark. Compton, California, USA, 2009.

Pg. 5. Prohibitionist Poster, c. 1918.

Pg. 6. New York City Deputy Police pour liquor into the sewer following a raid, c. 1920.

Pg. 7. Logo of the American Prohibition Party, ProhibitionParty.org.

Pg. 8. Women's Christian Temperance Union, Seattle Headquarters. Seattle, Washington, USA, 1914.

Pg. 10. Brian Clark. Long Beach, California, USA, 2009. Photograph by Shanti Williams.

Pg. 12. Tube Station. London, England, 1999. Photograph by Brian Clark.

Pg. 14. All-Seeing Hedge. Los Feliz, California, USA, 2013. Photograph by Brian Clark.

Pg. 15. Carlo Gambino, New York, New York, USA, 1930s. Photograph by The New York City Police Department.

Pg. 15. The Twin Towers Burning. New York, New York, USA, 2001. Photograph by Robert Levine.

Pg. 17. Battle of Dorylaeum, c. 1330–1340. Unknown, Guillaume de Tyr.

Pg. 17. Hail Satan, Dude. Walnut Creek, California, USA, 1993. Photograph by Brian Clark.

Pg. 18. Hippies. San Diego, California, 2007. Photograph by Jaycee Scragz

Pg. 18. Teenage Fans of Heavy Metal, 2006. Photograph by Jerzy Durczak.

Pg. 19. Breakfast. Denver, Colorado, USA, 2021. Photograph by Brian Clark.

Pg. 20. Adam Parfrey. Early 1990s. Photograph by Scott Lindgren.

Pg. 21. Books edited and/or published by Adam Parfrey. Feral House, 1990s–2000s.

Pg. 22. Jason Robards Jr., 1956. Photograph by Ben Schiff.

Pg. 22. Aldo Ray, 1955. Photograph by Edward Cronenweth.

Pg. 23. Henry Ford's. Portland, Oregon, USA, early 2000s. Photograph by i.heart.living.in.portland.oregon.

Pg. 24. Pipes. Denver, Colorado, USA, 2005. Photograph by Brian Clark.

Pg. 26. Truck. Saratoga, Wyoming, USA, 2018. Photograph by Brian Clark.

Pg. 27. Monkey Mania Flier. Denver, Colorado, USA, early 2000s. Illustrated by Josh Taylor.

Pgs. 27–39. Photographs of Ralph Gean. Texas, Utah, and Colorado, USA, 1950s-2000s. Courtesy of Ralph Gean.

Pg. 40. Fog Over the Westside. Hollywood Hills, California, USA, 2013. Photograph by Brian Clark.

Pg. 42. Ticas. Playa Junquillal, Guanacaste, Costa Rica, 2000. Photograph by Brian Clark.

Pg. 43. Hotel Iguanazul logo, 2000. Designed by Brian Clark.

Pg. 43. *Hotel Impossible* program webpage screenshot, 2013. TravelChannel.com (archived).

Pg. 44. Hotel Iguanazul. Playa Junquillal, Guanacaste, Costa Rica, 2000. Photographs by Brian Clark.

Pg. 45. Condemned Hotel. Silver Lake, California, USA, 2013. Photograph by Brian Clark.

Pg. 47. Edificio Metrópolis. Madrid, Spain, 2001. Photograph by Brian Clark.

Pg. 48. Passport Photograph, 1999.

Pg. 50. Faustine. Saint-Jean-de-Luz, Pyrénées-Atlantiques, France, 2001. Photograph by Brian Clark.

Pg. 52. El Templo de Debod. Madrid, Spain, 2001.

Pg. 52. Brian Clark. Madrid, Spain, 2002. Photograph by John K.

Pg. 53. Brian Clark. Madrid, Spain, 2001. Photograph by Elizabeth Gonzales.

Pg. 55. John K. and Brian Clark. Madrid, Spain, 2002. Photograph by E.K.C.

Pg. 57. Brian Clark. Madrid, Spain, 2002. Photograph by E.K.C.

Pg. 59. Malasaña Graffiti. Madrid, Spain, 2001. Photograph by Brian Clark.

Pg. 60. Smug John. Madrid, Spain, 2002. Photograph by Brian Clark.

Pg. 61. The Film Professor. Madrid, Spain, 2002. Photograph by Brian Clark.

Pg. 61. El Rastro. Madrid, Spain, 2018. Photograph by Zarateman.

Pg. 62. Somewhere in Madrid. Madrid, Spain, 2001. Photograph by Brian Clark.

Pg. 63. Plaza Dos de Mayo. Madrid, Spain, 2001. Photograph by Brian Clark.

Pg. 65. Brian Clark. Segovia, Castilla y León, Spain, 2002. Photograph by E.K.C.

Pg. 65. El Alcázar. Segovia, Castilla y León, Spain, 2002. Photograph by Brian Clark.

Pg. 66. Hermine and Brian. Madrid, Spain, 2002. Photograph by E.K.C.

Pg. 66. Toledo street. Toledo, Castilla-La Mancha, Spain, 2002. Photograph by Brian Clark.

Pg. 66. Gates of Toledo. Toledo, Castilla-La Mancha, Spain, 2002. Photograph by E.K.C.

Pg. 67. Museo del Jamón. Madrid, Spain, 2001. Photograph by Brian Clark.

Pg. 68. Palacio de Cibeles. Madrid, Spain, 2001. Photograph by Brian Clark.

Pg. 72. American Forces Network screenshot, c. 2001.

Pg. 73. Brian Clark. Either Lisbon or Porto, Portugal, 2002. Photograph by John K.

Pg. 73. Rabelo Boat. Porto, Portugal, 2002. Photograph by Brian Clark.

Pg. 74. Francesinha. Photograph by Ali Berlinski.

Pg. 74. Castelo de São Jorge. Lisbon, Portugal. Photograph by John K.

Pg. 75. Brian Clark. Sintra, Portugal, 2002. Photograph by John K.

Pg. 75. "Tostada," Luis Sánchez de Ybargüen, and Vicente Pascual de la LLana. Madrid, Spain, 2002. Photograph by Brian Clark.

Pg. 76. Office Work. Compton, California, USA, 2009. Photograph by Brian Clark.

Pg. 98. Lawn Ornament. Silver Lake, California, USA, 2016. Photograph by Brian Clark.

Pg. 100. Fire Pit. Denver, Colorado, USA, 2018. Photograph by Brian Clark.

Pg. 115. Shadow. Madrid, Spain, 2001. Photograph by Brian Clark.

Pg. 117. Concrete Jack-o'-Lantern. Hollywood, California, USA, 2011. Photograph by Brian Clark.

Pg. 121. Crow. Hollywood Hills, California, USA, 2014. Photograph by Brian Clark.

Pg. 122. Faux Hipster, 2017. PxHere.com.

Pg. 123. Die Hipster Website Banner, 2009. DieHipster.com (archived).

Pg. 124. Emos vs. Punks. Azteca Noticias, YouTube screenshot, 2008.

Pg. 124. Stilyagi. Russia, 1950s.

Pg. 125. The Worst Country on Earth. Screenshot, 2009. The Economist.com (archived).

Pg. 126. Children in a Bangladesh Slum. Kallyanpur, Dhaka, Bangladesh, 2010. Photograph by Kibae Park.

Pg. 127. Bunny. Denver, Colorado, USA, 2005. Photograph by Brian Clark.

Pg. 128. Matt Skiba. Germany, 2006. Photograph by Dan Andriano.

Pg. 129. Matt Skiba. Cleveland, Ohio, USA, early 2000s. Photograph by Heather Hannoura.

Pg. 130. Matt Skiba. Tinley Park, Illinois, USA, 2007. Photograph by Eric Mueller.

Pg. 131. Matt Skiba, c. early 2000s.

Pg. 132. The Owl Tree Bar. San Francisco, California, USA, 2010s. Photograph from OwlTreeSF.com.

Pg. 133. Cemetery. Inisheer, Aran Islands, Ireland, 2001. Photograph by Brian Clark.

Pg. 135. Moon Trees. Los Angeles, California, USA, 2014. Photograph by Brian Clark.

Pg. 136. Brian Clark. Los Feliz, California, USA, 2013. Photograph by Howard Karp.

Pg. 137. Hallway. Los Feliz, California, USA, 2010. Photograph by Brian Clark.

Pg. 138. Kid with cat. Concord, California, USA, 1987. Photograph by E.K.C.

Pg. 144. Elanor Abernathy. Illustrated by Tito (ITTOworkshopUS), based on a character created by Matt Groening.

Pg. 148. Adult Male Smallpox Victim. Minnesota Department of Health, c. 1924.

Pg. 149. Dingo. Denver, Colorado, USA, 2019. Photograph by Brian Clark.

Pg. 152. Attic Ape. San Francisco, California, USA, 2003. Photograph by Brian Clark.

Pg. 161. Palm Trees. Long Beach, California, USA, 2009. Photograph by Brian Clark.

Pg. 162. Joe Bunik and Brian Clark. Boston, Massachusetts, USA, 2002. Photograph by E.K.C.

Pg. 162. Shanti Williams and Brian Clark. Denver, Colorado, 2006. Photograph by Lorin Partridge

Pg. 162. Aaron E. Olson and Brian Clark. Long Beach, California, USA, 2009. Photograph by Ranae Griego.

Pg. 163. Jessica Devine and Brian Clark. Saint-Jean-de-Luz, Pyrénées-Atlantiques, France, 2001. Photograph by Faustine.

Pg. 163. Ralph Gean and Brian Clark. Denver, Colorado, USA, 2004. Photograph by Josh Taylor.

Pg. 163. Christa Wiley, Martina Silverman-Hecht, and Brian Clark. Los Angeles, California, USA, 2014.

Pg. 163. Greg Santos and Brian Clark. Los Feliz, California, USA, 2015. Photograph by Alyssa Mann.

Pg. 163. Adam Parfrey and Brian Clark. Denver, Colorado, USA, 2013. Photograph by Robert Ferbrache.

Pg. 164. Jennifer Treza and Brian Clark. Denver, Colorado, USA, 2005. Photograph by E.K.C.

Pg. 164. Gidget Gein and Brian Clark. Hollywood, California, USA, 2007. Photograph by Matt Skiba.

Pg. 164. John K. and Brian Clark. Madrid, Spain, 2002. Photograph by E.K.C.

Pg. 165. Vanessa Leigh and Brian Clark. Denver, Colorado, USA, 2008. Photograph by Zhawna Siegwarth.

Pg. 165. Shaun Partridge and Brian Clark. Portland, Oregon, USA, 2003. Photograph by Kaleidoscope Partridge.

Pg. 165. Sarah Froelich, Erica Silzle, and Brian Clark. Long Beach, California, USA, 2009. Photograph by Aaron Olson.

Pg. 165. Don Pie and Brian Clark. Long Beach, California, USA, 2009. Photograph by Aaron Olson.

Pg. 166. Rosie O'Laskey and Brian Clark. Los Feliz, California, USA, 2011. Photograph by Matt Skiba.

Pg. 166. Frank Kelly Rich, Stanley McHale, and Brian Clark. Las Vegas, Nevada, 2006. Photograph by E.K.C.

Pg. 166. Little Fyodor and Brian Clark. Denver, Colorado, USA, 2008. Photograph by Gregory Daurer.

Pg. 166. Sid Pink and Brian Clark. Denver, Colorado, 2005. Photograph by E.K.C.

Pg. 167. Alyssa Mann and Brian Clark. Los Feliz, California, USA, 2015. Photograph by Amber Maykut.

Pg. 167. Matt Skiba and Brian Clark. Hollywood, California, USA, 2007. Photograph by Gidget Gein.

Pg. 167. Lisa Jones and Brian Clark. Denver, Colorado, USA, 2005. Photograph by Franklin Bell.

Pg. 167. Luis Sánchez de Ybargüen and Brian Clark. Madrid, Spain, 2002. Photograph by John Strege.

Pg. 167. Robert Ferbrache and Brian Clark. Denver, Colorado, USA, 2013. Photograph by Adam Parfrey.

Pg. 168. Meghan McGuinness and Brian Clark. Granada Hills, California, USA, 2016. Photograph by Thomas W. Brown.

Pg. 168. Dennis Lorence and Brian Clark. Hollywood, California, USA, 2008.

Pg. 168. Cara Chenworth and Brian Clark. Los Angeles, California, USA, 2015. Photograph by Magdalena Herrera.

Pg. 168. Jesse Peper and Brian Clark. Denver, Colorado, USA, 2005. Photograph by Andrew Novick.

Pg. 169. Matt Buster and Brian Clark. Concord, California, USA, 2002.

Image Credits

Pg. 169. Amber Maykut, Brian Senegal, and Brian Clark. New York City, New York, USA, 2015.

Pg. 169. Vicente Pascal de la Llana and Brian Clark. Madrid, Spain, 1999. Photograph by Elizabeth Gonzales.

Pg. 170. Gregory Daurer and Brian Clark. Denver, Colorado, USA, 2008. Photograph by Gregory Daurer.

Pg. 170. John Lawton, Boyd Rice, Mike Zoller, and Brian Clark. Denver, Colorado, USA, 2006. Photograph by Shanti Williams.

Pg. 170. Lauren Julia Dukes and Brian Clark. Denver, Colorado, USA, 2007. Photograph by Zhawna Siegwarth.

Pg. 171. Luke Schmaltz and Brian Clark. Denver, Colorado, USA, 2004. Photograph by Shanti Williams.

Pg. 171. Claudine Rousseau and Brian Clark. Denver, Colorado, USA, 2004.

Pg. 171. Rory Hinchey, Stephanie Gaunt, and Brian Clark. Ottawa, Ontario, Canada, 2011.

Pg. 171. Vadge Moore and Brian Clark. Denver, Colorado, USA, 2006. Photograph by Shanti Williams.

Pg. 171. Diego Sabanés and Brian Clark. Madrid, Spain, 2001. Photograph by Jessica Devine.

Pg. 172. Douglas Jenkins and Brian Clark. Eugene, Oregon, USA, 1997. Photograph by Joe Bunik.

Pg. 172. Franklin Bell, Karl Christian Krumpholz, and Brian Clark. Las Vegas, Nevada, USA, 2006. Photograph by E.K.C.

Pg. 172. Joe Choo and Brian Clark. Concord, California, USA, 2003.

Pg. 173. Rob Enbom and Brian Clark. Denver, Colorado, USA, 2003. Photograph by Josh Taylor.

Pg. 173. Zhawna Siegwarth and Brian Clark. Denver, Colorado, USA, 2007.

Pg. 173. Terry Campbell and Brian Clark. Denver, Colorado, USA, 2004. Photograph by Claudine Rousseau.

Pg. 173. Howard Karp and Brian Clark. Hollywood, California, USA, 2016. Photograph by Kristin Brooks.

Pg. 174. Josh Taylor and Brian Clark. Denver, Colorado, USA, 2004. Photograph by Amy Szychowski.

Pg. 174. Sherry Crawford and Brian Clark. Denver, Colorado, USA, 2008. Photograph by Zhawna Siegwarth.

Pg. 174. Andrew Novick and Brian Clark. Denver, Colorado, USA, 2007.

Pg. 175. The Mulholland Memorial Fountain. Los Feliz, California, USA, 2014. Photograph by Brian Clark.

Pg. 181. Oh La La Burlesque. Las Vegas, Nevada, USA. 2004. Photograph by Brian Clark.

Pg. 183. Franklin Bell. Las Vegas, Nevada, USA. 2004. Photograph by Brian Clark.

Pg. 184. Brian Clark. Las Vegas, Nevada, USA. 2004. Photograph by Franklin Bell.

Pg. 184. Sid Pink. Las Vegas, Nevada, USA. 2004. Photograph by Brian Clark.

Pg. 185. Drunks. Las Vegas, Nevada, USA. 2004. Photograph by Brian Clark.

Pg. 185. Oh La La Burlesque. Las Vegas, Nevada, USA. 2004. Photograph by Brian Clark.

Pg. 186. Lorin Partridge and Brian Clark. Las Vegas, Nevada, USA. 2004. Photograph by Franklin Bell.

Pg. 187. Ray Dennis Steckler and Brian Clark. Las Vegas, Nevada, USA. 2004. Photograph by Franklin Bell.

Pg. 187. Radiator Service. Las Vegas, Nevada, USA. 2004. Photograph by Brian Clark.

Pg. 187. Six-Man Beer Bong. Las Vegas, Nevada, USA. 2004. Photograph by Brian Clark.

Pg. 188. Lorin Partridge and Franklin Bell. Las Vegas, Nevada, USA. 2004. Photograph by Brian Clark.

Pg. 189. Eric The Pope and Brian Clark. Las Vegas, Nevada, USA. 2004. Photograph by Franklin Bell.

Pg. 191. Franklin Bell. Las Vegas, Nevada, USA. 2004. Photograph by Brian Clark.

Pg. 192. Backstreet. San José, Costa Rica, 2000. Photograph by Brian Clark.

Pg. 195. Demolition. Somewhere in southern Spain (probably Córdoba), 1999. Photograph by Brian Clark.

Pg. 197. Henry Rollins Caricature, 2009. VanityFair.com (archived).

Pg. 198. G-20 Protestors. London, England, 2009. Photograph by Kashfi Halford.

Pg. 202. George W. Bush, 2003. Photograph by Eric Draper.

Pg. 202. John McCain, 2009. Photograph by Frank A Fey.

Pg. 203. Jim Carrey and Jenny McCarthy, c. 2009. Screenshot from *Frontline*, "The Vaccine War," 2010, pbs.org.

Pg. 204. Kirk Cameron. Washington D.C., USA, 2012. Photograph by Gage Skidmore.

Pg. 204. Joe Rogan, c. 2009. Publicity photograph, Global Talent Booking.

Pg. 204. Coldplay, c. 2003. Oxfam International's "Make Trade Fair" awareness campaign.

Pg. 205. Tom Cruise. San Diego, California, USA, 2019. Photograph by Gage Skidmore.

Pg. 206. Henry Rollins. Hultsfred, Sweden, 1993. Photograph by Pelle Sten.

Pg. 207. Tunnel. Glendale, California, USA, 2016. Photograph by Brian Clark.

Pg. 211. El Alhambra. Generalife and Albayzín, Granada, Spain, 1999. Photograph by Brian Clark.

Pgs. 212–212 Jessica Devine at El Museo de Cera. Madrid, Spain, 2001. Photographs by Brian Clark.

Pg. 214. Roots. Guanacaste, Costa Rica, 2000. Photograph by Brian Clark.

Pg. 217. Royal Tomb. San Lorenzo de El Escorial, Cuenca del Guadarrama, Spain, 1999. Photograph by Brian Clark.

Pgs. 218–219. The Mimes. Long Beach, California, USA, 2011. Photographs by Lindsey Karnopp.

Pg. 220. Teardown. Denver, Colorado, USA, 2017. Photograph by Brian Clark.

Pg. 221. Monkey Mania. Denver, Colorado, USA, 2003. Photograph by Brian Clark.

Pg. 222. Bedroom-Closet. Denver, Colorado, USA, 2003. Photograph by Brian Clark.

Pg. 222. Showspace. Denver, Colorado, USA, 2003. Photograph by Brian Clark.

Pg. 223. Lightning Bolt. Denver, Colorado, USA, 2003. Photographs by Ben Brunton, from MonkeyMania.net (archived).

Pg. 224. Hale Zukas. Denver, Colorado, USA, 2003. Photograph by Brian Clark.

Pg. 227. Halloween. Denver, Colorado, USA, 2003. Photographs by Toshimi Ichiki.

Pg. 228. Homeless. Denver, Colorado, USA, 2003. Photograph by Claudine Rousseau.

Pg. 229. Josh Taylor. Denver, Colorado, USA, 2003. Photograph by Brian Clark.

Pgs. 230–231. Jean-Louis Costes, *et al.* Denver, Colorado, USA, 2003. Photographs by Brian Clark.

Pg. 231. Amy Szychowski, Josh Taylor, and Claudine Rousseau. Boulder, Colorado, USA, 2003. Photograph by Brian Clark.

Pg. 232. Wives. Denver, Colorado, USA, 2003. Photograph by Brian Clark.

Pg. 232. Hale Zukas. Denver, Colorado, USA, 2003. Photograph by Brian Clark.

Pg. 234. Mr. Pacman. Denver, Colorado, USA, 2003. Photograph by Ben Brunton, from MonkeyMania.net (archived).

Pg. 235. Fuckery. Denver, Colorado, USA, 2003. Photograph by Brian Clark.

Pg. 237. Get Your Going. Denver, Colorado, USA, 2004. Photograph by Ben Brunton, from MonkeyMania.net (archived).

Pg. 238. Ralph Gean. Denver, Colorado, USA, 2004. Photograph by Brian Clark.

Pg. 239. T-Man. Denver, Colorado, USA, 2004. Photograph by Brian Clark.

Pg. 240. Ralph Gean. Denver, Colorado, USA, 2004. Photograph by Brian Clark.

Pg. 241. Zombie Zombie. Denver, Colorado, USA, 2004. Photograph by Ben Brunton, from MonkeyMania.net (archived).

Pg. 242. Little Fyodor. Denver, Colorado, USA.

Pg. 243. Monkey Mania illustration by Grux, from MonkeyMania.net (archived).

Pg. 245. Drunks. Denver, Colorado, USA, 2004. Photograph by Brian Clark.

Pg. 245. Glass Candy. Denver, Colorado, USA, 2004. Photograph by Justin Simoni, from MonkeyMania.net (archived).

Pg. 246. Weather. Denver, Colorado, USA, 2004. Photograph by Andrew Novick, from MonkeyMania.net (archived).

Pg. 246. The Hot Rock. Denver, Colorado, USA, 2004. Photograph by Andrew Novick, from MonkeyMania.net (archived).

Pg. 246. Magic Cyclops. Denver, Colorado, USA, 2004. Photograph by Andrew Novick, from MonkeyMania.net (archived).

Pg. 247. Smash Club. Denver, Colorado, USA, early 2000s. Photograph by Ben Brunton, from MonkeyMania.net (archived).

Pg. 248. The Microphones. Denver, Colorado, USA, early 2000s. Photograph by Ben Brunton, from MonkeyMania.net (archived).

Pg. 248. Sonic Youth. Denver, Colorado, USA, 2004. Photograph by Ben Brunton, from MonkeyMania.net (archived).

Pg. 249. Planes Mistaken for Stars. Denver, Colorado, USA, early 2000s. Photograph by Claudine Rousseau, from MonkeyMania.net (archived).

Pg. 250. Department of Motor Vehicles. Lakewood, Colorado, USA, 2017. Photograph by Brian Clark.

Pg. 252. Clouds. Hollywood Hills, USA, 2013. Photograph by Brian Clark.

Pgs. 253–261. Crisis Photographs. England, late 1970s. Courtesy of Apop Records.

Pg. 262. Metro Tunnel. Madrid, Spain, 2001. Photograph by Brian Clark.

Pg. 264. Mr. Romance. Minimal collage by Brian Clark, 1997.

Pg. 269. Brian Clark with Meat Clock. Eugene, Oregon, USA, 1997. Photograph by Joe Bunik.

Pgs. 276–278. Artworks by Brian Clark, 1995–1998.

Pg. 281. Burning Garbage. Concord, California, USA, 2000. Photograph by Brian Clark.

Pg. 283. Freeways. Los Angeles, California, USA, 2013. Photograph by Brian Clark.

Pg. 285. Lake Statue. Barcelona, Spain, 1999. Photograph by Brian Clark.

Pg. 288. Office Complex. Dublin, California, USA, 1998. Photograph by Brian Clark.

Pg. 291. Toothless and Ruthless. Los Feliz, California, USA, 2011.

Pg. 294. Cementerio General de San José. San José, Costa Rica, 2000. Photograph by Brian Clark.

Pgs. 295–298. Brian Brushwood photos courtesy of Schwood.com.

Pg. 300. Roadway. San Lorenzo de El Escorial, Cuenca del Guadarrama, Spain, 1999. Photograph by Brian Clark.

Pg. 301. El Alcázar. Segovia, Castilla y León, Spain, 2002. Photograph by Brian Clark.

Pg. 302. Denver Gentlemen's Pipe Smoking League Logo designed by Brian Clark.

Pg. 303. Denver Gentlemen's Pipe Smoking League insignia illustrated by Karl Christian Krumholz.

Pg. 304. Roman Aqueduct. Segovia, Castilla y León, Spain, 2002. Photograph by Brian Clark.

Pg. 307. Rocky Beach Rivulets. Aran Islands, Ireland, 2001. Photograph by Brian Clark.

Pgs. 308–309. Spicy Bean Dip. Photographs by Brian Clark.

Pg. 310. Cocktail Glasses. Designed by Brian Clark.

Pg. 311. Driftwood Arch. Fairhaven, Massachusetts, USA, 2016. Photograph by Brian Clark.

Pg. 313. Skull Ring. Denver, Colorado, USA, 2004. Photograph by Brian Clark.

Pg. 319. Walkway. Somewhere in southern Spain (probably Seville), 1999. Photograph by Brian Clark.

Pg. 328. Farmacia Destruida. Somewhere in eastern Spain (probably Valencia), 1999. Photograph by Brian Clark.

Please notify the publisher of any image credit errors or omissions at Admin@DiscriminateMedia.com.

— Index of Works Referenced, Consulted, or Alluded To —

Books

Ariely, Dan. *Predictably Irrational: The Hidden Forces That Shape Our Decisions*. HarperCollins, 2008.

Batchelor, David; Wood, Paul; Fer, Briony. *Realism, Rationalism, Surrealism: Art Between the Wars*. Yale University Press, 1993.

Baumeister, Roy; Tierney, John. *Willpower: Rediscovering the Greatest Human Strength*. Penguin Press, 2011.

Bloom, Howard. *The Lucifer Principle: A Scientific Expedition into the Forces of History*. Atlantic Monthly Press, 1995.

Bowyer, Richard. *Check Your Vocabulary for Military English: A Workbook for Users*. Peter Collin Publishing, 2001.

Brockman, John. *What Is Your Dangerous Idea?: Today's Leading Thinkers on the Unthinkable*, Simon & Schuster, 2006.

Brushwood, Brian. *Cheats, Cons, Swindles, and Tricks: 57 Ways to Scam a Free Drink*. Self-published, 2000.

Brushwood, Brian. *The Professional's Guide to Fire Eating*. Bizarre Magic, 2002.

de Botton, Alan. *Status Anxiety*. Hamish Hamilton, 2004.

de Botton, Alan. *The Consolations of Philosophy*. Penguin Books, 2000.

de Sélincourt, Aubrey. *The World of Herodotus*. Little, Brown and Company, 1962.

Dostoevsky, Fyodor; Ginsburg, Mirra (trans.). *Notes from Underground*. Epoch, 1864 / Bantam Books, 1974.

Durant, Will. *The Story of Philosophy*. Simon & Schuster, 1926.

Evans, Richard. *Richard Evans' Quote Book*. Publishers Press, 1971.

Gale, Matthew. *Dada & Surrealism*. Phaidon, 1997.

Gilovich, Thomas. *How We Know What Isn't So: The Fallibility of Human Reason in Everyday Life*. The Free Press, 1993.

Gladwell, Malcolm. *The Tipping Point: How Little Things Can Make a Big Difference*. Little, Brown and Company, 2000.

Glover, Jonathan. *Humanity: A Moral History of the Twentieth Century*. Yale University Press, 1999.

Hemingway, Ernest. *The Sun Also Rises*. Charles Scribner's Sons, 1926.

Hitchens, Christopher. *God Is Not Great*. Twelve Books/Hachette, 2007.

Huelsenbeck, Richard; Neugroschel; Joachim (trans.). *Memoirs of a Dada Drummer*. The Viking Press, 1974.

International Bible Society. *The Great News: The New Testament, New International Version*. International Bible Society, 1984.

Juno, Andrea (ed.); Vale, V. (ed.). *Angry Women*. Re/Search Publications, 1992.

LaVey, Anton. *The Stanic Bible*. Avon Books, 1969.

Legman, Gershon. *Rationale of the Dirty Joke: An Analysis of Sexual Humor*. Grove Press, 1968.

Lehrer, Jonah. *How We Decide*. Houghton Mifflin, 2009.

Levine, Robert. *The Geography of Time: The Temporal Misadventures of a Social Psychologist*. Basic Books, 1998.

Marcus, Greil, *Lipstick Traces: A Secret History of the Twentieth Century*. Harvard University Press, 1990.

Mencken, H.L., *A Mencken Chrestomathy: His Own Selection of His Choicest Writing*. Knopf Doubleday, 1982.

Milgram, Stanley. *Obedience to Authority: An Experimental View*. Harper & Row, 1974.

Morin, Jim. *Ambushed!: A Cartoon History of the George W. Bush Administration*. Routledge, 2008.

Morton, Jim (ed.); Rice, Boyd (ed.). *Incredibly Strange Films*. Re/Search Publications, 1985.

Nietzsche, Friedrich; Kaufmann, Walter (trans.). *The Portable Nietzsche*. Penguin Publishing Group, 1977.

O'Rourke, P.J. *Give War a Chance: Eyewitness Accounts of Mankind's Struggle Against Tyranny, Injustice and Alcohol-Free Beer*. Atlantic Monthly Press, 1992.

O'Rourke, P.J. *Holidays in Hell: In Which Our Intrepid Reporter Travels to the World's Worst Places and Asks, "What's Funny about This?"* Atlantic Monthly Press, 1988.

Orwell, George. *Down and Out in Paris and London*. Victor Gollancz, 1933.

Orwell, George. *Homage to Catalonia*. Secker and Warburg, 1938.

Parfrey, Adam (ed.). *Apocalypse Culture: Enlarged and Revised Edition*. Feral House, 1990.

Parfrey, Adam (ed.). *Apocalypse Culture II*. Feral House, 2000.

Parfrey, Adam (ed.). *It's a Man's World: Men's Adventure Magazines, The Postwar Pulps*. Feral House, 2003.

Parfrey, Adam (ed.); Lunch, Lydia (ed.). *Sin-a-Rama: Sleaze Sex Paperbacks of the Sixties*. Feral House, 2004.

Powell, John. *How Music Works: The Science and Psychology of Beautiful Sounds, from Beethoven to the Beatles and Beyond*. Little, Brown and Company, 2010.

Richter, Hans. *Dada: Art and Anti-Art*. Oxford University Press, 1965.

Ronson, Jon. *The Psychopath Test: A Journey Through the Madness Industry*. Riverhead Books, 2011.

Rousseau, Jean-Jacques. *Discourse on the Origin and Basis of Inequality Among Men*. Marc-Michel Rey, 1755.

Sagan, Carl. *The Demon-Haunted World: Science as a Candle in the Dark*. Random House, 1995.

Sanford, John. *Evil: The Shadow Side of Reality*. Crossroad Publishing Company, 1982.

Schneider, Charles (ed.). *CAD: A Handbook for Heels*. Feral House, 1992.

Shermer, Michael. *Why People Believe Weird Things: Pseudoscience, Superstition, and Other Confusions of Our Time*. Henry Holt and Company, 1997.

Tolkien, John Ronald Reuel. *The Lord of the Rings* (single volume edition). George Allen & Unwin, 1968.

Toole, John Kennedy. *A Confederacy of Dunces*. Louisiana State University Press, 1980.

Tzu, Lao. *Tao Te Ching*. Penguin Classics, 1964.

Veblen, Thorstein. *The Theory of the Leisure Class: An Economic Study of Institutions*. Macmillan, 1899.

von Franz, Marie-Louise. *The Problem of the Puer Aeternus*. Spring Books, 1971.

Periodicals

Adbusters. Published in Vancouver, British Columbia, Canada, 1989 to present.

Book Your Own Fucking Life. Published in San Francisco, California, United States, 1992 to 2019.

Disabled American Veterans. Published in Cincinnati, Ohio, United States, 1960 to present.

The Economist. Published in London, England, 1843 to present.

Exotica/Etcetera. Published in Raleigh, North Carolina, United States, 1996 to 1998.

The Guardian. Published in London, England, 1959 to present.

Le Gai pied. Published in Paris, France, 1979 to 1991.

MAXIMUM ROCKNROLL. Published in San Francisco, California, United States, 1982 to present.

Modern Drunkard. Published in Denver, Colorado, United States, 1996 to present.

National Geographic. Published in the District of Columbia, United States, 1888 to present.

NME: New Musical Express. Published in London, England, 1952 to present.

Playboy. Published in New York City, New York, United States, 1953 to present.

Rock & Blues News. Published in Sacramento, California, United States, 1998 to 2001.

Scientific American. Published in New York City, New York, United States, 1845 to present.

Search & Destroy. Published in San Francisco, California, United States, 1977 to 1979.

Slash. Published in Los Angeles, California, United States, 1977 to 1980.

Speak Up! Published in Madrid, Spain, unknown to present.

Vanity Fair. Published in New York City, New York, United States, 1983 to present.

Westword. Published in Denver, Colorado, United States, 1977 to present.

Print Articles, Essays, Interviews, and Reviews

Barakat, Ghazi. "The Late, Great, Aesthetic Taboos," *Apocalypse Culture II*, edited by Adam Parfrey. Feral House, 2000.

Boroditsky, Lera. "How Language Shapes Thought: The Languages We Speak Affect Our Perceptions of The World," *Scientific American,* Vol. 304, No. 2, Feb. 1, 2011.

Brown, Walter. "Ancient Sleep in Modern Times," *Scientific American Mind*, Vol. 17, No. 6, Dec. 2006.

DeWitt, Howard. "Ralph Gean: Psycho-billy is alive in Denver in the 1990s," *Rock & Blues News*, No. 1, Dec. 1998/Jan. 1999.

DeRogatis, Jim. "Nazis Or Not? Censorship Keeps Fans from Deciding" *Chicago Sun Times*, Dec. 17, 2003.

Dickie, Tony. "Death In June: An Interview with Douglas P.," *Compulsion*, No. 1, 1992.

Haddow, Douglas. "Hipster: The Dead End of Western Civilization," *Adbusters,* No. 79, Sept./Oct. 2008.

Juno, Andrea. "Diamanda Galás Interview," *Angry Women*, Re/Search Publications, 1992.

Krugman, Paul. "Why Most Economists' Predictions Are Wrong," *Red Herring*, No. 55, Jun. 10, 1998.

McEvilley, Thomas. "Art in The Dark," *Artforum*, Vol. 21, No. 10, Summer 1983.

Parfrey, Adam. "Aesthetic Terrorism." *Apocalypse Culture: Enlarged and Revised Edition*, edited by Adam Parfrey. Feral House, 1990.

Peek, Preston. "Ralph Gean: Reviewed," *Exotica/Etcetera,* No. 11, Nov. 1997.

Tyrangiel, Josh. "Can Bono Save The World?," *Time Magazine*, Vol. 159, No. 9, Mar. 4, 2002.

Zerzan, John. "The Case Against Art," *Fifth Estate*, No. 324, Fall 1986.

Zimbardo, Philip. "The Mind Is a Formidable Jailer" *The New York Times*, Apr. 8, 1973.

Zimbardo, Philip. "When Good People Do Evil: 45 years ago, Stanley Milgram's classic experiments showed that, under orders, decent human beings will do anything," *Yale Alumni Magazine*, Vol. 70, No. 3, Jan./Feb. 2007.

"Reviews: A Star Unborn," *MAXIMUM ROCKNROLL*, No. 176, Jan. 1998.

Online Articles, Essays, Interviews, and Reviews

Adam, David. "Can A Parasite Carried by Cats Change Your Personality?" *The Guardian*, Sept. 25, 2003, theguardian.com/science/2003/sep/25/medicineandhealth.thisweekssciencequestions1.

Baker, Brian. "The Alkaline Trio Keeps Going and Going," *Cincinnati CityBeat*, Jun. 29, 2000, citybeat.com/2000-06-29/music.shtml.

Brown, August. "After Ghost Ship and a Crackdown, L.A.'s DIY Music Scene Plans its Response," *The Los Angeles Times*, Dec. 17, 2016, latimes.com/entertainment/music/la-et-ms-diy-panel-20161216-story.html

Conklin, Ellis. "For Adam Parfrey, Publishing the Unabomber's Book Is All in a Day's Work," *Seattle Weekly*, Nov. 23, 2010, seattleweekly.com/news/for-adam-parfrey-publishing-the-unabombers-book-is-all-in-a-days-work/.

Delmar, Sari. "Alkaline Trio: Matt Skiba Interview," *Truth Explosion*, 2006, truthexplosion.com/live/interviews/interviews.php?id=116.

Dowden, Bradley. "Fallacies," *Internet Encyclopedia of Philosophy*, Mar. 27, 2003, iep.utm.edu/fallacy/

Dunning, Brian. "Animal Earthquake Prediction," *Skeptoid*, Oct. 23, 2018, skeptoid.com/episodes/4646.

Grillo, Ioan. "Mexico's Emo-Bashing Problem," *Time*, Mar. 27, 2008, time.com/archive/6908826/mexicos-emo-bashing-problem/

Guerrero, Juan Carlos. "Ghost Ship Timeline: How the Investigation into the Deadly Fire Unfolded," *ABC7 News*, Jul. 31, 2029, abc7news.com/timeline-how-the-ghost-ship-fire-investigation-unfolded/5414390/

Home, Stewart. "We Mean It Man: Punk Rock and Anti-Racism; or, Death In June not mysterious," *Datacide*, Summer 2000, stewarthomesociety.org/dij.htm.

Klosowski, Thorin. "Sonic Youth at Monkey Mania: Remember That? What a Night That Was, eh?," *Westword*, May 7, 2010, westword.com/music/sonic-youth-at-monkey-mania-remember-that-what-a-night-that-was-eh-5713004

Koch, Cynthia. "The Contest for American Culture: A Leadership Case Study on The NEA and NEH Funding Crisis," *Public Talk: Online Journal of Discourse Leadership*, 1998, upenn.edu/pnc/ptkoch.html.

Kreps, Daniel. "Anti-Emo Violence Plagues Mexico as Attacks Increase," *Rolling Stone*, Mar. 27, 2008, rollingstone.com/music/music-news/anti-emo-violence-plagues-mexico-as-attacks-increase-80654/

Maglaty, Jeanne. "When Did Girls Start Wearing Pink?" *Smithsonian Magazine*, Apr. 7, 2011, smithsonianmag.com/arts-culture/when-did-girls-start-wearing-pink-1370097/.

Moss, Corey. "Alkaline Trio Won't Let Spinal Tap Curse Slow Them," *MTV News*, Jul. 24, 2001, mtv.com/news/articles/1445360/07232001/alkaline_trio.jhtml.

Murphy, Tom. "Remembering The Last Night at the Great Monkey Mania," *Westword*, Mar. 20, 2015, westword.com/music/remembering-the-last-night-at-the-great-monkey-mania-6602550

Paul, Aubin. "Interviews: Matt Skiba (Alkaline Trio)," *Punk News*, May 2, 2005. punknews.org/article/12426/interviews-matt-skiba-alkaline-trio

Roberts, Michael, "Ralph Gean: Mystery Man," *Westword*, Sept. 12, 1996, westword.com/music/mystery-man-5056682.

Rollins, Henry. "Change You Don't Have to Believe In, Just Deal With," *Vanity Fair*, Apr. 3, 2009, vanityfair.com/online/politics/2009/04/change-you-dont-have-to-believe-in-just-deal-with.html.

Smith, Stephanie. "Researchers Say They Found Malaria's Origin: In Chimps," *CNN.com*, Aug. 3, 2009, cnn.com/2009/HEALTH/08/03/malaria.origins/index.html.

Tolosa, Conrad; Julia Zulia, Julia. "Alkaline Trio – Matt Skiba," *Decapolis*, 2001, fastgodstuff.com/musicreviews/interviews/alkaline.shtml.

"A Different Perspective on the Controversy at the Death in June Show in Chicago," *Chicago Indy Media*, Dec. 20, 2003, chicago.indymedia.org/archive/newswire/display/34629/index.php.

"Evidence Is Mounting to Link Toxoplasmosis with Schizophrenia," *News-Medical.net*, Oct. 18, 2005, news-medical.net/?id=13866.

"The Worst Country on Earth: Piracy, Poverty and Perdition: Somalia Takes Our Unwanted Prize," *The Economist*, Nov. 13, 2009, economist.com/news/2009/11/13/the-worst-country-on-earth.

"Sodomy Laws in the United States," SodomyLaws.org, accessed Dec. 2, 2011, glapn.org/sodomylaws/usa/usa.htm

"Summer of the Shark," *Wikipedia*, Wikimedia Foundation, accessed Aug. 9, 2009, en.wikipedia.org/wiki/Summer_of_the_Shark.

"Toxoplasmosis," *Wikipedia*, Wikimedia Foundation, accessed Aug. 9, 2009, en.wikipedia.org/wiki/Toxoplasmosis.

Academic, Governmental, and N.G.O. Papers and Reports

Bugl, Paul. "History of Epidemics and Plagues," *Syllabus: Epidemics and AIDS*, University of Hartford, Oct. 2001, uhaweb.hartford.edu/bugl/histepi.htm.

Carnahan, Thomas; McFarland, Sam. "Revisiting the Stanford Prison Experiment: Could Participant Self-Selection Have Led to The Cruelty?," *Personality and Social Psychology Bulletin*, Vol. 33, No. 5, Apr. 17, 2007.

Gaskell, Elizabeth, *et al.* "A Unique Dual Activity Amino Acid Hydroxylase in Toxoplasma Gondii," *PLoS One*, Mar. 11, 2009, journals.plos.org/plosone/article?id=10.1371/journal.pone.0004801.

Cooperman, Alan (ed.). "The Global Religious Landscape: A Report on the Size and Distribution of the World's Major Religious Groups as of 2010," Pew Research Center's Forum on Religion & Public Life, Dec. 2012.

Klatsky, Arthur. "Moderate Drinking and Reduced Risk of Heart Disease," *Alcohol Research & Health*, Vol. 23, No. 1, 1999.

Miller, Peter; Anton, Raymond; *et al.* "Excessive Alcohol Consumption and Hypertension: Clinical Implications of Current Research," *The Journal of Clinical Hypertension*, Vol. 7, No. 6, Jun. 2005.

Nissani, Moti. "A Cognitive Reinterpretation of Stanley Milgram's Observations on Obedience to Authority," *American Psychologist*. Vol. 45, No. 12, 1990.

Subramanian, Rajesh. "Alcohol Involvement in Fatal Motor Vehicle Traffic Crashes, 2003," U.S. Department of Transportation, National Highway Traffic Safety Administration, National Center for Statistics and Analysis (Technical Report), Mar. 2005.

Thoman, Evelyn. "Co-Sleeping, An Ancient Practice: Issues of The Past and Present, And Possibilities for The Future," *Sleep Medicine Reviews*, Vol. 10, No. 6, Dec. 2006.

"A Decade of Discoveries in Veterinary Protozoology Changes Our Concept Of 'Subclinical' Toxoplasmosis," *Veterinary Parasitology*, Volume 132, Issues 3 – 4, Sept. 30, 2005.

"Basic Information: HIV/AIDS," U.S. Department of Health and Human Services: Centers for Disease Control, Sept. 3, 2008, cdc.gov/hiv/topics/basic/.

"Diarrhoea: Why Children Are Still Dying and What Can Be Done," The United Nations Children's Fund (UNICEF)/World Health Organization, 2009, iris.who.int/bitstream/handle/10665/44174/9789241598415_eng.pdf.

"Male Circumcision: Global Trends and Determinants of Prevalence, Safety and Acceptability," World Health Organization, Dec. 14. 2007, who.int/hiv/pub/malecircumcision/globaltrends/en/index.html.

"Toxoplasmosis Parasite May Trigger Schizophrenia and Bipolar Disorders," *ScienceDaily*, University of Leeds, Mar. 11, 2009, sciencedaily.com/releases/2009/03/090311085151.htm.

Films and Movies

Bartleby. Directed by Jonathan Parker. Parker Film Company, 2001.

The Blair Witch Project. Directed by Daniel Myrick and Eduardo Sánchez. Haxan Films, 1999.

Bram Stoker's Dracula. Directed by Francis Ford Coppola. American Zoetrope, 1992.

But I'm A Cheerleader. Directed by Jamie Babbit. Ignite Entertainment, 1999.

Expelled: No Intelligence Allowed. Directed by Nathan Frankowski. Premise Media Corporation, 2008.

Fahrenheit 9/11. Directed by Michael Moore. Dog Eat Dog Films, 2004.

Friends Forever. Directed by Ben Wolfinsohn. Plexifilm, 2003.

Hell House. Directed by George Ratliff. GreenHouse Pictures, 2002.

The Incredibly Strange Creatures Who Stopped Living and Became Mixed-Up Zombies. Directed by Ray Dennis Steckler. Fairway International Pictures, 1964.

In Search of Beethoven. Directed by Phil Grabsky. Seventh Art Productions, 2009.

Les Quatre Cents Coups (The 400 Blows). Directed by François Truffaut. Les Films du Carrosse, 1959.

Lost Highway. Directed by David Lynch. Asymmetrical Productions, 1997.

Monty Python's Life of Brian. Directed by Terry Jones. HandMade Films, Cinema International Corporation, 1979.

Nixing The Twist. Directed by Frank Kelly Rich. Unreleased.

Police Academy. Directed by Hugh Wilson. The Ladd Company, 1984.

Pulp Fiction. Directed by Quentin Tarantino. A Band Apart, 1994.

Raiders of The Lost Ark. Directed by Steven Spielberg. Lucasfilm, 1981.

Rat Pfink a Boo Boo. Directed by Ray Dennis Steckler. Craddock Films, 1966.

Scream. Directed by Wes Craven. Woods Entertainment, 1996.

Seven. Directed by David Fincher. New Line Cinema, 1995.

Wesley Willis's Joyrides. Directed by Chris Bagley. Eyeosaur Productions, 2008.

Television Shows, Programs, and Series

All in the Family. Developed by Norman Lear, CBS, United States. 1971 to 1979.

American Idol. Created by Simon Fuller, Fox, United States. 2002 to 2016; 2018 to present.

Bar Rescue. Created by Darrin Reed, Spike, United States. 2011 to present.

Ben Casey. Created by James E. Moser, ABC, United States. 1961 to 1966.

Beverly Hills 90210. Created by Darren Star, Fox, United States. 1990 to 2000.

Girls Gone Wild. Created by Joe Francis. GGW Brands. United States. 1997 to 2013.

He-Man and the Masters of the Universe. Created by Lou Scheimer, Filmation Associates, United States. 1983 to 1985.

The Kids in the Hall. Produced by Lorne Michaels and Joe Bodolai, CBC Television, Canada. 1989 to 1995.
Kitchen Nightmares. Developed by Daniel Kay, Fox, United States. 2007 to 2014; 2023 to present.
Leave it to Beaver. Created by Joe Connelly and Bob Mosher, CBS/ABC, United States. 1957 to 1963.
Lifestyles of The Rich and Famous. Created by Al Masini, TPE / Leach Entertainment Features, United States. 1984 to 1995.
Married... with Children. Created by Michael G. Moye and Ron Leavitt, Fox, United States. 1987 to 1997.
MTV Cribs. Developed by Nina L. Díaz, MTV, United States. 2000 to 2010; 2017 to 2018; 2021 to present.
MTV Sports. Created by Patrick Byrnes, MTV, United States. 1992 to 1997.
Operación Triunfo. Created by Toni Cruz, TVE, Spain. 2001 to 2011; 2017 to 2020; 2023 to present.
Popstars. Created by Jonathan Dowling, ITV, United Kingdom. 2001 to 2002.
The Real World. Created by Mary-Ellis Bunim and Jonathan Murray, MTV, United States. 1992 to 2019.
Scam Nation (Scam School). Created by Brian Brushwood, Revision3, United States. 2008 to present.
Scooby-Doo, Where Are You!. Created by Joe Ruby and Ken Spears, Hanna-Barbera/CBS, United States. 1969 to 1970; 1978.
The Shock of the New. Written and presented by Robert Hughes, British Broadcasting Corporation, United Kingdom. 1980.
The Simpsons. Created by Matt Groening, Fox, United States. 1989 to present.
South Park. Created by Trey Parker and Matt Stone. Comedy Central, United States, 1997 to present.
Xena: Warrior Princess. Created by John Schulian and Robert Tapert, Renaissance Pictures/Universal, United States. 1995 to 2001.

Television Episodes

"Show 9," *So It Goes*, Series 1, Episode 9, produced by Chris Pye, Granada Television, United Kingdom, Aug. 28, 1976.
"Tropical Termites" *Hotel Impossible*, Season 3, Episode 31, The Travel Channel, United States, Sept. 2, 2013.

Online Videos

Ariely, Dan. "Are We in Control of Our Own Decisions?" *TED*, Dec. 2008, ted.com/talks/dan_ariely_are_we_in_control_of_our_own_decisions
Ariely, Dan. "Our Buggy Moral Code" *TED*, February 2009, ted.com/talks/dan_ariely_our_buggy_moral_code
Brushwood, Brian. "Break Out of Police Issued Handcuffs!" *Scam Nation*, Dec. 29, 2009, youtu.be/5-O2jJWAfK8
Brushwood, Brian. "Mind Control Scam." *Scam Nation*, Dec. 29, 2009, youtu.be/qc5FgDNgkVM
Brushwood, Brian. "The Phantom Quarter." *Scam Nation*, (reupload) Aug. 10, 2015, youtu.be/pvipZ71zPQk
Brushwood, Brian. "Stick It To 'Em with The Funnel." *Scam Nation*, Dec. 29, 2009, youtu.be/onJPTWaKR_o
Gladwell, Malcolm. "Choice, Happiness and Spaghetti Sauce." *TED*, Feb. 2004, ted.com/talks/malcolm_gladwell_choice_happiness_and_spaghetti_sauce

Theatrical Productions, Plays, and Performances

Costes, Jean-Louis. *Holy Virgin Cult*. Monkey Mania, Denver, Colorado, 2003.
Finley, Karen. *Yams*. LACE, Los Angeles, California. 1986.
Porter, Cole. *Kiss Me Kate*. Shubert Theatre, Philadelphia, Pennsylvania, 1948.
Roberts, Keenan. *Hell House*. Abundant Life Christian Center, Arvada, Colorado, 1995.
Uhry, Alfred. *Driving Ms. Daisy*. Playwrights Horizons Studio Theatre, New York City, New York, 1987.

Artworks

da Vinci, Leonardo. *Mona Lisa*. Circa 1503 to 1506, Louvre, Paris.
Manzoni, Piero. *Merda d'artista*. 1961, various museums.

Musical Albums, EPs, and Singles

Amon Tobin. *Supermodified*, Ninja Tune, 2000.
Aphex Twin. *Selected Ambient Works Volume II*, Warp Records, 1994.
At the Gates. *Slaughter of the Soul*, Earache Records, 1995.
Autechre. *Amber*, Warp Records, 1994.
Beastie Boys. *Check Your Head*, Grand Royal, 1992.
Beastie Boys. *Cooky Puss*, Rat Cage, 1983.

Index of Works Referenced, Consulted, or Alluded To

Beastie Boys. *Hello Nasty*, Grand Royal, 1998.

Beastie Boys. *Ill Communication*, Grand Royal, 1994.

Beastie Boys. *License to Ill*, Def Jam Recordings, 1986.

Beastie Boys. *Paul's Boutique*, Capitol, 1989.

Beastie Boys. *Some Old Bullshit*, Grand Royal, 1994.

Beck. *Sea Change*, Geffen Records, 2002.

Bikini Kill. *Yeah Yeah Yeah Yeah*, Kill Rock Stars, 1993.

Black Flag. *Damaged*, SST Records, 1981.

Black Math Horseman. *Wyllt*, Tee Pee Records, 2009.

The Cardigans. *Life*, Minty Fresh Records, 1995.

Case, Neko. *Blacklisted*, Bloodshot Records, 2002.

Cheap Trick. *Cheap Trick*, Epic Records, 1977.

Cheap Trick. *Heaven Tonight*, Epic Records, 1978.

Cheap Trick. *In Color*, Epic Records, 1977.

Circle Jerks. *Group Sex*, Frontier Records, 1980.

Coldplay. *A Rush of Blood to the Head*, Parlophone Records, 2002.

Coldplay. *Parachutes*, Parlophone Records, 2000.

Crisis. *Holocaust Hymns*, Apop Records, 2005.

Crisis. *We Are All Jews And Germans*, World Serpent, 1997.

Danzig. *Danzig*, Def American Recordings, 1988.

Depeche Mode. *Violator*, Mute Records, 1990.

Electric Wizard. *Dopethrone*, Rise Above Records, 2000.

Eydie Gormé y Los Panchos. *Eydie Gorme Canta En Español Con Los Panchos*, Columbia Records, 1964.

Gean, Ralph. *A Star Unborn or What Would Have Been If What Is Hadn't Happened: The Amazing Story Of Ralph Gean*, World Serpent, 1997.

Gean, Ralph. *One Night In San Antonio / Hey Dr. Casey*, Gallant Records, 1964.

Gean, Ralph. *The Amazing Ralph Gean – His Music, His Story*, Discriminate Audio, 2007.

Gean, Ralph. *Weeping Willow Tree / Experimental Love*, Lori Records, 1962.

The Go-Go's. *Beauty and the Beat*, I.R.S. Records, 1981.

Gogol Bordello. *Multi Kontra Culti vs. Irony*, Rubric Records, 2002.

Guns N' Roses. Appetite for Destruction, The David Geffen Company, 1987.

Hilton, Paris. *Paris*, Warner Bros. Records, 2006.

Interpol. *Turn On the Bright Lights*, Matador Records, 2002.

Iron Maiden. *Iron Maiden*, EMI Records, 1980.

Iron Maiden. *Killers*, EMI Records, 1981.

Jesu. *Jesu*, Hydra Head Records, 2004.

Little Fyodor. *Dance Of The Salted Slug*, Elephant Six Recording Co., 1994.

Los Bunkers. *Vida de Perros*, La Oreja, 2006.

M.Kourie. *The Dreams Of M.Kourie*, Chrome Peeler Records, 2006.

Madonna. *Ray of Light*, Maverick Records, 1998.

Metallica. *Kill 'Em All*, Megaforce Records, 1983.

Milemarker. *Frigid Forms Sell*, Lovitt Records, 2000.

My Chemical Romance. *Three Cheers for Sweet Revenge*, Reprise Records, 2004.

Necronomitron. *Necronomitron*, Load Records, 2003.

New York Dolls. *New York Dolls*, Mercury Records, 1973.

Nikki and The Corvettes. *Nikki and The Corvettes*, Bomp! Records, 1980.

Nine Inch Nails. *Broken*, Nothing Records, 1992.

Nine Inch Nails. *Fixed*, Nothing Records, 1992.

Nine Inch Nails. *Pretty Hate Machine*, TVT Records, 1989.

Noxagt. *Turning It Down Since 2001*, Load Records, 2003.

Plastikman. *Consumed*, M-nus, 1998.

Portishead. *Dummy*, Go! Discs, 1994.

The Ramones. *Ramones*, Sire Records, 1976.

The Raveonettes. *Lust, Lust, Lust*, Vice Records, 2008.

The Rezillos. *Can't Stand the Rezillos*, Sire Records, 1978.

Rollins Band. *Liar / Disconnect*, The Imago Recording Company, 1994.

Satan's Pilgrims. *Satan's Pilgrims*, MuSick Recordings, 1999.

Screeching Weasel. *My Brain Hurts*, Lookout Records, 1991.
She Wants Revenge. *She Wants Revenge*, Perfect Kiss, 2006.
Slayer. *Seasons in the Abyss*, Def American Recordings, 1990.
The Smashing Pumpkins. *Siamese Dream*, Virgin Records, 1993.
The Strokes. *Is This It*, RCA Records, 2001.
The Sword. *Age of Winters*, Kemado Records, 2006.
T. Rex. *The Slider*, EMI Records, 1972.
Various Artists. *Rock Against Bush Vol 1*, Fat Wreck Chords, 2004.
Weezer. *Weezer*, DGC Records, 1994.

Songs and Musical Compositions

Alien Ant Farm. "Smooth Criminal." *ANThology*. New Noize, 2001.
Anal Cunt. "You Keep A Diary." *I Like It When You Die*. Earache Records, 1997.
Armstrong, Louis. "What a Wonderful World." *What a Wonderful World / Cabaret*. ABC Records, 1967.
August and The Spur of The Moment Band. "The I-95 Asshole Song." *Lost Horizons / The I-95 Asshole Song*. Pantera
    Records, 1983.
The Beatles. "I Want to Hold Your Hand." *I Want to Hold Your Hand / I Saw Her Standing There*. Parlophone Records, 1963.
Beastie Boys. "Girls." *License to Ill*, Def Jam Recordings, 1986.
Beastie Boys. "Hey Ladies." *Paul's Boutique*, Capitol, 1989.
Beastie Boys. "Intergalactic." *Hello Nasty*, Grand Royal, 1998.
Beastie Boys. "Root Down." *Ill Communication*, Grand Royal, 1994.
Beastie Boys. "So What'cha Want." *Check Your Head*, Grand Royal, 1992.
Berry, Chuck. "Johnny B. Goode." *Johnny B. Goode / Around and Around*. Chess Records, 1958.
Berry, Chuck. "Rock and Roll Music." *Rock and Roll Music / Blue Feeling*. Chess Records, 1957.
Big Black. "The Ugly American." *Racer-X*. Homestead Records, 1984.
Bikini Kill. "White Boy." *Yeah Yeah Yeah Yeah*, Kill Rock Stars, 1993.
Carter, Anita "(Love's) Ring of Fire." *Anita Carter Sings Folk Songs Old And New*. Mercury Records, 1963.
The Clash. "Rock the Casbah." *Combat Rock*. CBS Records, 1982.
The Clash. "Should I Stay or Should I Go." *Combat Rock*. CBS Records, 1982.
d'Urfey, Thomas (original); Nettlingham, Frederick (modern lyrics). "Old MacDonald Had a Farm" ("In the Fields in Frost
    and Snow"). *The Kingdom of the Birds* (1706); *Tommy's Tunes* (1917).
Devo. "Freedom of Choice." *Freedom of Choice*. Warner Bros. Records, 1980.
DiMucci, Dion. "Runaround Sue." *Runaround Sue / Runaway Girl*. Laurie Records, 1961.
DiMucci, Dion. "The Wanderer." *The Majestic / The Wanderer*. Laurie Records, 1961.
Dion and the Belmonts. "A Teenager in Love." *Presenting Dion and the Belmonts*. Laurie Records, 1959.
The Eagles. "Hotel California." *Hotel California*. Asylum Records, 1976.
Exodus. "Low Rider." *Fabulous Disaster*. Combat Records, 1989.
Folk, Robert. "Police Academy Theme." *Police Academy: Original Motion Picture Score*, 1984.
Gean, Ralph. "Electricity." *A Star Unborn: The Amazing Story Of Ralph Gean*. World Serpent, 1997.
Gean, Ralph. "Goddess Of Love." *A Star Unborn: The Amazing Story Of Ralph Gean*. World Serpent, 1997.
Gean, Ralph. "Hard To Be A Killer." *A Star Unborn: The Amazing Story Of Ralph Gean*. World Serpent, 1997.
Gean, Ralph. "Here I Am." (Unreleased.) Ray Doggett Productions, 1962.
Gean, Ralph. "Homicidal Me." *A Star Unborn: The Amazing Story Of Ralph Gean*. World Serpent, 1997.
Gean, Ralph. "Kill For A Cigarette." *A Star Unborn: The Amazing Story Of Ralph Gean*. World Serpent, 1997.
Gean, Ralph. "You're Drivin' Me Crazy." *A Star Unborn: The Amazing Story Of Ralph Gean*. World Serpent, 1997.
Godflesh. "Like Rats." *Streetcleaner*. Earache Records, 1989.
Hale, Sarah Josepha; Roulstone, John. "Mary Had a Little Lamb." 1830.
Higley, Brewster; Kelley, Daniel. "Home on the Range." Pre-1874.
Joel, Billy. "My Life." *52nd Street*. Columbia Records, 1978.
The Kingsmen. "Louie Louie." *Louie Louie / Haunted Castle*. Wand Records, 1963.
Kraftwerk. "Autobahn." *Autobahn*. Philips, 1974.
Kraftwerk. "Musique Non-Stop." *Electric Café*. Kling Klang/EMI, 1986.
McDonald, Michael "I Keep Forgettin' (Every Time You're Near)." *If That's What It Takes*. Warner Bros. Records, 1982.
Metallica. "The Prince." *Harvester Of Sorrow*. Elektra Records, 1988.
Minor Threat. "Straight Edge." *Minor Threat*. Dischord Records, 1981.
Momus. "I Want You, But I Don't Need You." *Ping Pong*. Le Grand Magistery, 1997.

Moondog and the London Saxophonic. "New Amsterdam." *Sax Pax for a Sax*. Atlantic Records, 1997.

Mötley Crüe. "Kickstart My Heart." *Dr. Feelgood*. Elektra Records, 1989.

Mozart, Wolfgang Amadeus. *The Requiem in D minor*. 1791.

Mozart, Wolfgang Amadeus. *The Symphony No. 25 in G minor*. 1773.

Nelson, Willy. "Always on My Mind." *Always on My Mind / The Party's Over*. Columbia Records, 1982.

Nirvana. "Smells Like Teen Spirit." *Nevermind*. DGC Records, 1991.

Oasis. "Cum On Feel the Noize." *Don't Look Back in Anger*. Creation Records, 1996.

The Ohio Express. "Cowboy Convention." *Cowboy Convention / The Race (That Took Place)*. Buddha Records, 1969.

Parker, Trey; Shaiman, Marc. "Blame Canada." *South Park: Bigger, Longer & Uncut – Music from and Inspired by the Motion Picture*. Atlantic Recording Corporation, 1999.

Pet Shop Boys, "Always on My Mind." *Always on My Mind / In My House*. Parlophone Records, 1988.

Presley, Elvis. "Always on My Mind." *Separate Ways / Always on My Mind*. RCA Records, 1972.

Rogers, Roy. "Happy Trails." *Happy Trails / The Yellow Rose Of Texas*. RCA Victor Records, 1952.

Slayer. "In-A-Gadda-Da-Vida." *Less Than Zero (Original Motion Picture Soundtrack)*. Def Jam Recordings, 1987.

The Sugarhill Gang. "Rapper's Delight." *Rapper's Delight*. Sugar Hill Records, 1979.

Sunforest. "Lighthouse Keeper." *Sound of Sunforest*. Decca, 1970.

Sunny & The Sunliners. "That Night In San Antonio." *Tear Drop Presents Sunny & The Sunliners*. Tear Drop Records, 1966.

The Swingin' Medallions. "Double Shot (Of My Baby's Love)." *Double Shot / Here It Comes Again*. 4 Sale, 1965.

Taylor, Jane; *et al.* "Twinkle, Twinkle, Little Star" ("*Ah! vous dirai-je, maman*"). 1806 / 1740.

Tchaikovsky, Pyotr Ilyich. *Shchelkunchik (The Nutcracker)*, 1892.

Thee Headcoatees. "Teenage Kicks." *Punk Girls*. Sympathy For The Record Industry, 1997.

Thomas, B.J. "Raindrops Keep Fallin' On My Head." *Raindrops Keep Fallin' On My Head / Never Had It So Good*. Scepter Records, 1969.

van Beethoven, Ludwig. *Bagatelle No. 25 in A minor* (*Für Elise*), 1867.

van Beethoven, Ludwig. *Egmont*, Op. 84, 1810.

van Beethoven, Ludwig. *The Piano Sonata No. 14 in C-sharp minor* (Moonlight Sonata), 1802.

van Beethoven, Ludwig. *The Symphony No. 3* (*Eroica*), 1805.

van Beethoven, Ludwig. *The Symphony No. 5 in C minor* (*Schicksalssinfonie*), 1808.

van Beethoven, Ludwig. *The Symphony No. 7 in A major*, "II. Allegretto,"1813. Performed by The Boston Symphony Orchestra, conducted by Leonard Bernstein. Deutsche Grammophon, 1992.

van Beethoven, Ludwig. *The Symphony No. 9 in D minor*, "IV. Finale," ("*An die Freude*"), 1824.

Van Halen. "Panama." *1984*. Warner Bros. Records, 1984.

Vance Charles and The Sonics. "Closer To Me." *Closer To Me / Let's Fall In Love*. Lori Records, 1964.

The Violent Femmes. "American Music." *Why Do Birds Sing?*. Reprise Records, 1991.

Wagner, Richard. *Der Ring des Nibelungen* (The Ring of The Nibelung), "Die Walküre," (The Valkyrie), 1870.

Warren G. "Regulate." *Regulate... G Funk Era*. Violator, 1994.

The Weather Girls. "It's Raining Men." *It's Raining Men*. Columbia Records, 1982.

The Who. "My Generation." *My Generation*, 1965.

Williams, Hank. "Ramblin' Man" *Ramblin' Man / Pictures from Life's Other Side*. MGM Records, 1951.

Yankovic, "Weird" Al. "I'll Be Mellow When I'm Dead." *"Weird Al" Yankovic*. Rock n' Roll Records, 1983.

ZZ Top. "Legs." *Eliminator*. Warner Bros. Records, 1983.

Music Videos

Beastie Boys. "Hey Ladies." Directed by Adam Bernstein, 1989.

Beastie Boys. "Intergalactic." Directed by Adam Yauch, 1998.

Beastie Boys. "Sabotage." Directed by Spike Jonze, 1994.

Electric Six. "Danger! High Voltage." Directed by Tom Kuntz and Mike Maguire, 2002.

Rollins Band. "Liar." Directed by Anton Corbijn, 1994.

Podcasts

Cordkillers. Hosted by Brian Brushwood and Tom Merritt. Acast, 2023 to present.

Great Night. Hosted by Brian Brushwood and Justin Robert Young. Patreon, 2021 to present.

The Joe Rogan Experience. Hosted by Joe Rogan. Spotify, 2009 to present.

SciAm Podcast (now *Science Talk*). Hosted by Steve Mirsky. *Scientific American*, 2008 to present.

Weird Things. Hosted by Brian Brushwood, Andrew Mayne, and Justin Robert Young. Patreon, 2008 to present.

— About the Author —

Brian M. Clark is an avocational writer and musician who has authored a couple of books besides this one and released various musical recordings. He runs the independent record label Discriminate Audio, through which he puts out his own music as well as that of other recording artists. At the time of this book's publication, Brian resides in Denver, Colorado, where he works as an attorney. More information about Brian is available on his website, BrianMclark.com.

www.ingramcontent.com/pod-product-compliance
Lightning Source LLC
Chambersburg PA
CBHW081753110426
42740CB00058BA/2900